The Language of Sex

The Chicago Series on Sexuality, History, and Society

Edited by John C. Fout

The Language of Sex

FIVE VOICES FROM NORTHERN
FRANCE AROUND 1200

John W. Baldwin

The University of Chicago Press
Chicago and London

John W. Baldwin is the Charles Homer Haskins Professor of History at The Johns Hopkins University. Among his books are *Masters, Princes, and Merchants: The Social Views of Peter the Chanter and His Circle* and *The Government of Philip Augustus: Foundations of French Royal Power in the Middle Ages*.

The University of Chicago Press, Chicago 60637
The University of Chicago Press, Ltd., London
© 1994 by The University of Chicago
All rights reserved. Published 1994
Printed in the United States of America
03 02 01 00 99 98 97 96 95 94   1 2 3 4 5

ISBN 0-226-03613-8 (cloth)

Library of Congress Cataloging-in-Publication Data

Baldwin, John W.
    The language of sex : five voices from Northern France around 1200
/ John W. Baldwin.
        p.   cm. — (The Chicago series on sexuality, history, and
society)
    Includes bibliographical references and index.
    1. Sex customs—France, Northern—History—13th century—Sources.
2. Sex customs—France, Northern—History—13th century.   3. Sex in
literature.   4. France—Social life and customs—To 1328.
I. Title.   II. Series.
HQ18.F8B28   1994
306.7'0944'09022—dc20   93-6040
                                                                         CIP

For
Christopher

CONTENTS

---————————— ❧ ————————————

PREFATORY WORDS . . .

To Readers

Individual readers who pick up a book about human sexuality situated at a
particular historical moment may bring to it different expectations. Those
who are primarily interested in the subject matter might begin the present
work at Chapter 3 after they have taken notice of the general orientation in
the first half of the Introduction. Those who are also interested in the medieval context of the five discourses will find Chapter 2 pertinent. Those
who recognize, as many do today, the import of the methodological and
theoretical implications of such an investigation may find the second half
of the Introduction of interest as well as the Conclusion.

Readers who demand demonstration and wish to consult the texts for
themselves will, of course, refer to the Notes, for which the following instructions will be of assistance. The primary texts used frequently in this
study are listed by author and short title among the "Texts" in the list of
"Short Titles." Each entry includes the edition employed in the original
language and a modern translation where it is available. In order to avoid
duplication and reduce the quantity of Notes, all citations of primary texts
are to the editions in the original language. Wherever possible the citation
gives the internal division to book, chapter, section, verse, etc., to enable
reference to both the edition and the translation. For example: Augustine,
De civitate dei XIV, 17, 18; Jean Renart, *Roman,* vv. 14–15. In most cases
both the original text and the translation can be located through these citations. Where confusion may result, further reference is given to the edition.

As will immediately become apparent to the most casual reader, this
book consists largely of paraphrases and translations of a wide assortment
of medieval texts in Latin and the vernacular French, many of which have
already been translated into modern languages. I bear full responsibility
for the accuracy of all renditions in the book, but I should acknowledge my
debt to the extant translations cited in the list of "Short Titles."

To Colleagues

This study of sexuality in northern France at the turn of the twelfth and thirteenth centuries attempts to bring together five distinct discursive genres, each of which has generated a long tradition, a discrete scholarly discipline, and a massive bibliography. Among the five I can only bring prior experience to the theologians from my study of Pierre the Chanter of twenty years ago. In the present work I have been able to add to the publication of the vast store of his, as yet, unedited texts in Latin. Because of the scope of the enterprise, however, I have gratefully welcomed help wherever it was available in the other four genres as well as among the theologians. I have, therefore, availed myself of the now standard works of James A. Brundage on canon law, of John T. Noonan, Jr., on contraception, of Michael Müller and Hans Zeimentz on the theologians, of Danielle Jacquart and Claude Thomasset on the physicians, and Per Nykrog on the fabliaux. (Theirs and other works important for this study can be found in the "Studies" of the list of "Short Titles.")

Beyond the published literature, I have taken the liberty to call upon colleagues directly. To compensate for my deficiencies in medicine I have been fortunate in having close neighbors in the Welch Medical Library and the Institute of the History of Medicine at Johns Hopkins. From the latter, Jerome J. Bylebyl and Owsei Temkin read the medical sections and offered helpful suggestions. Monica Green, then at the Institute of Advanced Study in Princeton and now at Duke University, also read the medical sections and generously allowed me access to her text of *Cum auctor* from the corpus of Trotula of Salerno which she is editing. Margaret Switten of Mount Holyoke College read my sections on romance and offered counsel on Jean Renart's lyrics. Werner Hamacher of the Johns Hopkins University advised me on the texts of Gottfried von Strassburg. David F. Hult of the University of Virginia not only shared his expertise in Old French by helping with difficult passages, but he has also been willing to discuss with me at length all problems theoretical and practical, great and small. As before, I have counted heavily on his faithful friendship throughout the project. The History Seminar at Johns Hopkins fulfilled its habitual and essential role by considering a paper on sexual desire which became the nucleus of Chapter 4. When toward the end of the project I began to worry about my critical stance, I was able to recruit a platoon of colleagues who could advise me, if not reassure me, about the concerns of theory for which Johns Hopkins remains renowned. I trust that the disclosure of their identities will not cause embarrassment: Jeffrey Brooks, Toby L. Ditz, Frances Ferguson, R. James Goldstein, Stephen G. Nichols, Mary L. Poovey, Gabrielle M. Spiegel, and Judith Walkowitz. With characteristic generosity Robert W. Hanning of Columbia University shared the helpful comments he prepared for the Press on the entire typescript. Patricia Stirnemann of the Centre National de la Recherche Scientifique in Paris procured a photograph of the manuscript used for the cover. I wish to express my deep gratitude for all of this direct and personal help.

This book originated as a chapter in a projected study on the chivalric ethos in northern France around 1200 but then took on a life of its own. I wish to acknowledge gratefully a fellowship from the National Endowment for the Humanities and a sabbatical leave from Johns Hopkins which funded the initial stage of this enterprise.

When the last of our children left by the front door, my wife Jenny Jochens closed the door to her study and plunged into a truly monumental project on the image and reality of women in the medieval Old Norse tradition. As her work progressed, she permitted me to read articles and chapters which convinced me of the importance and feasibility of investigating sexuality and gender from medieval sources. Her project, begun earlier and now completed, is certainly of greater scope, ambition, and significance than mine. To her I owe the underlying impulse for the present study as well as supportive reading throughout.

One of the pleasures of parenthood is to welcome the return of children as colleagues and potential readers. Despite Peter's escape to twentieth-century Europe I am hopeful that this aspect of the remote Middle Ages might elicit his historical interest. Ian, our sociobiologist, accepted to read the sections on the medieval perceptions of anatomy and physiology but, I suspect, he put them down with bemused bewilderment. Had Birgit, our literary scholar from Yale, been able to peruse my reading of the romances and fabliaux, I imagine that she would have blushed at my hermeneutic shortcomings. It remains our perduring pain that she is no longer among our readers. Christopher, however, who eschewed the contemplative life of academia for the activity of electronics, remains our autonomous child. To this authentic layman from a family of clerics, I offer a book on one of the defining and delightful functions of the laity in any age.

INTRODUCTION

In the year 1200 in northern France the dénouement of a sexual scandal broke suddenly and dramatically on the entire population of the royal domain. On 13 January Pope Innocent III levied a solemn interdict on the royal lands because of the king's matrimonial behavior. The reigning king, Philip (II) Augustus of France, had departed on the Third Crusade in 1190 as a recent widower and the father of a sickly infant son. When he returned in 1191, he was determined to remarry and reinforce the royal lineage with another son. His choice of a bride in the Danish princess Ingeborg puzzled contemporary chroniclers as it has modern historians, but whatever his reasons he formed a total aversion to his new spouse on the wedding night of 14–15 August 1193. Starting immediate proceedings for separation, he contracted a new marriage with a Bavarian noblewoman, Agnès de Méran (Andechs-Meran), to remove all doubt about his resolve to be rid of the Danish princess. Although his initial and formal ground for separation was close parentage within the prohibited degrees established by the church, his evident motive was sexual incompatibility because he steadfastly refused to grant her conjugal rights throughout his lifetime. (Later in the proceedings he accused her of bewitching him and rendering him impotent.) The papacy sought to counter this blatant mockery of sacred matrimony at the highest level of society by defending Ingeborg and asserting its jurisdiction over the king's marriage. When Philip ignored a succession of papal delegations and warnings, the pope imposed the interdict upon the royal domain. For nine months the doors of churches were closed by decree until the king agreed to separate from Agnès, to become publicly reconciled with the queen, and to submit his quarrel to a church court. When the faithful throughout the royal lands were deprived of the church's ministry, their attention was directed to the king's personal and sexual problems.[1] This was not the first marital démêlé of the French monarchy within memory nor was it to be the last in French history; but the king's subjects of northern France in 1200 as sexually active humans needed no spectacular scandal to remind them of the subject of sexuality, which remained as ubiquitous as the connubial bed or forest glade and as frequent as nightfall and the afternoon tryst. It is nonetheless true that until recently modern historians have paid little attention to this universal and vital activity except as it has surfaced in the notorious conduct of the highborn.

Within the past decade, however, a veritable torrent of books containing the words "sexuality" and "gender" in their titles has flowed from American presses. If the term "desire" favored by literary scholars is added to this nomenclature, the stream attains flood proportions. All of this afflux is convincing testimony to the primal springs and sustaining force of the women's moment in the 1970s. When our contemporary concerns in sexuality and gender are applied to the European Middle Ages, however, they encounter resistance from surviving source materials. The predominant Christian ideology harbored a negative evaluation of sexuality as inherently evil, appraised the act itself as shameful, and raised inhibitions over the expression of the subject except to condemn it. Although articles treating limited topics or proposing broad hypotheses have proliferated, sustained studies have been less abundant. In order to demarcate the present study within the burgeoning field of sexuality and gender, I shall offer a brief overview of current medieval scholarship.

The importance of the Middle Ages was noticed almost by inadvertence by Michel Foucault in volume 1, *La volunté de savoir* (1976), of his influential *Histoire de la sexualité*. Seeking to examine the appearance of modern sexuality in the eighteenth century as the product of converging technologies of power exercised by doctors, educators, and psychiatrists, he was led to recognize a preexisting "traditional technology of the flesh" founded on Christian ideology and promulgated by the medieval penitential system. By the end of the volume, it became clear that the modern revolution required a more substantial prehistory. This discovery was followed by a long pause. When Foucault resumed the project in 1984, he had completely reversed his chronology and proposed three additional volumes which approached the Middle Ages from the other side. Volume 2, *L'usage des plaisirs* (1984), treated the Classical Greek period of the fourth century B.C.E.; volume 3, *Le souci de soi* (1984), the pagan Greek and Latin texts of the first two centuries C.E.; and a fourth volume, *Les aveux de la chair,* unachieved at his tragic death in 1984, proposed to explore the teaching and pastoral practice of the Christian church.[2] From frequent asides and anticipations, it became clear that his ultimate interest was directed to the Christian society of the late Antique and medieval eras.

The pause between volumes 1 and 2 also transformed the underlying approach to his subject. Volume 1 was akin to his previous studies on prisons and madness in which he analyzed the nature of discourse and related it to the production of power. Modern sexuality, therefore, was the product of multiple discourses fashioned by doctors, educators, and psychiatrists in contrast to the Middle Ages in which discourse was markedly unitary. Now approaching the medieval period from the far side in volumes 2 and 3, he exchanged a preoccupation with conceptualization for a more descriptive stance. Although he did not repudiate the approach of the first volume, he nonetheless proceeded to read the ancient texts in a more expository mode. By examining the philosophical and medical discourses of high culture (to which he added the literary discourse of Hellenistic romance in volume 3), he recounted the sexual conduct and self-representation embedded in the discourses of the two ancient epochs which he called the forms, modalities, or "techniques of the self." Because of the overwhelming masculine orientation of these discourses, he adopted their male perspective—particularly its homoerotic interests—and thereby paid little attention to the discursive production of women. Even their pronounced absence went unnoticed except as an extension of the male self.[3]

In one sense, the gap left by Foucault's unexpected death was soon filled by Peter Brown's *The Body and Society: Men, Women, and Sexual Renunciation in Early Christianity* (1988) which explored the sexuality of Christians in late antiquity.[4] With the empathy and eloquence that have become his hallmark, Brown sought to study sexual behavior through a discourse that proposed its permanent abnegation. The varieties of virginity would be an equally fitting subtitle to his work, because early Christians were ingenious in generating a wide range of strategies to renounce sex that cast light on the nature of their sexuality and the structure of their society. Brown is particularly adept in encouraging compassion for preoccupations that may seem bizarre to the modern readers; nonetheless, the ascetics and Church Fathers of late antiquity formulated a discourse that remained the foundation for understanding sexuality in the medieval era. That this discourse was pervasively prescriptive and exclusively voiced by male writers resulted in scant attention to the specific needs of women and afforded Brown little opportunity to offer a sustained treatment of gender.[5]

Because of the restricted number of surviving treatises dealing with sexuality, both Foucault and Brown limited their attention to a narrow range of discourses: Foucault to three learned discourses at most, Brown to a single kind of ascetic writing. Both extended the scope of their inquiries to large units of space and time. Foucault devoted one volume to a broad century centered on Athens and the other to two centuries of Greek and Latin writing in the Roman Empire. Brown traversed the entire Mediterranean world, both Greek and Latin, over four centuries. If such strategies were required to assemble coherent choruses of ancient voices, they were deemed even more necessary for the vast millennium of the Middle Ages comprising diverse peoples across Western Europe. For this period scholars have devised a common approach of focusing on one discourse or activity over extended geographic and chronological areas.

Actually medievalists have applied this strategy for over a century. Since 1883 when the French philologist Gaston Paris coined the term, literary scholars have traced the single theme of "courtly love" or *fin'amors* in vernacular texts from its first imputed appearance in the Provençal troubadours at the end of the eleventh century, through the *trouvères* and romances of northern France in the twelfth century, to the German Minnesingers of the thirteenth century, and finally as it fanned out across Europe by the fourteenth century.[6] Throughout the past century scholars have rarely agreed on the proper name of the phenomenon, its origins, its essential characteristics, or whether it was a historical code of conduct for the aristocracy or rather a contrived game of poets. Of interest to us is the particular controversy whether *fin'amors* involved sexual consummation or was limited to spiritual ennoblement.[7] In recent years, however, literary critics have turned their attention from looking at literature for evidence of sexuality to looking at representations of sexuality for literary purposes. The *topoi* of sex have been seen as furthering preoccupations with language and rhetoric.[8]

Although interest in "courtly love" may have subsided in recent years, the underlying strategy of focusing on a single discourse over extended space and time continues. In *Sexualité et savoir médical au moyen âge* (1985), for example, Danielle Jacquart and Claude Thomasset wrote a pioneering introduction to medical theories on sexuality in Western Europe ranging from the ancient Hippocratic corpus through the thirteenth century.[9] Shortly thereafter James A. Brundage published his *Law, Sex and Christian Society in Medieval Europe* (1987) which offers an authoritative and comprehensive survey of the canon law on sex from antiquity through the sixteenth century.[10] Before the appearance of these studies historians had virtually ignored the phenomenon of sexuality except as it was exercised in the institutions of family and marriage.[11] Another solution to demarcating the vast terrain was to look at perceived transgressions. In *Christianity, Social Tolerance, and Homosexuality: Gay People in Western Europe from the Beginning of the Christian Era to the Fourteenth Century* (1980), for example, John Boswell exploited what few texts are available to uncover evidence of homoerotic behavior across the greater part of the Middle Ages.[12] Others, such as Leah L. Otis in *Prostitution in Medieval Society: The History of an Urban Institution in Languedoc* (1985), have mined the documents of a specific region in the late Middle Ages to reveal the practices of professional sex, but these two works treat only limited segments of the sexual population.[13]

These studies of medieval sexuality have mirrored the gender orientation of their sources. Since the physicians and canon lawyers were exclusively male, their preoccupations were predominantly masculine. The
search for homophilia has uncovered very little lesbian expression. Since
one of the characteristic tenants of "courtly love" was the idealization of
the aristocratic lady, literary scholars have devoted more attention to the
female image, but admittedly it was largely mediated through the eyes of
male poets.[14] The forms of prostitution that have been studied involved
mainly women, but again entirely at the service and control of their masculine clients. The emergence of histories of women in the Middle Ages
has opened possibilities for gender analysis, but few of these studies have
focused specifically on female sexuality.[15]

In contrast to these treatments of one discourse over extended space and
time, I seek to distinguish the present study by limiting its geographic
scope to northern France and its chronological span to the three decades
that pivot on the year 1200 (1185–1215).[16] Rather than concentrating on
one discourse, I have listened simultaneously to five, three in Latin and two
in the vernacular, each the voice of a distinct tradition, all conversing and
interacting together. The proper subject of the study is solely and simply
discourses about sexuality and their attendant consequences for the construction of gender. In other words, it is about talking about sex in the
double sense of the English word as both eroticism and gender. It is not
about sexuality as a metaphor for language, rhetoric, or power. Nor have I
centered this study on love. As an emotion or a sentiment, love extends
beyond the fleshly to the spiritual and includes more than sex. I would be
the first to recognize the intrinsic importance of love for sex, but to keep
this study within manageable limits I have deliberately excluded it from
direct consideration. Sexuality, to be sure, implicates love, but the refined,
nonsexual dimensions of love are not my primary focus. In sum, this study
attempts to encompass the full range of the physical manifestations of sex
as they were perceived in northern France around 1200 without privileging either prevailing or transgressive types of behavior.

The first discourse on sexuality in the Middle Ages was recorded by
churchmen in Latin. The Church Fathers, who were preoccupied with the
ideals of virginity, formulated it in late antiquity and conveyed it to the
early Middle Ages through monastic writers. Scholars at the school of
Laon assembled it into biblical commentaries and monographs on marriage at the beginning of the twelfth century; Pierre the Lombard inscribed
it into the standard collection of theology, and Gratian entered it into the
science of canon law at the middle of the century. Since churchmen sought
to bring all matters pertaining to sexuality and marriage under their exclusive jurisdiction, they promulgated their doctrines through preaching and
the confessional and applied them with spiritual sanctions in their courts.

Attempting to fashion a unified doctrine, their discourse was prescriptive in method and hegemonic in character. Impressed by the church's pervasive influence over medieval society, modern historians have usually assumed that the ecclesiastical voice, in fact, regulated human sexuality throughout the Middle Ages.

A second discourse emerged in the second half of the eleventh century in southern Italy when physicians began to translate ancient medical treatises into Latin and compile epitomes which were derived from Arabic versions. These writings circulated in schools offering instruction in medicine. A third Latin discourse appeared at the beginning of the twelfth century when clerics in the grammar schools wrote for their own amusement love poetry and plays modeled on the erotic poetry of Ovid, the acknowledged authority of sexual love in the Middle Ages. It should be remembered that these three discourses were transcribed in Latin, the official language of the church and scholarship and the nearly exclusive monopoly of clerics who, for the most part, were presumed to be destined to a celibate life.

The vast majority of the laity, to whom churchmen assigned sexuality and reproduction as primary functions, undoubtedly talked about sex in the vernacular. Whatever the contents and rhetoric of this oral discourse were, it is lost to us until it was first reduced to writing early in the twelfth century. Chief among the first compositions to emerge in vernacular French were epic poems loosely entitled *chansons de geste*. Concentrating on martial deeds recited before crowds of warriors assembled in the great halls of powerful lords, these narratives were little concerned with sexual matters. When, however, during the second half of the century, a new genre of vernacular romance was written down and spoken for a more intimate audience of the chamber where ladies were also present, love and sexuality emerged as clear preoccupations of romance literature. Since the great lords and barons of noble society commissioned the romances, we may presume that they also constituted the audience accompanied by entourages of knights and ladies—all demanding entertainment that conformed to the refined conventions and language of the aristocratic court. By the end of the twelfth century, however, the fabliaux, a new kind of vernacular entertainment, surfaced in writing. Although its audience was identified less specifically, it appears to have included lesser knights and ladies and the bourgeoisie of the towns. Reacting against high aristocratic sensibilities, this literature offered short narratives that took delight in speaking about sexuality in direct and crude language.

Around the year 1200, therefore, a multiplicity of texts appeared for the first time in which modern historians can read a variety of discourses talking about sexuality. Within the vast corpus of Latin writing, the production of monks gave way to the secular clergy of the schools and parishes. Alongside the Latin of churchmen and schools, a vernacular literature was written down expressly for the laity. Unlike the early monks who wrote mainly for the secluded cloister, this multiplicity envisaged expanded audiences. It is difficult to be precise about the full extent for each of the five, but distinct elements can nonetheless be distinguished. The theologians, canonists, physicians, and masters of arts wrote for clerics in the schools, but by addressing their treatises to the secular clergy as well they extended their potential audience to the lay parishioners in the world. The romanciers composed for the lay aristocracy both high and low. The lesser aristocracy and townspeople may be singled out within the fableor's audience. Only the masses of the peasants in the countryside were not directly addressed except as they appeared among the secular clergy's parishioners. The school clerics and secular clergy consisted exclusively of males, but the audiences of the parish clergy, the romanciers, and the fableors included women as well.

To represent this discursive heterogeneity at this historical moment, when the king's sex life drew the attention of the inhabitants of the royal domain, I shall select five voices from northern France within the three decades surrounding the year 1200. Each will have a principal spokesman who articulated a discrete tradition to designated audiences. ("Spokesman" remains the appropriate term because all were male except for two females.) Each tradition, if not the spokesman himself, has been the object of sustained modern scholarship. It cannot be demonstrated whether any one of the five conversed personally with the others, but they all participated in the common cultural context of northern France. The theological-canonistic tradition of Augustine is represented by master Pierre the Chanter (d. 1197) and his two direct students, master Robert of Courson (d. 1219) and master Thomas of Chobham (d. 1233–36) who taught theology at the schools of Paris and wrote Latin treatises designed to guide priests for hearing confessions. Galen's legacy as mediated through Salerno is articulated by the anonymous *Prose Salernitan Questions,* which collected Latin medical questions composed for learned physicians in the schools of England and northern France. The classical tradition of Ovid is conveyed by the enigmatic André, chaplain of the French king, who composed a Latin treatise on love for the clerics who frequented the schools and the aristocratic courts. The vernacular tradition of romance is represented by Jean Renart from northeastern France, who composed two romances and a lai for Baudouin VI, count of Hainaut (d. 1205), and Milon de Nanteuil, prévôt of the cathedral chapter of Reims (d. 1234), and their courts of knights and ladies. The Tristan legend, Marie de France, and Chrétien de Troyes provided Jean's immediate literary inspiration. And, finally, Jean Bodel (d. 1210), a jongleur from Arras, wrote a handful of vernacular fabliaux articulating perhaps ancient folkloric traditions for the amusement of townspeople and the lower aristocracy. As the first identified fableor, his production was small, but his corpus has been supplemented with a selection of fabliaux which resemble Jean's and appear to belong to the early thirteenth century.

To compensate for the inherent limitations of focusing on a single spokesman, I have accompanied each with a discussion of the preceding tradition which serves to supplement his discussion and to place him in his respective context. In addition to the spokesman, each tradition was alive and active around the year 1200. Augustine and Ovid, for example, were represented by more manuscripts at the time than their contemporary spokesmen Pierre the Chanter and André the Chaplain. In the imagery of the twelfth-century conceit, the spokesmen were not dwarfs perched on the shoulders of giants but dwarfs bearing the burden of gigantic traditions.[17] A nagging doubt will always persist that I have neglected some other spokesman whom historians will consider equally noteworthy; nonetheless, I proceed on the assumption that, when each of the five is considered within his tradition, other voices will not likely surface to alter the present conclusions significantly. By juxtaposing five current spokesmen and their discursive traditions within a restricted place and time, I propose to open a window on the articulation of sexuality in northern France around 1200.

The five available spokesmen were all male. To help alleviate the masculine timbre of their voices, I have included Marie de France from the previous generation of romance writers (second half of the twelfth century) and Marie d'Oignies (d. 1213) who spoke for the monastic-theological tradition as a protégée of Jacques de Vitry, himself a direct student of Pierre the Chanter. The first Marie wrote with unusual subtlety and nuance, and the second possessed a distinctive personality, but with few exceptions the two women did not differ markedly from their male contemporaries. Like previous studies, this present work is, therefore, subject to the overwhelming masculine bias of the surviving source materials. The male spokesmen constructed paradigms of gender relations in accordance with their underlying interests. As feminist critics have detected from traditional and patriarchal discourse, their language was pervasively phallologocentric, and their presumptions were heterosexual. Male-female relations were translated into formulations that were both binary and reifications of foundational categories. According to R. Howard Bloch, they voiced the traditional misogynistic speech act in which woman is the subject, and the predicate is a more general term (either negative or positive) that essentializes or abstracts the feminine condition. In medieval terms, women were polarized as the "Bride of Christ" modeled on the Virgin Mary and the "Devil's gateway" patterned on Mother Eve. It was not a situation of either/or but both/and. Simultaneously idealized and condemned, women were overdetermined and trapped in double jeopardy.[18] Rooted deep in society and pervasively expressed in language, a presumption of underlying asymmetry underlay gender relations within the five discourses. I shall seek to make these gender assumptions explicit in the course of discussing sexuality, but I reserve my overall conclusions for the final chapter.

* * *

Completing this study in the 1990s, I find it impossible to ignore what might be considered my theoretical stance. From my training as a historian I began reading the five discourses before considering their theoretical implications, but I was soon convinced that a virtue could be made of a necessity. As I proceeded, I discovered that the theorems of poststructuralism which colleagues and students had been recommending to me in fact accorded well with the nature and scarcity of medieval evidence and discourse. Although such propositions are well-known throughout literary and feminist circles, I found the formulations by feminist scholars to be the most helpful.[19] They may be stated as five axioms to be taken as hypotheses.

1. *Discourse.* This project places discourse at the center for the simple reason that it remains our chief access to sexuality in the distant past. For my purposes I have adopted a broad rendering of the term as organized utterance generated by historically current languages. Obviously a linguistic phenomenon, discursive practices are produced historically, socially, and institutionally. Since they are products of political and social power, they may also embody conflict. Derived from the Latin *discursus/discurrere,* meaning running to and fro, discourses can vacillate between extremes.[20] Neither fixed or intrinsic, they must be evaluated according to context. They convey meaning with various degrees of transparency but usually contain silences. Often their meanings can be constructed from what they exclude as well as what they contain. Characteristic of most medieval discourse, all but one of our five contained an integral oral component. Pierre the Chanter, for example, delivered lectures on the Bible to students in his classroom which were written down as his scriptural commentaries, and he debated the pros and cons of theological propositions which resulted in written *questiones.* Presumably the written versions of the *Prose Salernitan Questions* were associated with comparable oral pedagogy. However the fabliaux were actually composed, there is abundant evidence that jongleurs such as Jean Bodel performed the fabliaux to audiences. Like the fabliaux, the romances were composed in octosyllabic rhymed couplets.

Although they were probably written down first, they were meant nonetheless to be rehearsed before aristocratic audiences. Larding his narrative with numerous lyrics, Jean Renart, for example, declared that his *Roman de la rose* was to be read and sung (vv. 16–23, 5643–52). Yet it is obvious that, whatever the oral component, these discourses have reached us only after they were recorded in written texts. Alone among our spokesmen, André the Chaplain composed his treatise as a written missive to a designated reader. The Chanter's biblical lectures and disputations were written down by a student *reportator*, edited by the Chanter or a scribe, and re-copied in numerous manuscripts. Jean Renart's romances, like those of his predecessors, were similarly committed to writing (*mis en écriture, Escoufle*, v. 45); otherwise, his signature concealed in an anagram would have been erased. As a result of oral performances, the texts of our spokesmen are not stable. The Chanter's scriptural commentaries comprise several versions, and his *questiones*, especially those on marriage not yet incorporated by the editor, are extant in differing fragments. Certain fabliaux that circulated in multiple copies demonstrate that they were adapted for diverse audiences, and most romances, except for those preserved in single manuscripts, are riddled with variations that are not insignificant for understanding the poem.[21]

2. *Heterogeneity*. Unlike many previous studies, the underlying strategy of this investigation is to multiply discourses, producing a polyvalence of approaches and meanings. Such heterogeneity may be found not only within differing texts of a single poem but also with differing voices assumed by a single poet. For the most part, however, the five distinct discourses produce discord. Although this is true in a general sense, we shall see that on occasions—often unanticipated—the diverse voices can concur at specific points. These multiple discourses nonetheless interact, compete, and ignore each other simultaneously.

3. *Constructs*. It is no longer unusual to assert, as I do in this study, that sexuality and gender are considered to be cultural constructs.[22] Such constructs, however, do not exclude other realities. Sexuality and gender, for example, exist both as cultural constructs and biological phenomena. Sex in both meanings of the word cannot be separated from the biology of human anatomy and physiology, but this biology must be constantly interpreted. Since it is impossible for me to determine which element predominates in the perpetual interaction between biology and culture in the distant past, my attention will be directed exclusively to questions of cultural construction or how the body was interpreted. No greater contrast can be discerned than between the medical conceptions of anatomy and physiology of the Middle Ages and those of modern science. Although patent fictions, these cultural constructs are not mere illusions as

opposed to a biological reality. Nor do they, however, supplant biological reality. As reenacted experience, these constructs nonetheless possess a "reality" of their own through repeated deed, and they constitute the sole object of my investigation.

4. *Nonessentialism.* Such cultural constructions help to obviate attempts to achieve essentialist, ontological, reified, and foundational explanations. Although anatomy and physiology remain essentially present, interpretations of sexuality and gender are not thereby essentialized. This hypothesis, I believe, permits me to ignore modern essentialisms that have been applied anachronistically to the Middle Ages. The ideology most frequently employed in sexuality is that of Sigmund Freud who postulated an unchanging psyche. Although medievalists have not been immune to Freud or his French interpreter Jacques Lacan, who laid particular stress on language, I shall not avail myself of their insights.[23] In a similar manner, aesthetic essentialism has attributed transhistorical value to works of art, and has undergirded literary criticism with ontological explanations of enduring beauty, but I shall not participate in these considerations.

5. *Alterity.* Refusing modern ideologies, my exploration of medieval sexuality and gender seeks, in the last analysis, to furnish an exercise in the study of alterity. Considering these five discourses as articulations of humans living during a time and under conditions remote from my own, I shall be prepared to hear voices "other"—both foreign and unaccustomed—than my own. This attentiveness thereby eliminates a commonsense approach based on personal experience. When medieval discourses do speak to me, this is, in itself, not warranty that I understand them; nor can I exclude meanings I find strange.

Whereas all texts are, to varying degrees, subject to interpretative processes, the issue of hermeneutics becomes acute in literary texts. As critical theories have evolved during the past half century, the interpretations of medieval texts have followed these fashions. Although Jean Renart has not been considered as central to medieval literature as Chrétien de Troyes or Guillaume de Lorris, the critical reception of his romances nonetheless illustrates the diversity of hermeneutics. When Rita Lejeune devoted the first book-length study to Jean Renart in 1935, she adopted a positivist approach. Literary texts were considered to be objective and commensurate with history. Written in a common language, they could refer to history and in turn be interpreted from a historical context. Although Jean Renart's romances were works of imagination, they were nonetheless *réalistes* and represented the reality of life without idealization or caricature.[24] In 1972, however, Paul Zumthor affirmed in his influential *Essai de poétique médiéval* that the literary text does not imitate life but is self-reflexive, taking itself as its objective. In 1979 Michel Zink applied this approach to Jean

Renart by showing that the *Roman de la rose* is a work of pure imagination which produces an illusion of reality and refers ultimately not to historical reality but to the nature of the literary text itself.[25] Roger Dragonetti pushed this approach to an extreme in 1987 when he declared that Jean Renart's romances, like all medieval literature, were nothing more than artifices of rhetoric which intended to falsify. Not only were they self-referential, but they profited from the polyvalent and indeterminate character of medieval language to engage in subversive and destructive wordplay—to play with (*jouer*) and to frustrate (*déjouer*) their meaning.[26] In effect, therefore, recent interpreters have seriously challenged Jean Renart's role in communicating information about his historical context. Medieval romance has thereby become irrelevant to history. When R. Howard Bloch (1986) recently suggested that the fabliaux were not about sexuality but about language, he adopted a comparable approach.[27] On the other hand, critics such as Per Nykrog (1973) and Charles Muscatine (1986) reaffirmed a position closer to Rita Lejeune that the fabliaux were rooted in the real world and should be taken seriously as evidence for cultural history.[28] Such isolated examples, however, do not necessarily announce any discernible trend but merely illustrate the complexity of modern hermeneutics.

As a historian, my response to critical fashion is to reaffirm that medieval literary texts need not be irreconcilably incommensurate with history. I find sufficient for my purposes a working definition of literature as those texts that are read more than once over time and with pleasure. My underlying criterion for distinguishing literature is, therefore, the historical process. Through the pleasure of hearing and reading, certain works were written down, reread, and recopied; others were not. The explanation of why certain texts survived and others did not pertains to literary critics and is not my task. One feature, however, that makes literature rereadable over time is that it does not propose a single and unequivocal meaning but can be read at many levels. As the embodiment of poetic language, literature invites multiple approaches and different interpretations. The more "literary" a text, the deeper its receptivity to hermeneutic probing. Perhaps our own generation has attained the limits in the poststructuralist movement to "deconstruct" the text by showing how the very language of the text (as in Dragonetti's practice) undercuts and destabilizes its own apparent meaning. This multiplicity of readings makes literature attractive to different audiences over time but especially to critics. A text that supports only one meaning quickly becomes a bore and is not reread. A rich text engages a succession of readers and excites critics to proliferate their interpretations. Multi- or in-determinacy, in effect, nourishes literature and keeps critics active. It is the nature of literature, therefore, to sustain multiple interpretations, but this polyvalence does not exclude any one level, not the least the most superficial.

Although medieval exegetes rarely matched the sophistication of post-structuralist critics, they also developed a praxis of multiple hermeneutics which they applied to classical and biblical texts in particular. As early as Origen among the Greek Fathers, and Jerome, Ambrose, and Augustine among the Latins, scriptural commentators proposed a spiritual inter-pretation of the Bible that sought to avoid the obscurities and absurdities of a literal understanding. Among the earliest, Origen had wholly rejected the literal for the spiritual. Although Ambrose's recommendation of the spiritual had been instrumental in convincing the young Augustine to take the Scriptures seriously, in actual practice the Latin Father preferred to di-vide his own commentaries between the two approaches.[29] By 1200, scriptural scholars had adopted a threefold hermeneutics. In addition to the literal, the spiritual or figurative was divided between the allegorical which related to theology and the tropological which pertained to moral-ity. Pierre the Chanter, for example, explicitly distributed most if not all of his biblical exposition among the three interpretative modes of *historice* (or *ad litteram*), *mistice* (allegory), and *moraliter*.[30] The twelfth-century exe-getes, as well as the Church Fathers, developed nuanced views as to which level they preferred, but in the twelfth century the school of Saint-Victor at Paris placed special emphasis on the literal as the necessary foundation for the spiritualizing or figurative understanding. Until the literal, gram-matical, and historical meaning was established, all further hermeneutic superstructure was insecure. The Apostolic statement that "the letter kills but the spirit gives life" (2 Cor. 3:6) was determinative for Augustine, but Hugues de Saint-Victor was persuaded by another dictum that "that was first which is fleshly, afterwards that which is spiritual" (1 Cor. 15:46). "Do not despise what is lowly in God's word," Hugues continued, "for by lowliness you will be enlightened to divinity. The outward form of God's word seems to you, perhaps, like dirt, so you trample it under foot, like dirt, and despise what the letter tells you was done physically and visibly. But hear! that dirt, which you trample, opened the eyes of the blind! Read Scripture then, and first learn carefully what it tells you was done in the flesh."[31] Hugues's disciple André de Saint-Victor formulated an exegetical program founded on *iuxta superficiem littere* (according to the surface of the letter).[32] Pierre the Chanter valued the interpretative freedom afforded by the multiple approaches of allegory and tropology, but he nonetheless based his own commentaries on the literal exegesis of Hugues and André and thereby maintained that the truth of the spiritual or figurative could only be guaranteed by its grammatical and historical foundations.[33]

Positing the foundations of a literal reading, the twelfth-century commentators nonetheless proceeded to erect an exegetical structure of spiritual interpretations. Following the example of the Victorines and the Chanter, I, too, have chosen the fleshly surface-literal level as my point of entry, but unlike them I shall be satisfied to remain there. The reasons for this strategy are admittedly practical. As a historian, I am ill-equipped linguistically and hermeneutically by training to contribute to a literary reading. And even if I should presume to try, I have selected too many texts from diverse genres to explore the depths of their multiple, not to speak of their subversive, readings within the confines of one volume. The poststructuralist approach works best, it seems to me, when applied to single texts. Realizing that the literal level itself is not simplistically innocent, but entails different interpretations as well, I have attempted to reduce it to the sense of historical information. Just as Pierre the Chanter read the Old Testament for historical data about the ancient Jews (whatever his ultimate designs to allegorize or moralize), I shall read my texts for information about sexuality. The Tristan legend in its different versions, for example, can be read at complex and aesthetically stimulating levels, but it also concerns the practice of adultery and contains a narration of that subject. The recounting of the seduction of a naive girl in the fabliau, *La damoisele qui ne pooit oïr parler de foutre,* undoubtedly delighted its listeners beyond the surface of the narrative with outrageous parody, humor, and double entendres, but it also explicitly spelled out both a literal and euphemistic lexicon of the sexual body. It will be my underlying hypothesis, therefore, that this literal-surface reading was both intended by its authors and understood by its listener-readers, and that I, too, can achieve a degree of comprehension at that level. Certainly the medical and theological discourses in the expository modes of commentary and debated questions were understood at this level, but the literary discourses were as well. The fableor Jean Bodel may raise fewer difficulties, but even the convolutions and parody of André the Chaplain and the rhetoric and wordplay of Jean Renart could make sense to their audiences at the narrative surface. By remaining at the literal level, I by no means intend to deny the historical possibility of numerous other readings. Medieval authors, listeners, and readers were capable of exploring the riches of multiple interpretations, just as modern critics have had the pleasure of discovering them for themselves. Hermeneutic complexity was itself a medieval phenomenon, but it need not exclude the validity of the more simplistic surface level for audiences both medieval and modern. The stance I have adopted for this study, therefore, approximates what used to be called "content analysis." As a "flat" reading, it will offer little of interest to modern literary critics who cultivate a penchant for "richly textured" meaning. Unresponsive to the nuances of language and rhetoric, I shall concentrate on the distinctly audible and banal, thereby slighting irony, satire, humor, and all the poetic inventions that intrigue critics. Although I have frequently found myself laughing at passages in Jean Renart or the fabliaux, I have refrained from signaling elements of humor because I can never be assured that I share a sense of the comic with medieval audiences. While the surface interpretation at which I dwell undoubtedly impoverishes the beauty and charm of literary works, it has become my strategic choice, and I hypothesize it as a plausible reading at the time the works were composed.

However modern critics may understand a particular text of medieval literature, the modern historian is ultimately concerned with its reception by a medieval audience. How did contemporary men and women hear, read, and understand not only the literary but also the other discourses? Moreover, although poststructuralist critics often exclude context from their agenda, and literary scholars in general have discharged their duties when they have proposed a reading of a text, historians may not avoid the central issue of the relationship between text and history. How well do these theological, medical, as well as literary, discourses disclose the historical "reality" of sexual behavior and gender differentiation, the one which is so private and both which are so universal? These important historical questions of audience response and the relation of discourse to reality raise assumptions that should be made explicit, but they are best deferred to the conclusion of this study after the five voices have been heard.

As universal functions, sexuality, reproduction, and their implications for gender have been and remain of highest concern to humans everywhere. Discoveries about these matters, even from remote epochs, continue to bear on present policy. Among political activists today one often hears that no study of the past can be value-neutral and that present situations, attitudes, and politics significantly shape our perceptions of the past. Although I would agree that neutrality toward history is not fully attainable, I would judge the obverse reaction to be unacceptable. The deliberate imposition of present concerns upon the past violates the historian's respect for alterity and impedes historical understanding. Whatever my personal political stance as a twentieth-century male, husband, father, and feminist, therefore, I shall seek to count these commitments as irrelevant to an investigation of sexuality and gender in northern France around 1200. My conscious goal is to minimize all impulses toward present politics however they succeed in reemerging unintentionally.

For the chapters that follow I shall relate the apparent sense of five discourses on sexuality and gender as they were enunciated in northern France around 1200. I have selected and arranged their contributions to follow a simple topical progression. After introducing each spokesman with his accompanying texts, context, orientation, and audience (Chapter 1), I have turned to a sociology of those who were depicted as sexually active and classified them according to their physiological, social, marital, and marginal configurations (Chapter 2). The sexual body, perceived in learned writing and concealed and exhibited in literary discourses (Chapter 3), provides an entry to sexuality itself, which I then pursue through desire (Chapter 4) to coitus (Chapter 5), with its ultimate biological consequences in children (Chapter 6). Having disclosed in as great detail as possible the contents of the five discourses on these subjects, I draw together conclusions as they pertain to sexuality, gender, and finally history.

1

THE FIVE DISCOURSES

Pierre the Chanter and the Augustinian Tradition

Pierre the Chanter originated from the lords of Hodenc-en-Bray, a family of petty nobility in the Beauvaisis. He appeared in Paris as a master of theology by the 1170s, perhaps after receiving an early education at Reims. In 1183 he became chanter of the cathedral of Notre-Dame by which title he was known for the rest of his career. An unsuccessful candidate for the bishopric of Tournai, and perhaps also of Paris, he was elected dean of Reims in the last year of his life but died in 1197 before assuming office. The popes frequently appointed him as judge-delegate while he was chanter of Paris to decide numerous cases of litigation in northern France, including King Philip's divorce. As a teacher at the cathedral school of Notre-Dame, he lectured on the Bible and became the first theologian to produce commentaries to the entire Scriptures. In addition, he debated practical problems of moral theology recorded in the form of *questiones* which were collected in a work entitled *Summa de sacramentis et de animae consiliis* organized around the sacraments but left unfinished. When the sacrament of penance was reached, the organization dissolved and the manuscripts merely transcribed questions on moral theology and casuistry without logical order. Addressing commentaries and questions to his students and colleagues, he also popularized his ideas to a broader clerical audience in a moral treatise, entitled the *Verbum abbreviatum,* whose near hundred extant manuscripts indicate wide circulation.[1]

Pierre's distinctive interests in moral theology and practical ethics attracted a dozen students or more, including perhaps Lothario di Segni, the future Pope Innocent III. Characteristic of recruitment to the Parisian schools, almost half of the circle came from the British Isles, two of whom, Robert of Courson and Thomas of Chobham, were numbered among his closest disciples.[2] Of obscure origins, Robert was a master in Paris by 1200, canon of Noyon by 1204, and of Paris by 1209. Like his teacher, he, too, was frequently appointed as papal judge-delegate in numerous lawsuits including the king's tiresome plea for divorce. Pope Innocent III undoubtedly met Robert in Paris and elevated him to the rank of cardinal-priest of Saint Stephen in Mount Celius in 1212. The following year the pope announced his intention to convoke a universal council at the Lateran Palace in 1215 and commissioned the newly created cardinal as papal legate for France to prepare for the forthcoming event. In discharge of these duties, Robert held numerous local councils, became embroiled in local disputes, and drafted statutes for the newly emerging university in Paris in 1215. The summons to the council finally removed him from France. He died at the siege of Damietta in 1219 while participating in the Fifth Crusade to Egypt. He incorporated the results of his teaching in a *Summa* of *questiones* containing the incipit: *Tota celestis philosophia* . . . Not only did he acknowledge his debt to his teacher throughout, but the entire work was organized according to the sacraments, as the Chanter's *Summa*.[3]

An illegitimate son, most likely of a parish priest at Chobham in Surrey, England, Thomas's origins were as undistinguished as Robert's. Surfacing first as a master and cleric of the bishop of London, Thomas transferred his services to Salisbury where he rose to subdean of the chapter and the bishop's *officialis* before his death in 1233–36. Although his academic career is difficult to date, it may be inferred from his writings. Among attributed sermons one survives, entitled an inaugural lecture when he began teaching theology at Paris. Since it borrowed from the Chanter's *Verbum abbreviatum,* it indicates Thomas's close association with the master. This suggestion is confirmed by Thomas's *Summa confessorum* which also drew heavily on Pierre's *questiones* and applied the master's solutions to practical issues. The hundred surviving manuscripts indicate as wide a circulation as Pierre's *Verbum abbreviatum*.[4]

Pierre the Chanter and his two associates discussed sexuality within the sacrament of marriage, the chief approach open to the Christian theologian. Each contributed in a characteristic manner. Pierre forged the basic elements in his scriptural commentaries and the *Verbum abbreviatum,* but he apparently had not yet written down his *questiones* on marriage. Still involved with the complexities of penance, the compilers of the *Summa de sacramentis* omitted sustained discussion of marriage. Robert's treatment of the sacrament, however, not only incorporated the Chanter's arguments and terminology but frequently referred explicitly to the opinions of "our master the Chanter," noting "as the Chanter was wont to affirm." On one occasion he specified that "just as the aforesaid Chanter, our master, asserted in the last year of his life when it was vigorously disputed . . ."[5] We are, therefore, justified in viewing Robert of Courson's *Summa* as the final version of the Chanter's on the subject of marriage in which he reduced the master's concepts to the form of the *questio*. Thomas of Chobham, for his part, adopted the Chanter's analysis and solutions and reformulated them as advice to the priest who administered penance in the confessional, particularly to those in England. Common questions, solutions, and vocabulary demonstrate that the three constituted a coherent theological school.

Among the theologians at Paris, the Chanter and his students comprised only one of three or four flourishing schools descended from Pierre Abélard, Gilbert de la Porrée, Hugues de Saint-Victor, and Pierre the Lombard in the first half of the twelfth century. In addition, canonists inspired by Gratian's authoritative *Decretum* compiled at Bologna also discussed questions pertaining to marriage.[6] In the school debates, however, the Chanter's group ignored some, disagreed with others, took cognizance of the canon lawyers, but usually followed Pierre the Lombard most closely. Pierre the Lombard's *Libri sententiarum,* completed around 1154, was doubtless the Chanter's principal source of inspiration on marriage. By the turn of the century, theologians accepted it as their authoritative textbook, just as the canon lawyers chose Gratian's *Decretum*. On marriage and original sin the two collected and systematized the vast body of materials generated by the most influential of Church Fathers, Augustine of Hippo. The Lombard himself depended on the work of Gauthier de Mortagne, bishop of Laon (d. 1174), who, in turn, was a later disciple of the theological school at Laon founded at the beginning of the century by Anselme de Laon (d. 1117) and Guillaume de Champeaux (d. 1122). Anselme and Guillaume began the monumental task of collecting and organizing patristic opinion according to subject matter, which were assembled in two basic formats. On the one hand, they appended the materials to the text of Scriptures as interpretative commentary, thus producing the *Glossa ordinaria,* which became the standard commentary for Bible study. On the other, they collected varied opinions of the Church Fathers, particularly of Augustine, in *Sententie* devoted to specific topics such as marriage and original sin. Treatises on these subjects became the first monographs of a nascent scholastic theology.[7] By a laborious process of collecting and sifting, the school of Laon prepared the Augustinian materials for Pierre the Lombard, who transmitted them directly to the Chanter and his students.

Augustine's were not the sole views to be considered by the twelfth-century theologians, but they were the chief authority for the theological tradition inherited by Pierre the Chanter and his school. Although the Church Father's analysis was undoubtedly shaped by his own sexual experiences, so poignantly revealed in his *Confessions,* it was equally informed by the controversies that agitated the post-Constantinian Christians of the fourth and fifth centuries. His first sustained treatments were the *De bono conjugali* and the *De Genesi ad litteram* composed in the first decade of the fifth century to establish a middle position between two opposing extremes. On one side were the Manicheans, who, as radical dualists, sharply separated the goodness of spirit from the wickedness of matter and condemned sexuality, procreation, and marriage as ineradicably evil. On the other was the Roman priest Jovian, who depreciated the value of holy virginity and asserted that the married state was equally meritorious. Against the former, Augustine argued for the divine institution and positive value (*bonum*) of marriage; against the latter, he sought to demonstrate the corruption of human sexuality through the Fall into sin. Marriage, therefore, directly implicated the nature and propagation of original sin. Two decades later, when the British monk Pelagius had proposed a doctrine of the Fall that defined original sin as merely following a bad example rather than a corruption of human nature, Augustine replied with a polemic, *De nuptiis et concupiscentia,* against the contemporary Pelagian bishop, Julian of Eclanum. In this and other anti-Pelagian tracts, he deepened his exploration of sexuality and the transmission of original sin throughout the human race. About the same time, he included a summation within the fourteenth book of his monumental *De civitate dei,* which constituted his final and most sustained analysis.[8]

The appearance of heterodoxy in France in the twelfth century gave new life to the fifth-century arguments over sexuality and marriage. The Paterini around Arras and the Cathars in the south, for example, rehabilitated Manichean dualism to impute evil to sexuality, propagation, and marriage.[9] Once again the theologians revived Augustinian doctrine to contest these opinions. Although Pierre the Chanter did not engage the heretics in polemics directly, he was aware of their positions. Commenting on the Genesis (1:28) passage where God commanded the first parents to replenish the earth, he noted that God thereby instituted marriage between man and woman which, in turn, confuted the Manichean doctrine that no intercourse could be conducted without mortal sin. To the classic Pauline passage on marriage (1 Cor. 7) he added that Christ's presence at the wedding of Cana contradicted heretics who claim that marriage is not good. In another context he identified the *Cathari* as those who claim to be pure through opposition to second marriages but are, in fact, impure in contrast to their name. Robert of Courson denounced as semiheretics those who invoke the routine liturgical calendar to exclude the laity from having sexual relations throughout the week.[10] As in the fifth century, the threat of dualist heresy in twelfth-century France compelled the theologians to reexamine the basis for human sexuality and marriage.

Pierre the Chanter and his circle were the last spokesmen for the Augustinian tradition of sexuality and marriage before it was challenged from the new direction of Aristotle. From the early Middle Ages into the first half of the twelfth century, the Greek philosopher was known chiefly as a logician. Throughout the second half of the century, however, his treatises on metaphysics and natural science were gradually translated into Latin from Arabic sources. Although they were probably available to the masters of arts and the theologians, those of the Chanter's school largely ignored them. When, however, they came to the full attention of theologians during the first decade of the thirteenth century, they encountered sharp hostility. The immediate circumstances were connected to a local investigation that uncovered a group of heretical clerics, some who had studied theology at Paris. Although the group held various heterodox views, the two chief members, master Amaury de Bène and master David de Dinant apparently shared common inclinations to pantheism. Robert of Courson and perhaps even Thomas of Chobham were among three theologians commissioned to investigate. In 1210 master Pierre de Corbeil, archbishop of Sens and a former theologian, and Pierre de Nemours, bishop of Paris, convoked a provincial church council at Paris which formally condemned the doctrines of Amaury and David. The *Quaternuli* of David de Dinant were to be brought to the bishop and burned, and it was further decreed that the books of Aristotle on natural philosophy and their commentaries were forbidden to be taught publicly or privately under penalty of excommunication. Robert of Courson renewed the substance of these decrees in 1215 as papal legate when he drafted the statutes of the university. [11]

Among the views the contemporary chroniclers imputed to these clerics, few pertained directly to sexuality. Apparently some had asserted that fornication or adultery committed in charity or while possessed by the Holy Spirit were not sins. [12] More important was the close connection between David de Dinant's condemnation and the prohibition against Aristotle which is now apparent from the fragments of David's *Quaternuli* which have been recovered. These include not only doctrines of philosophical materialism but also copious extracts from Aristotle's vast corpus on natural science and philosophy. We shall see that these writings contained new views about nature, sexuality, and women that challenged twelfth-century thought and eventually shaped the scholastic theology and philosophy of the thirteenth century. [13] Pierre the Chanter and his colleagues, therefore, flourished at a moment just before the upsurge of Aristotelianism which engulfed the later Middle Ages.

As ecclesiastics, the theologians were fully committed to the church's program on matrimony. During the tenth and eleventh centuries, churchmen had begun to assert exclusive jurisdiction over all matters pertaining to marriage—and by extension to sexuality—in an effort to replace local and familial customs with a universal and uniform ecclesiastical law. By 1200 this jurisdictional supremacy had been carefully formulated, but the problem remained to persuade the laity's acceptance.[14] In France churchmen started at the highest level of society with the royalty. Reviewing and contesting the marital arrangements of the kings Robert the Pious and Philip I in the tenth and eleventh centuries, these clerical interventions culminated at the turn of the twelfth century in the imbroglios between King Philip Augustus and Queen Ingeborg. After the hesitant initiatives of the aged Celestine III, the youthful Innocent III decided to open his pontificate with decisive action. Entering the dispute at the request of Ingeborg, the pope occasionally neglected his suppliant's plight to assure his ultimate goal of uncontested jurisdiction over the affair. Although Philip was able to bargain for personal accommodations, at each crucial stage he was forced to concede that Innocent enjoyed the final right to judge his marriage.[15] Confirming this principle at the inconvenience of both the king and queen, Innocent undoubtedly hoped that the victory at the summit of royalty would facilitate the church's jurisdiction down through society.

By asserting exclusive jurisdiction, churchmen also assumed responsibility for defining this fundamental human institution with extreme care. At the end of the twelfth century, the canonists and theologians had come to a consensus over the major contours of a matrimonial model applicable to the laity. Circumscribed by a series of inalterable restrictions, Christian marriage was to be monogamous (limited to one husband and one wife), exogamous (exclusive of close relations defined by blood or other marriages), and indissoluble (terminated only by the death of one of the partners). It was the exclusive domain for sexual activity thereby rendering all extramarital behavior as subject to punishment. And finally, it was to be freely contracted by both parties, which raised an important question still under debate among canonists and theologians during the first half of the century:[16] Was the ultimate foundation constituting marriage consent or intercourse? Posed in this fashion, the question highlighted the function of sexuality within marriage.

Those who argued for intercourse evoked the Pauline passage that marriage is a sacrament symbolizing the union between Christ and the church. The sexual union between husband and wife, therefore, represents the mystical union between Christ and the church, thus linking intercourse with indissolubility. The canonist Gratian, the foremost proponent of this position, proposed a two-stage process in the formation of marriage: first, the exchange of words that conveys consent and, second, consummation that completes or perfects the marriage bond. The latter creates the mutual obligation to pay the marital debt as the Apostle Paul exhorted and is necessary for the constitution of marriage. Gratian's authoritative support for the theory of copulation, however, did not calm critics. Not only had ascetics like Peter Damian long objected to privileging the iniquitous sexuality at the center of matrimony, but canonists themselves' found the double solution unsatisfactory.[17]

Those who argued for consent alone drew upon Roman law and added support from the biblical example of Mary and Joseph. Since, by this time, theologians had agreed that Jesus' parents had never had sexual relations, their marriage, which was not open to question, could only have been founded on mutual consent. Maintaining that copulation affected neither marriage or its indissolubility, Pierre the Lombard forcefully decided for consent alone. His solution required a further distinction between consent through future words (*verba de futuro*), or engagement and consent through present words (*verba de presenti*), or the marriage agreement itself. What truly constitutes a marriage is the exchange of words or signs in the present tense that express the full consent of a man and woman. Formulated in the *Libri sententiarum,* this position was accepted by influential church leaders, including the canonist Huguccio and Popes Alexander III and Innocent III, who devoted unusual attention to the subject of marriage. By siding with consent to the exclusion of all other elements, the popes attempted to free marriage from the influence of families and lords and to place it entirely within the partner's free choice guaranteed by ecclesiastical law.[18] With the resolution of this question, the major definitions of marriage were settled by the turn of the twelfth and thirteenth centuries.

Pierre the Chanter and Robert of Courson had both collaborated with the popes to assert jurisdiction over Philip Augustus's marriage.[19] Neither, however, was directly involved in the canonists' and theologians' enterprise to define the nature of marriage. Coming late to the scene, they merely accepted the consensus formulated by the Lombard. Their contribution to the issues of sexuality and marriage was to develop the science of casuistry. Pierre raised practical and specific cases in his lectures and debates. His arguments and solutions were finally written down by Robert of Courson and adapted for pastoral use in the confessional by Thomas of Chobham and others. The importance of this casuistry and these guides to confessors was immeasurably increased when Pope Innocent III decreed at the Lateran Council of 1215 that all the faithful of both sexes were to say confession and submit to penance at least once a year.[20] This legislation instituted a vast technology for imposing ecclesiastical discipline upon the moral lives of the laity throughout Western Christendom. Implementation of the program required time and varied according to place, but by preparing handbooks for the growing needs of confessors the Chanter and his school extended their influence far beyond the confines of Paris and northern France.

Pierre the Chanter's audience was not limited to the students and priests who attended his classes and read his treatises but also reached out to all who heard the preaching of his students. Pierre himself left no sermons of his own but inspired a group of active preachers who propagated his teachings throughout northern France, chief among whom were Foulques de Neuilly and Jacques de Vitry, two of the most celebrated preachers of the day. Jacques, the Chanter's student by 1187, had earned his master's degree by 1193 and was ordained a priest shortly thereafter in Paris. By 1211 he appeared in the diocese of Liège drawn by the personality and reputation of Marie d'Oignies, a remarkable woman who was to become the patron saint for a new movement of female spirituality. [21]

Marie was born in 1176 to a wealthy family from the Liégeois town of Nivelles. Exhibiting signs of precocious sanctity from birth, her childhood was so different from other girls that her parents wondered "what sort will our daughter be?" Nonetheless, they arranged a marriage for her at age fourteen. Soon after she persuaded her husband Jean to discontinue their conjugal rights and to pursue a chaste life of asceticism and charity in the service of lepers in nearby Willambroux. When their fame attracted numerous admirers, they retreated to the house of Augustinian canons of Saint-Nicholas in the neighboring town of Oignies where Marie entered as a lay *conversa*. In a cell near Saint-Nicholas Marie performed miracles, acts of sanctity and ascetic austerities that undoubtedly shortened her life. On 23 June 1213, at the age of thirty-six, she died before the altar of Saint-Nicholas after refusing food for fifty-three days. [22]

Despite her flight from publicity, her deeds attracted numerous clergymen to Oignies, including Foulques, bishop of Toulouse, exiled from his diocese by the Albigensian heretics, and masters and preachers from Paris, chief among whom were Jean de Nivelles, Jean de Liro, and, as we have seen, Jacques de Vitry, who made Saint-Nicholas a base for preaching throughout the diocese of Liège. [23] When Jacques encountered difficulties in his ministry, Marie encouraged him to persist and to extend his preaching against the Albigensians and on behalf of the Holy Land. [24] As reward for his latter efforts, the canons of Acre elected him bishop in 1216. From 1218 to 1221 he participated in the Fifth Crusade against Egypt, and in 1229 he was elevated to the dignity of the cardinal bishop of Tusculum in which post he remained until his death in 1240. [25]

Jacques de Vitry composed a biography, the *Vita Mariae Oigniacensis,* addressed to Bishop Foulques of Toulouse shortly after her death when his recollections were still vivid. [26] This remains our chief source for her life. He left no hint that Marie understood or wrote Latin. During her last ecstasies, for example, she expounded the Scriptures and the *Magnificat* of the Virgin Mary in versified French; her knowledge of theology was gained from the preachers resident at Saint-Nicholas.[27] Through the instrument of biography, therefore, Jacques was her mouthpiece. Although the *Vita* undoubtedly reflects attitudes imparted by Jacque's teacher at Paris,[28] it was also informed by close association with and admiration for the saintly woman herself. The question of authenticity, therefore, can be resolved if we consider Marie's voice as the hyphenated expression of "Marie-Jacques." By recording Marie's life, Jacques created a model for female sanctity and spirituality and drafted the *Vita,* the founding charter for the movement of beguines that introduced new institutions for shaping female life. After Marie's death, houses of beguines appeared at Oignies and Nivelles and spread into the Lowlands and Rhineland throughout the thirteenth century. With less-structured institutions and independent of the established monastic orders, these beguinages extended semimonastic protection and the opportunity to lead lives of chastity and worldly renunciation to expanding numbers of lay and married women.[29]

Marie's *Vita* circulated in numerous manuscripts, but, when Vincent de Beauvais, the Dominican encyclopedist, incorporated it into his influential *Speculum historiale* in the mid-thirteenth century, Marie became a prototype of the *mulier religiosa/sancta* who renewed the ideals of ascetic sanctity for women in the thirteenth century.[30] Marie's chastity was anchored in the traditions of monastic virginity formulated in the gnostic theories of early Christianity and transmitted to the West through Eastern monasticism. Her spiritual comportment closely followed the traditional elements of the ancient virgin monks.[31] If monks were reputed to lead angelic lives through chastity, Marie herself was continually aware of the presence of angels. Like early monks, she adopted poverty and insisted on supporting herself with the work of her hands. She healed the sick and received visions; her prophecies were notable for accuracy in detail.[32] Like preceding saints, she could detect the unconsecrated host or even the host consecrated by unworthy priests. Equally striking was the extremity of her alimentary practices—for example, her constant refusal of food and her deriving nourishment from the eucharist.[33] Of particular concern is the transferal of these saintly practices, which had been limited to virgins in traditional monasticism—that is, to those who have never had sexual relations—to married women. Marie's exemplary chastity followed a movement initiated by monastic reform in the previous century. The regular canons, the Carthusians, and particularly the Cistercians, for example, began to modify their policies of recruitment. Renouncing oblates—that is, children offered to monasteries to be raised as monks and nuns—they accepted into their ranks only adults who chose the monastic vocation freely. Presumably, they did not refuse men and women who had had previous sexual experience as long as they were willing to submit to vows of chastity for the future.[34] As a *mulier religiosa,* therefore, Marie d'Oignies exemplified the new religious life that opened the monastic calling to adult and married women.

The Prose Salernitan Questions and the Galenic Tradition

The *Prose Salernitan Questions* is the title modern editors ascribe to manuscripts circulating around 1200 that contain collections of scientific and medical questions originating in the schools of Salerno. The manuscripts contain other materials as well, and, despite Salernitan inspiration, the geographic distribution of the collections denotes a provenance from Northern Europe, especially England and France. Not only are the majority and most extensive collections of English provenance, but the only named contemporary masters are five Englishmen, three from Hereford, one of whom became bishop of the see in 1216. Another important manuscript (*Questiones Alani*) was copied for the chapter of Notre-Dame in Paris by the fourth decade of the thirteenth century.[35] This association with France is further reinforced by the medical tradition from which the collections developed. The immediate source for the *Prose Salernitan Questions* is Guillaume de Conches whose *De philosophia mundi* (1125–35) was later revised and expanded in his *Dragmaticon* (1146–49). Reminiscent of Isidore of Seville's encyclopedia, these treatises were cosmologies of natural philosophy that included sexual matters which, in turn, were quoted by the *Prose Salernitan Questions* and constituted a point of departure for discussion. The *Dragmaticon* was dedicated to Geoffroi le Bel, the count of Anjou, while Guillaume was apparently in his entourage, but Guillaume's later scholarly work was composed while he was at Paris.[36]

A faculty of medicine emerged at Paris at the turn of the twelfth century. By 1213 those who taught medicine (*physica*) were distinguished from theology, canon law and Roman law, and the masters of arts. Not long before this date Alexander Neckham had copied a list of textbooks for each of the faculties active at Paris.[37] By 1193 the most prominent master teaching medicine at Paris—indeed, the only master whose name has survived— was Gilles de Corbeil, who forged personal links with the medical traditions of Salerno and contemporary theologians at Paris. Originating from the French royal domain, he learned his elements of medicine at Salerno, then passed to Montpellier where he disagreed vigorously with the doctrine taught there, and finally established himself at Paris, an enthusiastic proponent of the Salernitan medical theories. His treatises, composed in Latin verse as a mnemonic device for teaching, treated the standard subjects of uroscopy and pulse measurement as well as pharmacology, diagnosis, and symptomatology. The first two achieved authoritative status by the first decade of the thirteenth century when they circulated in numerous copies and attracted commentaries. In addition, Gilles composed a long satirical poem, *Hierapigra ad purgandos prelatos* (literally: "pills to purge prelates"), which shared moral concerns with Pierre the Chanter and excerpted important passages directly from the latter's *Verbum abbreviatum*. As a poet Gilles was also sensitive to competition from clerics who wrote amatory verse. Dedicating his treatise on pharmacology to a certain Richard, he pleaded with his patron to urge young students to recognize the merits of his work over the frivolities and lascivious loves of Ovid. Although Gilles's extant medical corpus contained no treatise devoted expressly to sexuality, the subject appeared tangentially. In a work on pharmacology, for example, he discussed the aphrodisiac *Diasatyrion* which offered an opportunity to expatiate on the frenzies of sexual excess. The moral concerns of the *Hierapigra,* moreover, led to excurses on the libidinal life of the clergy.[38]

Salerno enjoyed a reputation as the foremost center of medical learning in Western Europe throughout the twelfth century. In Chrétien de Troyes' *Cligès,* for example, the heroine's dissimulation of death through pharmacology may have duped the local doctors but not three visiting physicians from Salerno (vv. 5745–47). When the lovers in Marie de France's *Les deus amanz* require a potion to surmount an ordeal, they also apply to Salerno (vv. 95–142). As exemplified by Gilles de Corbeil's journey from Salerno to Paris, the English and French continuators of Guillaume de Conches founded their learning on the medical theory of the celebrated Salerno. Until the second half of the eleventh century the Italian seaport had been known chiefly for its health spa and center of healing, but, by the 1070s with the arrival of Constantinus Africanus, a drug merchant from Tunis, the physicians of Salerno began to expand their interests from the practice to the theory of medicine. In addition to elixirs, Constantinus's luggage contained Arabic medical treatises which he translated into Latin when he became a Christian and entered the monastery at nearby Monte Cassino. His prolific production supplied Western Europe with a series of monographs on a broad range of subjects. The *De coitu* (On male sexual intercourse), for example, was translated from a treatise by Ibn al-Jazzār who was best known for his widely circulating compendium *Viaticum* (*Zād al-Musāfir [wa qūt al-ḥāḍir]*). Constantinus also translated the *De genitalibus membris* (On the sexual organs [both female and male]) from 'Alī ibn al-'Abbās al-Majūsī's *Pantegni* (*Kamil aṣ-Ṣina 'a [aṭ-Ṭibbīya]*) which circulated further as a separate treatise. Closely related to these works was the Salernitan *Liber minor de coitu* which focused on sexual dysfunctions and therapy.[39] The revival of theoretical learning further stimulated the composition of anatomical studies at Salerno. The *Prose Salernitan Questions* did not concern themselves directly with anatomy, but they appear to have accepted the conclusions of the Salernitan anatomists such as the *Anatomia Richardi Salernitani* and the *Anatomia magistri Nicolai* whose manuscripts circulated in France and England.[40] The brief *Isagoge Iohannicii* translated from *Masā 'il fi ṭ-ṭibb* became the standard introduction to Salernitan medicine throughout the Latin West. The list of books that Alexander Neckham recommended for medical study at Paris included the *Viaticum*, the *Pantegni*, and the manual of Johannicus, all elementary texts of the Salernitan corpus.[41]

By translating Arabic treatises, Constantinus recovered the ancient medical authority of Galen of Pergamum (d. ca. 200). Prodigious and verbose, Galen's vast corpus of writings encompassed not only the full range of medicine but also delved into natural science and philosophy. Although unable to avoid a certain amount of eclecticism, he was thoroughly knowledgeable in medical traditions ranging from the ancient Hippocratic corpus (late fifth to early fourth century B.C.E.) to contemporary Hellenistic anatomists. Generally favorable to Hippocrates and often critical of Aristotle, he founded his own opinions on impressive experimental evidence. In general, he did not align himself directly with the contemporary sect of "empiricists," who concentrated on therapy based on the accumulated experience of individual practitioners, but was more disposed toward the "dogmatists," who sought to combine observation with reason and speculation in order to explain the "hidden causes" (etiology) of health and disease. With other Hellenistic scientists he shared common premises such as the four elements, the four qualities, and rudimentary human anatomy, but on specific theories such as human conception he held independent opinions. Since he wrote in Greek, his voluminous production was unavailable in the West until the Salernitans translated it into Latin from Arabic sources.

Within the vast corpus of his writings Galen had not devoted a monograph to the subject of gynecology. By the end of the twelfth century, however, an anonymous work, identified by its incipit *Cum auctor*, surfaced within Salernitan circles which applied Galenic principles to the cure of female disorders, relying primarily on the *Viaticum* and *Pantegni* of Constantinus. In the manuscripts this work was frequently associated with two other treatises devoted to women, *De curis mulierum* and *De ornatu*. By the end of the thirteenth century the three were often ascribed to the authorship of a certain Trot or Trotula.[42] Already by the beginning of the thirteenth century Trotula (Troculeus) was identified in the French vernacular commentary to Ovid's *Ars amatoria* as one who gave instruction on the nature of women.[43] During the course of the century, the name was increasingly attached to a female physician and authority on women's diseases who flourished at Salerno at an undetermined period. Her emerging reputation as a gynecological authority stimulated the copying of manuscripts of the three works attributed to her by the late Middle Ages (extant in over 110 manuscripts). Although *Cum auctor* cannot be attributed to Trotula with any certainty, it was nonetheless known to the Salernitan circles of England and northern France around 1200. (At least two manuscripts have survived from this period.) A reference to a queen of France treated for amenorrhea further attaches the work to a French milieu.[44]

Within the field of gynecology Galen's opinions differed significantly with those of another Greek authority, Soranus of Ephesus, who wrote at the beginning of the second century. Adhering to the sect of the "methodists" who distinguished themselves from both "empiricists" and the "dogmatists" to whom Galen belonged, Soranus felt it sufficient to know only the general conditions of the body in order to apply pragmatic remedies. Caelius Aurelianus paraphrased Soranus's *Gynecology* in Latin in the fifth century, and a certain Muscio addressed it to midwives in the sixth. Although Muscio's version circulated more widely, Caelius's has survived in only one manuscript, but it was one to which physicians in northern France may have had access. A volume in the great library of master Richard de Fournival, chancellor of the chapter of Amiens in the second quarter of the thirteenth century, contains the unique copy of Caelius Aurelianus as well as Muscio's version and other gynecological treatises. This volume may have been copied from a similar collection located at the nearby abbey of Saint-Amand. Since Richard was himself a physician, and the son of the personal physician to King Philip Augustus, these medical collections contained works that may have been more widely available to the medical profession in northern France around 1200.[45]

By and large, the Galenic tradition transmitted through Salerno to Northern Europe embodied a vast synthesis of ancient medical science. Although containing Aristotelian elements, it was not directly based on Aristotle's writings. At the end of the twelfth century, however, Aristotle's natural scientific treatises did become directly known to Western Europe through Latin translation of Arabic versions and accompanying commentaries. We have seen that the initial reaction at Paris to this direct access was hostile. The provincial council at Paris in 1210 condemned David de Dinant's *Quaternuli* containing excerpts from Aristotle's natural works, and the books of Aristotle on natural philosophy and their commentaries were forbidden to be taught under the penalty of excommunication.[46]

As Aristotle became better known through his direct works, his Arabic commentators were also made available in Latin. Chief among them was Avicenna (Ibh Sīnā, d. 1037), who not only transmitted important

Aristotelian treatises but also wrote an important medical treatise which Gerald of Cremona translated into Latin at Toledo under the title of the *Liber canonis*. Combining Aristotelian with Galenic elements, the *Liber canonis* was a systematic and organized encyclopedia in contrast to Galen whose multiple monographs lacked overall coherence. Comprehensive in scope and well delineated in organization, it provided Western Europe with the most extensive summary of ancient medicine available in Latin to its date. Although Gerald's translation was completed by the time of his death in 1187, Avicenna's manual did not come into use until the second quarter of the thirteenth century, after which time it became the standard medical text in Paris and elsewhere. Since the *Prose Salernitan Questions* were collected at the turn of the twelfth century, they yield virtually no recognition either to Aristotle's natural treatises or to Avicenna's compendium.[47] Thus positioned, the *Salernitan Questions* stand at the eve of an era when Galen predominated, and before the dawn of the new Aristotle and his Arabic interpreters who reshaped the scientific world of the thirteenth century.

Composed for the learned physicians in the schools devoted to fundamental science, the *Prose Salernitan Questions* offered scant help for medical practitioners. Except for a brief allusion to lovesickness, they displayed little interest in the morbidity, dysfunction, and therapy of sexuality. Instead, they assumed an attitude akin to the ancient Galen, and transmitted by the Salernitans, who was not unsympathetic to the "empiricists" (those who concentrated on therapeutics) but hostile to the "methodists" (those who advocated mastery of a short canon of rules) and strongly in favor of the "dogmatists" or "rationalists" who sought to investigate the underlying causes of health and disease. In this spirit, for example, the Salernitan anatomists sought to describe the body systematically. Because anatomical dissection of humans had been abandoned in Antiquity even before Galen's time, they proceeded not in the order of dissection but in a logical sequence that classified and arranged the parts of the body for teaching purposes. With similar goals, the *Prose Salernitan Questions* sought to understand the physiology and psychology underlying sexuality, privileging logic and analogy over empirical observation and explanation over description. After a long period of disinterest during the early Middle Ages, attention to theoretical issues reemerged in the twelfth century.

Iohannicius's *Isagoge,* the standard manual for beginning students in the twelfth century, framed the study of medicine within the vast cosmology of science. By applying a series of logical divisions that separated the component parts, Iohannicius attempted to organize the entire discipline into a comprehensive scheme of categories. A brief and selective sketch will merely suggest the scope of the enterprise: medicine is divided between theory and practice. The former treats natural, nonnatural (environmental), and contranatural (pathological) conditions. Natural factors can be divided into fundamental elements, mixtures, compositions, members, virtues, operations, and spirits to which the distinctions of age, color, figure, and difference between the sexes may also be added. There are four elements each with a pair of corresponding qualities: fire (hot and dry), air (hot and moist), water (cold and moist), and earth (cold and dry). There are four compositions, also called humors, each with a pair of characteristic qualities and a corresponding complexion: blood (hot and moist, sanguine), phlegm (cold and moist, phlegmatic), red bile (hot and dry, choleric), and black bile (cold and dry, melancholic). The principal members of the body also number four, each served by a corresponding network: the brain by nerves, the heart by arteries, the liver by veins, and the testicles by the spermatic ducts. Derived from the principal members are the secondary organs of the stomach, kidneys, and intestines. There are three virtues or forces: animal (*anima* = soul), spiritual (that is, spirit), and natural. Among the last are those which minister and others which are ministered to, that is, to generate, nourish, and feed. There are also three spirits: the natural which flows from the liver through the veins, the vital from the heart through the arteries, and the animal (soul) from the brain through the nerves. Age consists of childhood, youth, maturity, and old age, and color involves skin and hair each with characteristic complexions. Sexual difference likewise entails complexion. Men are hot and dry; women cold and moist. Even the seasons of the year can be arranged under this basic classification: spring (hot and moist), summer (hot and dry), autumn (cold and dry), and winter (cold and moist). Treated in rapid succession, other subjects include sleep and sexual intercourse (*coitus*) which normally dries and cools the body through the diminution of natural virtue. When exercised rapidly, however, the body is heated. In a few introductory pages, Iohannicius thus linked the physiology of sexuality with the scientific cosmos as understood within the Galenic tradition. Guillaume de Conches and the *Prose Salernitan Questions,* however, applied special interest to the sexual realm.[48]

When Constantinus Africanus translated the basic corpus of Arabic-Greek medical texts, he also transmitted attitudes toward sexuality—especially the nonprocreative aspects of contraception and abortion—that opposed current religious beliefs in Western Europe. Not following his Arabic and Greek sources word for word, he edited them by selectively retaining and omitting phrases and passages. The result was neither full fidelity to the non-Christian sources nor unquestioning respect for Latin theological opinion but a different and independent stand on sexuality.[49] The *Prose Salernitan Questions* retained this stance a century later in northern France and England. In the first redaction (*De philosophia mundi*), Guillaume de Conches had hesitated to pursue treatment of a sexual matter because of fear of offending the sensibilities of monks who might reject his work. In the second version (*Dragmaticon*), his interlocutor resumed the discussion by objecting that since sexual intercourse is not decent matter, it should not be discussed further. Guillaume replied spiritedly that nothing natural can be shameful because it is the gift of creation. Only hypocrites avoid such matters, abhorring names rather than reality. Repeating Guillaume's repost verbatim, the *Prose Salernitan Questions* began to propose alternatives to theological theses on sexuality. We shall see that the delight experienced in coitus, for example, can be understood both by the theological theory of concupiscence and by the concentration of nerves in the genitals. Alongside the biblical doctrine of the Fall can be placed a medical-natural theory (*secundum phisicam*) that explains the origin of sin through the destruction of a balanced temperament. Like Constantinus Africanus, therefore, the physicians of the *Prose Salernitan Questions* did not so much oppose the theologians as propose independent and alternative theories.[50]

André the Chaplain and the Ovidian Tradition

André the Chaplain's treatise *De amore* discloses four items about its author: he was named André, was chaplain of a royal hall (*aulae regiae capellani*), wrote after 1 May 1174 (the last date noted), and for the personal benefit of a young man named Gautier.[51] Although these constitute the most reliable data available on authorship, they find scant confirmation outside the text. Since all events mentioned in the text take place within France, the king must be French, but no André has yet been found among the chaplains of the Capetian court.[52] The chapel in the royal hall, however, may not have been attached to the perambulating central *curia regis*, but rather at one of the castles or palaces throughout the royal domain whose chaplains were rarely named. An André the Chaplain does appear between 1182 and 1186 at the court of Marie, countess of Champagne, who plays an important role in the treatise.[53] The treatise also mentions a king of Hungary, who might be identified with Bella III, who came into prominence in France during the negotiations leading to his wedding in 1186 to Marguerite, half-sister of Philip Augustus.[54] In 1186—to continue the line of reasoning—when André dropped from sight at Troyes, he may have transferred to royal employment. On these tenuous grounds scholars usually date the treatise to the mid-1180s (1182–86, for example), but firm evidence for dating does not occur until 1238–45, when the work was first unmistakably quoted by another author.[55] The linkage with the king of

France nonetheless receives further corroboration from the royal archives where the treatise was deposited with the king's registers and appears in the first inventory of 1348.[56] Because of this royal association, a favorite candidate for the young Gautier in modern scholarship is the royal chamberlain Gautier, called "the Young" to distinguish him from Gautier his father. Although a layman, this Gautier may be presumed to have been sufficiently literate to read André's Latin treatise because he was credited with reconstituting the royal archives after their loss in 1194, which, in turn may explain how the book finally entered the archives.[57] The identification of Gautier the Young with André's dedicatee nonetheless remains conjectural. Despite these uncertainties, we can still situate André the Chaplain's *De amore* within a royal milieu in northern France during the reign of Philip Augustus.

If the author's figure remains shadowy, the principal contours of his treatise are distinct—at least from a distance. In the tradition of Latin school texts, the books and chapters are clearly delineated and rubricated.[58] André addressed a preface to Gautier in response to his request to be instructed in love. The treatise is divided into three books, of which the first defines love by posing three standard scholastic questions: What (*quid*) is love? Who (*quis*) can love? How (*qualiter*) may it be acquired?[59] The second book demonstrates how love can be preserved with practical advice. Having fulfilled the dedicatee's petition, the third book (*De reprobatione amoris*) reverses itself by marshaling seventeen arguments against love, compiling a misogynistic catalogue of female failings, and finally urging Gautier to reject love altogether.

As the reader approaches the treatise more closely, however, he becomes aware of numerous and lengthy detours. After announcing five ways of acquiring love in chapter 6 of Book I, at the third (eloquence) André divagated to divide society into four classes (three lay and one clerical) and proceeded to enlist one man from each of the three lay classes (townsmen, nobility, and upper nobility) to engage in conversation women from each of the classes in an effort to seduce them. This produced eight out of nine possible extensive dialogues in which the man attempts to employ eloquence (or perhaps, more accurately, argumentation) to persuade the woman to accept his love. The convoluted conversations in chapter 6, therefore, occupy more than half (55%) of the entire treatise.[60] André embedded two further digressions within this detour. As the nobleman engages the noblewoman, he proposes treatment of three kinds of ladies (loving, promiscuous, and prudish), according to three elaborate allegories: the three gates to the god of love's palace, three companies of women on horseback, and three concentric gardens (vernal, wet, and arid), and concludes this excursion with twelve precepts of love. The argument between the higher nobleman and the noble lady was decided by an epistolary exchange with the countess of Champagne who decrees that love is incompatible with marriage. The practical advice of Book II includes further important digressions. Chapter 7 provides twenty-one cases of love casuistry that are adjudicated by noble ladies, including Queen Eleanor, and the countesses of Champagne, Narbonne, and Flanders. (This consumes 7% of the total text.) Chapter 8 contains a Latin version of a vernacular romance narrating the capture of a sparrow hawk by a knight, which, in turn, concludes with a scroll containing thirty-one precepts of love.

Within this allegedly simple but actually imbricated framework, André crammed a burgeoning encyclopedia of love lore drawn from the broadest range of sources. Among our five spokesmen he was certainly the most widely learned. As an ordained priest, he intoned the standard theological arguments on sexuality and marriage, sharpening them to the point of caricature in Book III. Recent scholarship has shown that his casuistic treatment was profoundly, if not obviously, informed by the canon law of marriage, particularly within the collection of love judgments.[61] Although not always accurate, he also revealed a modicum of medical knowledge. From training in the arts of grammar and rhetoric, he discoursed within the literary tradition of allegory flourishing in both Latin and vernacular. Equally notable was his familiarity with vernacular French literature not formally part of the Latin school curriculum. Including a romance about a sparrow hawk and recalling the names of Fenice, Iseut, and Blancheflor, heroines in the vernacular, the De amore resonated with contemporary French literary modes.[62] Beyond his sensitivity to the vernacular, André could not avoid the obvious and fundamental influence of his Latin schooling in the arts. Although infrequently quoted, the ancient poet Ovid was the supreme master of André the Chaplain, whose De amore faithfully replicated both the goal and triune structure of the Ars amatoria, Ovid's classic of love.

Given the divagations and heterogeneity, it is not surprising that André's encyclopedia of love appears to be riddled with contradictions.[63] Not only does overt antagonism separate the first two books from Book III which summarily rejects all that precedes, but attentive readers have detected numerous discrepancies and anomalies, particularly during the eight dialogues. In the last two, for example, between the man of the higher nobility and the noble woman and the woman of his own class, André enunciated his most controversial propositions about sexuality and adultery. As the man attempts to seduce the woman, he shifts arguments with disconcerting sophistry to gain advantage, thus obliging his opponent to match his convolutions.[64] In the last dialogue, she even changes her persona from a young maiden, to a mature widow, and then back to a woman with no sexual experience, while the man slips from wedlock to a beautiful wife to the clerical state. At times within these twists and turns it becomes difficult to ascertain the interlocutor's own opinions, not to speak of the author's. The fundamental anomaly nonetheless remains that of an ordained chaplain openly and learnedly discoursing on sexual love and occasionally appearing to argue for adultery. It is no wonder that modern exegetes have been prone to regard the whole treatise as an elaborate spoof.

Long after André's day, the attraction of his theme has generated wide and varied audiences for the *De amore*. Doubtlessly a result of the inconsistencies, the diversity of interpretation was matched by the heterogeneity of the audience. His first attested reader was the married layman, Albertanus of Brescia, who sought to incorporate him into a pious Latin treatise on the Christian love of God and neighbor between 1238 and 1245. In 1277 the bishop of Paris, Etienne Tempier, found no redeeming merit in André's pages, condemned them unequivocally along with a treatise on sorcery, and enjoined reading under pain of excommunication. The first recorded vernacular reader was probably the author of the *Livre d'Enanchet,* who responded ambiguously as he attempted to adopt André as an example of secular love. By 1290, however, a cleric, Drouart de la Vache, found it funny, or at least it made him laugh, when he wrote a French version.[65]

This legacy of widely varying responses has persisted into modern times. When Gaston Paris invented the concept of "courtly love" in 1883, he assumed that André the Chaplain had written the textbook. Paris and his followers simply accepted the *De amore* as an accurate and contemporary statement on aristocratic love in the twelfth century.[66] Reacting to this position, later scholars have been unable to read him without interposing distance between the author and his audience. As exemplified by D. W. Robertson, Jr., a dominant fashion has seen the work as skillfully constructed irony in which André was actually parodying the love he seemed to be proposing. Others have preferred to regard it simply as an elaborately contrived joke. The penchant for humor has led some to read André's scholastic Latin as a string of obscenities and double entendres for the ribald amusement of a clerical audience. Until recently, modern readership has been preoccupied to find authorial unity behind the divagations and inconsistences of the text—to explain how a single mind could have tolerated so many contradictions—but the present critical climate probably renders futile any further attempt to find pervading integrity within the text.[67] For my part, I have abandoned the search for overarching consistency and am content to accept the work as an encyclopedia rich in amatory lore, replete with contradictions, perhaps irony (whether intentional or not), and maybe even humor. For me the parts of the *De amore* are greater than the whole, and I am no longer interested in deciphering contradictions to uncover authorial coherence. André may well have intended his contradictions to be an elaborate parody on current theological, medical, and erotic doctrine which his clerical audience fully appreciated, but I shall refrain from applauding his comedy. André's importance for my purposes is to bear witness to the tradition of the twelfth-century clerical schools where Ovid was taught.

Equally compelling to creating sense out of André's inconsistencies is the historical task to identify his immediate audience at the end of the twelfth century. The larger group to whom the treatise was addressed was personified by André's friend Gautier. Was he a royal chamberlain and a literate layman? If so, those of his social peers who could understand André's elaborated Latin and appreciate his school learning were limited in number. If, however, Gautier was a cleric who was contemplating love or even compromising his clerical ambitions through marriage, André would find a larger and more comprehending audience. The De amore was not unaware of the sexual problems facing the clergy. In one brief chapter (Book I, ch. 7) proclaiming that the clerical status is higher and more noble than the three lay estates, André was remarkably complacent about clerical love. In the conversation immediately preceding, moreover, the man of the higher nobility, who has attempted to seduce his lady peer, turns out to be a cleric himself. Despite the fact that the treatise was composed in the clergy's language, it nonetheless devotes considerably more attention to the laity as is seen in the disproportionate length of the eight dialogues, and the sensitivity to the idioms, conventions, and genres of vernacular literature written expressly for the laity. Like his overarching theme, André's audience is, therefore, equivocally located at the borders of two worlds, clerical and lay—where knights and clergy mingled freely. This was, in fact, the world of the great aristocratic courts, perhaps even of the king himself.[68]

Whatever the internal anomalies, the De amore fitted comfortably into the clerical schools of arts where Ovid was accepted as an important text. In this milieu, its direct forerunner was a poem entitled Facetus, composed in the mid-twelfth century (1170 at the latest) by an author who called himself Aurigena, doubtlessly a pseudonym. The term facetus implies not only wit but also the inculcation of refinement, elegance, or courtliness. Although in verse, it shared striking traits with André. Addressed to both a clerical and a lay audience, the poem divided society into classes and professional groups including clergy, physicians, judges, and soldiers. Within this instruction on courtliness was embedded an ars amatoria, a treatise on how to make love, which often circulated separately in the manuscripts. Along with straightforward advice on physical techniques were models for conversations and final instructions for disabusing oneself of love. A popular work (over thirty extant manuscripts), its doggerel lines were obviously produced for clerical amusement.[69]

Clerics also amused themselves by composing love lyrics in Latin that blended Ovidian inspiration with vernacular modes of sentiment and poetic expression. These efforts were preserved in collections such as the Cambridge Songs and the *Carmina Burana*.[70] Clerics in the Loire valley, however, took equal delight in writing plays in Latin, which scholars have found difficult to define as a genre. In poetic form some approximated the ancient elegiac comedy, but their bawdy content often approached the vernacular fabliaux. Taking Terence as their model for drama, they enthusiastically selected Ovid as their exemplar for love. Three of them may serve as samples of those most directly concerned with love and sexuality. *Alda* is the straightforward story of a young girl's sexual initiation by a young man. Its author, Guillaume de Blois, composed the work between 1167 and 1169 as abbot of Santa Maria di Manico in Sicily, but like his brother, the renowned humanist and letterwriter Pierre de Blois, he originated from and received his literary training in the Loire region. Arnoul d'Orléans, an Ovidian commentator at the school of Orléans, was the probable author of *Lidia* (ca. 1175) which related a cynical tale of a wife's blatant infidelities with her paramour before her husband's eyes. And finally, *De tribus puellis,* written late in the twelfth century or early in the thirteenth, was an elaborated parody of Ovid's celebrated love tryst with Corrina recounted in the *Amores*.[71]

Behind the Latin school exercises was the ancient teacher himself, Ovid, the foremost *magister* of love. Through the circulation of manuscript copies of his works, the Roman poet was present in the twelfth century. By the turn of the century his *Metamorphoses,* the acknowledged authority on mythology, was the most popular in terms of extant manuscripts (twenty-five manuscripts have survived in France before the thirteenth century), but his love poetry circulated in significant numbers as well. At least seventeen manuscripts of the *Ars amatoria* have survived and eleven each for the *Remedia* and the *Amores*. These French manuscripts, moreover, included some of the earliest, most complete, and best texts of the amatory poems.[72]

These texts were energetically studied in the schools where a series of commentaries or glosses accompanied by introductions or *accessi* were produced. The early exercises concentrated on grammar and mythology, but in time Ovid was recognized primarily as an authority on love. According to one French *accessus,* the principal intention of the *Ars amatoria* was to instruct boys and girls by precept and to render them expert in love. Ovid became the specialty of the French schools, particularly those of Orléans, where introductions and glosses can be attributed to Arnoul d'Orléans, Foulques, *écolâtre* of the cathedral school, and Guillaume d'Orléans, author of the *Bursani ovidianorum*.[73] Paris itself was not immune to the poet's spell. Not only did Gilles de Corbeil resent Ovid's competition, but among texts on which Alexander Neckham reported Parisian lectures were Ovid's elegies, his *Metamorphoses,* and especially (*precipue*) his *Remedia amoris*. Responsible teachers, however, were to see that the *carmina amatoria* (certainly the *Ars* and perhaps the *Amores*) were kept from adolescent hands.[74] The poet's success found further echo in the well-publicized trial of the heretics in 1210. Caesar of Heisterbach, who reported the event in detail, attested that the heretics not only denied the doctrines of the eucharist and resurrection, but they even claimed that God spoke through Ovid as he had through Augustine.[75] (Whether or not the charge is accurate, it nonetheless confirms the poet's popularity and the apprehension he created for contemporary observers.)

Ovid himself was born to a wealthy family of equestrian rank and came to maturity during the age of Augustus. Married three times, he first devoted the *Amores* to his early affairs in the demimonde of Rome, particularly to a courtesan identified as Corrina. Composed in elegiac couplets, these were a series of short stanzas that purported to narrate his erotic experiences in the style of the Roman elegists Gallus, Tibullus, Propertius, and Catullus. Around the years 2 B.C.E.–2 C.E., as a middle-aged man, he turned his hand to the *Ars amatoria,* a veritable manual for seduction, in the didactic style of Lucretius and Vergil. Originally intending two books for the instruction of fellow males, he addressed himself to three questions: how to find a girl, how to win her, and how to keep her love. At the end of the second he decided to add a third for the edification of women, namely, how to make themselves more pleasing to men. For those men who achieved conquest he wrote a sequel, the *Remedia amoris,* on how to disabuse oneself of the lady. With consummate skill Ovid played games with his poetic techniques and love making, producing both dazzling verse and a virtual *seductio ad absurdum*. In the process he did not neglect to make fun of Augustus's earnest program of moral reform and sobriety that attempted to restore ancient family values among the Roman elite. The result was exile for the poet who so robustly preached adultery. Years at the perimeter of the Black Sea afforded Ovid ample opportunity to reflect on his miscalculation.[76]

Not only were his *Ars* and accompanying poems admitted to the clerical schools of the twelfth century, but they were welcomed into aristocratic circles as well. In her lai *Guigemar* Marie de France depicted a "chapel" decorated with paintings of Venus, including one in which the goddess consigns Ovid's *Remedia* (not the *Ars*) to flames (vv.232–44). In a well-known passage opening *Cligès,* the romancier Chrétien de Troyes declared that he had translated the precepts of Ovid (*commandemanz d'Ovide, Remedia[?]*) and *L'art d'amors* into French (vv.2–3). Although these two works have been lost, a *Maistre Elie* rendered parts of the first two books of the *Ars* freely into verse at the opening of the thirteenth century, transferring the poem's setting from ancient Rome to medieval Paris.[77] Also early in the century (1214/15–1230), a full translation of the first two books, entitled *L'art d'amours,* was made into French prose, interwoven with an extensive commentary, and prefaced with an *accessus.*[78] Although the text, gloss, and preface followed the tradition of the Latin schools, the language was nonetheless vernacular, approaching the diction of the fabliaux. In the manner of a Latin commentary the introduction attempted to situate the work within the educational curriculum of both liberal and nonliberal arts. The former was represented by the traditional seven arts of the clerical schools (trivium and quadrivium) to which medicine (*phisique*) and theology were substituted for rhetoric and astronomy. In addition to the arts proscribed by worldly justice (poisons, sorcery, and divination) were also those that the church had specifically prohibited to the clergy, namely, gaming and attending tournaments and other contests.[79] Frequent references to tournaments and round tables, knights and squires, dances and ladies, as well as the insertion of popular proverbs and lyric verse—all in the vernacular—nonetheless leave no doubt that the intended audience was lay aristocracy. However André the Chaplain had envisaged his audience as he treated Ovidian themes in Latin, the prose French translation and commentary rendered the Latin school text more directly accessible to the laity habituated to the vernacular. Like André, therefore, the prose author positioned himself at the border of the clerical and aristocratic worlds.

Unavoidable but unexpressed questions remained: How could a hedonistic manual for seducers, which so vigorously recommended sex and adultery, be taught in the Middle Ages, an era when ecclesiastics closely linked sexual desire with sin and unequivocally condemned sexual activity outside of marriage? How could it be taught, moreover, in schools established for training clergymen ultimately destined for the celibate life? The prose vernacular commentary provided answers for the laity. In an effort to classify all learning, the commentary made distinctions not only between liberal and nonliberal arts but also between those permitted and prohibited. Those arts that are neither totally prohibited nor expressly conceded included astronomy without divination (*sors*), necromancy, and, most significantly, the art of love. This art is neither totally excluded nor permitted for two chief reasons: if some had not read or heard about love, they will have no desire or will to love; if some are injured by love, moreover, they will not know how to seek healing and health and might fall into depraved sins against nature leading finally to death. In other words, because neither love nor healing can exist without being taught, the art or teaching of love is, in the final analysis, morally indifferent. It is nevertheless a true art according to the understanding and etymology of the term. Women and young men learn it by nature, the poor and *ribaus* by custom, peasants by pride, but clerics acquire it through learning (*par aprison*) as they read stories and books, especially the precepts of the ancients— undoubtedly those of Ovid himself.[80]

Within the clerical schools, however, it remained for the theologian and rigorous moralist Pierre the Chanter to face the problem squarely. In a *questio* from his classroom that was not included in the major collections of his *Summa,* we find rough notes for the expressed question of whether the *ars amatoria* could be taught in school. Although the *questio* has not been reworked in a polished form, it is worth quoting in full. Following scholastic technique, he raised and discussed arguments pro and con:

> All knowledge comes from God. Since the art of love is knowledge, it comes from God, is good, and its use is good. If its use were bad, it would be bad in itself and therefore could not be said to come from God, because nothing bad comes from God. We reply that the art and its precepts must be considered as good in themselves (*in se*). But there is nothing good that does not also bring harm, as, for example, when Ovid seeks out a girl to seduce in the *Ars amatoria* (I, vv.35, 42).
>
> It may be argued (*ratione*) that the precept should serve the choice of one's manner of life. Similarly, if the precept is to speak with women, and like matters, we say that all of this can be done for good. Even that very act by which one is united with a prostitute is good in itself, and from God, as well as all of its predicable properties. For another but identical act can be meritorious in essence. If a woman is married, and by that act the man renders the marriage debt, he does not sin.
>
> The art of love is good in itself, but we abuse it and change it to worse use. The master himself says that the art itself is good, but the use is bad. The logician's rule does not follow that the use of a good is good. Poison is good, for example, because it comes from God, but its use is bad. He who teaches the art of love, however, is he not using it and therefore teaches (*tradit*) it? He who corrupts women through it, uses it, but the teacher (*doctor*) teaches it, not for use, but as a warning (*ad cautelam*).[81]

In effect Pierre argued that, originating from God, the *ars amatoria* is morally good in itself, but its use, like that of poison, can be bad. He who teaches it does not use it to seduce women but to warn his students against its ill-effects. "As a caution or warning" (*ad cautelam*) was a standard expression among confessors in administering penance. Ovid himself had proposed a *Remedia* to his own *Ars amatoria,* not to repent of his success, to be sure, but to free himself of his conquest. This cure nonetheless implied a rejection of former actions. The twelfth-century commentators interpreted the sequel as a remedy for the excesses of the *Ars.* One *accessus,* for example, alleged that Ovid's youthful friends had so perverted his teaching by seducing matrons, relatives, and married women, as well as maidens, that Ovid had repented of this misuse and provided his friends with medicine to protect themselves against illicit loves. As a good doctor he had prescribed both for the sick and the well to caution (*precavere*) the latter from taking ill.[82] André the Chaplain came even closer in concurring with the Chanter's argument. He baldly asserted that a cleric was to be preferred over a layman as a lover because the former was more cautious and wise (*cautior et prudentior*) through greater knowledge and skill in the Scriptures. Indeed, he himself had been able to avoid the snares of love when he was tempted to seduce a nun because of his own mastery of the art and remedies of love. More important, he affirmed in his preface that he had agreed to his friend's request for a treatise because he believed that, once instructed in the doctrine of love, Gautier would be more cautious in practice (*quod docto in amoris doctrina cautior tibi erit in amore processus*). In the final and violent palanode of Book III André repeated this theme: he had acceded to Gautier's desire for a little book, not that his disciple could adopt the lover's life but for the purpose that, nourished by its doctrine and instructed on how to arouse a women's love, he would gain eternal reward by abstaining from such action (*a tali provocatione abstinendo*). He who avoids the opportunity of sinning pleases God more than the one who lacks the power.[83]

André's protestation that he wrote his treatise as a remedy for love is, of course, integrally linked to the framing device of Book III which categorically repudiates the previous books. Modern interpreters have been reluctant to accept this framing device as well as the specific protestation, reminding the Chaplain of his own words, "that it is indeed a prodigy if a man is placed in a fire and does not burn."[84] It is nonetheless noteworthy that Pierre the Chanter's solution of *ad cautelam* appears to accept André's statements in his preface and conclusion and accordingly to lend credance to the Chaplain's ingenuous declarations. That the Chanter took the proposition of *ad cautelam* at face value encourages me to take André's declarations seriously as one (if not the only one) of the readings the author intended.

Jean Renart and the Tradition of Romance

As is characteristic of many authors of romance, Jean Renart's identity is virtually limited to his name. Of three works attributed to him with reasonable certainty, he spelled out his name *Jehan Renart* in one and concealed it in an *engin,* or an anagram, in the two others.[85] Jean Renart, like the English equivalent John Fox, doubtlessly hides his historical identity behind a pseudonym. He may well have taken it from the *Roman de Renart* to which he pointedly alluded (*Roman,* vv. 5420–21). The three works consist of two extensive romances and a short lai. From reciprocal citations they may be set in chronological order and assigned approximate dates appropriate to their dedicatees and internal references: *Escoufle* (1195–1202, most likely 1200–1202), *Le lai de l'ombre* (1200–1202), and *Le roman de la rose* (1202–18, probably 1209–14).[86]

The romance *Escoufle* divided into two parts. In the preliminary story Richard, called count of Montivilliers (but ostensibly duke of Normandy), departs on a crusade to the Holy Land, defeats the Turks in two battles, and negotiates a truce. Returning home through Italy, he meets an unnamed emperor of the Germans who complains of difficulties in ruling the Empire because of insubordination of servile officials. Richard accepts the emperor's appointment as imperial constable, recruits a company of French knights, subjugates the officials, and is rewarded with lands and a wife. Not long after, a son is born to Richard on the same night that a daughter is born to the emperor, and thus begins the principal narrative of the young couple Guillaume and Aelis, who are raised together as brother and sister at the imperial court in Rome. The emperor wants Guillaume to marry his daughter and succeed him, but this *mésalliance* is opposed by the empress and the imperial princes who seek to separate the children. Having fallen in love, the children elope together and attempt to return to Normandy, Guillaume's fatherland. Passing through Lorraine in the vicinity of Toul, the couple take a siesta after an idyllic *dejeuner en herbe.* While they sleep, a buzzard (*escoufle*) steals a purse and ring given to Guillaume by Aelis. The former's efforts to recover the gifts separate the couple, and the rest of the story recounts their mutual wanderings in search of each other from Normandy through Lorraine to Montpellier. The two finally arrive in Montpellier where Aelis has established a sewing shop and has made the acquaintance of the count of Saint-Gilles. Through the offices of the latter the lovers are reunited, escorted to Normandy where they marry and inherit the duchy, and finally come to Rome where Guillaume succeeds to the imperial throne through his wife's inheritance.

Le lai de l'ombre was a short but exquisite tale of seduction recounted with economy, delicacy, and psychological insight. An ardent knight finally overcomes the scruples of a virtuous married lady by casting his ring to her image reflected in the depths of the well. Unlike the romances, neither principal was named nor was a historical context provided except that the knight comes from the marches of the Empire between Germany and Lorraine. Jean noted that no one can equal him from Châlons to Perthois in Champagne (vv.51–59).

Jean Renart's *Roman de la rose* (often known as *Guillaume de Dole*) was devoted to the conventional romance theme "of arms and of love" (vv.24). It opened with an introduction to Conrad, the young emperor of the Germans. Although he and his court are the mirror of chivalry, Conrad has paid little attention to his imperial duties to marry and produce an heir. Rather, the emperor passes his time in frivolous amusements as illustrated by a hunt in the verdant forest where Conrad pursues the ladies back in the tents as ardently as the boar and stag. To recall him to his duties one hot summer day, his jongleur draws for him a verbal portrait of a beautiful maiden Lïenor and her brother, a chivalrous knight, Guillaume de Dole. So convincing is the jongleur that the emperor falls in love with her mere description. To test the courtesy and prowess of her family, Conrad summons her brother to court and holds a festive tournament at Saint-Trond near Liège, where Guillaume's skill in arms captures the honors of the day. After setting the stage at length with hunt and tournament, Jean Renart finally turned to the principal story of love. Thus reassured, the emperor entertains a secret intention to marry Lïenor at an imperial assembly soon to be held at Mainz. Among the barons who suspect this project of blatant *mésalliance* is the imperial seneschal who schemes to foil the emperor's plans. Traveling secretly to Dole, he tricks Lïenor's mother into revealing that the girl has a rose-shaped birthmark on the inside of her thigh (thus the name of the romance). Armed with this compromising information, he is able to convince the emperor that he had debauched Lïenor and rendered her ineligible for marriage. Not accepting her fate, however, Lïenor suddenly appears at the assembly of Mainz. Through a complicated stratagem she compels the seneschal to submit to an ordeal which, in turn, effectively demonstrates her innocent of the calumny, and the romance concludes with Lïenor's and Conrad's rapturous marriage.

Jean Renart opened this work with a declaration of literary craft: "He who transformed this story into romance/French has transcribed fine songs to be remembered. . . . Just as one colors cloth with dye to increase its value, so he has added song and music to the *Roman de la rose*. It is an original work and different from the others because it is embroidered here and there with beautiful verse. . . . One might think that he who wrote the romance composed all the lines of the songs because they fit so well into the story" (vv.1–29). In fact, Jean included a repertory of some forty-six lyrical pieces composed of *grands chants courtois,* dance songs, pas-tourelles, and *chansons de toile,* mostly anonymous, but many from identi-fied and well-known poets. So abundant was this lyrical repertory that it became virtually impossible to integrate all of the songs into the narrative. Some pieces do accord well with the plot of the romance, as Jean claims, but the relevance of many others is difficult to discern.[87] Jean's final goal, however, was comparable to an operetta or musical comedy where song and music unite with dramatic narrative to tell a story of love.

Among the identified *grands chants courtois,* those most frequently em-ployed were composed by Gace Brulé and the Châtelain de Coucy, both trouvères from nothern France at the turn of the twelfth and thirteenth centuries. Beyond these near contemporary and neighboring poets who wrote in *langue d'oil,* Jean reached back to an earlier age of troubadours from southern France who composed in Provençal or *langue d'oc.* Quoting French versions of the opening stanzas of Jaufré Rudel's *Lan que li jor sunt lonc en may* (vv.1301–7), Bernart de Ventadorn's *Can vei la lauzeta mover* (vv.5212–27), and the *Bele m'est la voiz altane* (vv.4653–59) of uncertain authorship, Jean evoked some of the best-known lyrics of two previous generations of troubadour poets.[88] Bernart de Ventadorn was especially known in northern France through Queen Eleanor's patronage who was both duchess of the southern province of Aquitaine, and queen of England and duchess of Normandy through marriage to King Henry II. While the emplacement of these three poems in the *Roman de la rose* is puzzling, they nonetheless recalled to his listeners the rich tradition of *fin'amors* embedded in Provençal lyric. The southern troubadours had formulated the lexogra-phy and conventions of a new style of love that prepared the way for the trouvères and romanciers of northern France. Although Jean himself did not fully accept the themes of troubadour love, he nonetheless acknowl-edged their contribution to the expression of desire by those who wrote in the vernacular for aristocratic audiences in northern France during the second half of the twelfth century.

Within the lyrical repertory, Jean Renart also included two fragments of pastourelles (*Roman,* vv.3403–6, 4568–83). Like the lyrical poetry this genre also reached back to Provence where the troubadour Macrabru wrote early examples, but it flourished most vigorously in northern France at the turn of the twelfth and throughout the thirteenth century. Several complete specimens can be attributed to Jean Bodel, our spokes-man for the fabliaux. Situated in an idyllic country setting, these poems involved a young shepherdess and a man who, upon discovering her, at-tempts to seduce her with varying success. Most often a narrative format was combined with dialogue between the principals, but all was expressed in poetic diction and style thoroughly consonant with romance.[89]

Jean Renart further exhibited his literary culture by making rapid comparisons to personages and events drawn from the entire repertory of vernacular literature. In recounting Count Richard's victory over the Turks, for example, he naturally compared it with Roland's exploits at Roncevaux. After the tournament at Saint-Trond when the minstrels started to sing of Perceval and Roncevaux, the emperor did not want to hear about Charlemagne, only about his newfound love Liënor. Reminiscences from the *chansons de geste* included not only the celebrated *Roland* but also *Guillaume d'Orange* and a stanza from *Gerbert de Metz*.[90] The embroidery on Liënor's wedding gown included scenes from the *Roman de Troie*, but *Alexandre* was also invoked from other *romans d'antiquité*. In addition to Perceval, perhaps echoing Chrétien de Troyes, he rehearsed other names from the Arthurian cast of characters, including Gauvain, Keu, and Sagremor as well as the venerable king himself. Breton lais were represented by the anonymous *Graelent Muer* and Marie de France's *Lai de Lanval*. The story of Piramus and Thisbe recalled either Latin versions (including Ovid's) or the French twelfth-century poem. Jean undoubtedly delighted in alluding to the *Roman de Renart* cycle if only to call attention to his own name.[91] These allusions, however, were scattered and fleeting when compared to one source that thoroughly informed all three works. In terms of citations and themes, the legend of Tristan and Iseut emerges as the dominant literary inspiration for Jean Renart's oeuvre. The romance authors that best prepared Jean Renart's conceptions of sexuality, therefore, included Marie de France, and especially Tristan, the latter mediated by Chrétien de Troyes.

When Jean Renart sought comparisons for Conrad's night of nuptial bliss (*Roman,* vv.5511), among a score that come to mind was the knight Lanval and his fabulous lady. With this name Jean evoked the *Lai de Lanval* of Marie de France and signaled acquaintanceship with her work.[92] A collection of twelve lais, a larger group of animal fables, and the *L'espurgatoire Saint Patrice* bear the name of Marie as author.[93] The fables were dedicated to a certain Count Guillaume, but the lais, of importance to us, were addressed to a king. The most solid biographical evidence about this Marie derives from the literary production itself. At the end of the fables she affirmed simply: "My name is Marie and I am of France." Writing in a distinctively Anglo-Norman dialect, she claimed literacy in Latin and familiarity with English. From circumstantial evidence various historical candidates have been proposed for Count Guillaume and for Marie herself, among the latter abbesses in England and noble families in Normandy, but none with conviction. Perhaps the best that can be said is that she wrote within the Anglo-Norman milieu during the second half of the twelfth century, most likely for King Henry II, the one monarch best able to appreciate her work.

Marie's lais were predominantly centered on Brittany with occasional excursions into Normandy and across the channel to Wales, Cornwall, and the Scottish marches, but all within the domain of King Henry. Brittany's setting permitted supernatural forces to intervene like Lanval's dream-like lady and Guigemar's magic stag and ship. Although Marie shared the conventional themes of arms and love with romance, her lais, being shorter, focused more sharply on the individual personal strategies of the scores of knights and ladies who inhabited her stories. Within this universe she explored a great variety of love situations—married and unmarried, young and old, happy and tragic—but with sustained emphasis on social status and the permutations of extramarital love, particularly adultery and the nuances of *drürie* (amorous dalliance). Most important, Marie's self-presentation as a woman was rare among contemporary discourses but unique within the romance tradition. By comparing her stories, themes, and language with her male colleagues of romance we have a remarkable opportunity to explore an authentic female voice within a predominately masculine discourse.

The score of famous couples to whom Jean Renart compared Conrad's and Lïenor's wedding night also included the most celebrated of all lovers, Tristan and Iseut. "When Tristan loved Iseut and could take pleasure with her by embracing, kissing, and the *sorplus* that accompanied it . . . , then you can be sure that one would not easily be able to compare their happiness with [Conrad's and Lïenor's]" (*Roman*, vv.5507–15). Tristan and Iseut became the constant standard of comparison for Jean's couples in all three works. The knight of the *Lai de l'ombre*, for example, excelled Tristan as a courtier at fencing and chess (vv.101–5). When he dissembled madness, Tristan did not experience a third of the knight's suffering for the love of his lady (vv.124–27). The celebrated lovers are evoked at all crucial junctures throughout the *Escoufle* to provide examples for Guillaume and Aelis. After their separation has been decreed, Guillaume laments that Aelis does not have Iseut's experience nor has he Tristan's guile, wisdom, or *engin* to plot their reunion (vv.3122–37). At one desperate point in the search for Aelis he refuses death, blaming the love potion for Tristan's tragic end (vv.6352–59). When finally reunited, their hearts were intertwined as Iseut's and Tristan's never were (vv.7820–23).[94] Toward the beginning of the preliminary story, Count Richard presents to the church of the Holy Sepulchre in Jerusalem a magnificent gold chalice containing enameled illustrations of major scenes from the lovers' legend. Despite the apparent incongruity of this gift, Jean's careful description (vv.579–616) constitutes the fullest resumé, and his oeuvre contains the most numerous citations of the legend for its day.[95]

The legend of Tristan and Iseut may never come clearly into focus because the extant versions are not only incomplete but also circulated in diverse forms.[96] Recounting Tristan's birth, life, and death, the German Eilhart von Oberge (1170–90) offered a version both comprehensive and condensed. The rest survived only in fragments. That of the Anglo-Norman Béroul (1180–1200) presented a coherent section from the middle that corresponded to Eilhart but lacked a beginning and an end. The extant passages of the Anglo-Norman cleric Thomas of Britain's (1170s) depicted the hero's exile and tragic death but departed substantially from Eilhart and Béroul. Gottfried von Strassburg (ca. 1210) amplified Thomas in German, but his conclusion has been lost. Marie de France, for her part, embroidered a single episode in her *Lai de chevrefoil*. Evidently aware of the confusion, most authors claimed authority for their particular account. The tale is told in many ways, Thomas observed, but he will keep to one version (p.119, vv.835–51). Those who tell the story, Béroul asserted, do not know the true story, but he remembers it better (vv.1265–70). Marie also heard the story many times, but wanted to report the truth (*Chevrefoil*, vv.1–10). Likewise aware of many authors who misunderstood the story, Gottfried referred to his own researches in French and Latin and proposed Thomas's authentic version (vv.149–54).

The numerous episodes of the legend, well-known today as they were in the twelfth century, contained equivocal, if not contradictory, elements. At the core was an adulterous triangle: Marc, king of Cornwall married to the Irish princess Iseut, who, in turn, was reciprocally in love with Tristan, Marc's nephew and heir; these eventually squared into two couples with Tristan's marriage to another Iseut, distinguished as Iseut aux Mains Blanches. The final situation was a pair of thwarted lovers destined to die, each bound to an unhappy spouse. The original adultery, however, was the result of a magic potion the lovers unwittingly drank on board ship. In Béroul's version the illicit love was entirely due to the magic drink. When its effects wore off after three years, the lovers sought to discontinue their unlawful liaison. In Thomas's version, however, the potion was more a symbol than the cause of their love, but the couple's responsibility remained ambiguous because of the magic drink. Because of mutual devotion and fidelity Tristan and Iseut's love nonetheless proposed a celebrated example for all lovers, yet one beclouded by tragic death.

Transmitted in both French and German, the legend floated along the linguistic frontier of France and the Empire, precisely in Jean Renart's geographic domain whose patrons were in Hainaut, the Rémois, and perhaps Liège. When Jean convoked the French and German parties to a fictional tournament, it was situated at the Liégeois town of Saint-Trond precisely at this border. Writing in Francien French, Jean recorded with amusement the Germanic names (*Boidin, Wautre, Roman*, vv.2168–69) and words (*wilecome, godehere*, vv.2594–96) heard as the German knights and their retinues arrived in the town.[97] Jean was familiar with the French versions of Thomas, Béroul, and perhaps others, but in contrast to Béroul's Tristan, whose death was necessitated by the potion (*medecine*), he had his hero Guillaume declare that he will not be compelled (*Escoufle*, vv.6352–59).[98] Rather than tragedy Jean adopted the exemplary and positive qualities of the youthful Tristan's and Iseut's love; rather than adultery he preferred to marry both pairs of lovers. Undoubtedly Jean accepted the version of the famous legend mediated by Chrétien de Troyes.

As has become characteristic of romance authors, fullest information about Chrétien was supplied by the author himself.[99] He revealed his own name (*Erec*, v.9) and those of two patrons, Marie, countess of Troyes (d. 1198) (*Charrete*, v.1), and Philippe, count of Flanders (d. 1191) (*Graal*, L., R. v.13). Although written in Francien, a trace of Champenois dialect supports his origins from Troyes. His second romance, *Cligès* (vv.1–10), offered a catalogue of early works, now mostly lost, which included French versions of Ovid's *comandemanz* (*Remedia amoris*) and the *art d'amors* (*Ars amatoria*). He took the story of *Cligès* itself from a book, most likely in Latin, possessed by the cathedral of Saint-Pierre de Beauvais. Its purpose was to demonstrate that both chivalry and learning originated in Greece, were transmitted by Rome, and now flourished in France (vv.25–42). The emphasis on Latin school texts, chronicles, and clerical learning suggests that Chrétien at least enjoyed a Latin clerical training, whether or not he was a master in the schools, as was later asserted. The chronological order of his romances can be determined more readily than the precise dates. *Erec et Enide* was the first (already mentioned in *Cligès*), then *Cligès*, followed by *Le chevalier au lion (Yvain)* and *Le chevalier de la charrete (Lancelot)*, written concurrently, and concluded by *Le conte du graal (Perceval)*, left unfinished. The period of composition extended from the 1150s into the 1180s.

In *Le conte de graal* Chrétien combined the story of the grail, most likely inspired by contemporary crusades, with a *Bildungsroman* of the young Perceval who set out to become both a knight and a lover. Jean Renart's early attempt to construct a similar development for his young hero Guillaume suggests familiarity with Chrétien confirmed by double allusions to Perceval in the *Roman de la rose* (vv.1746–48, 2880–81).

Also included in the catalogue of lost works in *Cligès* was the *roi Marc et d'Ysalt la blonde* (v.5), a citation that indicated Chrétien's early fascination with the Tristan legend and its concomitant subjects of adultery and marriage. He dealt directly with the adultery of Lancelot with Queen Guenièvre in *Le chevalier de la charrete* undertaken at the expressed command of Marie, countess of Troyes. Why Chrétien left the story to a cleric, Godefroi de Leigni, to complete (v.7102) is not yet clear, but he may have had misgivings about the theme. Whatever his personal feelings, the two adulterous couples were linked together in the massive prose versions of *Tristan* that flourished in the thirteenth century. Already in *Erec et Enide* (vv.2021–23) Chrétien had voiced doubts about the Tristan legend, but *Cligès* itself constituted a direct reply to the celebrated tale. He incorporated the elements of the adulterous triangle (Alis, emperor of Constantinople, married to Fenice, princess of Germany, who reciprocally loves Cligès, nephew of the emperor) and magic potions but with opposing results. On three occasions (vv.3107–14, 5199–5211, 5249–56) Fenice openly and resolutely refuses to follow Iseut's example and employs a potion to delude her husband into thinking that he has consummated the marriage. Technically a virgin, therefore, she uses a second potion to dissimulate death, which allows her to join her lover in a secret hideaway. Despite obstacles and tribulations, the lovers are finally united in matrimony, thus achieving the goal of Erec and Enide and Yvain and Laudine in *Le chevalier au lion*. A neo-Tristan, if not an anti-Tristan, Chrétien's *Cligès* directly challenged the adulterous example of the famous legend and proposed marriage as the desirable goal, a resolution quickly endorsed by Jean Renart.

The Tristan authors, Marie, and Chrétien, Jean's three major sources, situated their tales in the mythical space and time of King Arthur and peopled them with personages drawn directly from the Arthurian cast of characters. Although Marie might occasionally allude to specific places in northeastern France, and Chrétien located parts of *Cligès* in Germany and Constantinople, by and large most action radiated out from Brittany (great and minor) to adjacent lands. Congruently most characters took their names from the fictional universe of the Arthurian court. In direct contrast, Jean Renart placed his works in geographic space that was immediately recognizable to audiences in northeastern France. *Escoufle,* for example, opened and closed in Normandy around centers such as Rouen, Montivilliers, Caux, Pont de l'Arche, and Arques. Count Richard's itinerary follows the established crusading route across St. Bernard's pass, through Lombardy to Brindisi and thence by boat to Acre. Beyond Italy and Normandy the lovers' wanderings are confined to the middle space between the French royal domain and the Empire: Normandy, Lorraine, Montpellier, and Saint-Gilles. In the *Lai* the knight's renown extended through the imperial marches and Lorraine (from Châlons to the Perthois in Champagne). In the *Roman* he delimited the geographic terrain with greater precision. In addition to the imperial cities and castles of Mainz, Cologne, Kaiserwerth, and Maastricht in the valleys of the Rhine and Meuse, Jean evoked numerous places—Dinant, Huy, Nivelle, Looz, and Namur—all contained within the diocese and principality of Liège. At Saint-Trond, not far from Liège, he located Guillaume's lodgings at a crossing of two roads next to the market place (vv. 2068–71) that have left traces in the present topography of the city.[100]

Jean's selection of characters further enhanced this search for verisimilitude. Although the principal figures in his tales were patently fictional (with the possible exception of Conrad), a Norman count Richard de Montivilliers, related to the count of Toulouse, who confided his lands to an archbishop, and departed on a crusade to the Holy Land where he obtained a truce, could only be a thinly disguised Richard, king of England and duke of Normandy. Even if certain features were inaccurate or counterfactual, the audience would still have recognized the contemporary Richard by the designation of *cuers de lyon* (v. 298), the king's renowned epithet. Similarly, the emperor Conrad may have reminded Jean's audiences of the young Otto IV of Brunswick, the contemporary Welf candidate to the imperial throne, particularly when the blazon on Conrad's shield corresponded closely to Otto's.[101] In the *Roman* moreover, the fictional principals were surrounded with secondary personages all selected from the contemporary scene. The bishop of Chartres with a brother, the dukes of Geneva and Burgundy, and the counts of Luxembourg, Savoie, and Forez were placed in plausible contexts. The penchant for contemporary identification intensified at the tournament of Saint-Trond. The victorious German knights consisted of members of the Welf party known to have supported Otto's election to the imperial throne. Although defeated, the opposing French side was more numerous and composed of identified French knights and barons, led by the champion Michel de Harnes, all faithful to Philip Augustus. To distinguish his romances from the patently Arthurian space and characters, Jean Renart therefore cast them in settings and with personages that contemporary audiences could immediately recognize.

The chief audiences for all romances were those who assembled in the aristocratic courts. Chrétien fashioned the formulaic phrase in his first romance *Erec*: "before kings and before counts" (v. 20), modified to "told in the royal court" in the *Graal* (L. v. 65, R. v. 64). Jean Renart reproduced the same phrase in *Escoufle* (v. 9076) and with variations elsewhere (*Lai,* v. 49; *Roman,* v. 5646). The word *conte* was especially appealing because it was a homonym for both count and story and permitted Jean to play on all its forms: *K'a cort a roi n'a cort a conte/Ne doit conteres conter conte* (*Escoufle,* vv. 21–22). Marie addressed her lais to an unnamed king, probably Henry II of England, but Chrétien identified the counts in his two romances as Marie de Troyes and Philippe de Flandre. In like manner Jean identified the three magnates to whose courts he addressed his works: *Escoufle* to Baudouin VI, count of Hainaut, *Roman* to Milon de Nanteuil, prévôt of the chapter of Reims, and the *Lai de l'ombre* to a bishop-elect, perhaps Hugues de Pierrepont, bishop of Liège. Although kings and counts convoked these courts, the assemblies themselves were undoubtedly crowded with knights and ladies to whom Marie's Guigemar, Lanval, and Fresne as well as Chrétien's Lancelot, Yvain, and Laudine were representative figures. Jean Renart accentuated this orientation toward the lesser knights and their women. When Count Richard proposes to aid the emperor against his servile officials, he recruits a company of *bons chevaliers* from France to accomplish the task (*Escoufle*, vv.1562–66). Similarly, the Emperor Conrad reckons his riches in the supply of good knights on whom he lavishes gifts of horses and garments. No *bon chevalier* crosses his lands without offers of lands and castles in return for service (*Roman*, vv.92–103). The splendid tournament at Saint-Trond draws the best knights of the Empire and France at which Guillaume de Dole becomes the champion of the day. The knight Guillaume de Dole and the belle Lïenor, both of modest lineage, stand, respectively, for the "arms and love" in Jean's *Roman*.

To entertain common audiences the romanciers adopted common modes of expression and language. All were composed in octosyllabic lines with rhymed couplets, a scheme that arose in the mid-twelfth century to distinguish romance from the octosyllabic lines grouped in *laisses* or paragraphs of the *chansons de geste*. In this metric form the romances were undoubtedly meant to be heard aloud by audiences as well as to being written down on parchment—hence their preservation for posterity. Marie de France acknowledged this symbiosis in her prologue, remembering the Breton lais that she heard (v.33) and attesting to glosses of Priscian written in ancient books (vv.7–16). Similarly in *Cligès*, Chrétien noted that the *conte*, which he speaks and his audience hears, was found in a book at Saint-Pierre de Beauvais (vv.18–21). In the *Graal* he asked his audience to listen to rhyming of a tale found in a book furnished by Count Philippe (L., R. vv.61–68). In the *Charrete* he promised Countess Marie that he would place the materials of the tale into a book (vv.24–29). Because of the importance of musical lyrics Jean Renart intended the *Roman* to be sung, yet at the end the archbishop of Cologne had the story written down. For this reason Jean insisted in the prologue that his romance must be both read and sung (vv.16–23, 5643–52). He also proposed to place *Escoufle* in writing (v.45); otherwise the authorship of both romances would have been lost to the public since his name was concealed in a scribal anagram.

Also shared was a sense of linguistic propriety that distinguished romances as *courtois* from other modes that were *vilain*. In the *Graal* Chrétien praised Count Philippe for not tolerating coarse jokes or demeaning words (L., R. vv.21–22). In the prologue to the *Lai de l'ombre* (vv.8–12) Jean Renart expanded Chrétien's phrase by contrasting the *vilain* who makes jokes with his own *cortoisie* to fashion a pleasant work without spite or ugliness. In the *Roman* Jean simply noted that *vilains* could not appreciate his fine lyrics (vv. 14–15). These vague protestations against *vilain* expression might simply be read as aristocratic disdain for peasants, but, when the language of romance is compared with that of the fabliaux, it appears that the antagonism operated at a linguistic level as well. We shall see that in matters of the body and sexuality the fabliaux used a vocabulary of direct, even crude, expression that was entirely absent in the romance which preferred the euphemisms of *joie, delit,* and *deduit*.[102] Although the fableors were familiar with romance vocabulary, the romanciers consistently avoided the characteristic words of the fabliaux with rare exceptions. Since the romances appeared to have been written down at least a half-century before the fabliaux, the problem is thereby complicated, but the vulgar speech recorded in the fabliaux doubtless circulated long before it was committed to writing. Whatever the precise relations, the linguistic medium of romance by its compulsive purity and by its conscious recognition of an opposing *vilain* speech reacted vigorously against the vulgarity which the fableors later took delight in flaunting.

Jean Bodel and the Fabliaux Tradition

The fabliaux were the last of the five discourses to appear in writing. Possessing scant tradition that might expose their origins and sources of inspiration, these brief but racy stories surfaced as a literary phenomenon shortly before 1200 in northern France, flourished throughout the thirteenth century, and disappeared as a genre by 1340. They were not transcribed or collected until the late thirteenth or early fourteenth centuries. Emerging in the 1190s, Jean Bodel from Arras became the first identifiable author.[103]

The second richest manuscript collection of fabliaux also contained a story entitled *Richeut* which may be considered a forerunner of the genre by at least a quarter of a century. It told of Richeut, a woman who abandons her calling as a nun to become a prostitute and "mistress of lechery." In order to increase her fortune she engenders a son with whomever she can find, imputes paternity to three rich clients—a priest, a knight, and a townsman—and collects substantial endowments through blackmail. Her son, Samson, imitates her successful career by also abandoning the monastic vocation and perfecting the skills of lechery learned from his mother. The two pit their amatory wiles against each other in a climactic struggle, but the mother wins out when she contrives his seduction and fleecing. Three anomalies raise obstacles to unqualified inclusion of this piece among the fabliaux. It is too long (1,300 verses), too early (1159–89), and employs a different metrical pattern (the *cauda* stanza), but in subject matter and outlook it fully fits the genre.[104]

Jean Bodel, the first known author of a fabliau, can be linked with the personage whose name appeared in the necrology of the confraternity of the jongleurs and bourgeois of Arras and who died of leprosy in 1210. A resident, jongleur, and most probably a sergent of the *échevinage* of Arras, he gained literary fame by composing in a wide variety of genres which, if used retrospectively, can help to reconstruct his career. His contraction of leprosy induced him in 1202 to write the *Congés,* a lyrical poem of adieu to his friends. Earlier he had written two major pieces, a play, the *Jeu de Saint Nicolas* (ca. 1200), and a lengthy epic, the *Chanson des Saisnes* (1197–1200), as well as a handful of pastourelles, as we have seen. His earliest writings, however, were nine fabliaux, eight of which he listed at the opening of the last, probably in the order in which they were composed during the 1190s. In the same passage he acknowledged his debt to Jean de Boves, another trouvère from the Amienois, and implied the existence of other competitors as well. (None of their works have survived.) These nine pieces, therefore, represent both the earliest examples of fabliaux (with the possible exception of *Richeut*) and the largest number assigned to a single author.[105]

Jean Bodel's fabliaux stimulated an entirely new literary genre of which at least 150 examples have survived in about three dozen manuscripts. Although difficult to date precisely and to assign authorship, most were produced in the thirteenth century. Jean Bodel's initial sample, although formative, was also small. Of the nine, only four are devoted to sexual themes. In *Le vilain de Bailluel* a peasant nearly dead from hunger returns home to witness his wife making love to the local priest before his very eyes. Two clerics accept hospitality from a peasant in *Gombert et des deus clers* and repay their host by sleeping with his daughter and wife during a dark night of frenetic activity. When a merchant returns to his wife after a lengthy business trip in *Li sohaiz des vez,* he responds to her pent-up ardor by falling asleep. She compensates for his inattentiveness by dreaming of a market where the male amatory equipment, so urgently desired, is spectacularly and plentifully displayed for sale. In the longest and most involved of Jean's fabliaux, *Barat et Haimet,* a peasant and his wife foil the machinations of two thieves to rob them of a prized ham. To compensate for the smallness of this sample, I have increased the number of fabliaux to fifty from the available repertory of undated examples in the thirteenth century. I have selected those especially centered on sexual matters but have avoided tales from named authors of the later period (Rutebeuf, Gautier Le Leu, and Jean de Condé, for example) and those bearing indications of late composition. All in all, I have attempted to constitute a concomitant corpus that will enhance Jean Bodel's characteristic traits that were expressive of the initial stages in the early thirteenth century.[106]

Jean Bodel's nine pieces established the salient characteristics of the new genre which were also self-consciously articulated in the prologues and conclusions of the anonymous corpus. Although the narrative told a story (*conte*) like the romance, it was designated by the specific terms *fabliaus* or *fablel* first coined by Jean Bodel. At least sixty of the total extant stories identified themselves by this term.[107] In contrast to the romances which usually comprised between 5,000–10,000 verses, the fabliaux were short. Jean's ranged between 70 and 500. The scabrous *La crote* (p.46) asserted that brief fabliaux inflict less boredom on their audiences than the long. Like Chrétien's and Jean Renart's romances they were invariably composed in octosyllabic couplets *à rime plat*. When Jean Bodel identified himself in *Li sohaiz des vez,* he called himself a rhymer of fabliaux (vv.209–10). Among others, Jehan, the author of *Auberee* (vv.2–5), promised to put a fine story into rhyme line by line.

Frequently calling upon the audience to listen to a tale which had been heard, the fableor indicated that the dominant mode of transmission was oral-aural. In *Li sohaiz des vez* (vv.208–10), for example, Jean Bodel claimed that the husband reported his wife's dream on the morrow throughout Douai where the author himself heard it and converted it into rhyme. Guérin, who produced *Berengier au long cul* (vv.1–9), boasted that for the past two years he had been composing and telling so many fine stories and fabliaux that it was time to call a halt—if his audience would only listen to this last one. Others drew attention to specifically oral characteristics of their tales. Inviting his public to hear a wonder, Eustace d'Amiens (*Le boucher d'Abeville,* vv.1, 5–6) warned that a word unheard is a word lost. Milon d'Amiens told his audience that he had committed the story of *Le prestre et le chevalier* (p.46) to memory. The fact that Boivin de Provins (vv.377–80) received ten *sous* for telling his story and that Guérin who composed *Le chevalier qui fist parler les cons* (vv.1–2) was reimbursed a penny for each tale suggests that fableors could be jongleurs who, like Jean Bodel, gained their livelihood by performing their stories. When Guillaume le Normand, who wrote *Le prestre et Alison* (p.14), compared the act of committing the story to French and parchment to someone depositing money in a chest for safekeeping, he offered one of the few examples of an author self-consciously referring to writing. In fact, the surviving written evidence for the fabliaux did not appear before the end of the thirteenth century when, as a genre, they were in decline. Those fabliaux, moreover, that are extant in multiple copies contain significantly different versions and alterations under the same title—suggestive of oral transmission.[108]

After acknowledging reimbursement in *Le chevalier qui fist parler les cons* (vv. 4–6), Guérin claimed that his wares would bring comfort to the carefree and idle among his listeners if only they would keep quiet. The great majority of fableors offered explicit morals or examples (*essample*) with their tales. Jean Bodel concluded from the *vilain* of Bailleul (vv. 115–16) that he who believes his wife more than his eyes can only be a fool. The *essample* of Gombert (vv. 186–89) taught that whoever has a beautiful wife should not invite a cleric to spend the night. Most fableors followed this misogynistic penchant, but occasionally one offered the opinion that a young lover should keep trying (*Guillaume au faucon,* p. 113), and another advised the married to observe moderation when returning the marital debt (*La dame qui aveine demandoit pour Morel,* p. 329). Very few fabliaux, however, offered morals that could be considered either pious or decorous under normal circumstances.[109]

Jean Bodel's practice of signing his stories was rare, not to be imitated until late in the thirteenth century by Rutebeuf and Gautier Le Leu. The vast majority of fabliaux were anonymous or assigned to stereotypical first names (Jehan, Guérin, for example) or to authors identified by only one tale (Milon d'Amiens). Only one claimed to be a cleric (*Les trois dames qui trouverent l'anel,* v. 2), and only one devised a situation (*Le povre clerc,* p. 196) where a cleric was asked to recite a song or adventure. This was a rare case in which the story circulated in writing, but it is significant that a literate cleric was asked to read it.

The most common means of identifying each tale were proper names. Jean Bodel, for example, entitled fabliaux from the names of two thieves, Haimet and Barat, and the hospitable peasant Gombert. On the other hand, he used place names to identify other stories such as the peasant of Bailleul and the merchant from Douai. The names of characters (for example, Boivin de Provins) or of places (the fisherman of Pont-sur-Seine) became the characteristic device for distinguishing the tales. From this latter technique we can determine the geographic settings. It is clear that the fabliaux were limited to the northern half of France with a heavy concentration in lands neighboring Jean Bodel's Artois (for example, Abbeville, Bailleul, Douai, Amiens, Reims, and Ardres).[110] To give scope to his gargantuan talents, Samson, Richeut's son, travels throughout the known world, but the final contest between the two rivals, significantly enough, takes place at Beauvais in northeastern France.

If geography was limited, the social setting was broad. Although Richeut stems from a knightly family (vv. 274–75) and had served a novitiate with the nuns (vv. 36–43), her customers are drawn from the clergy, aristocracy, bourgeoisie, and peasants. "There was no occupation—no peasant, laborer, journeyman or forester—whose money she did not accept (vv.392–95)." Jean Bodel's world of peasants, townsmen, and clergy was perpetuated by his successors to which others, like the authors of *Guillaume au faucon* and *Le chevalier a la robe vermeille,* added the lower aristocracy of knights in stories that emulated courtly convention and language. Only barons and bishops, the high nobility of the laity and church, play inconsequential roles in the escapades.[111]

Within this social world, the fableors exhibited a pronounced interest—bordering on obsession—with the sexual life of their characters. Four out of nine of Jean Bodel's stories established the pattern. Our sample of 50 out of 150 fabliaux by no means exhausts the supply. One survey has estimated that erotic themes predominated over all other subjects by a proportion of two to one.[112] Not only does sexuality underlie most of the narratives, but the matter is treated in direct, uneuphemistic, and vulgar language. The fabliaux shared this penchant for sexuality with the elegiac comedies written in Latin by school clerics. Despite similarities, however, the differences remain important, thus obscuring affiliations between the two genres.[113]

A final trait of the fabliau relevant to sexuality was an unmistakable stance toward courtly literature. These tales competed so vigorously with romance in the vernacular that the two genres must be read together in symbiosis. Since courtly literature was composed nearly a half-century before the fabliaux, the latter expected its audience to be familiar with the former. Reciting tales in octosyllabic rhymed couplets, the same rhyme adopted by the romances, the fableors knew and could imitate courtly style and themes. Comprised in his mastery of lechery, Samson in *Richeut* (vv.617–24), for example, learned not only the school techniques of dialectics but also courtly fashions to make songs and *rotrüanges* to deceive women. Jean Bodel's list of his fabliaux in *Deus chevaus* (vv.1–15) parodied Chrétien's enumeration of his romances in *Cligès* (vv.1–24). He tellingly renamed his first tale *Morteruel*—gruel of milk and flour fit only for peasants—to distinguish his stories from the elegant fare of the nobility. The evocation of the astounding masculinity of the apprentice in *Le fevre de Creeil* (vv.14–17) echoed Enide's beauty in Chrétien's *Erec* (vv.411–13). Both were produced by nature's careful attention. *L'Aloul* (vv.41–55) opened on a garden scene in the springtime like any standard romance. The judgments of the fabliaux—*Les trois dames qui trouverent l'anel,* for example—recalled the love decisions in courtly literature. In *Li sohaiz des vez* Jean Bodel promised his audience an *aventure* (v.1), redolent of romance, which *La borgoise d'Orliens* specified as *une aventure assez cortoise* (v.2).[114]

Language, however, was the crucial terrain over which the two competitors battled. Jean Bodel, himself, was well versed in courtly diction. When his merchant from Douai returns home, for example, his wife greets him with the romance euphemisms of love. The aristocratic lovers in *Guillaume au faucon* further express their feelings with refined delicacy. But Jean alternated courtly sensibility with the crudest of speech to designate the genitals and the sexual act. The four-letter words of spoken French— *vit* (prick), *coilles* (balls), *con* (cunt), *cul* (asshole), and *foutre* (fuck)—which were all banned from the literary language of romance, now detonate in the verse of the fabliaux. Jean Bodel's title *Li sohaiz des vez* was confused for *Li sohaiz desvez* (Wild Desires), but it simply meant "the dream of pricks" as confirmed in his catalogue when he renamed it *Songe des vis*.[115] Such obscenity became the hallmark of the new vernacular genre. By voicing *vilain* language so offensive to courtly ears, the fabliaux challenged the romances on linguistic grounds. "He who tells the tale of Richeut," the story itself averred, "cannot speak in a courtly way" (*par cortoisie*, vv.70–71). The damoiselle who faints at the sound of the word *foutre*, in the fabliau of the same title, was a girl conditioned by courtly language. Her eventual seduction is both sexual and linguistic. Decades before Jean Bodel's appearance, romances had responded to *vilain* language— undoubtedly encountered in oral speech—by erecting linguistic barriers. At the end of the century, however, the fabliaux, in turn, reacted to this "outbreak of decency" in romance.[116] Thereafter the gauntlet was cast between the two modes of speaking. Out of interaction between the two genres arises the problem as to which first prompted the other. The fabliaux could have long preceded the romances as an oral subculture, thereby provoking the romance's response in polite language, to which the fabliaux that were written down, in turn, continued to taunt with offensive reposts. At whatever point the cycle of action and reaction was set in motion, the fabliaux, read in the context of the romances, can be seen as attempts to shock their audiences, like naughty children crossing a forbidden boundary.[117]

The prologues to the fabliaux offer little help in identifying the audiences to whom the stories were directed. Occasionally the listeners were addressed as "lords" (*seigneurs*), a term no more specific in medieval speech than *messieurs* in modern French.[118] The world within the tales, as we have seen, unfolded over the entire spectrum of medieval society, excluding only the high ranks of aristocracy and church. This vagueness has encouraged modern critics to speculate. The first to devote serious attention to the question was Joseph Bédier, who, impressed by the linguistic antagonism to courtly literature, decided that they were directed to the emerging bourgeoisie exemplified by Jean Bodel's milieu at Arras. Per Nykrog countered this thesis by showing they cannot be extricated from courtly literature and concluded that they were essentially addressed to an aristocratic society. In arguing their respective positions, however, both scholars actually blurred the sharpness of the dichotomy. Most recently, Charles Muscatine has argued for an essentially mixed audience that did not decompose into class components. Jean Rychner had proposed this nuanced position when he noted that the various manuscripts of a single fabliau often differed according to the intended audience. One version of *La damoisele qui ne pooit oïr parler de foutre,* for example, was directed to a more refined courtly audience, another to a more vulgar peasant public. In all events, those who collected and transcribed the fabliaux in manuscripts of the late thirteenth century included them with Jean Renart's *Lai de l'ombre,* courtly romances, religious verse, and other genres—suggestive that they belonged to a unified audience.[119]

We may suspect that despite offense to morality, language, and good taste, the fabliaux nonetheless reached the ears of those most likely to be outraged. Within the casuistry collected by Pierre the Chanter and his circle appeared occasional cases that echoed the hyperbolic situations of the fabliaux. Both Pierre and Robert of Courson cited an example worthy of a fableor's talents. When an adulterous couple are surprised by the husband's return, the wife hides the lover in a chest. The husband nonetheless discovers the culprit and mayhem ensues.[120] That the fabliaux reached courtly audiences as well may be confirmed not only from the tales themselves but also from accounts emanating directly from aristocratic society. When Lambert d'Ardres extolled the accomplishments of Count Baudouin II of Guines (d. 1206), he noted an extensive library in French, many volumes of which were translated from Latin, because Baudouin was technically illiterate in Latin. The catalogue included not only Augustine in theology and pseudo-Dionysius in philosophy but also chansons de gestes (*in cantilenis gestoriis*), aristocratic *aventures* (*sive in eventuris nobilium*), and even ignoble fabliaux (*in fabellis ignobilium*), so that he was thought to rival the most renowned jongleurs.[121] When, moreover, Jean Renart pictured the emperor Conrad, the very mirror of courtliness, calling for entertainment after dinner, the repertory was the same. Minstrels appeared to recite a romance about Perceval and a chanson de geste about Roncevaux, but the program culminated with the performance of three or four chansons and fabliaux by the jongleur Juglet (*Roman,* vv. 1745–65). Apparently the emperor was an habitué of such stories because he was unable to guard himself against vulgarity. When impatient to marry the belle Lïenor, he lets slip a malodorous *vilain* proverb: "ass (*cus*) pulls harder than rope" (v. 5300).[122]

2

PARTICIPANTS: THE SOCIOLOGY OF SEXUALITY

As our five spokesmen narrated the variety of sexual behavior, they took note of the participants and classified them on grids of defining categories. Following differing traditions, each discourse possessed distinctive predispositions for organizing the schema. The physicians, for example, were naturally concerned with the physiological parameters. André the Chaplain and the fableors were attentive to the diversity of social categories, whereas the romanciers preferred to concentrate on their own aristocratic world. Asserting supreme jurisdiction over marriage, the theologians were preoccupied with the institution of matrimony and how sexuality separated the clergy from the laity. From these diverse observations and orientations we can construct a kind of sociology of sexuality as it was perceived at the turn of the twelfth century. Underlying all classification was, of course, the differentiation between male and female. Because of its ubiquity, however, we can only note gender wherever it occurs and reserve our conclusions to a final chapter.

The Physiological Parameters

Among the possible parameters, the most evident was anatomical, which, in turn, raised the question of sexual orientation. Licit sexual relations were undisputably limited to those between men and women, thereby proscribing all homoerotic practices. Although each of the discourses assumed this heterosexual orientation, it was most fully articulated by the theologians. Whatever homophilia was practiced in antiquity, the theologians revived a long-established Hebraic-Christian tradition that vehemently opposed sexuality within the same gender. Preoccupied with procreative sex necessary to assure racial survival, the ancient Jews had formulated in the Levitical legislation anathemas against homophilia so severe that they included the death penalty. This underlying attitude was reechoed in lists of sinful practices compiled by early Christians in the New Testament, but it remained for Paul the Apostle to articulate at length a rational argument that sex between persons of the same gender was wholly against nature.[1] During the early Middle Ages the penitentials undertook the task of applying these principles to a great variety of homoerotic practices. By mid-twelfth century, however, the standard compilations of canon law by Gratian and of theology by Pierre the Lombard curiously ignored this long-established tradition, except for a brief mention against the unnatural use of women.[2] However this omission can be explained, the Third Lateran Council nonetheless kept the ancient homophobic tradition alive when it convened at Rome in 1179 and decreed that clerics guilty of incontinence against nature were to be degraded and consigned to a monastery for penance, and laymen were to be excommunicated and separated from the faithful.[3]

Pierre the Chanter played an important role in the revival of homophobia at the end of the twelfth century. Both the long and short versions of the *Verbum abbreviatum* constituted the most extensive discussion of the subject for its time.[4] As an energetic biblical scholar, he collected virtually all of the available scriptural references to expose what he considered to be the enormity of the problem. Those who offended God at Sodom and Gomorrah (Gen. 13 and 18) were identified as homosexuals. Since God created male and female for the perpetuation of the human race, homoerotic practices were judged equivalent to racial murder for which the Levitical law assigned death as the appropriate punishment. How God dealt with the inhabitants of the region is a measure of the depravity of the practices. When sins are minor, God sends ministers to correct them, but the cry of the men of Sodom and Gomorrah was so great that God himself intervened as he did for the crimes of homicide and pride. Divine fire so thoroughly destroyed the region of the Pentapolis that the sea itself became dead, unable to support fish, fowl, or ships. Trees bearing comely fruit turned to ashes at mere touch. The church punishes lightly today, Pierre complained, those whom the Lord chastised so heavily in the Old Testament. So vehemently did the Chanter oppose homosexuality that the next generation of theologians imputed to him the rehabilitation of one homophobic legend in particular. According to the Dominican compilation of scriptural glosses of the 1230s, Pierre claimed to have found in Jerome's commentaries that all sodomites died on the night of Christ's birth because it was fitting that the enemies of nature could not endure the advent of the author of nature himself.[5]

Amidst the thunder of these diatribes we can perceive specific homosexual practices. The Chanter was careful to separate hermaphrodites from direct blame. God had created humans as male and female to ensure that both would join together; not of one kind so that man consorted with man and woman with woman. Although the Lord may permit a fetus to be born *androgeos,* that is, not exclusively masculine or feminine, but with instruments for both acting and receiving, the church grants the option of choosing that sex which is best aroused and to marry accordingly. Once established, however, never is a hermaphrodite permitted to change roles.[6] Among practices that Pierre singled out for condemnation in his own day were men who took the female role, men who preferred boys, and those who committed the sin of Onan (Gen. 38:8–10). The last named was slain by God when he refused to procreate with his deceased brother's wife, as his father commanded, but spilled his seed on the ground.

Closely related to nonprocreative sex was extravaginal sex, that is, the avoidance of the female member naturally designed for intercourse, a practice strongly condemned by Augustine in a statement collected both by Pierre the Lombard and Gratian. In his *questiones* the Chanter raised the case of a man who sought to copulate with his wife, not in the natural receptacle but according to the practice of the sodomites. The wife's refusal might incite the husband to return to male lovers. If the wife could prove that she remained a virgin, she could request the church to compel him to perform naturally, but if she were a widow, to whom the remedy was inapplicable, her last recourse was to assume the natural position and with her hands force his penis into her vagina.[7] Drawing upon the practical orientation of the early medieval penitentials, Thomas of Chobham expanded the classification of the sin against nature into four ascending categories: (1) shameful, in the place not designated or in the position not observed by nature; (2) more shameful, lustful abuse with one's own members (masturbation); (3) most shameful, men with men and women with women; and (4) diabolical, men and women with brutish animals.[8]

Throughout the discussion in the *Verbum abbreviatum* the Chanter relied heavily on scriptural authority, paying less attention to the argument against nature except as formulated by the Apostle Paul. His contemporary, Alain de Lille, however, began to elaborate the natural rationale in his poem *De planctu nature.* Personifying nature as a woman, Alain depicted her garments as shredded by human disobedience to the natural law of sexual conduct, in particular, by homosexual practices. As did the *Carmina burana,* Gautier de Châtillon, Gautier de Coincy, and other contemporaries, he chose to represent sexual abberations in terms of elaborate metaphors based on grammar. Although both nature and grammar distinguish between the two genders, natural construction links unlike genders of male and female, but grammar requires the monstrous solecism of joining the same gender. Gilles de Corbeil, the Chanter's medical colleague, echoed Alain's sentiments in the *Hierapigra,* his advice to prelates. Against rational boundaries erected by nature, certain men abandon the active role of their sex and become passive women, and women, in turn, commit solecisms, as in grammar. Elsewhere he complained that, whereas animals follow the natural laws of sex, many men perform the execrable practice of the grammarians to unite the same gender, thus annihilating reproduction. Syntax requires the same gender, but nature demands the coupling of opposites.[9] After Aristotle's natural treatises were rediscovered in the early thirteenth century, the concept of nature was more clearly expanded and reified. Thus clarified, it was increasingly employed as the salient argument against homosexuality by theologians throughout the thirteenth century, most notably Albert the Great and Thomas Aquinas. Increased attention from the theologians, in turn, spawned legislation that sought to obliterate homoerotic practices from Western Europe.[10]

Starkly formulated by the theologians, uncompromising homophobia was the one position, and indeed the only position, with which the other four discourses agreed unequivocally. If Ovid had confessed that he had little interest in boys, his vernacular translator in the thirteenth century commended the *Art d'amours* as a remedy for vile sins against nature. The royal chaplain André further aligned himself with the theological tradition by asserting that love exists only between persons of different sexes, blushing to embrace what nature forbids. Although the medical treatises did not limit their discussion to procreation, they nonetheless assumed without exception that coitus took place exclusively between members of the opposite sex. Like the Tristan legend and Chrétien de Troyes, Jean Renart was totally silent on genital activity between the same sex. For at least two generations, however, the romance tradition had harbored infrequent but strongly expressed aversion to homoeroticism. Among the *romans de l'antiquité,* for example, the knight-hero of *Eneas* was open to the defamation that he preferred boys over females if he chose to ignore the advances of powerful women. In Marie de France's *Lanval,* a story Jean himself cited, the spurned Queen Guenièvre accuses the young knight of having no desire for women but of delighting only in beautiful boys.[11]

The fabliaux were also reticent about homophilia despite the abundance of sexual activity they recorded.[12] A rare exception in *Le prestre et le chevalier* by Milon d'Amiens, however, is sufficient to reveal an antipathy more virulent than in the romances. The priest of the story is thoroughly inhospitable, ungenerous, avaricious, and lecherous, the very antithesis of Christian and chivalric virtue. So great is his greed that nothing escapes sale—not even the sexual services of his niece and concubine—but when he is personally obliged to submit his own body to the passive sexual act, he utterly refuses and agrees to pay any price to escape. Even if he were given the cities of Péronne or Roie, Nevers or La Charité, he swears by God that he will never take the place of a woman under a man. Whatever the priest may think about heterosexual incontinence, bedding with another man is unthinkably *sodomite* and *contre nature*. Male abhorrence of the passive role has a long tradition extending deep into Antiquity. In addition to its expression by Alain de Lille and Gilles de Corbeil among the theologians, Pierre de Poitiers's guide to confessors introduced an explicit distinction between the active and passive roles. At the turn of the twelfth century, therefore, the fabliaux joined with theologians to reinforce contemporary homophobia and to decry the passive male in particular. Apart from the theologians' blanket proscriptions, lesbian practices went unnoticed in the other discourses. [13]

The commencement of sexual activity was naturally subject to the physical conditions of puberty. Guillaume de Conches offered a physiological rationale for the Galenic tradition that coitus began at age fourteen in both boys and girls. We shall see that, according to the physicians, intercourse depended on the proper mixture of heat and moisture. Although children possess the requisite heat and moisture, they cannot cohabit because the bodily ducts are restricted, which prevents the transmission of sperm. A child, moreover, absorbs its total food supply in bodily growth and repair leaving nothing for other functions such as sexual desire. [14] The canonists likewise prescribed a minimum age not only because marriage initiated sexual activity but also because the free consent essential to the bond of wedlock required the parties to reach the age of discretion. By the turn of the century, churchmen in general adopted age fourteen for boys and twelve for girls as established in contemporary Roman law. Some suggested that, since this was only a minimum (*semiplena*), the full age of puberty should be raised to seventeen, but others argued that puberty depended less on chronological age than on physiological maturity. Thomas of Chobham summarized current opinion in the Chanter's circle by accepting fourteen and twelve, justifying the lower limit for girls because women attain the fleshly desires more quickly than men. [15] André the Chaplain likewise accepted the ages of fourteen and twelve but strongly preferred eighteen for the accomplished male lover, because boys are inhibited by excessive blushing and instability before that age. [16]

Ovid set a pattern for the imaginative literature of the twelfth century by recommending himself, a mature man, as the archtypical example of the sexual lover, although he preferred the more vernal years for women. [17] Among the lively sexual activity within the fabliaux, most of the men and women are physiologically mature. Only rarely did the authors indulge in stories of the sexual initiation of young boys and girls. [18] Although the aristocratic lais of Marie de France and the romances of Chrétien de Troyes were populated with mature lovers (Gualadun/Eliduc, Guenièvre/Lancelot, Lunette/Gauvain, and Enide/Erec, the last whose age is given as twenty-five), the legend of Tristan and Iseut provided a potent model to explore the sexuality of young couples. In common with other young heroines, Iseut's age was not revealed in the romances, but Tristan enters his amatory career after receiving knighthood at fourteen. Marie de France did not divulge the age of her young couple in *Les deus amanz*, nor Chrétien that of Perceval, his naive initiate, but Cligès, Chrétien's counterpart to Tristan, is fifteen and "in the flower of his age" when he embarks upon his adventures.[19] Whatever the attraction to young love, however, the romance tradition rarely transgressed the age boundaries set by medical and ecclesiastical authority.

Jean Renart's narration of Guillaume's and Aelis's love in *Escoufle* is the principal exception which explores the age limits of incipient love inspired by Tristan's and Iseut's example. Born on the same day as Aelis (vv. 1764–66), Guillaume is moved into Aelis's chamber after he has been weaned from his nurse at age three (vv. 1801–3). After two years together in the same nursery, the children discover love behind the words *ami/amie* which they hide under epithets of brother/sister (vv. 1976–91). More precocious than Tristan, Guillaume acquires courtly skills by ten (vv. 2018–51), which confirms the emperor's resolution to make Guillaume his heir through marriage to his daughter. The objections of the imperial princes are founded not only on *mésalliance* but also on the impropriety of raising youthful lovers in the same chamber. The emperor protests that they are not yet of age—witness Aelis's small breasts (vv. 2320–31)—and that they will be married when they attain the legal limit (vv. 2712–15). After an undisclosed period of time passes, the imperial constable revives the princes' objections. "No one dares tell you," he argues, "what kind of life these two lead: they lie together the whole night" (vv. 2818–25). When the emperor himself confronts Guillaume with the charges, the youth admits intimacies but denies guilt because of his intention to marry Aelis.[20] Evoking their literary forebears Tristan and Iseut, Guillaume and Aelis scheme to reunite in flight (vv. 3122–31). Jean Renart took advantage of the ambiguities of the romance rhetoric to leave doubt over the exact age of the young couple and over the extent of their lovemaking, but he thereby provides his audience with a continuous narrative of nascent sexuality as his lovers cross the threshold from childhood to pubescence.

If sexuality depends on heat and moisture, then, according to Guillaume de Conches, the ensuing coldness of old age debilitates coitus. Since old people are naturally cold and dry, continued a Salernitan question, they are not prone to sex. If they do have intercourse, this raises the level of heat which is retained longer in their denser bodies, and they find it difficult to abstain from sexual activity.[21] Neither the doctors nor the canonists, however, presumed to speculate at what age natural coldness extinguishes sexuality, but André the Chaplain, apparently thinking of precedent in

Roman law, decreed sixty for men and fifty for women. To the loss of heat he added the increase of body humors that produce discomfort and illness.[22] André further recorded Queen Eleanor's judgment which classifies sexual preferences according to age: the natural libidos of younger men prefer older women, older men prefer younger women, and all women prefer younger men. Although Ovid had disparaged the pretensions of aging lovers—old men are an embarrassment in love as in war—apparently this group offered little interest to the sensuality of the fableors or to the glamor of the romanciers, because as lovers the aged are virtually absent in the pages of vernacular literature.[23]

Since consummation played an important role in the legal definition of marriage, the canonists were obliged to consider the possibility of male impotence and vaginal restriction that prevented a marriage from taking place. Thomas of Chobham's *Summa,* for example, summarized the physiological and psychological factors, ranging from the congenital size of the sexual organs to castration and magical incantations, resulting in frigidity in women and impotence in men. To these André the Chaplain added blindness and immoderate libido that disabled the accomplished lover.[24]

The Social Parameters

Beyond the physical parameters, sexual life in twelfth-century France could be organized on grids of social categories and interests by which dominant groups sought to regulate and control society. Churchmen, for their part, had made use of canon law to define and implement their theories of marriage. We have seen that for centuries ecclesiastics strove to contain sexuality within the institution of matrimony which, by definition, was extended to embrace all the laity. This vast category, comprehensive of the overwhelming majority of the population, admitted no social distinctions. Within marriage, inclusive of all sexual matters, lay men and women were virtually social equals. This was one consequence of emphasizing the free choice of partners over the marital bond that excluded all considerations of social class as long as the contracting spouses were at liberty to consent to their union. The social dimension was recognized only when mistakes over status entered nuptial contracts, called *errores conditionis.* If, for example, a freeman unknowingly marries a servile woman, his marriage can be annulled; not because of social disparity but because his freedom to contract a marriage was vitiated by ignorance.[25] The fundamental social division lay between the laity to whom sexuality was permitted and the clergy to whom it was increasingly prohibited.

To those who could read Latin, Ovid's love poetry transmitted the social assumptions of his ancient Roman milieu into the late twelfth century.

The poet acknowledged that at the pristine beginnings of the world men and women copulated equally like beasts without Venus's instruction, but in his own civilized age Ovid offered himself as the exemplary model of the consummate lover. His personal status of freeborn (*ingenuum*), therefore, translated to the medieval context a social distinction that excluded servile classes from instruction in the art of lovemaking. The poet, moreover, revealed that, although not of ancient lineage, he was of the knightly (*eques*) class.[26] If Corrina's origins were not entirely clear, his partner in the game of love was presumably of comparable social status. The business connotations implied in the ancient class of *equites,* however, most likely escaped medieval readers, who would have been led to associate the poet with the chivalric class of knighthood (*miles*). This anachronistic interpretation was undoubtedly corroborated by the military imagery that pervaded the ancient Latin love elegy. What Propertius and Tibullus termed the *militia amoris,* Ovid transmitted as a knight with new arms in his *Ars amatoria.* By ancient authority, therefore, *amor* had become the unique specialty of the medieval *miles* or knight, but this awareness may have been limited to the clerics who read Latin.[27]

The twelfth-century school clerics who composed amatory comedies in Latin for amusement usually adopted vaguely classical or exotic settings (*Alda*), occasionally specified as Rome (*Miles gloriosus*) or Constantinople (*Milo*). When identified, their lovers were entitled a young *miles* (*Miles gloriosus*), or an *eques (Lidia)* who could be accommodated into medieval society, or a married priest (*Babio*) who was patently anachronistic.[28] Absorbed with the affairs of the heart, contemporary Latin love poetry was, for the most part, oblivious to social milieu.

Written for the courts of kings and counts, romance literature was, like Ovid's poetry, also limited to the upper reaches of society. The social world of Marie de France's lais virtually excluded all notice of nonaristocratic elements. When a merchant is mentioned by inadvertence (*Equitan,* vv. 150–52), his occupation is immediately disparaged.[29] Although townspeople, clerics, and even occasional *vilains* appear on the peripheries of Chrétien's and Jean Renart's vision, these authors consistently omit nonnoble figures as lovers. Within these boundaries, however, the full breadth of aristocratic society appears in the writings of Marie, the Tristan legend, and Chrétien. At the highest level, royal lineage is represented by lovers like Guenièvre, King Marc, and Marie's King Equitan. Arthurian heroes, such as Erec, Yvain, Gauvain, and even Tristan, conceived out of wedlock, bear royal blood in their veins, as do the heroines Blancheflor (Gottfried) and Iseut. In Chrétien's *Cligès,* the level rises to imperial heights in Alexandre and Cligès, both heirs to the throne at Constantinople, and Fenice, daughter of the German emperor. The middle baronial rank is represented by the lady's unnamed husband in Marie's *Yonec,* Rivalin, lord of Parmenie (Tristan legend), and Laudine, daughter of the duke of Laududet (Chrétien's *Yvain*). Beyond the *éclat* of these dignitaries the lower aristocratic levels are equally present in the knights comprising Marie's young heroes (Guigemar and Lanval, for example) as well as Chrétien's Lancelot, Perceval, and Enide, daughter of a poor vavassor. All secondary figures likewise remain within these confines. Jean Renart's characters span the same aristocratic spectrum. At the top is the imperial lineage of Aelis, heiress to Rome, and Conrad, emperor of the Germans. At the middle are Richard the count of Montivilliers and the lady of Genoa who engender the hero Guillaume, whose rank is shared by his cousin the count of Saint-Gilles and the latter's paramour the lady of Montpellier. The lower level of knights is represented by the two lovers in the *Lai de l'ombre* and, of course, most exemplarily by Guillaume and Lïenor de Dole, of the petty aristocracy of the Lorraine.

André the Chaplain inherited the Ovidian preoccupation with the free-born *miles* instructed in love, but he drew upon other traditions as well. From diverse sources his *De amore* achieved the most differentiated and elaborated taxonomy of the social world of sexuality in its time. As a cleric André was not ignorant of the trifunctional scheme, long established in ecclesiastical circles, that divided all society into three orders (*ordines*) according to distinctive functions: the *laborator,* the peasant who works; the *bellator,* the knight who fights; and the *orator,* the cleric who prays. To the traditional terminology of *ordo* he added *genus* (class), and *gradus* (grade) to demarcate social groupings without making clear distinctions among them. (In addition, *genus* was also used to designate family or lineage.)[30] Like Pierre the Chanter and his theological colleagues, however, André declined to restrict himself to three groupings and expanded his scheme by refining functions.[31] He substituted the class of *plebs* (townspeople) for the peasants among the *laboratores* and divided the order of *bellatores* into two groups, the *nobilis* (noble) and *nobilior* (the more noble). The cleric thereby became the fourth or *nobilissimus* class. Because the four groups are unequal they can be ranked in an ascending hierarchy: (1) townspeople, (2) simple nobility, (3) high nobility, and (4) clerics.

After discussing social dimensions, André explained why peasants were not to be included among the *plebs* and thus excluded from the court of love. Finding solace in manual labor associated with the hoe and plowshare, they are driven to sexuality by bestial nature like horses and mules. If they were ever taught the refinements of love, they would be so distracted by actions alien to their nature that the fields would lie uncultivated. (Ovid's thirteenth-century translator, however, felt that peasants work so hard that they are too tired for love, thus allowing their wives opportunity to sport with *amis*.)[32] Should a man qualified for love be obsessively attracted to a peasant woman, he will find that his blandishments will pierce her rough exterior only with difficulty. Having selected an opportune place and not neglecting to complement her profusely, he should not delay to take what he wants even though it requires force.[33] That André condoned rape in this situation clearly underscored Ovid's social barrier between the unfree peasants unsuited for love and other groups to whom love is appropriate.

The lowest level of those fit for love is called plebs (*plebeius, plebeia*), which, André noted at the first occurrence of the term, should be sufficiently clear to the reader. The classical word suggested commoners inferior to patricians, but the medieval context became apparent when the plebs justifies a livelihood gained from merchandising. Although he works the whole week at trading, allowing only one day for love's leisure, his business profits are nonetheless honorable.[34] André's plebs is, therefore, a merchant who normally inhabits the town, or, in medieval terminology, he belongs to the townspeople or the bourgeoisie. André defined the class of *nobilis* as those descended by blood from vavassors or barons or their wives, thus constituting a hereditary caste. Vavassor occurred frequently in vernacular romance and also can be found designating the lowest level of aristocracy in the contemporary registers of King Philip Augustus. By contrast, the *nobilior* (more noble) class originates exclusively from barons for which André cited counts/countesses and marquis/marchionesses as examples. Evidently the countesses of Champagne and Flanders and Ermengard of Narbonne, whose casuistic judgments were quoted, were taken to be historical personages belonging to the higher nobility. These three levels applied equally to men and women with the distinction that a woman's rank changed in marriage to that of her husband's but not vice versa.[35]

Having distinguished three classes suitable for love, André invented conversations between a man from each class with a woman from the three groups. Of the nine possibilities, eight were recorded; only the dialogue between the nobleman and woman from the higher nobility was omitted. The avowed objective of each conversation is seduction. André supplied each man with words appropriate to his class to persuade the woman to consent to his love as well as the responses delivered by each woman. The actual results of these verbal exercises, however, were discouraging for the male lover. Only the plebian man wins any semblance of hope from the plebian woman. The sole conquest of the higher nobleman is aided by arbitration from the countess of Champagne. In all other instances the women reject or ignore the suits. (Perhaps the nobleman's failures with the plebian and woman of his own class rendered further attempts fruitless.)

Occupying over half of André's treatise, the amorous strategies and arguments of the men encounter skillful resistance and subversion from the women.[36]

Although addressed to more diversified audiences than André's Latin treatise was, the fabliaux also revealed awareness of the traditional clerical doctrine of the three orders, which they reexpressed with characteristic satire and crude humor. As early as *Richeut,* for example, when the eponymous prostitute looks for clients to fleece, she singles out one from each of the three orders: a priest (v.154) and a lord knight (vv.230–31), but, like André, she substitutes a rich bourgeois (v.309) for the peasant. A second example, *Des chevaliers, des deus clercs, et les villains,* returned to the traditional schema. Two knights come across a charming clearing in the forest. "If only we had a barrel of wine and good paté," they exclaim, "we could have more pleasure than at high table in the great hall." But having neither, they depart regretfully. They are followed by two clerics who find the place perfect for amorous dalliance with their ladyloves: "One would be a coward, if he couldn't take his pleasure here." But lacking such company, they also depart. Finally, two *vilains* appear burdened with tools of labor, who exclaim, "What a beautiful place to take a crap!" Having full bowels, they do. The point of this exemplary tale, the author concluded, is that *vilains* find no other pleasure than in shitting. Although this opinion explicitly retails traditional contempt for peasants, the two higher orders themselves do not escape unscathed. Knights whose duty is to fight think characteristically of eating, and clerics who should be praying dream of their girlfriends.

A third fabliau, *Les putains et les lecheors,* however, uncovered sharp rivalry between the two traditional ruling classes. When God created the world, the story went, he established three orders: to the knights he endowed lands, to the clerics he gave alms and tithes, and to the peasants he gave the work there is to do. When the riffraff (*tricheors*) that was left over protested that they had been forgotten, God gave the lechers to the knights to provide for and the whores to the clerics. The knights treat their charges shamefully, clothing them poorly and quartering them with dogs, but the whores receive fine robes, drink freely, and sleep with the clerics, all paid by church tithes and revenues. The truth of the story, the fabliau summed up, is that clerics are saved, but knights are damned. Once again, a story that ajudged the two ruling orders on how they favor the world of vice and preferred the clergy who spend church revenues on making themselves comfortable with prostitutes can hardly be innocent praise.

Since the fabliaux portray hundreds of sexually active characters, it is possible to plot a rough sociodemography from their numbers.[37] Jean Bodel's sample of four is, of course, too small to be statistically representative, but the figures sketched of *vilains,* bourgeoisie, and clerics are none-theless suggestive of social divisions found throughout the fabliaux. The knight is the major category missing in Jean. Our larger corpus of fifty fabliaux shows that the treatment of sexuality was not confined to the tra-ditional three orders which the fableors held up to ridicule. Like André the Chaplain they admitted the bourgeoisie, but unlike André they did not ex-clude peasants; nor were they much concerned with divisions within the nobility. The social spectrum that emerges in the fabliaux is more diverse than in André. Within the corpus of fifty fabliaux, almost two-thirds (thirty-two) treat the sexual activity of the nonnoble classes. Ten contain peasants, nineteen bourgeoisie, and three craftsmen. These crude statistics are not mutually exclusive, nor are they offered in any precise sense, but only to suggest relative importance among the groups.

The fabliaux recounted tales that confirmed André's conviction that peasants are bestial by nature. In *La crote* (The turd), for example, a *vilain* and his wife sit cozily by the fire and amuse themselves with guessing games involving their genitals and excrement. We shall see, however, that in the fabliaux the sexual behavior of peasants did not differ appreciably from that of the bourgeoisie, a class whom André admitted to love's in-struction. Most common, peasants were identified by the term *vilain* as, for example, Jean Bodel's characters Travers, Gombert, and the *vilain* of Bailluel who appear in rural settings. Occasionally the term is less precise and cannot exclude ambiguity about the farming activities of the individ-ual in question.[38] The bourgeoisie can be identified through their occupa-tions or the urban setting of their homes. The husband in Jean Bodel's *Li sohaiz des vez,* for example, who returns home to Douai after three months on a business trip, can be associated with the largest segment of towns-people in the fabliaux, the traveling merchant whose frequent absences provide opportunities for the spouse's amorous adventures.[39] To money changers, fishermen, butchers, and millers who supply local commercial needs can be added those who are specifically craftsmen, such as black-smiths, cobblers, and a carver of crucifixes.[40] At times the townspeople are simply designated *borgois/borgoise;* occasionally, they are honored with aristocratic epithets of *prodon* and *prudefame.*[41] Although absent from Jean Bodel's tiny sample, the great majority of the principal characters in the twenty fabliaux recounting aristocratic *amours* are called knights or vavassors (with only an occasional châtelain) all corresponding to André's classification of *nobilis.* A solitary count emerges in the *La dame escolliee* to represent André's *nobilior* category.[42] Unlike the romances which aspired to entertain the brilliant courts of kings and counts, therefore, the authors of the fabliaux were largely content to represent only the lower levels of the aristocracy.

Because both the fabliaux and André report a richly diversified social scene with each status distinctly defined, the theme of *mésalliance* or social disparity dominated both discourses. When applicable in André, for example, *mésalliance* becomes the single major obstacle to the lover's suit. The fullest discussion of these discrepancies arose in the earlier dialogues when the plebian man seeks love from noble and higher noblewomen. The noblewoman replies that the reason class distinctions have existed among humans since earliest times is to encourage each to remain content with his or her order. No one should exceed the limits of rank, but each *preudom* (*probus*) of the lower order should seek the love of a woman of the same rank. The offense to the woman of the higher nobility is greater when more than one grade has been bypassed.[43] The most ancient of class distinctions is that of nobility itself which arises from ancient lineage. Against the higher noblewoman's reasoning, the plebian man asserts that these distinctions appeared in antiquity only because the unworthy needed protection—just as the Scripture says, the law is not for the just but the unjust.[44] His case for dismantling class barriers involves three factors: the equalizing forces of birth, love, and *probitas*. Against noble lineage he asserts to the noble lady that all are sprung from Adam's stock. In love's army all do equal service without exceptions for beauty, class, gender, or inequality of blood; the only measure of distinction is aptitude to bear love's arms. Most important, the true measure of worth is not noble blood but *probitas* derived naturally from common human origins. First defined as one's mold of character, probity comes close to the classical virtue of *honestas*. The cultivation of probity admits one to the ranks of nobility because nobility is more dependent on character than on blood. In response, the woman of higher nobility admits that probity can ennoble a plebian in a moral sense but cannot change his order and make him a vavassor or a baron. The power of the prince, however, can confer nobility on persons of worthy character.[45] In social practice André, therefore, concluded that, despite equalizing theories of birth, love, and moral character, class boundaries remain determinative, subject to alteration only by the prince.

By enregistering social groupings and by according attention to the aristocracy, the fableors, like André the Chaplain, also confronted the central problem of *mésalliance*. In a world pulsating with sexuality, their characters nonetheless remain acutely aware of social barriers. The most extreme case of class disparity is that of Berengier, noble lady (*gentis dame*) and daughter of a châtelain. The father's indebtedness has forced him to marry his daughter to the son of a rich and usurious *vilain*. Although dubbed a knight, this man is totally unfit for chivalry. Disguising herself in armor, Berengier challenges her imposter-husband to a joust, defeats him roundly, and avenges her humiliation by making him kiss her ass. Since the social gulf is deep, the remedy is extreme, but Berengier's predicament, if not her solution, was not unusual among other noblewomen in the fabliaux. In *Jouglet,* for example, Lord Girart, a vavassor in debt, marries his daughter Meheut to young Robinet, whose inexperience and dimwittedness qualifies him only for sheepherding. Similarly, another vavassor gives his beautiful and noble (*bele et gente*) daughter in marriage for a sum of money to Aloul, a rich *vilain* who is excessively miserly and jealous. The young bridegroom in the former case is decommissioned on his wedding day by a mischievous jongleur who administers an overdose of emetics in the form of pears, while the second lady invites the neighboring priest into her bed. This latter recourse was not unusual among female nobles who were forced to submit to disparity with peasant men; it reoccurs in another fabliaux (*Le prestre ki abevete*) from our sample.[46] While marrying downward could be painful to noblewomen, it also occurred among noblemen in the fabliaux but for romantic reasons. The single example of higher nobility in the fabliaux (*La dame escolliee*) made its appearance when a count falls in love with the beautiful daughter of a wealthy knight, although he must thereby suffer an impossible mother-in-law, who is incapable of saying yes. (The father finally subdues his wife by threatening to marry the daughter beneath her station.) A bourgeois son falls in love with and likewise wishes to marry his neighbor's daughter who is presumably of the same class but poorer. The son's father, planning an upward alliance with better lineage, forbids the marriage. In the meantime the girl is wedded to another bourgeois recently widowed. The quandary is finally resolved through the skill of Auberee, an old *entremettreuse,* who enables the young lovers to keep company without the husband's knowledge, thus satisfying all parties.[47] Although these fabliaux provide examples of downward mobility for both women and men, an important gender difference appears comparable to André's dictum that men retain their social status after marriage but women are obliged to accept that of their husbands. Men, both noble and bourgeoisie, who marry downward for the sake of love do not leave the noble or bourgeois strata, but the noblewomen who take *vilain* husbands to recover wealth for their impoverished families are forced to cross a deep chasm. The depth of this humiliation can be gauged by the extremity of their reactions.

Mésalliance was no less present among the romances. Like Tristan and Iseut and the numerous couples from Marie de France, ideally lovers should be social equals. Although they never search for partners outside aristocratic society, within these limits the range of gradation once again poses the problem of social disparity as in André the Chaplain and the fabliaux. Like the solitary count of the fabliau, romantic love moves men of high lineage to seek marriages with lesser-born women. Marie de France's

King Equitan falls in love with his seneschal's wife; Chrétien's Erec, a king's son, with the impoverished Enide, although she is also a count's niece. Occasionally, it is the woman who wishes to marry down, as Marie's royal daughter Guilliadun, who loves a knight Eliduc. Chrétien called attention to the gulf separating Erec and Enide by accentuating the meanness of the damoiselle's clothes (*Erec*, vv.1532–47). Marie's heroines express this consciousness of social disparity most forcefully. Princess Guilliadun is fully aware of her social superiority (*Eliduc*, vv. 345–47), but the seneschal's wife repeatedly recognizes her own vulnerability as a paramour of lower status (*Equitan*, vv.121–24, 133–36, 215) for which she attempts to compensate through marriage. In Jean Renart, however, where the principal love stories entail imperial personages, the social disparity becomes greatest, and *mésalliance* moves squarely to the center of the story. In *Escoufle*, the emperor wishes to marry his daughter Aelis to her childhood companion, the son of the count of Montivilliers; in the *Roman*, the emperor Conrad falls in love with Liënor, daughter of a lowly knight of Dole. Like Marie's lais, Jean conferred upward mobility to both a man and to a woman. As Aelis crouches on a windowsill, about to leap into elopement, *sens* and *amors* struggle together for her decision. *Sens* upbraids her for disgracing her *lignage* and consenting to concubinage, but love finally wins her for her *ami* (vv.3891–3963). Both marriages are resolutely opposed by the princes and high men of the empire. Guillaume is denounced as a parvenu (vv.2792–93), and Liënor declares that the seneschal has always despised her family (v.5063). In both, the princes propose either the king of France (*Escoufle*, v.2166) or his daughter (*Roman*, vv.3040, 3515). (In the days of Louis VII, the Capetians were reputed to have an abundant supply.)[48] In both romances, social disparity generates the conflict that sets the principal narrative in motion; in both, love finally overcomes the distance.

How aloof churchmen remained from aristocratic preoccupations with class and *mésalliance* can be seen in a case raised by Robert of Courson. From all the casuistry of the Chanter's circle, the closest that one came to the issue was Robert's example in which a prince marries the servant of an emperor's daughter believing that she is the daughter herself. The issue at stake is not the invalidity of the marriage because of social disparity but a mistake in identity. Since the prince had not consented to the fraud, he had not actually married the servant and was guiltless of adultery. *Conditio* or social status only enters ecclesiastical consideration when it is implicated in error or fraud that nullifies the free will of the marriage contract.[49]

Since antiquity, the solemn vow to chastity closed sexual relations to the regular clergy, both monks and nuns. From the eleventh century, church reformers had also attempted to introduce celibacy into the secular clergy (exclusively male), beginning with bishops and descending through holy orders (priests, deacons, and subdeacons). Only those at the lower levels of minor orders were permitted to marry and thereby exercise their sexuality. The ecclesiastical tradition, therefore, had long attempted to erect an impenetrable sexual barrier between the lay and clerical populations. The only question left open at the turn of the twelfth century was the precise lower limits of holy orders—in other words, whether the subdeacon belonged to holy orders and was thereby subject to celibacy.[50]

In the twelfth century clerics in the schools questioned this prohibition of sexuality and raised a potential antagonism between the *clericus,* to whom love was denied, and the *miles,* who was celebrated as the exemplary lover. In the opening passage of his autobiography, Abelard adumbrated this conflict when he contrasted the belting of knighthood and the pomp of military glory inherited from his father through primogeniture with his own heroic choice of the vocation of learning. He had, in effect, forsaken arms for letters, the court of Mars for the lap of Minerva.[51] In the Ovidian tradition Abelard nonetheless narrated a tale of love and seduction in which he embellished his amatory prowess despite its tragic and cautionary dénouement. During the first half of the century, clerics extrapolated Abelard's suggestions to their logical conclusion and created a new literary genre entitled "Debates between the cleric and the knight" as to who was the better lover.[52] From the citadel of the schools, clerics, therefore, defied the knights on the erotic field, thus challenging not only their ecclesiastical superiors but also their social competitors.

In the last dialogue between two members of the higher nobility, André the Chaplain disconcertedly altered the persona of his interlocutors. The woman passes from one without experience to a widow and the man from married to clerical status and proceeds to press his suit as a clergyman. This passage combined with two succeeding chapters, in which André briefly summed up his views on the love of clerics and of nuns, therefore dealt with the clergy as a whole, the last class remaining to be treated. Reinforced by personal experience, André's position on nuns was unequivocal. The seduction of nuns provokes God's wrath and is contrary to both public law under penalty of death and to the law of love, which disallows dalliance with those to whom marriage is legally forbidden. (Presumably the same reasoning equally proscribes monks from sexual encounters.) He recalled an occasion when he himself was tempted to apply his amorous skills on a nun. Coming to his senses at the last moment, he extricated himself only with difficulty from the catastrophe of lapsing from good sense. Stay clear of secluded places or private conversations with nuns, he warned his friend Gautier, because they easily lead to criminal acts.[53]

André's opinions on the sexuality of clerics, however, were not unequivocal. Above the plebs, nobles, and higher nobles, the clerics constituted the fourth and highest grade, the *nobilissimus* of society. Derived not from blood but from God, their dignity could be abrogated not by secular power but by God alone. Since the sacred nobility of their order clearly excluded sexuality, any further discussion appeared pointless, but clerics were nonetheless subject to greater bodily temptations than the laity because of long exposure to leisure and abundance of food.[54] This brief passage merely summarized the conclusions of the preceding dialogue between the cleric and the woman of higher nobility, where André directly considered the ecclesiastical requirement of clerical celibacy.

When the woman discovered her suitor's clerical status, she immediately pointed out the incongruity. The man replied that although he shared the cleric's lot, like all men he was conceived in sin and subject to carnal lapses. Since God did not remove fleshly promptings and sinful fires from the clergy, why is the cleric required to preserve bodily chastity anymore than the laity? Rather than rejection, the interlocutor would prove a contrary proposition with compelling reasons: clerics should be chosen as lovers in preference to laymen. A cleric is more cautious and prudent, orders his affairs with greater moderation and control, and possesses greater knowledge through training in the Scriptures. At this point the dialogue began to follow the familiar path of the debates between clerics and knights as to who was the better lover. Unimpressed with the cleric's case, the woman counters with arguments drawn from the chivalric code. If clerics enjoy superior dignity to laymen, they also share greater moral responsibility to avoid sin. More to the point, love requires the qualities of knighthood—physical beauty, unbounded largess, and martial prowess. In contrast, the cleric wears women's clothes, disfigures his head with the tonsure, is without means to practice largess unless he steals from others, and is prone to idleness and enslavement of his belly. In riposte, the cleric responds to each point: because of their dignity clerical lapses are exaggerated; their peculiar dress is worn to distinguish them from other men; they are capable of generosity, and their order forbids them to shed blood. When the cleric reaches excessive idleness and eating, he lays the responsibility on Eve whose gluttony introduced sin into the world.[55] At the introduction of this familiar misogynistic argument, the debate takes leave of clerical love to pursue another path, but in the following chapter André concluded that, if a cleric persists in entering love's warfare, he should enlist at the order and rank of his birth and adopt the appropriate discourse.

The encyclopedic *De amore* approached the task of accommodating church proscriptions with conflicting traditions of Ovid and the contemporary schools. The ecclesiastical attempt to create an absolute division between the laity and the clergy in sexual matters is countered with the school tradition of the clerical lover adumbrated by Abelard's personal experience and defended in the "Debates between the cleric and the knight." Although André continued to accept celibacy as a clerical goal, in practice he was willing to condone the activities of the clerical lover because of fleshly weakness. His treatise, therefore, represented an attempt to accommodate ecclesiastical restrictions on clerical sexuality with the love doctrine of the schools.

Within our selection of fifty fabliaux, twenty-three contain sexually active clergymen, a number comparable to that of the knights (twenty) and townsmen (including craftsmen: twenty-two). So ubiquitous is the churchman-lover that his behavior assumes patterns that can serve as a taxonomy for clerical sexuality. Jean Bodel's two stories establish the pattern by the turn of the century. In *Gombert* a *vilain* offers hospitality to two itinerant clerics which the guests repay by seducing the peasant's daughter and wife. In utter blackness of night, one cleric persuades the girl with a gift of a gold ring (actually an iron ring stolen from the fireplace), and the other diverts the husband, who arises to answer the call of nature, from his wife's bed by shifting the crib of the couple's infant. The *Meunier* repeated the essential features of Jean's tale, including the ring and the baby. At least eight other fabliaux recounted similar escapades of amorous clerics. In four of the accounts the clerics attend schools, in one at Paris; in the *Meunier* they are identified as deacons. In all cases it is clear that they are young and without permanent attachment to the community. So conventional is the figure of the young, wandering clerical lover that it is not surprising that of the three versions of *La damoisele qui ne pooit oïr,* a story of a girl so prudish that she must be taught the language and deeds of love, one included a clerical preceptor.[56]

Even if the young men are committing fornication or adultery, they are not violating sacred vows because celibacy was not required of simple clerics below holy orders. More numerous than the wandering cleric, however, is the local priest who appears in fourteen fabliaux. Mature and well-established in the community, he has taken a vow of celibacy at his ordination, which amplifies the scandal. Occasionally, he keeps a concubine at the rectory (*Bouchier* and *Prestre et le chevalier*), but most often he is the adulterous lover of someone's wife. In the *Vilain* (later imitated in the *Prestre ki abrevete*) Jean Bodel pressed the limits when he has the priest make love to the wife in full view of the husband, convincing the latter that what he sees is not happening.[57] More plausibly in the other fabliaux, the wife is accustomed to entertain her lover at table, in the bath, and in bed in the spouse's absence.[58] Often the husband returns to surprise the lovers, but occasionally to be punished for his intrusion. Equally common, the priest does not escape unscathed, at times suffering loss of genitals.[59] Since monks were cloistered and, therefore, protected from the world, their appearance in these compromising situations is less common; only one appears in our corpus (*Segretain moine*).

The literary topos of the clerical lover adumbrated by Abelard, embroidered in the school debates, and justified by André the Chaplain, found ample attestation among the clerics and priests who crowd the tales of the fabliaux. Here the knight is faced with a worthy rival in the quest for amorous fame, but the objects of conquest are quite distinct. Clerical seduction is invariably aimed at wives and daughters of peasants and townsmen. Rarely does the cleric or priest approach a noblewoman, nor does the knight hunt among the *vilains* or bourgeoisie. The competition between the two orders came to a climax in the *Prestre et le chevalier*. When the priest abuses the obligation of hospitality, the knight takes revenge by demanding the priest's niece and concubine and by threatening to sodomize the priest's own body, the ultimate humiliation.[60] Despite direct confrontation within this single fabliau, the sexual worlds of the two champions were usually kept separate. Class barriers remain high in the fabliaux between the nobility on one side and the bourgeoisie and peasants on the other, where the clerical lover freely roams.

The school image of the clerical lover corroborated in the vernacular fabliaux suggests that the reform program on celibacy was far from achieving its goal at the turn of the twelfth and thirteenth centuries. This impression is further confirmed by a brief note in the Salernitan medical questions on the appropriate seasons for coitus. Five contemporary English physicians were named and characterized by their sexual appetites and capabilities. Master Hugh de Mapenore, for example, has small appetites but great energy, whereas master Philip Rufus of Cornwall possesses the reverse, but master Johannes Burgensis has appetites to match his capabilities. That master Hugh later became the bishop of Hereford (1216–19) and the other two are found in the documents of the episcopal entourage confirm a presumption raised by the master's title—that these men were clerics bound for ecclesiastical careers. It poses, moreover, the intriguing question of how and why their sexual diagnostics entered the medical literature.[61] This abundance of sexual energy imputed to the clergy may help to explain why churchmen at the time could still be found at Paris who questioned the wisdom of extending celibacy further.

Voices protesting the extension of celibacy can be heard in Paris since 1074, when a local council declared that the requirement was insufferable and unreasonable. In Pierre the Chanter's day, master Pierre Comestor of the previous generation was reported to have declared to his students that celibacy restrictions should be reduced.[62] Members of the Chanter's own circle likewise questioned the requirements and focused on deacons and subdeacons, the borderline between holy orders held to chastity and the lower orders free to marry. Pope Alexander III (1159–81) had dealt with the problem by granting dispensations or "dissimulations" which allowed subdeacons to marry under special occasions and difficult circumstances. Within the Chanter's circle Thomas of Chobham advised clerics in minor orders to marry secretly (Abelard's solution) because it was less sinful to deceive one's bishop than to commit fornication and violate the divine commandment. Renouncing temporary and oblique solutions, Robert of Courson preferred to face the problem squarely and summon a general council of the church to deliberate on the limits of celibacy. He raised the specific case of a young deacon, sorely tempted by sexual desire and fearful of succumbing to fornication, who petitioned the pope for a dispensation to marry. Did he not have a better cause for marriage than the aged clerics beyond carnal promptings whom papal letters nonetheless permitted to enjoy wives? As a matter of fact, Robert continued, many deacons and subdeacons in remote kingdoms as well as in France were married claiming papal indulgence. Although leaving the border undefined, Robert clearly proposed reduction of celibacy for the lower clergy. This call for a council was similarly echoed by Gerald of Wales, also of the Chanter's circle. Pierre the Chanter's extant writings were silent on the question, but Robert of Courson reported that his teacher was accustomed to assert that a general council be convoked to abolish intolerable burdens laid on the clergy.[63] Like the subject of marriage, this was apparently one of his favorite causes at the time of his death in 1197.

Those surrounding the Chanter called for a return to the primitive church when the lower clergy were permitted to marry. Speaking for the group, Raoul Ardent averred that the church was better served by married ministers than those tempted to fornication, adultery, sodomy, and incest.[64] This program, of course, would not have exonerated the behavior of clerics and priests in the fabliaux, who, for the most part, indulged in adultery, but by channeling the sexual energies of increasing numbers of clergy into the legitimate bonds of marriage they hoped to treat the cause, not just the symptoms. The contemporary papacy still under the sway of the reform momentum of the eleventh century, however, ignored their solution. In 1208 Innocent III commissioned the papal legate Guala to hold a council at Paris which decreed excommunication of all priests and other clerics who had contact with women in or outside their houses. So undefined were the terms that they provoked protests from Gilles de Corbeil, and the pope himself was obliged to issue special directives to French bishops for absolving those implicated. In 1207, however, Innocent defined the subdiaconate as formally included within holy orders and thereafter subject to celibacy. The long-awaited Lateran Council summoned all bishops from Latin Christendom in 1215, but if the Parisian masters had hoped for change, they were severely disappointed. When it closed, the requirements of chastity upon holy orders through the subdeaconate were further strengthened with sanctions.[65] Pierre the Chanter's program for alleviating the burdens of clerical celibacy was, therefore, relegated to the lost causes of history.

The Marital Parameters

By insisting that all human sexuality be contained within the institution of matrimony, churchmen attempted to set the most inviolate of all parameters for sexual conduct. At mid-twelfth century, Pierre the Lombard determined the course of theological discussion at Paris when he included marriage among the seven sacraments of the church and defined a sacrament in Augustinian terms as a sign of a sacred thing. Through the mutual consent of souls and the joining of bodies, husbands and wives thereby signified the union of Christ with his church. Since death prevented Pierre the Chanter from completing his *Summa de sacramentis,* it was left to Robert of Courson to include marriage within his extensive discussion. To the Lombard's union of Christ and the church, Robert added that human marriage was also a sign of the most sacred and ineffable *copulatio* between divinity and humanity in the Virgin's womb. The marriage of every man and woman gave expression to the mystery of the Incarnation, the Word becoming flesh in Christ Jesus, who was both God and man.[66]

Having laid stress on the sacramental character of marriage, ecclesiastics attempted to remove all possible doubt that sexual activity was permitted only between a man and woman married to each other.[67] All pre- or extramarital sexuality was condemned as fornication or adultery. Following generations of canonist discussion, Pierre the Chanter defined simple fornication as illicit intercourse between an unmarried man and an unmarried woman and condemned it with scriptural authority and reasons linking it to bestiality. Against those who held that simple fornication was only a venial sin because of frequency, Thomas of Chobham argued that it was indeed a mortal sin but of a lesser kind.[68] In the Chanter's discussion adultery was twofold: simple, involving an unmarried with a married partner; and double, between two married partners. Like sodomy, the crime was equated with murder as suggested by the death penalties which the Old Testament assigned to adultery. Once again, the church errs by not observing this penalty for adultery, although thieves are so punished, a measure not found in Scripture. Lest this recourse serve to justify an injured husband's revenge on a peccant couple, Thomas of Chobham disagreed with his teacher's opinion and argued that the Gospels finally abrogated the death penalty for adultery. Whereas secular law had permitted the husband to kill the wife, it now sanctions only the castration of the lover. The contemporary canonists likewise forbade outraged husbands to kill delinquent partners.[69]

Within Latin discourse the extremity of the Chanter's position on extramarital sexuality was matched by the adultery championed by the ancient preceptor Ovid. Presenting himself as the exemplary lover in the *Amores,* the poet is not only married but his mistress Corinna has a husband, whose existence Ovid tolerates with annoyance. His handbook on seduction taught the amorous disciple how to deal with the inconvenience of the husband while conquering the lady. In this Ovidian tradition, none of the lovers in the Latin school comedies are married to each other, and at least four of the works enact adulterous scenarios.[70]

Since marriage was normally denied to clergymen except at the lowest rank, sexual love was equally barred by ecclesiastical authority, notwithstanding clerical ambition to compete with knights. In the debate literature, one maiden rejects the cleric for the knight on the grounds that the latter is free to marry. Abelard's seduction of Heloise was technically fornication, but his attempt to resolve the dilemma through secret marriage was accepted only under protest by his young wife. Marshaling an arsenal of authorities from Scripture, ancient philosophers, and the Church Fathers to dissuade the philosopher-monk, Heloise resisted the name of wife with its coercive connotations (*vinculi nuptualis*) for the title of *amica,* more dear to her and more honest for him. She continued this theme in her first letter to Abelard after their separation. Protesting that she had sought neither dowry nor marriage bond (*matrimonii foedera*), she preferred the word *amica,* indeed concubine or even prostitute. In a rhetorical flourish, she proclaimed that even if the Emperor Augustus himself honored her with marriage and authority, she would choose to be Abelard's whore (*meretrix*) rather than the empress herself (*imperatrix*).[71] This defiance of the sacrament of marriage and articulation of uncoerced sexual love outside the matrimonial bond was without parallel in the Latin discourse of the Middle Ages.

The encyclopedic character of the *De amore* permitted André the Chaplain to assemble diverse and contradictory elements of the Latin school tradition. Book III, where he summarily and categorically refuted all of the love doctrine previously discussed, contained the traditional ecclesiastical position: in both Testaments God detests and orders the punishment of all sexual acts and desires outside of marriage. If God had conceded that fornication could be performed without sin, it was without cause that he decreed marriage to be celebrated, because his people could have reproduced more rapidly without restraint through fornication than through matrimony.[72]

André usually did not reveal the marital status of the three pairs of inter-locutors in Book I, but in the dialogues between members of the aristo-cratic classes (*nobilis* and *nobiliores*) the question of extramarital sexuality was explicitly raised. During the convoluted conversation between the two higher nobles the woman raises the case of a maiden to whom the loss of virginity through lovemaking threatens future marriage. Since the girl is unmarried at the time, it raises at least the possibility of fornication. The man dismisses the problem by noting numerous maidens in literature who had loved but had not suffered, among them the celebrated Anfelis (Fenice?), Iseut, and Blancheflor. A good husband will never refuse as wife a woman who is well taught in the commands of love.[73]

The important question for the aristocratic discussants, however, is adultery, which the seventh dialogue explicitly invoked where the *nobilior* suitor discovers that the *nobilis* woman has a husband. The man tries to neutralize her defense by making a distinction between the marital affec-tion found in marriage and the name of love which he proposes. The latter can play no role between wedded partners because matrimony excludes jealousy, secret embraces, and uncontrolled desire, the essentials of true love. In response, the woman attempts to reunite the functions of husband and lover by arguing that married couples do in fact enjoy secret embraces and carnal desire, but the man continues to belabor the point that jealousy can play no part in married life. To clinch his case he evokes the ancient opinion, transmitted by the Church Father Jerome, that a husband who is an ardent lover of his wife is an adulterer. Confronted with the extremity of this argument, the noble woman finally accedes to the arbitration of Marie, the countess of Champagne, to whom a letter is dispatched. Marie's reply is not only noteworthy for its terse solution ("We declare and confirm that love cannot exist between two married people"), but it is re-markable also for the arguments advanced. Employing the traditional and legal vocabulary of matrimony, Marie, like Heloise, contrasts the coercion of marriage with the liberty implicit in love. Beyond the practical consid-erations of embraces and jealousy, married people are "yoked together" (*duos iugales vires*)—compelled by the marriage obligation to submit to mutual will and in no way able to deny themselves to each other. (We shall see that this refers to the Pauline doctrine of the conjugal debt in sexual relations.) By contrast, lovers freely lavish everything on each other driven by no necessity whatsoever. Adopting Ovidian military imagery appro-priate to aristocratic audiences, the countess concludes that the king of love will crown no married woman with a prize unless she has enlisted in love's army outside the marital bonds.[74]

In Book III André not only rejects Marie's decision, as we have seen, but he also turns her own arguments against her conclusion. Because of jealousy and desire, it is now love that coercively binds one in arduous slavery. Between its first appearance and final refutation, however, André repeatedly involved Marie's famous judgment as authoritative. When the higher nobleman admits to the higher lady that he has a beautiful wife, he distinguishes between the love he presently offers and the marital affection with which he cherishes his spouse, but he justifies his extramarital suit on the countess's decision. Because love between husband and wife is impossible, he is compelled to seek love outside the nuptial bond, thus compounding the coercion. In the later chapter proposing options for terminating love, a subject of obvious Ovidian inspiration, André asserted that the marriage tie assuredly puts love to flight. First among the concluding set of regulations for love was the dictum that matrimony is not a justified excuse for refusing love. At least three cases submitted to the courts of love are resolved according to Marie's decision. Among them Ermengarde, lady of Narbonne, explicates the radical difference between marital affection and the true love of lovers on philosophical grounds.[75] Although Marie, Ermengarde, and through them André himself are primarily concerned with the controversial question of adultery, unlike Heloise who was only implicated in simple fornication, their discussions are nonetheless founded on the basic distinction between bondage and freedom in matrimony and love so eloquently articulated by Abélard's young mistress. Within these games of adultery André saw little difference whether they were played by married men, women, or both. The thirteenth-century translator of Ovid, however, was less sure of this reciprocity. Glossing his text, he allowed husbands to deceive wives but warned wives not to enter the game.[76] Behind the high seriousness of André's discussion loomed the sardonic leer of Ovid, the ancient authority and patron of all adulterers.

The animated sexual scene in the fabliaux encompassed the full range of possibilities defined by churchmen. Alongside vigorous extramarital activity, married sexuality was not neglected. In our corpus of fifty tales, at least twelve recount the experiences of married couples.[77] Jean Bodel's contribution of four fabliaux contains the major theological categories, including marital love. The merchant and his wife in *Li sohaiz des vez,* for example, are secure in their fondness for each other. Only when extreme fatigue causes the husband to neglect his marital duties does the wife lapse into lubricious reveries, but upon awakening he quickly recognizes his failings and compensates for lack of attention. "That night," Jean Bodel concluded, "they had it good together." A similar situation occurred in the *Pescheor* where a fisherman and his wife love each other *de bone amor.* He fishes, feeds his wife well, and services her vigorously in bed. When the wife shows signs of discontent, however, he feigns castration and then recovery, which revives her appreciation of his sexual contribution. In fact, a recognizable type appeared in the fabliaux of married couples whose sexual appetites exceed normal bounds. A Norman *vilain* and his wife, for example, are granted four wishes by St. Martin for faithful service. The latter may well have been surprised by the wife's request to have all her mate's skin covered with multitudinous sexual equipment, but in response the husband wishes his spouse to be furnished reciprocally. An ill-considered third wish eliminates the organs altogether, but the fourth boon fortunately remains to reestablish the status quo ante quem.[78]

Although unhappily married couples abound among all social classes in the fabliaux, examples of robust, cheerful, marital sexuality are limited to peasants and townspeople. Whenever aristocratic matrimony was represented, the sexual relations were rarely seen in a positive light. The lady in *Le chevalier a la robe vermeille* sleeps with her husband in order to deceive him; the noble youth from Normandy, who rashly aspires to polygamy (at least twelve wives), ruefully learns that one is sufficient (*Vallet aus douze fames*). Although circumstances suggest that the wife in *Guillaume au faucon* is satisfactorily married to the châtelain, in the end she consents to love Guillaume, the young and courtly suitor.[79]

Despite concessions to the existence of connubial bliss—at least among the lower classes—the conclusion nonetheless persists that the overwhelming number (thirty-seven) of fabliaux in our corpus furnish stories of extramarital love. At least nine stories contain cases of simple fornication. In Jean Bodel's *Gombert* (followed closely by the *Meunier*) a cleric shares the bed of the host's unmarried daughter. Two versions of the seduction of the girl who couldn't abide unvarnished language contain an unmarried *vallet* as well as the inevitable cleric. The astute butcher of Abbeville takes revenge on his ungracious host by corrupting not only the priest's concubine but also his servant girl, a feat replicated in *Le prestre et le chevalier*. Since the seducer's marital status is unrecorded, he may have been unmarried and his actions, therefore, limited to fornication.

Within this extramarital scene, the clear majority of fabliaux (twenty-eight) recounted tales of simple adultery among all levels of society where one partner is married. Among the peasants, Jean Bodel's *vilain* of Bailluel (imitated in *Prestre ki abevete*) must observe his wife and her lover.[80] Among the townspeople, as would be expected, the frequent and prolonged travels of the merchant provide the classic opportunity to the unfaithful wife. Invariably the husband returns home to find his spouse and her lover cozily engaged at table or in the bath. Even when the husband uses his absence to snare the lovers at home as in the *Borgoise d'Orliens,* he is caught in his own trap, beaten for his presumption, and forced to acquiesce to his spouse's domestic arrangements.[81] The class restrictions informing the fabliaux required that the lover of peasant and bourgeois wives invariably be a clergyman. Occasionally he is an itinerant cleric, as in Jean Bodel's two clerics who lodged with the peasant Gombert. While the one is busy with the daughter, the other is with the wife.[82] We have seen that the preferred lover of the peasant or bourgeois wife was the local priest who is ever ready to make pastoral house calls. The conventional features of this scenario may be illustrated by *Le prestre qui fut mis au lardier,* in which the beautiful wife of Baillet the cobbler was in the habit of entertaining a handsome priest whenever the husband was away. On one occasion after the wife had prepared a meal and bath for her visitor, Baillet, tipped off by his young daughter, returns home unexpectedly. The priest is quickly concealed in a meat larder which provides the cobbler a convenient container to transport the interloper to the market where he is sold to the priest's brother for an exorbitant price. In some stories neither the priest nor the husband so readily escapes injury or embarrassment, but the ten fabliaux containing priestly lovers demonstrate the ubiquity of the situation.[83] Ovid's recommendation of adultery was, therefore, represented to lay audiences of the fabliaux with the same enthusiasm as to the clerical readers of the love treatises.

Whereas André's treatment had intimated that adultery was the specialty of the nobility, the fabliaux demonstrate that it was by no means their monopoly. Love is nonetheless segregated at the level of aristocracy. We have seen that the noble wife who has been forced to marry a *vilain* beneath her station takes a clerical lover in the fabliaux. In addition, at least seven more tales introduced noble wives who are as eager for adventure as their lower-class sisters. For example, in *Les trois dames qui trouverent l'anel* three ladies compete for the prize of a ring to see who is most ingenious in deceiving their husbands. The most prevalent story, however, involved the classic triangle of a lady, a husband, and a knight replacing the cleric as lover. Occasionally they degenerate into burlesque situations where the husband returns home and the lover must be hidden (*Chevalier a la robe vermeille*). When the lover contrives to humiliate the husband in *Les tresces,* outrageous pandemonium breaks loose reminiscent of peasant and bourgeois scenarios. At the other extreme—close to the courtly romances— the young *damoiseaux* Guillaume eventually wins the love of the châtelain's wife through refined sentiments (*Guillaume au faucon*).[84]

Throughout this endless parade of adulterers one constant held firm: in Pierre the Chanter's terms all can be classified as simple adultery, involving only one married partner, the woman. In the peasant and bourgeois scenes, where the male lover is most frequently a young cleric, his legal status is presumed to be unmarried. In four fabliaux where the lover is a layman, he is invariably characterized as unwed or young.[85] In all cases involving aristocratic ladies, the paramour is either young like the *vallet*

Guillaume, or a knight whose marital status is unspecified. Apparently the male authors of the fabliaux found it difficult to talk about married men who trespassed matrimonial bonds, unlike André's higher nobleman, and preyed upon equally married women of the same rank.

When Pierre the Chanter proposed the Old Testament punishment of death for adulterers and Thomas of Chobham declared its contemporary commutation to castration, they assumed, of course, that the penalties were to be administered by legally constituted authority. Recourse to such measures by outraged husbands and family, however, remained an ever-present danger, as Abelard discovered and against which canon lawyers inveighed. The mutilation of the guilty organs (or the threat thereof), however, presented the fableors with the most dramatic of scenarios. One of the most vivid cases (*Prestre crucifié*) occurred when a sculptor of cruci-fixes surprises his wife with a priest. The latter adopts the ingenious, if not totally convincing, stratagem of placing himself on a cross in the work-shop. Unfortunately, sharp tools are close at hand, and the priest saves his life only at the sacrifice of his amatory equipment.[86] Despite similar close calls, none of the principal lovers, both clerical and lay, is killed, although a knight barely escapes in *Les tresces*. We hear of a priest who has been drowned by a jealous husband only because the fisherman of Pont-sur-Seine has snagged him in his net. Two fabliaux (*Estormi* and *Le segretain moine*), however, recount conspiracies of married couples to employ their wives' charms to ensnare priests whom they rob and murder. Audiences may have understood these examples of private revenge to be fitting justice for adulterous clergy.

Although the romance tradition inherited by Jean Renart reduced the social scene to the aristocracy, within that scope it nonetheless encom-passed the full variety of heterosexual activity classified by ecclesiastical authority. Chrétien's two couples, the adulterous Lancelot and Guenièvre and the married Erec and Enide, epitomized the extreme limits. Within this broad spectrum, however, the Tristan legend exercised a potent, if ambiguous, force. By her marriage to King Marc, Iseut is an unqualified adulteress, a situation underscored by Gottfried (following Thomas) when he has the king share both Brangane (Iseut's maid) and the queen herself on his wedding night in Tristan's company (vv.12, 435–463). When Tristan marries Iseut aux Mains Blanches with the church's blessing (Thomas, p.49, vv.369–84), the simple adultery is compounded to double (even though the latter marriage is not consummated). Yet the versions of Eilhart and Béroul attempted to mitigate the scandal by assigning primary responsibility to the magic potion. When its power dissipates after three years the young pair are extricated from their dilemma. This fundamental ambiguity in the Tristan legend was conveyed by Béroul's use of the terms *drüerie/dru*.[87] Akin to *amors/ami,* these words could be applied to a whole range of affective relations involved in love and friendship. Although Béroul could attribute *drüerie/dru* to the most refined and delicate of courtly sentiments, it also denoted baseness (*vilanie*). In its first occurrence, Iseut affirms that she would rather be burned and have her ashes scattered than to submit to the *drüerie* of adultery (vv.33–38). After the magic philtre has worn off, Tristan likewise asserts that he shall no longer continue in *drüerie* that turns to *vilanie* (vv.2228–30).

Within the romance tradition Marie de France was perhaps the most susceptible to the spell of Tristan. If the two husbands, the seneschal in *Equitan* and Bisclavret, believe their marriages to be secure at the opening of the stories, they are quickly disabused. The sexuality that absorbed Marie's attention in all twelve of her lais takes place outside matrimonial limits with a particular preference for adultery.[88] The young Guigemar who loves the wife of a jealous old man, King Equitan who covets his seneschal's wife, Queen Guenièvre who eyes the young Lanval, the paradigmatic Tristan and Iseut (*Chevrefoil*) are the most noteworthy of a succession of adulterers and adulteresses.[89] Marie herself was fully cognizant of the opprobrium directed against her lovers. When a fearful storm at sea threatens the lives of the wedded Eliduc and the young Guilliadun, the sailors demand that the *drue* be thrown overboard to appease divine wrath (*Eliduc,* vv.814–52).[90] A frequent word in Marie's lexicon, *drüerie* connoted broadly varied sentiments as in Béroul, but Marie made frequent use of it in adulterous and compromising circumstances. Equitan's relationship with the seneschal's wife (v.82) and the queen's infatuation for Lanval (vv.265–67), for example, are termed *drüerie*. Since Eliduc has not technically consummated his love for Guilliadun, he can protest that there was no *vileinie* in his *drüerie* which was, in fact, limited to talking and the exchange of gifts (vv.575–80).[91]

Whether or not Marie's audience included the Angevin kings of England, the latter undoubtedly shared her amorous vocabulary. King Richard's orientation as a lover may be unclear, but he was occasionally linked romantically to ladies in his day. In 1190 he confirmed by charter to his constable in Normandy several properties which the latter held through his wife Gisèle. The constable's attention was probably drawn to the terms of the charter, but if his wife had examined the seal closely, she would have noticed that it was attached by a ribbon into which a declaration of love was woven: *Jo sui drüerie / ne me dunez mie / ki nostre amur deseivre / la mort pui si ja receivre*.[92] "I am '*drüerie*.' Do not give me to one who might separate our love. May he then instantly incur death." In all likelihood, many of these "valentines" were produced, thus illustrating the wide circulation of the romance lexicon of love.

Against this background it is not surprising that Jean Renart explored the theme of adultery in his *Lai de l'ombre* where a knight pursues a married lady. The sport was also practiced by secondary characters in his two romances. When the count of Saint-Gilles and the lady of Montpellier were pictured as openly exchanging *gages d'amour* in the *Escoufle* (vv.5674–5709), or the seneschal and the (fictitious) châtelaine of Dijon are engaged in similar flirtations in the *Roman* (vv.4297–4312), Jean provided two couples compromised by suspicion of double adultery (if we assume that the latter pair were also married to different spouses as were the former).[93] The word *drüerie* comes quickly to the seneschal's lips who was well practiced in the art of womanizing. When he hears the young emperor singing of *fine amors,* he immediately suspects *drüerie* (v.3202) with the sister of Guillaume de Dole. To loosen the tongue of Guillaume's mother he pays her court and offers *par drüerie* (v.3345) a precious ruby mounted on a costly gold ring. The parlance of love fed on equivocation in which words like *drüerie* and *amors* both concealed and suggested illicit intentions.

Beneath adultery were other levels of ambiguity in the Tristan legend. If the famous couple's love was unlawful, it also comprised an awakening of two young people for the first time. Such nascent love likewise risked the dangers of fornication. Exploring the sexual initiation of Guigemar and Lanval, Marie de France has the *drüerie* (vv.55–62) of the youthful pair in the *Deus amanz* end tragically like Tristan's and Iseut's. Youthful sexual initiation, however, was an apt setting for equivocacy. Perceval, Chrétien's adolescent *nice,* steals a kiss from the damoiselle of the tent, protesting that it is innocent (*Graal,* L. vv.691–709, R. vv.696–711), but the girl's protective *ami* has doubts. "No one will believe that he took a kiss without going further; one thing leads to another" (L. vv.3839–47, R. vv.3857–65). When the hero later climbs into bed and holds the noble Blancheflor in his arms and "mouth to mouth until the morning came" (L. vv.2055–64, R. vv.2057–69), he may only have been following his mother's instructions to limit his lovemaking to a kiss. Whether or not these young initiates crossed the ecclesiastical line demarcating fornication, Chrétien is surely testing the subtlety of the boundary.

We have seen that Jean Renart repeatedly evoked the tradition of Tristan and Iseut throughout *Escoufle,* but all but one allusion was restricted to the theme of young love.[94] Born on the same day and raised in the same nursery, Guillaume and Aelis conceal their maturing love under the names of brother and sister until imperial politics force them to elope. As with Chrétien's Perceval and the damsel, it is not clear how far the young couples' sexual experiences have developed when they separate. At Guillaume's and Aelis's joyous reunion in Montpellier their beds are nonetheless placed next to each other—recalling a similar scenario for Tristan and Iseut. Jean did not mention whether Guillaume imitates Tristan's leap, but he coyly remarked: "I do not know about Guillaume and his *amie* or how they had it together, but he who sits shivering before the fire warms himself by moving closer. The beds were so close that there was only room for a wooden plank" (vv.7863–81). The boundary between the young couple's love and the ecclesiastical definition of fornication was, indeed, as thin as the plank.

However Jean Renart chose to veil Guillaume's and Aelis's love, he was not reticent about young Conrad's in the *Roman de la rose*. Refusing marital responsibilities, the emperor thinks only of youthful pleasures. The summer hunt deep in the forest furnishes opportunities for him and his companions to find new *amies*.[95] Profiting from the hunters' absence, the youths return to the tents and await the ladies with open arms. *Chevaliers aux dames* (v.223) is the joyous call to battle between the sheets. Jean frankly acknowledged that their pleasures are not innocent: "Since they afford no thought for their souls, they have no need for churches, bells, or chaplains, but only the sweet songs of birds" (vv.224–28). With all of the sheen of romance the author embellished what churchmen denounced as fornication, if not adultery.

We have also seen that *Cligès* was Chrétien's principal attempt to deal with the fundamental ambiguity in the Tristan legend. The hero of the romance is the product of Alexandre's and Soredamor's youthful love and legitimately born after their marriage. Fenice, for her part, explicitly rejects Iseut's adultery. Citing the Apostle's admonition to remain chaste (vv.5264–69), she refuses to imitate the celebrated lovers and flee to Brittany with Cligès. Like the legend, however, her solution requires magic— both to preserve her virginity and to feign her death. How well these artifices assuaged the basic ambiguity, the contemporary audience could best judge, but Chrétien's ultimate solution to young love and adultery is to dispose of the husband by death and unite the lovers in marriage. "Cligès makes his *amie* his wife and called her both *amie* and wife, for they lost nothing thereby, loving each other as lovers" (vv.6633–38). In direct denial of Countess Marie's dictum, marriage and love were reconciled.

From open adultery to the nuances of fornication—all inspired by Tristan and Iseut—Jean Renart encompassed the full spectrum bequeathed by romance tradition. His major characters, however, adopted Chrétien's solution in *Cligès* where marriage offers the final resolution to young love, a response reinforced by *Erec et Enide* in which the couple are also ceremoniously wedded. That night, unlike the Tristan legend, no Brangane is substituted for the bride (vv.2021–25). All three of Jean Renart's principal couples likewise consummate their love in festive weddings. In *Escoufle* Count Richard de Montivilliers marries the lady of Genoa (vv.1704–37); a son is conceived, who finally weds the emperor's daughter at Rouen (vv.8329–33). Despite Conrad's youthful indiscretions, lawful marriage has also become his sole concern after he falls in love with Lïenor. Once the obstacles are removed, the emperor's impatience can only be satisfied by an immediate wedding. Ignoring Tristan's and Iseut's illicit example, Jean Renart's characters conclude with the destiny Chrétien assigned to Cligès and Erec. After youthful hesitation, Conrad, like Guillaume, submits his sexuality to the discipline of matrimony. Jean Renart's matrimonial solution must have well pleased his powerful patron, Baudouin, count VI and IX of Hainaut and Flanders. Like Guillaume and Aelis of *Escoufle,* which was dedicated to Baudouin, the count was a mere youth (age thirteen) when he espoused Marie de Champagne, an equally young bride (age twelve). The court chronicler Gislebert de Mons expressly noted that Baudouin was a young knight who lived chastely and spurned all other women. He was satisfied with his wife alone whom he began to love with a fervent love (*amare amore ferventi*) which, the chronicler remarked, is rarely found in other men. Since his wife was the daughter of the Marie de Champagne quoted by André the Chaplain, it is evident that the count did not agree with his mother-in-law's celebrated dictum about love and marriage.[96] Gislebert was fully aware of the rarity of this behavior because he recorded the numerous bastards recognized by Baudouin's father and grandfather as well as other nobles. Despite Tristan's allure, the climactic marriages of Guillaume and Conrad accorded best with Jean Renart's princely patron and perhaps with many of the high nobility. Although Jean's solution coincided with ecclesiastical authority, his motivation may have been prompted less by piety than by a concern for progeny and lineage which preoccupied, as we shall see, the high aristocracy.

Although occasionally accepting the churchmen's rationale for containing sexuality within marriage, the French aristocracy did not entirely concur with the ecclesiastical definition of the institution. By 1200 the canonists had established a series of defining limitations: Christian marriage was to be heterosexual for the purpose of procreating children, monogamous, and indissoluble. As we have seen, its primary foundation was the mutual consent of both spouses. Legitimate marriages could be prevented by special conditions known as impediments. The handbooks of Thomas of Chobham and Robert of Flameborough summarized these as the sacred vows of chastity taken by former monks, nuns, and clergy, errors of person and condition (serfdom, for example), violent coercion (including rape), infamous crime, and physiological incapacity (frigidity and impotence). Most important, these impediments included relationships by blood (consanguinity) and by marriage (affinity) and godparentage (compaternity).[97] According to the impediment of consanguinity, persons were prohibited from marrying if they were related within the seventh degree, that is, possessing a common ancestor within seven generations. In complex fashion, affinity and compaternity were divided into three kinds to which varying degrees of exclusion applied. The definition and enforcement of these multifarious regulations pertained to the exclusive jurisdiction of churchmen and their courts.[98]

In contrast, the French royalty and aristocracy developed matrimonial practices which opposed the ecclesiastical program on specific points. This lay pattern can be best observed through the marital histories of the Capetian kings from Robert the Pious through Philip Augustus. Because of the need to transmit land (economic wealth) and lordship (political authority) through family, the French royalty and aristocracy could not accept the full implications of free and mutual consent between spouses. The decision over marriage partners was too important to leave to children and must remain the prerogative of the male members of the family, beginning with fathers and husbands and passing to sons and uncles in their absence. The incentive to accumulate wealth and authority within the family further encouraged the aristocratic and royal lords to oppose the thrust of the ecclesiastical program toward exogamy (marrying outside the family). The broad scope of the canonical definitions of consanguinity, affinity, and compaternity made it difficult to find permissible spouses outside the prohibited degrees. (Within the localized and immobile society of the peasants it was virtually impossible.) Taking advantage of this necessity, royal and aristocratic lineages pursued a policy of endogamy, to marry close relatives in order to reinforce the economic and political fortunes of their families. And finally, the ecclesiastical insistence on the indissolubility of the matrimonial bond was opposed by the frequent practice of divorce. The royalty and aristocracy profited from the practical necessity of marrying within the seventh degree to use this impediment as the legal basis for separating themselves from spouses as allowed in canon law. Of the seven generations of Capetians since 987, for example, four had availed themselves of this means. Within recent memory, Louis VII had repudiated Eleanor of Aquitaine on the grounds that she was related within the fourth and fifth degrees. Philip Augustus's current efforts to divorce Ingeborg of Denmark were originally justified by consanguinity within the fourth degree, an assertion that was patently fraudulent when applied to the Danish princess.[99]

Since matrimony was traditionally a family affair supervised by the couple's parents, it normally took place in the house of the bride's father where the essential rites of ring, dowry, and the bestowal of the bride were performed. As churchmen asserted exclusive jurisdiction over the institution, they wished to move it to a place where they were in a better position to enforce their regulations. By the end of the twelfth century liturgical *ordines* were drawn up in northern France, which, adopting Anglo-Norman precedents from the previous century, sought to transfer the nuptial ceremony from the family domicile to the entry of the church where the priest and the parents shared respective rites. Since free consent was the essence of Christian marriage, the priest's first and essential task was to verify whether both parties were in agreement. Then the father gave his daughter to the husband, and the spouses joined their right hands to signify their union. The ring or rings, which stood for their mutual faith, were blessed by the priest and placed on their fingers. Finally, pieces of money were handed over to the groom to represent the transfer of dowry. Only after these transactions had taken place did the couple and their families enter the church to attend mass, during which the priest bestowed the nuptial blessing while the pair knelt beneath a large canopy or veil. By moving the marriage rites to the church door and into the priest's presence, ecclesiastics hoped not only to assert jurisdiction but also to provide a setting appropriate for the sacrament.[100]

Although the fabliaux rarely divulge details about the marriage ceremony or site,[101] the weddings in our romance corpus are invariably held in the vicinity of a church or in the presence of the clergy. In Thomas's version (p.49, vv.372–76; p.51, vv.425–26) Tristan avers that he married Iseut aux Mains Blanches at the door of the church in the view of the people after which the chaplain said mass. Since Chrétien's Laudine is without family, she is given to Yvain by the hand of her chaplain accompanied by bishops and abbots (vv.2152–60).[102] Befitting their high station, all of Jean Renart's couples are wedded with elaborate ceremony including both ecclesiastical and public festivities. In *Escoufle* Count Richard and the lady of Genoa are conducted to a church at Rome (vv.1704–37), and their son Guillaume weds the emperor's daughter amidst public rejoicing at Rouen (vv.8329–33). Although the archbishop is not directly associated with the nuptial ceremony, he nonetheless plays a leading role in the final dénouement. In the *Roman* Jean Renart lavishly described the clothing, feasting, and rituals accompanying the imperial marriage at Mainz. Since Lïenor is to be crowned as well as married, the two ceremonies are closely bound together. The imperial barons lead the girl to the cathedral where its treasures are on display for the coronation. Proceeding to marry the imperial couple before crowning them, the archbishop chants the office of the Holy Spirit and Trinity (vv.5284–85).[103] Despite the competition of the coronation, it is perfectly clear that the emperor's marriage takes place in a church under ecclesiastical supervision.

That aristocratic marriages were conducted under church auspices did not thereby nullify the traditional role of the male family members in our corpus of vernacular literature. From a near score of such nuptials, well over half of the brides were explicitly given away by their fathers. This occurs in Marie de France (*Milun*, vv.126–27); among the romance heroines Iseut (Eilhart),[104] Fenice (*Cligès*, v.2631), and Aelis (*Escoufle*, vv.2150–52); and among aristocratic girls in the fabliaux (*Aloul*, vv.12–13; *Berengier*, vv.23, 38–40; *Damoisele qui ne pooit [I]*, vv.38–43; and *Jouglet*, vv.38–39). Because Lïenor's father is dead, Conrad must approach her family through her brother. Occasionally the bride's overlord acts in the absence of male representatives from the family, as, for example, when Guenièvre and Arthur give Soredamor to Alexandre (*Cligès*, vv.2302–6, 2312–15), or the emperor commands the lady of Genoa to marry Count Richard (*Escoufle*, vv.1696–99).[105] The vassals of the spouses could also be involved in the decision. Both of Jean Renart's emperors are obliged to seek the consent of the imperial princes (*Escoufle*, vv.2180–93; *Roman*, vv.5149–54), as well as the knight Gunrun from his vassals in Marie de France's *Le fresne* (vv.313–30). In Chrétien's *Lion* (vv.2083–2106) the châtelaine Laudine, who has just become a widow, quickly recognizes her vulnerability without a husband's sword and seeks her barons' consent to marry Yvain, as she had her first husband six years previously.

Whereas the bridegroom's agreement to the match was assumed, the arrangement was often imposed on the girl against her wishes. Marie de France's young brides in *Milun* (v.130) and *Yonec* (vv.45–50) are in great distress over their fate, as is Chrétien's Fenice (*Cligés*, vv.3098–99) when her father gives her to the emperor Alis. The contempt that the aristocratic girls heap on their lowborn husbands in the fabliaux *Aloul* and *Berengier* highlights their fundamental opposition to the arrangements. By contrast, however, the love matches between romance heroes and heroines expressed full consent by both parties according to the churchmen's prescriptions. Chrétien's Soredamor and Fenice ardently desire wedlock with Alexandre and Cligès as does Jean Renart's Aelis with Guillaume. If the marriage confers power and prestige as well, there is little doubt over the bride's consent. When Enide's father gives her to Erec, the maiden remains silent, but she is very happy because she realizes that she will become a queen (vv.684–90). Laudine quickly agrees to Yvain in order to preserve her seigneurie; the lady Genoa receives the emperor's command with joy because she has heard of Count Richard's high position (*Escoufle*, vv.1702–3); and the belle Lïenor is never unmindful of her personal advantage in marrying an emperor. Although the formality of female consent is maintained in these alliances, the bride's self-interest undoubtedly weighs heavily in her decision.

Throughout our vernacular corpus, the royalty and aristocracy appear to conform to the ecclesiastical regulations on monogamy, exogamy, and the indissolubility of marriage. No one seeks to have more than one spouse,[106] selects a partner who is identified by family relationship, or attempts to dissolve a marriage by legal proceedings. The closest example to this last resort was Marie de France's Equitan who attempts to murder his seneschal in order to marry the latter's wife, but it is not the spouse who acts, nor are the means lawful. The principle of monogamy may not have raised problems because of its evident advantages in the politics of lineage, as we shall see. While the adherence to exogamy and indissolubility may be due to the demands of particular romance narratives, and not altogether to conformity with the ecclesiastical program, these traits remain difficult to explain in other terms. We do not know why romance heroes never fall in love with cousins, nor why divorces never occur to them in difficult marriages. Arthur, Erec, and Laudine all had reasons to disavow their spouses, but Chrétien resolves their matrimonial difficulties by other means. Whatever the explanation, the recourse to endogamy and divorce was commonly practiced by French kings and nobility as abundantly seen in the Capetians' matrimonial history.

By the turn of the twelfth and thirteenth centuries, churchmen were well aware of the difficulty of applying their traditional program of exogamy up to the seventh degree of consanguinity.[107] In notorious and contested cases, popes such as Alexander III and Innocent III frequently granted dispensations allowing couples who were related in the third degree and beyond to contract legal marriages, or they refused by dissimulation to dissolve marriages which had been contracted within those limits. Pierre the Chanter narrated a personal reminiscence of two relatives married but related within the fifth and sixth degrees. When they came to him for advice, he sent them to the pope who followed Alexander III's procedure of referring them to the local bishop. They were sent to the archbishop of Sens and finally to Maurice de Sully, bishop of Paris, to receive final confirmation of their marriage.[108]

More important, the Chanter also acknowledged the contradiction between the ecclesiastical principles of exogamy and the indissolubility of marriage. Because the vast scope of consanguinity and affinity impeded most marriages, they could be dissolved by legal means. Pierre reported that a knight admitted to him in taking a wife: "She has a large dowry and is related to me in the third degree of affinity. If she doesn't please me, I can procure a separation."[109] When Innocent III obstructed Philip Augustus's plans to divorce Ingeborg because of consanguinity, the king complained that the papacy was treating him more severely than the emperor Frederick Barbarossa, King John of England, and his own father Louis VII, all who had secured separations on the grounds of blood relationships.[110] True to his own principles, the Chanter proposed to reform the marriage legislation of consanguinity by bringing it into conformity with the Bible. "The Lord has given," he affirmed in his *Verbum abbreviatum,* "certain and inviolable laws of matrimony which exclude twelve persons from marriage (Lev. 18:6–18 and 20:11–21), to which we have added as exceptions the fifth, sixth, and seventh degrees [of consanguinity] . . . [and] to these we have joined the second and third kinds of affinity."[111] On the authority of Scripture, therefore, the system of impediments should be discarded beyond the fourth degree of consanguinity and the first kind of affinity. Within the legislation on matrimony promulgated by the Fourth Lateran Council in 1215, Pope Innocent III fully accepted the Chanter's proposal for reform. Citing Pierre's prologue that human law varies with time, he enacted that impediments of consanguinity were henceforth reduced from seven to four degrees and those of affinity to the first kind.[112] These reductions did not fully conform to contemporary aristocratic practices of endogamy which sanctioned marrying of first and second cousins (second and third degrees), but it was a step in that direction. By eliminating impediments for remote consanguinity and affinity, it reduced the legal grounds for separation and thereby strengthened the indissolubility of matrimony.

On the Margin: Prostitutes and Holy Matrons

When the theologians—with ambivalent seconding from the romanciers—placed marriage at the center of the sexual universe, they created peripheries at either extremity. On the one side were the promiscuous; on the other, those who abstained totally. This was André the Chaplain's schema when he represented the palace of love as composed of four facades each with a door. The eastern side is the abode of the god of love and the southern of worthy ladies who prudently stand at the threshold and admit only worthy men. The western side, however, belongs to the promiscuous who mill around outside the wide-open door and the northern to the frigid whose closed door refuse men altogether. André repeated this distinction between the two extremes of women in his metaphor of the army of the dead and of the concentric circles in the delightful garden.[113] In the historical world shaped by the ecclesiastical institution of marriage, however, the promiscuous were usually motivated by venality and the abstainers by religious devotion. Both peripheries could count men as well as women, but at the turn of the twelfth century discussion was dominated by feminine concerns. Although male gigolos and pimps might be included, the female prostitute became the emblematic figure in the five discourses. Since the early Middle Ages the monastic orders likewise enlisted recruits among both male monks and female nuns, but in our period the traditional exhortations to masculine virginity had subsided in favor of new voices promoting the ideal of *mulieres sancte,* holy matrons devoted to chastity but enlisted not from the ranks of virgins but from the formerly married. With matrimony at the center, therefore, the prostitute and the holy matron came to occupy the margins.

To one side, therefore, stood the desolate figure of the prostitute, a woman whose sexuality was available to numerous clients for money or other remuneration. This profession was chiefly profitable where men gathered in numbers at the courts of great lords or in the growing populations of towns. Most historians agree that, at the turn of the twelfth century, prostitution was as yet fluid and unorganized throughout Western Europe and had not become institutionalized in designated bordellos and regulated by public authority as occurred during the fourteenth and fifteenth centuries.[114]

We shall see that prostitutes were the only women available to physicians for studying the subject of gynecology. Although their sexuality furnished a kind of laboratory for medical research, the doctors were largely unconcerned with their social or moral status. The legitimacy of prostitution, however, was sharply questioned in the two ancient traditions of Ovid and the ecclesiastics. The Latin poet, who certainly had no objection to abundant sexual activity, nonetheless protested that pleasure, not material gain, is the only reward worthy of love, and devoted a stanza of the *Amores* to chiding his mistress for cupidity over presents. When the work of Venus gives so much pleasure to both, why should one buy and the other sell? The prostitute, laboring for her greedy pimp, receives miserable payment for her body. If the former is coerced, why does Corrina do it by choice? Other than to complain about the expense of seduction, the poet made no mention of the practice in the *Ars amatoria.*[115] Ovid's twelfth-century interpreter, André the Chaplain, further elaborated this ancient distaste for venality: true love comes only from the heart's affection, pure grace, and genuine liberality. Any woman who offers herself for a gift is not a lover (*amatrix*) but a fraud (*falsificatrix*), worse than a whore, whose intentions, at least, are open. As for the latter, André simply warned his protégé to shun them, since these associations result only in defamation.[116] Apparently, his opinion was shared by the romanciers as a whole, because courtly and aristocratic literature is remarkable for the absence of women clearly identifiable as prostitutes.

Recognizing its extramarital character, the Parisian theologians condemned prostitution for entirely different reasons, yet their opposition did not inhibit careful definition and analysis of the profession's underlying functions. Roman and canon lawyers formulated initial principles; Pierre the Chanter raised specific and troublesome problems, which Robert of

Courson developed further; but it was Thomas of Chobham who assembled the discussion in the most comprehensive and organized form.[117] In Roman law Ulpian inaugurated the definition by insisting on the factor of promiscuity. A prostitute is a "woman who publicly earns money with her body." Her accessibility, however, is the crucial factor because even without gain she would still be a prostitute. Gratian's *Decretum* reinforced this emphasis with a formula from Jerome: "A prostitute is one who is open to the lusts of many."[118] Of the three progressively inclusive definitions proposed by Thomas of Chobham, the first comprised any woman who offers herself outside marriage—the equivalent of simple fornication—but the second specified one who is not content with just one person but is accessible to many, not denying herself to anyone. This promiscuity exposes her to the dangers of unknowing cohabitation with married men, excommunicates, priests, monks, Jews, fathers, brothers, or other incestuous relations. Following the Chanter's suggestions, Thomas extended the definition to both women and men. The woman is called a *meretrix* and the man a *scortator* in biblical terminology (Gen. 23:17), or, occasionally, *leccator* (lecher).[119]

Money or gain, the other element in Ulpian's definition, was reinforced by Gratian's citation of Augustine: "The Lord forbids one to be a prostitute or to approach a woman whose shame is for public sale." Thomas incorporated this factor into his third definition of "a woman who sells herself openly to the lusts of many." Elsewhere, he described the transaction as hirelings who rent their bodies for shameful uses. Living by their labor, they assume the form of public prostitutes or private, secret courtesans. If a woman sells herself in secret or just to one person, Thomas felt that the term *meretrix* did not strictly apply.[120]

This theological analysis was strikingly apposite to the picture of the prostitute found in the fabliaux. From the great quantity and variety of sexual activity reported in this literature, relatively little was transacted with prostitutes. One might be lead to conclude that as frequent as are the marital and extramarital couplings, few prostitutes are available to unmarried lovers, clerical or lay. (Married men, we remember, are rarely portrayed as philandering.) The notable exception was *Le prestre et Alison* in which a priest is advised to frequent the whore Alison in her bordello after he has been foiled and severely beaten for trying to seduce the daughter of a bourgeois woman. It should be noted, however, that the priest is, in fact, a victim of the bourgeois woman who has entrapped and despoiled him through the bait of her daughter—all an elaborate scheme that included the prostitute Alison and in character with her professional tricks. In other fabliaux, however, whores were treated in separate stories where they are also linked with male counterparts, called *lecheors*. In the *Putains et les lech-*

eors, for example, we remember that when God created the world, he assigned the *lecheors* to the knights and the whores to the clergy. The two notable fabliaux about prostitutes, however, were *Boivin de Provins* and *Richeut,* both of which featured not only prominent whores (Mabel and Richeut) but also worthy lechers as adversaries, for example, Boivin (v.1) and Samson, son of Richeut (v.629). Although the earlier of the two stories, *Richeut* offered the most developed tableau. In addition, an entire fabliau was devoted to the sexual prowess of a male character who is simply designated as "the fucker," *Le foteor.* The underlying ecclesiastical distinction between *meretrix* and *leccator* was, therefore, reproduced in the *putain* and *lecheor* of the fabliaux, and both characters were kept discrete in tales devoted to their exploits. In fact, both the churchman and the fableors were so preoccupied with comparable problems that their discussions can be arranged in dialogue.

In contrast to Ovidian disdain for money, this financial factor preoccupied the two other groups. Assuming that prostitution was fundamentally immoral, the theologians were led to consider whether such women could retain their earnings or were obliged to do restitution. Although Roman law offered a remedy for recovery of money from an immoral act, it also specified that if the giver, or the giver and the receiver, acted immorally, returning the money is not required. Roman law further stipulated that "a prostitute acts immorally for what she does, but she does not receive money immorally because she is a prostitute." For this reason also, the prostitute could keep her earnings. Pierre the Chanter, Robert of Courson, Thomas of Chobham, as well as the canonists, accepted this reasoning and argued that public prostitutes were not required to do restitution for their earnings in an open court of law. Thomas went as far as to maintain that since the woman works with her body, she is entitled to the gains of her labor.[121]

If prostitutes were entitled to their earnings, a corollary question arose as to whether they could thereby offer alms. Although some qualms were voiced as to the propriety of women of the street openly contributing to pious causes, in principle the theologians concurred that since their gains were licit, their alms were acceptable and even contributed to satisfaction in penance. Apparently a specific case had arisen at the cathedral of Notre-Dame in Paris. Without going into details, the Chanter had noted that certain active prostitutes had wanted to present chalices and stained-glass windows to the church in his time. Thomas expanded the discussion by revealing that the prostitutes of Paris had offered a magnificent stained-glass window. Although principle allowed them to contribute, discretion was advised. The Chanter urged that such gifts be made privately; Courson counseled only the gifts of secret prostitutes but not of public

women; Chobham reported that the bishop refused the women's benefi-
cence because open acceptance would seem to approve their profession.[122]

In Roman law Ulpian had observed that it should not be overlooked that
poverty might have forced a prostitute into her profession. Among the
theologians, only Thomas of Chobham took notice of this excuse by re-
marking that certain women are motivated by lust but others by indi-
gence. Although the former should be enjoined with solemn penance
because they were morally worse, the latter should be spared public discipline because they did not grow rich from the profession.[123]

In the view of the fableors, poverty was not the fundamental root of
prostitution, but the hallmark of harlotry was inordinate greed as represented by the two archtypes, Mabel and Richeut. The lecher Boivin is able
to excite Mabel's avarice by counting his money in front of her house, thus
convincing her of his wealth. Thereafter, the action of the story turns on
how Mabel and her accomplices will relieve Boivin of his purse. Even
though the women are finally duped by their wily adversary, their unre-
lenting goal remains his money. Richeut likewise plots single-mindedly to
amass a comfortable living by ruthlessly blackmailing her three affluent
clients with the imputed paternity of her son. "Richeut turns rich men into
beggars" (v.49), the narrator announced at the beginning of her cam-
paigns, and at each separate conclusion he detailed the swollen purse, fine
clothes, roaring fire, and good food and wine that rewarded her efforts
(vv.365–71, 526–31). Ovidian sexual pleasures are, naturally enough, the
least of her concerns. In tandem with the theologians' analysis of earnings,
therefore, the whores in the fabliaux share a sole passion for money.[124]

According to Thomas of Chobham, the most reprehensible of profits
were those received by a pimp for his wife's services. "Those who consent
to the adultery of their spouse for a price or some other gain should be
forever barred from the mass," Thomas reiterated.[125] Yet the exchange of
sex for money is frequent enough in the fabliaux that a reoccurring motif
was the husband who seeks to profit from his wife's sexuality by luring
wealthy lovers and relieving them of their money. In *Estormi*, for example,
Jehans, a poor *preudom*, makes his wife Yfame available to the lubricity of
three priests at the price of eighty *livres* to recoup lost fortunes. Similarly,
in *Le segretain moine*, a moneychanger Guillaume has been robbed while
returning from a business trip from Provins and Amiens. He recovers his
losses by offering his wife Ydoine to the sacristan of a monastery for a hundred *livres*. Although both men are murdered before the wives actually
commit adultery, it is doubtful whether this technicality would have exonerated them in the eyes of the theologians. That socially respectable men
were represented as plotting the murder of their victims highlighted the
enormity of the scenario. That these husbands also scheme to pimp their

wives pointed to a deeply rooted connection between sexuality and money. When Thomas of Chobham evoked the case of pimping one's wife more than once, this repetition suggests that the practice was not beyond the bounds of imagination.

Beyond obsession with money, the other dominating trait of prostitutes in both the theologians' analyses and the fabliaux narratives was proclivity to fraud. Such women are not obligated to restitution in principle, but, if they employ fraudulent techniques, they must restore to their customers to the extent of the deception. According to the Chanter, a woman, for example, might anoint her eyes with *stibio*, rouge her face with cosmetics, pretend that she is of noble birth, or declare her love above all others. A prostitute disguising herself as a simple girl might thereby raise her price from twenty to a hundred *sous*. Or, according to Chobham, if a woman is worth a pittance, but, because of her makeup or claim to be a knight's daughter, she demands a *denier,* she is required to restore the difference. Robert of Courson added that a prostitute owes a mature client nothing but an inexperienced boy full restitution. Because of the danger of deception, the Chanter concluded that private or secret women are more liable to restitution than public harlots.[126]

The whores' ruses to pass themselves off for honest women became a stock device of the fabliaux devoted to the profession.[127] In the *Prestre et Alison,* for example, the bourgeois mother bathes the harlot Alison and beds her in a dark room so that the priest will believe her to be the mother's virgin daughter. In *Boivin de Provins* Mabel not only pretends to be Boivin's niece to gain his confidence but also passes off her young accomplice Ysane as an intact maiden of honest family. In the titanic contest between Richeut and Samson as to who has best mastered the art of lechery, the mother profits from knowing her son's foibles to succeed in entrapping him by the rules of the trade. Richeut enlists her accomplice Hersent, bathes and dresses her richly, covers her face with white powder and rouge to make her beautiful (vv. 1036–47), and finally installs her in the upper room of the townsman's house, where the whore plays the knight's daughter who is learning to embroider with gold thread (vv. 1122–26). Samson catches sight of the damsel from the street, is lured into the chamber, where candlelight protects Hersent's disguise, and finally into bed where he is attacked, roundly beaten and fleeced by his mother's *lecheors.* From cosmetics to claims of gentle birth—all the tricks included by the theologians in their analysis were employed in this ribald tale.

The theologians' discussions and the fableors' portraits present a diversified and fluid picture of prostitution at the turn of the twelfth century. Jacques de Vitry's depiction of Paris during the days of Pierre the Chanter had the streets and squares teeming with such women. In a celebrated passage, so crowded was the Ile-de-la-Cité that teachers were obliged to share the same house with prostitutes where classes were held on the second floor while the women practiced their trade and quarreled with their procurers on the first. This social imbrication between harlots, townsmen, and clerics is further suggested by Richeut's career. Originating from a knightly family herself (vv. 274–75), she has easy access to the three dominant classes of society. Her son Samson, born of harlotry, is baptized at the church of Saint-Germain surrounded by requisite godparents (vv. 444–51). After her lying-in, she herself attends mass dressed ostentatiously (vv. 469–85). Pierre the Chanter assumed that prostitutes were allowed into church for the kiss of peace and the offering of prayers but were forbidden the eucharist. Thomas of Chobham reported that at Paris these women, although excluded from the mass, mixed with other women on Saturday vespers for the offering of candles. [128] Despite this intermingling, there were also signs of emerging segregation. The commercial town of Provins, a site of the famous fairs of Champagne, was the setting for the escapades of Boivin. Upon arrival the lecher goes straight to the street of the whores (*rue aus putains*) to find Mabel's house (vv. 20–21). This quarter resembled the "Hot Streets" at Montpellier and its suburb of Villanova at the end of the century. [129] Mabel's house accommodated not only herself and her accomplice but also a number of pimps. Thomas of Chobham devoted a separate chapter to such bordellos and their procurers, inclusive of both men and women. As advisors, their functions were to procure commerce, persuade customers with soft words, and enhance the women's attractiveness. Even more than prostitutes, these pimps were defamed as a profession and subject to solemn, public penance. [130]

As moralists, the theologians sought not only to analyze the activities of this infamous profession but also to promote measures of reform. Among the Chanter's students was Foulques de Neuilly who gained fame as a contemporary preacher and was particularly successful in persuading prostitutes to renounce their sinful lives. To induce conversion, he founded the Cistercian convent of Saint-Antoine on the outskirts of Paris in 1198 as a shelter for repentant women and raised a fund to supply dowries for other women who, fearing they could not remain continent, chose to marry. (According to one source, over 250 *livres* of silver were donated by scholars and a thousand *livres* by the bourgeoisie of Paris.) For at least a generation canonists had discussed the legitimacy of marrying repentant prostitutes, to which they usually responded in the affirmative. In the same year as the founding of Saint-Antoine, Pope Innocent III, also the Chanter's student, issued a decretal assuring all who rescued women from brothels and married them that they performed works meritorious for the remission of sin. [131]

A more severe approach was to enforce the consequences of the prostitutes' status as excommunicate. Although the Chanter and Chobham had acquiesced to their intermingling with others in church, Robert of Courson began to urge harder measures. Bishops and priests should publicly excommunicate all notorious and incorrigible prostitutes known by legal confession, conviction of witnesses, or notoriety of fact. If they remained incorrigible, they should be evicted from the city. When Robert returned to France as papal legate, he implemented his proposal at the Council of Paris in 1212. Treating the profession as a plague, he forbade them residence in the city under pain of excommunication and ordered their segregation outside the walls according to the custom of lepers. Perhaps for the first time at Paris prostitutes were consigned to a ghetto similar to contemporary measures in the south at Carcassonne and in the statutes of Pamiers.[132] This policy of ghettoizing may also have had repercussions in literature. We have seen that with rare exceptions the fableors treated prostitution in tales kept separate from other sexual activity. Adopting the theological distinction between *meretrices* and *scortatores/leccatores,* they designated women and men who participated in this form of venal sexuality as *putains* and *lecheors.* This separation within fictional narrative joined to expulsion from the city suggests that the integration of prostitutes within society had begun to dissolve.[133]

"Why does the church tolerate prostitutes," Thomas of Chobham queried, "when it is bound to eradicate all public and notorious sins and to coerce the incorrigible with judgment?" Augustine had reasoned that if prostitutes were removed from human society, unbridled lust would pose a menace, even to respectable matrons and other virtuous women. This opinion from an early work, *De ordine,* was not quoted directly by the Parisian theologians in their discussions, but they nonetheless concurred with the argument. In parenthetical statements Pierre the Chanter noted that the church tolerates public women to avoid more shameful desires. Just as Moses permitted divorce to reduce recourse to murdering wives, so harlots, who abound everywhere, are condoned to escape greater evil. Thomas of Chobham summed up by observing that the fleshly weaknesses of the present day render many prone to lust, and scarcely anyone can be persuaded to remain continent. The church, therefore, puts up with prostitutes and lechers to avoid worse passions.[134] Exactly what were the worse passions (*turpior/deterior libido*) is not specified, but the rationale enjoyed a long future. "To avoid a greater evil" became the chief justification for institutionalizing and regulating public brothels throughout Western Europe in the fourteenth and fifteenth centuries.[135]

* * *

Diametrically opposite to the sexually promiscuous were those on the other side of marriage, the monks and nuns who renounced sexuality altogether. From the monastic movement originated the oldest and perhaps most pervasive of all medieval social classifications that divided human society into three groups according to sexual practice: *conjugates* (married), *continentes* (continent), and *virgines* (virgins).[136] In other words, those who are sexually active, those who have ceased, and those who have never experienced. Originally the *continentes* stood for widows, but later this category was extended to the secular clergy. From the beginning, this trisexual schema comprised both men and women but attributed highest priority to the virgin monks and nuns who lived a nonsexual, angelic life on earth.

At the turn of the twelfth and thirteenth centuries the monastic life of chastity was practiced by thousands of monks and nuns in hundreds of cloisters across the kingdom of France. Many treatises had been composed on the virtues of virginity by the early twelfth century, but at the end of the century no new *De laude virginitatis* surfaced in northern France deemed worthy of transcribing. The intellectual preoccupations of monks lay elsewhere. When Pierre the Chanter's student Jacques de Vitry wrote his *Historia occidentalis* in the 1220s he surveyed the great variety of monastic orders that flourished in the West in his own day. Under his master's influence, however, he sought to expand the category of *ordo* to include the laity and to apply it to the trisexual schema. Not only did married people constitute a sacred order but the lay professions did as well. Knights, merchants, farmers, and craftsmen also had their institutions and regulations that qualified them as orders making up the church, the mystical body of Christ.[137]

Jacques's interest in the lay world was also enhanced by his association with Marie d'Oignies in the diocese of Lièges. In the *Vita Marie Oigniacensis* addressed to Foulques, bishop of Toulouse, he reminded Foulques that the bishop had been attracted to the Liégois region because of the fame of holy women. With a rhetorical flourish he recalled how the bishop had rejoiced when he saw not only holy virgins but also matrons who preserve their youthful modesty, widows who engage in fasting, prayers, vigils, and manual labor, and, equally important, holy women (*sanctas mulieres*) who remain in matrimony. These raise their sons in the fear of the Lord, keep their marriage bed pure, abstain for periods of prayer, but return to their spouses lest they be tempted by Satan. Many of them, however, with the consent of their husbands, even abstain from licit marital embraces and espouse the angelic life worthy of a great crown because, although they are placed in the fire of desire, they do not burn.[138] The most illustrious example of this last vocation was Marie herself, who did not live long in the matrimonial state before she and her husband Jean agreed to separate for higher service. Whereas they had been divided by carnal affection, now they were united through love in spiritual marriage. Appearing to Marie, God had promised that by avoiding fleshly commerce on earth they would repair their marriage in heaven. While unhappy couples were ashamed and terrified by the extramarital and illicit couplings around them, these two blessed young people abstained from even licit endearments and channeled their adolescent energies into religious fervor. Fighting fire with fire, they deserve the triumphal crown of martyrs.[139]

Although numbered among the multitude of women enrolled in the monastic life, Marie perpetuated the example of the monastic reform movements such as the Cistercians because she was not a virgin dedicated to her calling since early childhood, as was customary in the ancient model. Like the new monks, she was an adult woman who had experienced a sexual life but was prepared to transmute her energies to a higher plane of suprasexuality in an effort to efface sexual desire. Jacques de Vitry's commemoration of Marie attributed increased value to lay society among the theologians and the church hierarchy. Like most of the laity Marie had been married, yet her previous sexual experience did not disqualify her from higher service to God. As one of the *continentes*, Marie's example did not yet permit the same honor to the married woman who remained sexually active, but it was a step beyond the ancient scheme that limited the religious calling to virgins from birth. Through publicizing Marie's image of the continent laity, Jacques de Vitry extended the possibility of the religious calling to a larger segment of thirteenth-century society.

3

THE SEXUAL BODY

The Learned Body

Within the teaching of the schools, the sexual body came under the purview of both the theologians and the physicians, the former to explain how the body was originally created by God, the latter to describe its present function. For the most part, the theologians surrounding Pierre the Chanter paid little attention to the speculative issues involved in the biblical story of creation but were content to embroider Augustine's theories that were transmitted in the *Glossa ordinaria* and the *Sentences* of Pierre the Lombard. To summarize the views of the latter, God originally created the first humans each with a soul and body, both immortal. The body was fitted with genital organs that could be commanded at will according to the dictates of reason, just as the hands and feet move without lust or fleshly wickedness. After Adam and Eve disobeyed God and fell into sin, however, the genitals were infected with concupiscence, thereby debilitating volitional mastery over sexual activity. The final result of original sin was bodily corruption and eventual death.[1]

Augustine had asserted that the genital organs were called the *pudenda* because the first parents were ashamed of their loss of control over sexuality.[2] Commenting on the Genesis passage that Adam and Eve became aware and ashamed of their nakedness after their disobedience, Pierre the Chanter elaborated on Augustine's theme. Before sin our parents looked at their nudity as they would at their hands. It is only unbidden movement that causes shame. Children do not blush to have their genitals seen because at their age they do not experience embarrassing movements. Only after sin, however, were Adam's and Eve's eyes opened by lust, and they perceived that their members began to move against reason's higher dictates.[3] Bodily modesty and sexual shame were attributed directly to concupiscence resulting from disobedience to God. Equally significant, this shame which was manifested in the unseemly erection was modeled on the male body.

The English compiler of the largest selection of the *Prose Salernitan Questions* opened his collection with the theological question, Why had God created humans? Behind the turgid discussion that followed, the answer was simple: humans are the result of the sweetness of divine will. A second query as to what is a human being produced the definition: a rational, mortal animal, susceptible to instruction, a walking biped who represents the image and likeness of God both in soul and in body. The human body is connected with world as the microcosmos to the macrocosmos, consisting of the basic elements, humors, and spirits that unite soul to body. If the soul is more worthy than the body, a third question asked, Why are physicians more intent in examining the body than the soul? Because the soul has little that is demonstrable to theory and philosophy, it can be known only through faith. The body, however, whose nutrition and regime lies within the senses, is accessible to experience and human reason.[4] Despite this confidence in medical science, contemporary anatomists had made little progress over their ancient predecessors because from Antiquity (except for a brief period in Hellenistic Alexandria) the dissection of human cadavers was not practiced and was reinaugurated only at the end of the thirteenth century. A reliance on etymological reasoning and a preference for analogous explanations over pure description prevailed into the twelfth century. At the time, anatomical treatises drew heavily on Galen's teaching transmitted through Salerno, which, in turn, was largely derived from the dissection of pigs. The Salernitan anatomical treatises explained that although the external features of the human body resemble bears and monkeys, the internal organs are closer to pigs, especially in the case of the female uterus. Even the theologian Pierre the Chanter reaffirmed the anatomical similarities between humans and pigs.[5] Much confusion and vagueness, however, pervaded the anatomical literature of the late twelfth century. Without becoming enmeshed in specific uncertainties and controversies, we can nonetheless outline the major contours of the sexual body as it appeared to the learned physicians of Northern Europe by the late twelfth century.

Like Iohannicius's *Isagoge,* the Salernitan anatomies approached the human body through the hierarchy of the four principal members arranged from head to loins, each with a corresponding network. The first three (brain/nerves, heart/arteries, liver/veins) are called principal because the body cannot function without them. The fourth, the genitals (*testiculi, genitalia*), although dispensable for individual life, are essential for the propagation of the human race.[6] This comprehensive anatomical scheme, however, fell heir to a fundamental assumption in antiquity that the male body is normative to the female in anatomy. Although it could be more readily demonstrated that the three principal organs of the female are virtually the same as the male, when Aristotle and Galen arrived at the apparent genital differences, they suggested that female organs are merely homologues of the male. Thus the uterus corresponds to the scrotum, and the vagina to the penis. Noting these similarities, Aristotle nonetheless had asserted that males differ from females because they possess greater heat. Galen further elaborated these similarities but focused on the factor of heat to explain the differences. The male and female genitals differ one from the other only in position. The greater heat of men expels their organs to the exterior, whereas the colder female retains her organs inside the body. In short, a woman is merely an inverted man, one turned outside in.[7]

As heirs to ancient tradition, the Salernitans could not ignore these arguments for anatomical similarities. Alfanus, archbishop of Salerno, who had encouraged Constantinus Africanus's work in the eleventh century, also translated into Latin Nemesius of Emesia's *De natura hominis* which had clearly propounded the thesis. The Salernitan authority, Constantinus, himself further suggested that the female labia (*badera*) are protrusions of skin like the male prepuce.[8] With the one and important exception of the testicles, however, the Salernitan anatomies took little notice of the Galenic homologies. It was not until the appearance of Aristotle's natural treatises and Avicenna's *Canon* that the full force of the ancient hypothesis was reasserted. Along with Aristotle's physiology, David de Dinant revived the Galenic paradigm (attributed to Hippocrates here) that a woman's uterus is similar to a man's scrotum, her vagina to his penis, with the one difference that the former are turned inward and the latter outward. Avicenna opened his discussion of the anatomy of the uterus by asserting that the woman's instrument of generation is the uterus which was created fundamentally similar to the penis and its accompanying organs. While the latter is complete and extends outward, the former is diminished and retained inward, the very inverse of the male instrument.[9] Such explicit treatment of the similarities did not emerge in the Salernitan anatomies until the *Anatomia vivorum* which appeared in Paris no earlier than 1210 and most likely by 1225. With some knowledge of Aristotle, but heavily dependent on Avicenna, the *Anatomia vivorum* worked out in detail the correspondence between male and female genitals.[10] This Galenic homological paradigm, which reappeared in the thirteenth century, survived in European anatomy until the eighteenth century. In contrast, the *Prose Salernitan Questions* and the accompanying twelfth-century Salernitan anatomies, which antedated the Aristotelian and Avicennian revival, were more prone to explore sexual differences.

On one important subject the Salernitan anatomies did accept a fundamental homology—that of the equivalence between male and female testicles, the principal organs of generation. Galen had asserted that women like men possess testicles. Hot and moist in complexion, delicate and soft in substance, loose and spongy in composition, and with oblong rotundity in form, they are large in men but small in women, but in both they contribute to the generation of sperm. The Salernitan anatomies neglected to locate them in women, perhaps agreeing with Caelius Aurelianus and Muscio who placed them outside the cervix of the uterus on either side, or with Constantinus who located them to the right and left at the upper neck of the uterus just below protrusions called the horns. One of the *Prose Salernitan Questions* argued that the female testicles reside beneath the two kidneys to prevent dispersion of the seed.[11] This is the closest that the twelfth-century anatomists came to following Soranus and Galen in identifying the female ovaries. In men the testicles are easily located in the scrotum (*osceum*) or the purse, which protects them from the thighs, which, in turn, shield them from external injury. In not too clear fashion they are connected by networks of nerves, arteries, and veins with the principal organs. One nerve is called the *didimus* because its origin is doubtful.[12] In general, the testicles are supplied with blood and other materials for generating sperm by veins from the liver. One vein, named the *juvenilis,* is peculiar to men and passes from the brain behind the ear. If cut, a man no longer produces sperm. Finally, the testicles possess their own network of ducts for expurgating sperm.[13] Lacking details about the male vas deferens and the corresponding female fallopian tubes, the Salernitan anatomies most likely relied on Constantinus. Through two spermatic ducts the sperm exits both to the penis and the vulva. The male ducts are long to allow the sperm to be fully heated as it travels the route arising from the testicles and descending the penis. They are large to permit quick passage and hard to prevent rupture. In contrast, the females are short because of the testicles' proximity to the uterus, narrow because the sperm is thin, and soft because the route is short.[14]

The Salernitan anatomies paid little attention to the penis except to note that it is the male instrument for projecting seed into the uterus and that because of its extreme sensitivity it is called a tail of nerves (*cauda nervorum*) connected with the brain through the peritoneum and pubis and then through the dorsal spine.[15] Constantinus had been more explicit. As flesh permeated with nerves, the penis transmits the appetite of concupiscence by touch. It is also concave so that with the arrival of appetite it is filled with air and becomes erect. Lateral muscles on both sides prevent it from bending, so that the sperm is ejected directly into the vulva. Because of the proximity of the bladder, the penis is also the route by which urine is evacuated.[16]

Following Guillaume de Conches, the *Prose Salernitan Questions* pictured the female uterus (*matrix*) as a chest for receiving seed. Shaped like a wine flask, it has a large mouth above and a corpulent stomach below connected with a long slender neck. Its interior is fibrous (*villosa*) designed to retain semen.[17] The *Anatomia magistri Nicolai* described it as cold and dry in complexion but hard and solid at the center. In composition it is nervous and dense to resist the kicking of the fetus. It is oblong in shape to accommodate the fetus's size but round to avoid corners where waste products would cause harm. Smooth outside, it is hollow and fibrous inside. The interior is divided into seven cavities (*fossuli, cellulis*) where the fetus is generated—three to the right, three to the left, and the seventh in the center. This time, following the lead of Guillaume de Conches, the *Prose Salernitan Questions,* as well as the Salernitan anatomies, rejected Constantinus Africanus's bicameral structure of the uterus to adopt one of the remarkable curiosities of the twelfth-century anatomy—the seven-chambered uterus. Unknown to Constantinus and the Galenic tradition, it was perhaps inspired by Byzantine precedents. We shall see that it combined ancient physiology with numerological speculation to account for multiple births, hermaphrodites, and other congenital abnormalities.[18]

The Salernitan anatomies ignored Constantinus's complex analysis of the uterus to declare that it simply contained two orifices, one that is wide open (*patulum*) and the other that opens and closes (*patens*). After that point their agreement deteriorated, because their terminologies and descriptions became incompatible. The *Anatomia Ricardi Salernitani* appeared to equate the exterior orifice that is wide open with the neck of the womb or the vulva (*vulva*) where the nerves are collected and the concupiscence of coitus is experienced. The interior orifice, however, is open but closes so tightly after conception that it cannot be pierced with a needle. On the other hand, the *Anatomia magistri Nicolai* distinguished between an interior orifice that is more nervous and less fleshy but always wide open and an inferior orifice that is less fleshy and more nervous, opens and closes, and is equated with the vulva.[19] Both authors preferred to treat the vulva in terms of etymological analogies. To Richard it was named because of the desire (*volendo*) of concupiscence, because of the collection of nerves as in a vineyard (*vinea*), or because the penis flew (*volvitur*) in it like a wing (*vola*). Nicholas interpreted it as desire (*volo, vis*), turning around (*volvendo*), or as a swinging door (*valva, ianua*). The two authors, however, agreed that the orifice of the uterus (whichever one) contains, like the penis, a concentration of nerves responsive to coital concupiscence.[20]

Since the Salernitan anatomists found it difficult to distinguish between the neck or mouth (*collum* or *os matricis*) of the uterus and the vagina or vulva, these etymological speculations were the closest they came to representing the external genitals of the female. Caelius Aurelianus's Latin version of gynecology recalled that since ancient times women were reluctant to submit to male scrutiny, presumably leaving these matters to midwives. Transmitting the tradition of Soranus, Caelius and Muscio did, however, locate the vagina between the thighs and between the bladder and the rectum. It is a nervous membrane like an intestine, spacious on the inside but narrow at the exterior opening. The interior is connected to the neck of the uterus at the middle of the vagina, the exterior to the labia, buttocks, and the neck of the bladder. Called *connum* in the vernacular, it is where intercourse with men takes place. The outer lips are termed *pterigomata* in Greek or *pingnacula* in Latin, and at the middle of the higher parts is found the clitoris (*landica*). Constantinus's authoritative text was not more specific. The vagina (*natura feminea*) is a small space between the pubis and the anus, furnished with external protrusions of skin called the labia (*badera*), equivalent to the male prepuce, which protect the vulva from cold air. Its form and composition vary in time and state according to whether the woman is pregnant or a virgin, and to the extent of her sexual desire.[21]

Similarly, the Salernitan anatomists said little about the female breasts except to follow Galen and to trace the particular vein from the liver which bifurcates with one branch to the breasts and the other to the uterus, thus establishing direct connections between the two female organs. In the tradition of Soranus, Caelius likewise noticed that the uterus has a natural and common agreement with the breasts.[22] Adopting an attitude established by Isidore of Seville, the physicians neglected the erogenous character of the breasts to emphasize their nutritive function. In the eleventh century Constantinus had described the breasts (*mamillae*) as made from glandular flesh, soft and white in nature like milk. A mixture of both veins and arteries, they are placed in the chest near the heart where natural heat aids in cooking blood necessary for producing milk to nourish infants. Accepting this anatomical structure, the *Salernitan Questions* distinguished the male from the female breasts and summarized the latter's functions by relating them to three logical causes. The material cause is moisture of which women have an abundance by nature; the efficient cause is heat for digesting and cooking; but the final cause is to feed infants who are unable to assimilate solid foods.[23] Among the theologians, Thomas of Chobham also emphasized the nutritive function of the breasts. In a discussion of nursing and wet nurses, he asserted that God gave breasts to women and caused milk for the raising of children. Those women who by various means withhold their breasts frustrate God's work.[24]

Accepting Galen's assertion that both men and women possess testicles, the Salernitan anatomies equally assumed that both sexes produced sperm.[25] In antiquity the Hippocratic corpus had argued that both the father and mother ejaculated, that both experienced pleasure, and that both contributed seed to the generation of the embryo. Although the male seed was stronger than the female, either partner could dominate conception through the quantity of sperm contributed. Galen accepted this Hippocratic two-seed theory but emphasized that the female seed was extremely weak and of little assistance in generation. The *Prose Salernitan Questions,* however, ignored these nuanced qualifications and simply postulated a two-seed theory of generation without distinction to male and female. We shall see that their discussions of the specific features of prostitutes and rape assumed that both sexes experienced delight and both contributed seed necessary for conception without privileging one party over the other.[26] Although they were agreed that the testicles are the last stage in the process of creating sperm before it is transmitted to the penis and uterus, they were still aware of ancient controversy over how the sperm itself was generated. The *Anatomia magistri Nicolai* reported three theories, that of Hippocrates who argued for the brain, of Galen for the liver, and of others for the whole body, and concluded that all three contain truth. Since the incision of the *juvenilis* vein behind a man's ear can stop the production of sperm, this argues for the brain. Galen had noted that the liver furnishes nutrition for the entire body and, therefore, for the sperm as well. The prevailing opinion, however, favored the theory of pangenesis. Following Guillaume de Conches, the *Salernitan Questions* asserted that sperm or human seed is composed of a pure substance consisting of all members and fluids of the body, especially blood. Since nature requires that similars be born from similars—flesh from flesh, bone from bone—semen must be generated from the entire body. (Equally important, this explains congenital defects as well.) Fluid produced in the liver is transmitted through vessels to nourish the members of the body; fluid from the brain is led by veins behind the ears to the kidneys and thence to the testicles where it is whitened and transformed into sperm.[27]

Not long after the *Prose Salernitan Questions* were compiled, the appearance of Aristotle's natural treatises in Latin challenged directly the Hippocratic-Galenic doctrine of the two seeds. The *Quaternuli* of David de Dinant, condemned at Paris in 1210, reported Aristotle's theory that only the male emits sperm whereas the female produces no sperm but merely menstrual blood for the formation of the embryo. Inherent in his physiology was Aristotle's philosophical analysis that, as the efficient cause, the male confers form while the female is the material cause and contributes only matter. The male is active; the female is resigned to passivity. The reappearance of Aristotle's one-seed doctrine presented a major challenge to the Hippocratic-Galenic two-seed theory and revived contradictions that had long preoccupied Arabic physicians. Avicenna, for example, had sought to reconcile Aristotle's scheme of generation with Galen's discovery of the female seed.[28]

In the Middle Ages the single-seed doctrine found reinforcement from the Old Testament and Augustine. Throughout the entire biblical history all humans descended from Adam's seed, and the children of Israel were propagated solely by Abraham's seed and his patriarchal descendants.[29] Since Augustine himself had restrained his curiosity over the secrets of feminine sexual organs, his physiological assumptions about conception are not entirely clear. He did, however, appear to favor the single-seed theory because his preferred metaphor was that of the farmer sewing seed by hand. Like soil, the woman passively receives the male seed and produces fruit. This theory was reinforced by the predominance of phallic imagery—hand, finger, foot, etc.—in his sexual language. Debating with Julian of Eclanum, Augustine concluded that concupiscence, the essence of original sin, was transmitted entirely through Adam's vitiated seed and his male progeny.[30]

By the second decade of the thirteenth century, the Parisian anatomies attempted to accommodate the single-seed theory within the older Hippocratic-Galenic system. Not only did the author of the *Anatomia vivorum* revive the Galenic anatomical homologies reintroduced by Avicenna, as we have seen, but he also attempted to deal with the Aristotelian theory of sperm. Like Avicenna before him, he recognized that women possess testicles and produce sperm, but unlike the Hippocratic-Galenic theory that envisaged male and female sperm acting upon each other, the anatomist proposed the Aristotelian notion that the male sperm acts upon the female sperm in the uterus and imprints form which the female sperm receives. Some even say, he reported, alluding to Aristotle, that it acts not upon the female sperm but upon the menstrual blood.[31] To these doctrines about the single seed and their troublesome questions the *Prose Salernitan Questions* appear to have remained oblivious, assuming the truth of the Hippocratic-Galenic theory. Despite the implications of the Old Testament stories and Augustine's doctrine of concupiscence, the theologian Pierre the Chanter remained faithful to the two-seed tradition of contemporary medicine. Commenting on Psalm 50:7, "In iniquity was I conceived," Pierre reported a twofold conception, one of the body and the other of the soul. Of the former, the flesh is conceived when the seeds of two—a man and a woman—are united in the womb. This dual-seed theory was still held in ecclesiastical circles by the second decade of the thirteenth century when the Synod of Angers (1217–19) defined marriage as the voluntary effusion of seed both by the man and the woman.[32]

The discussions of anatomy and sperm bore far-reaching implications for the larger question of gendering the body into the male and female sex. The authors of the *Prose Salernitan Questions* wrote at a time too early to enregister the consequences of two influential paradigms that were to dominate the later Middle Ages. Revived by David de Dinant and later by Avicenna in the thirteenth century, the first was Aristotle's and Galen's anatomical theory that saw the female body as essentially homologous to the male but inverted inwardly. By holding that the male body is normative, it thereby implied that to a greater or lesser degree the inverted articulations of women are inferior to men's outward protrusions. We have seen that the *Prose Salernitan Questions* were largely unaware of this emphasis. Apart from parallels between male and female testicles, they felt free to explore and develop anatomical differences and to be unconcerned about ultimate superiority. Nor were the twelfth-century physicians interested in the Hippocratic and Galenic qualifications of the two-seed doctrine that privileged the male over the female. There is little doubt, however, that Aristotle's one-seed theory opened a radical division between the sexes and proposed the ultimate superiority of the male. David de Dinant faithfully reported the Greek philosopher's logical conclusion that the female is essentially an imperfect male, just as is a boy (*femina est mas imperfectus, quemadmodum et puer*), and the female sperm is, in reality, only undigested menstrual blood.[33] This directly contradicted the two-seed theory still espoused by the doctors of the *Prose Salernitan Questions* that permitted to males and females mutual contributions to the generative process. The twelfth-century physicians of England and northern France, therefore, left the scene too early to record Aristotle's notions that eventually lent scientific support to the biological superiority of men over women.

Beyond acknowledging divine creation, the theologians paid little attention to the sexual organs except when they malfunctioned. Like the canonists, Robert of Courson and Thomas of Chobham explored the diverse physical impediments to the consummation of marriage through congenital bodily defects, sorcery, and mutilation. Adopting the terminology of learned Latin, Thomas noted that the *virile membrum* could be too small or, if of sufficient size, could be impotent. The woman could be restricted, that is, her vagina (*vas muliebre*) was too small. Less concerned with clinical symptoms than the danger of collusive fraud in procuring unlawful annulments, Robert devoted more attention to the modes of proof and preferred examination by expert witnesses to the unsupported testimony of partners. Men claiming to be impotent should be touched and handled by beautiful women, and restricted women should be visually inspected and probed by expert women (*discretis mulieribus*), presumably midwives. While recognizing the existence of the sexual body through its malfunction, the theologians preferred to leave the details to professional experts.[34]

The Body Concealed

Like the theologians, Ovid also took notice of the sexual body when it failed to function properly. Reminiscing in the *Amores* of an occasion when he was bedded with a lovely and experienced girl, the ancient master of love found himself hopelessly and embarrassingly impotent. The recounting of the predicament, however, was limited either to clinical terminology—my wornout loins (*inguinis ineffeti*) and my member prematurely dead (*nostra . . . praematura membra*), denoted in the plural—or to a series of metaphors—inert trunk (*truncus iners*) and useless weight (*inutile pondus*). The girl's skilled kisses and caresses are, *hélas,* to no avail. He is not even aroused by the murmurs of dirty words, usually so effective, but which the poet dares not transcribe. Only as he is presently penning his verses does he revive, but discreetly. At a happier moment Ovid indulged in the fantasy that he had been transformed into the ring on the left finger of his mistress Corinna which enabled him to explore her breasts beneath her tunic and to accompany her to the bath. His member responds to the sight of her unclothed body but again solely in clinical terms.[35] Throughout his poetry the authority on love shied away from vulgarity and maintained a studied reticence about the male body.

As to the female body, however, the Roman poet found opportunity to visualize it in the celebrated account of a hot, summer afternoon in his chamber when he was awakened from his siesta by Corrina's entry. Impetuously disrobing her, the poet discovered no fault with her naked body, which he proceeded to describe in caressing detail: shoulders, arms, nipples fit to be pressed, a flat stomach beneath a small breast, and hips, but when Ovid descended to the youthful thighs, he stopped short: "What particulars should I relate? . . . Who doesn't know the rest?" (*Singula quid referam? . . . Cetera quis nescit?*). In the quiet afternoon of the poet's chamber the female body remains obscured in the semidarkness of the half-open shutters.[36] These feminine components remained consistent throughout the *Amores.* When Ovid codified his experiences for instruction in the *Ars amatoria,* the male body was entirely omitted, and the partial concealment of the female was canonized. Although breasts remain in full view, the mysteries of Venus are hidden. The goddess of love herself lays her robes aside, leans forward, and covers her pubic mound with her left hand. It is only right that the doors to our intimate chambers are closed, and our shameful parts are hidden under garments. When the instructor of love finally united his pair of pupils in the bed chamber, he hesitated on how to advise them to display their bodies. Let each woman choose her most favorable attitude. A woman, for example, whose thighs are youthful and breasts without blemish (like Corrina's) should lie crosswise on the couch while her lover stands—to be sure—unnoticed. Let not sunlight enter the chamber's windows, Ovid counseled; it is more suitable that most of the body be hidden. If one's intent, however, is to be anaphrodisiac, the *Remedia* recommended throwing open the windows so that the shameful members are exposed to the day's light. [37] The withdrawal of the male body, the downward description of the female but with genitals designated only by the euphemistic *cetera* (the rest), and all members partially concealed in half-light became the poet's formulaic legacy for the literary treatment of the body in the twelfth century.

Ovid's poetic mastery, therefore, enunciated a fundamental ambiguity about the feminine body. On one side, it is frankly sexual, concentrating on the terrain from the shoulders to the thighs; on the other, the torso is obscured in half-tones and studiously omits the central seat of love. In the twelfth-century schools, therefore, the Latin poets were induced to pursue both possibilities. Since it is difficult to date the works precisely, a general direction is not clear. Guillaume de Blois's early poem, the *Alda,* moved toward a more graphic representation of males, and at the end of the period the *De tribus puellis* looked more directly at females, [38] but a countermovement emerged in the second half of the century to raise the viewers' gaze toward the woman's head and to avert looking directly at her sexual parts. Even in the early and risqué *Alda,* Guillaume de Blois first introduced the heroine's beauty with a catalogue of attributes centered on the head: snow-white skin, rosy complexion, arching eyebrows, laughing eyes, golden hair, and rosy lips sweet for kissing. Arnoul d'Orléans described his Lidia in the same terms, culminating in a bosom adorned with a necklace of sparkling gems. As the description of the beautiful damoiselle in the *De nuncio sagaci* proceeds downward, it stops with the hands and echoes Ovid's telling refrain that the unmentionable has been reached: "What more shall I talk about?" (*Quid referam multa?*). In the *De tribus puellis* the author answered Ovid's question directly: "What particulars should I relate? . . . A thousand days would not suffice. . . . I know for certain that the best are concealed." [39]

These catalogues of feminine beauty were canonized by Mathieu de Vendôme and Geoffroi de Vinsauf in rhetorical handbooks for the use of Latin poets. In the earliest and fullest of the manuals Mathieu demonstrated how the description of Helen may serve as a model. Beginning with her head, he proceeded down her body to her feet: golden hair, cascading in disarray to her shoulders; a charming brow; a face without blemish; dark, arched eyebrows; eyes sparkling like stars; rosy hues competing with a snowy-white complexion; a well-lined nose; reddened, full lips smiling for kisses; straight ivory teeth; a white smooth neck leading to small breasts; a narrow waist descending to the swell of the abdomen; and finally small feet, fleshy thighs; and smooth hands delineate the extremities. Offering this portrait to Venus, Mathieu confessed that he describes the qualities of beauty he adores. Geoffroi's abbreviated but similar description in his *Poetria nova* and his *Documentum* helped to disseminate the stereotypical description. To the standard parts he added corresponding adjectives deemed appropriate: snowy teeth, flaming lips, honeyed taste, rosy visage, milky forehead, and golden locks. How canonical the model had become is illustrated by an elaborate parody by a twelfth-century clerical poet.[40]

While each segment coupled with a characteristic quality conveyed undoubted erotic significance, the Latin poets treated the patently erogenous zones of the mouth, breasts, and genitals with consistency. The lips are ripe for kissing, but the breasts are invariably small and firm. Echoing Ovid, for example, the author of the *De tribus puellis* explained that some girls constrict their full bosoms with bands to be more pleasing to men, but the breasts of the particular girl are attractively small.[41] Never, however, is the pudenda uncovered to the poet's gaze. After reaching the abdomen, Mathieu celebrated the storeroom of modesty, the delightful house of Venus. What lies hidden in Venus's realm can only be divined by an experienced judge. "I am silent about the lower parts," announced Geoffroi; "here the soul speaks more suitably than the tongue." "What are we to say of that most praiseworthy thing—proclaimed the mimicking twelfth-century cleric—when we cannot speak of that nobility hidden by englobing modesty?" Like the contemporary physicians reticent to examine the female genitals, the voice of the Latin poet trailed off as he approached the seat of love.

In direct contrast to the exuberance over female beauty, however, the male body remained unobserved. While the appraisal of the female form can be expanded, Mathieu de Vendôme postulated, the masculine body should be minimized, because, as Ovid has remarked, nonchalance is more suitable to men (*forma viros neglecta decet*).[42] Discretion reigned supreme over the male body.

The more a man burns with love, asserted André the Chaplain, the more he begins to think about a woman's features, to distinguish her members, to probe their secrets and functions, and to imagine his response. Despite an initial avowal of fascination, André evidenced scant concern for physical beauty except to list a pleasing form among love's requirements. As for the sexual body, he merely divided it into upper and lower parts like

Geoffroi de Vinsauf. If a woman's beauty excels all others, but if she is deficient in the lower regions, she will be totally rejected—a cynical remark he attributed to the woman of the higher nobility.[43] Despite allegiance to the Ovidian tradition, the Chaplain could not verbalize the sexual body beyond the clinical *membra*. Because of this inhibition the reader might be justified in scrutinizing André's metaphors for sexual imagery. The allegory of the three doors of the palace of love; for example, through which three kinds of women (discerning, promiscuous, and frigid) receive their lovers can be seen as the vagina, and the crystalline rod (*baculum, crystallina virga*) which the dreamer draws out, as he awakens in a shower of water, may represent the penis undergoing a wet dream.[44] Whatever the possibilities of metaphorical imagery, however, the sexual body remained obscure in André's prose vocabulary.

The writers of vernacular romance adopted the stereotypical beauty canonized by the Latin rhetoricians, but they further fused it with their own preoccupation with clothing.[45] Since romance heroes and heroines were nearly always garbed, the body was reduced to what can be perceived above or beyond the dress. Not only is it difficult to see the body behind the clothes, the naked body itself is shaped by the clothes, so closely do body and clothes coexist in symbiosis. Moreover, because clothing was the fundamental medium to distinguish the status and privilege of aristocratic society from all other groups, romanciers paid meticulous attention to what their characters wore.

The basic costume of French aristocrats in the twelfth century can be discerned from archaeological, iconographic, as well as literary sources.[46] As in the early Middle Ages, the nobility wore long garments to be distinguished from the short clothing of peasants and other workers. A common wardrobe was shared by both men and women. Next to the skin was the *chemise* or shirt, of light material, often linen. Over this was placed a *bliaut* (tunic or gown) or more costly material. (The term *bliaut* was also synonymous with rich cloth.) The woman's *bliaut* differed from the man's by a tightly fitting bodice descending low to the hips above a full skirt that fell away in folds. Only men wore *braies* (breeches) under their shirts. Outer garments were variously designated as *mantel, cote* (coat), and *surcot* (overcoat). They could differ widely as to form, materials, and length and breadth of sleeves, but the mantel was usually the nobles' distinctive garment and accorded the richest materials and ornamentation. The *surcot* was increasingly without sleeves. Both men and women wore close-fitting hosiery (*chauces*) and some kind of leather footwear (*soller*).

It seems likely that aristocratic men and women were accustomed to sleep nude which can be inferred from an episode in Chrétien's *Charette* when Lancelot insisted on wearing his chemise to bed to discourage the unwanted advances of his amorous hostess (vv.1202–15). It is confirmed in a passage of Jean Renart's *Escoufle* where Aelis spends a sleepless night thinking about her separated lover. When she arises from her bed, she is naked (vv.3280–81). Under night's cover the body was, of course, not depicted.

Within the romance tradition erotic encounters were occasionally enacted in déshabillé. When Marie de France's young Lanval approaches his fabulous lady on her rich bed in her sumptuous tent, she is dressed only in her chemise protected from the heat (!) by a mantel of white ermine, but her whole side is uncovered displaying her face, neck, and bosom (vv.97–105). When Chrétien's young Perceval retires to bed at Blancheflor's castle, he is visited by his hostess almost naked (L. v.1984, R. v.1986), that is, in a short *mantel* of scarlet silk worn over her chemise (L. vv.1950–51, R. vv.1952–53). Jean Renart, whose fascination with clothing was acute, furnished both his romances with an erotic scene in déshabillé. In *Escoufle* the count of Toulouse was accustomed to frequent the maiden's chamber each night where he relaxed and ate his fruit before the fire and where Aelis knew especially how to make him comfortable. Undressing to be scratched (massaged?), he wears nothing except his *braies* and chemise, over which she places a *surcot* (but not a light summer one) to protect him from the cold (vv.7021–39). She is also in déshabillé (*toute desliie*) with a *pliçon,* a furred garment without sleeves over her chemise. She thrusts her right hand through the opening of his *surcot,* while he nestles his head on her lap (vv.7048–57). Although the erotic relationship between the count and girl is ambiguous, the count is represented as naked (*nu,* v.7065), even completely naked (*tout nu,* v.7102), but the context implies that both he and Aelis are still garbed in undergarments.[47]

After the hunters are sent off into the forest in the *Roman,* Conrad and his two gallants return to the ladies in the tents who are wearing *chainses,* a kind of pleated chemise, tied by lacings and confected of light silks. Without mantels these flowing robes did little to conceal their beautiful bodies (vv.194–207). Their amorous exertions exhausted, the men and women emerge from the tents to don *cotes* and mantels of varied furs and embroideries (vv.232–39). A coquette damoiselle exchanges a ribbon from her chemise with a jeweled belt from the emperor (vv.247–58). They proceed to the fountains barefooted and with their sleeves unsewn. After completing ablutions, the girls produce needles and threads from their purses to reattach the tightly fitted sleeves (vv.259–76).[48] Throughout these dalliances the bodies of the lovers are represented as clothed, but the light *chainses* and chemises do not prevent the men from appreciating the women's noble bodies and breasts (vv.206–7).

Aristocratic clothes conveyed greatest import in public, at which time the canons of the Latin rhetoricians were joined to the sartorial fashions of the nobility. The Latin poets had ignored the male form, and physical portraits of men, such as Chrétien's depiction of the fifteen-year-old Cligès, were rare in vernacular romance.[49] Although the boy's beauty rivaled Narcissus, the details were limited to golden hair, rosy visage, and a well-formed nose, mouth, and shape of the body (vv.2721–42), all which could be perceived above and through his clothes. Only in the erotically charged Tristan legend did suggestions of the male sexual body emerge. Gottfried had Iseut examine the wounded and unconscious Tristan in the bath. "She kept looking at him, scanning his body with uncommon interest. She stole glance after glance at his hands and face and studied his arms and legs, which openly proclaimed what he tried to keep so secret. She looked him up and down; and whatever a maid may survey in a man pleased her well" (vv.9, 992–10,003, trans. Hatto). In a parallel passage in Marie de France's *Guigemar* the wife likewise closely examines the young knight's body and attends to the emblematic wound on his thigh (vv.295–96, 370–72), whereas in the *Lion* Chrétien further exploited the conceit when a damoiselle applies a whole box of ointment to the naked and demented Yvain from the forehead to the big toe (vv.2987–97). Jean Renart, however, never divulged the physical appearance of his heroes, Guillaume of *Escoufle,* Guillaume de Dole, or Conrad. When the emperor emerges from the ladies' tent, it is his attire that is noticed. Out of modesty he did not wish to appear better dressed than his companions. His robe consists of alternate bands of silk, distinguished only by the coquettish but simple ribbon from the damoiselle's chemise (*Roman,* vv.242–49).

Feminine beauty, however, elicited great fascination from the romanciers and provided abundant opportunities to exercise the rhetorical conventions. When Lanval's fabulous lady finally appears in Arthur's court to vindicate the youth's claims of her beauty, Marie de France followed the rhetorical canon closely: her neck is whiter than snow, her eyes clear, her face white, her mouth beautiful, the nose well-set, the eyebrows dark, the forehead elegant, and the head crowned with golden curls (vv.564–70).[50] Marie precedes this conventional picture, however, with a more daring glimpse usually denied by the rhetoricians. Her noble body and slim hips are revealed through the open laces along the side of her white *chainsil* and chemise (vv.559–63). As she approaches the king, she lets her mantel fall so that she can be better seen (vv.605–6). Everyone agreed with Lanval that she is the most beautiful woman in all the world (v.591)! In a similar mode, the comely body of Chrétien's Enide is perceived through the tears and rents of her frayed garments (vv.401–10, 1475–77). Chrétien likewise chose the codified format to depict his heroines in *Cligès.* Evoking the image of the plumed arrow to represent Soredamor's beauty, Alexandre delineates her with classic features: an admirable forehead, flashing eyes, well-formed nose, rose-tinted, lily-white complexion, laughing mouth, straight ivory teeth, and snow-white neck and chest. In conformance with rhetorical convention, Alexandre would gladly describe the arrow's shaft at this point, but it is hidden in the quiver of her *bliaut* and chemise (vv.761–849). Like most romance heroines Soredamor's body appears only through her attire. Chrétien later renounced the task of portraying Fenice's arms, body, head, or hands—a thousand years would not have sufficed. When she uncovers her head and face, however, her beauty shines like a brilliant gem (vv.2675–2711).[51]

With studied mimicry Jean Renart also made the jongleur Jouglet descant to the attentive emperor the glories of Lïenor's beauty transmitted through the codified format. The undulating curls of her blond hair encircle her face on which the rose's redness and the lily's whiteness are subtly infused; her eyes are clearer and brighter than rubies, her eyebrows well-arched, long but not joined; her teeth and nose fashioned masterfully. "It is not everyday that one has learned to describe and embellish so well," the jongleur interjects in mockery of the cliché he is patently following. Her visage is open, her neck and chest white, her arms and hands fine, and her body noble (*Roman,* vv.691–723). (Like many romanciers Jean was particularly susceptible to hair. As Lïenor prepares to enter the imperial court at Mainz, for example, she inadvertently uncovers her head before all the barons allowing her blond locks to cascade down to her shoulders and around her neck [vv.4722–27].) Despite—or perhaps because of—the rhetorical contrivance, the emperor falls hopelessly in love with the stereotypic portrait. The remark is no longer necessary that the heroine is, once again, fully dressed.

As in Latin poetics, so in courtly romance, the woman's sexual plexus remained unarticulated.[52] By diverting attention to the thighs, however, the erotically innovative Tristan legend circumvented the problem and established an alternate approach. When Gottfried first introduced Iseut's appearance, he concentrated on her garments of purple samite and white ermine tailored in the French fashion but added that her robe fits her intimately. Without bulging or sagging, it clings close to her body everywhere, even between her knees to the pleasure of all (vv.10, 900–923). In the ordeal convoked to cloak Iseut's adultery, Béroul has her carefully phrase the crucial oath that never has any man entered between her thighs or legs except her husband and the leper who carried her across the ford (vv.4205–13).[53] In another episode in Thomas, as Iseut aux Mains Blanches's horse rears up, water from a ditch splashes up her legs, causing her to laugh. Asked to explain her merriment, she confesses to her virginity by declaring that the water has touched her thighs higher than Tristan's hands or any other man (p.79, vv.249–55).

If Chrétien had remained discreet about the lower limbs, Jean Renart, ever responsive to the Tristan legend, adopted the female thigh as the central emblem of the *Roman de la rose*. Evoking the good days of King Marc, Jean's account of the spring hunt, we have seen, included a scene at the fountain where Conrad and his amorous gallants wash after disporting themselves. Lacking towels, they borrow chemises from their lady companions, which provides numerous opportunities for hands to touch white thighs. "I do not say that whoever asked for more could claim to be courteous," the narrator gaily interposed (vv.259–83). After this vernal prelude, however, the central issue of the romance was Lïenor's vindication of her virginity which the seneschal calumniated. His convincing proof to have taken her maidenhood is drawn from his knowledge of a birthmark on Lïenor's thigh which he has extracted from the girl's imprudent mother. "Never can one relate or see such a marvel as the red rose on her white and tender thigh," confides the mother, offering full particulars of its size (vv.3360–69). The rose on Lïenor's thigh, therefore, becomes the central emblem of the maiden's unplucked sexuality. After the ordeal discredits the seneschal's charges, Lïenor identifies herself by the celebrated mark, proudly proclaiming before the emperor and his assembled court: *Je sui la pucele a la rose* (I am the maiden of the rose, vv.5038–43). Jean Renart adopted this sign as the title of his romance. As the romancier elaborated the description of her robes in preparation for her victorious entry to the imperial court, her apparel does not conceal her low and slender hips (vv.4359–60). Around her waist is a belt with a gold buckle worth more than twenty-five *livres* (vv.4381–84). If Lïenor wore the belt according to twelfth–century fashion, the belt encircled the body twice, tied first at the side of the waist and knotted a second time in front of her loins. This knot, or perhaps even the buckle, marked the unmentionable *cetera* of Latin and romance convention.[54]

If the female thigh was not to be seen in romance—but only to be talked about—what was permitted to public view was the breast, which is always white, small, and firm, as prescribed in Latin poetics. It is often enhanced with sparkling gems, as in the case of Lidia's necklace.[55] In Gottfried's description of Iseut's French-styled robes, a string of pearls is inserted where a clasp normally closed the mantle. Iseut inserts her hand there, suggestively holding the mantle together, lest the opening reveals "this and that"—Gottfried coyly observed—meaning, of course, the ermine (vv.10, 900–956).[56] Chrétien's Alexandre offers a comparable glimpse of Soredamor: "From the collar to the clasp (*fermail*) at the opening of her robe, I saw an uncovered chest whiter than the snow" (*Cligès*, vv.834–37).

That which is revealed in décolleté became an obsession for Jean Renart. In *Escoufle* young Aelis's breasts had barely appeared when the emperor noticed them as he proposed marriage for the two children (vv.2320–21), but on her return to Rome for the coronation, Jean not only compared her once more to Iseut's beauty (v.8848) but fastened his listeners' eyes on the broach (*afiche*) that closed the collar of her black mantel. Composed of precious stones radiating the colors of summer flowers, it shines upon the whiteness of her chest (vv.8926–37). In like manner in the *Roman,* as Lïenor entered Mainz, she also carefully prepares her décolleté. Her triumphal appearance rivals the fabulous lady of Marie de France's *Lanval* (vv.547–93). Above her low and slender hips is the beauty of Lïenor's chest, a veritable work of nature. Her firm breasts fill out her silk gown; her neck is long, slender, white, and without blemish or wrinkle. To embellish her neck she places a clasp (*fermail*), richly carved in gold, a full finger below the opening of her chemise so that her chest, whiter than snow on a bough, adds to her beauty (vv.4359–80). As she mounts to ride to court in full view of the crowds, she adjusts both panels of her *mantel* to reveal her chest and body above her belt. Uncovering her face, she rides with one hand on the reins and the other at the string (*atache*) opening and closing her mantel. While she passes by the money exchange, the bourgeois are so intent to catch sight that a pickpocket could have easily relieved them of their purses (vv.4529–46). Finally standing before the emperor, she keeps her hand at the string of her mantel. As she attempts to remove it, it becomes tangled with her wimple, thus precipitating the cascade of her coiffure (vv.4716–29). Depicted in twelfth-century iconography, the heavy materials of the *bliaut* and outer garments were closely fitted to the shape of the bust, but the neckline, as well as that of the chemise, was modestly high.[57] Like Marie de France's fabulous lady, Jean Renart dispensed with a *bliaut* for Lïenor and placed a more simple *cote* over her chemise which permitted greater freedom to reveal her chest (vv.4355–58).[58] As before, he could employ the brooch and other attachments at the neck to play suggestively with the décolleté. The neckline, declining toward the breast, and delineated by the bejeweled brooch to which the heroine's hand invariably points, became the liminal boundary between the public image of the clothed woman of aristocratic romance and her sexual body concealed from view.

We shall see that the twelfth-century physicians assigned to the eyes an important role in the arousal of sexual desire, a theory that was accepted by André and most of the vernacular romanciers. Sexual pleasure was assuredly enhanced by the beauty of the human body. For Latin literature and vernacular romance this beauty was defined by Ovid in traditional conventions. The female head and hair were highly stereotyped; her torso was concealed behind aristocratic clothing which allowed only the breasts to be viewed. Since the male body was virtually ignored, the Ovidian vision established an elemental distinction between women and men that may be identified as the "male gaze," according to recent terminology.[59] So dominant was the influence of Ovid and his twelfth-century epigones that even Marie de France's potentially female perspective did not depart noticeably from the conventional picture.

"We are carried away by clothing," complained Ovid, in a remark often repeated in the twelfth-century schools. "Everything is hidden under gems and gold; the girl is the least part of herself."[60] After abbreviating Mathieu de Vendôme's vision of female beauty, Geoffroi de Vinsauf followed with a model for describing feminine clothing that directed attention to gold, gems, and jewelry.[61] Responding to increased trade in luxury cloth and ornaments as well as new styles from the East since the crusades, the writers of vernacular romance outdid each other in emphasizing the richness of silks, furs, and embroideries, the profusion of gold and gems, and the variety of colors. Chrétien illustrated Enide's transformation from a poor vavassor's daughter to a king's spouse by contrasting the simplicity and poverty of her former white chemise and *cheinse* with the furs, gold, stones, and clasps on the *bliaut* and mantel which the queen contributed to her wedding trousseau (*Erec,* vv.401–10, 1533–1622). Not to be outdone, Jean Renart detailed the ermine, gold, and gems on Aelis's *cote* and *mantel* worn for her coronation at Rome (*Escoufle,* vv.8914–25). As Li̇enor enters Mainz, the *cote* over her white flowered *chemise* is of green silk finely embroidered and trimmed with fur throughout the body and sleeves (*Roman,* vv.4350–58).[62]

It was the extremity of this luxury that attracted the particular animus of Pierre the Chanter as he inveighed "against the superfluity and costliness of clothing" in a chapter of the *Verbum abbreviatum.* Since contemporary fashions were usually modest in a sexual sense, Pierre's criticisms were diverted toward extravagance. Contemporary attire exceeds all decent measure in material, color, and form. As to material, even a serf today would be ashamed to wear the skins with which the Lord covered the nudity of the first parents in paradise. How these skins were prepared Pierre did not dare to say, but he believed them to be rude. Simple materials, such as animal skins, sheep wool, or the flax or hemp of linen would be tolerable, but humans proceed to cover themselves with the plumage of birds (that would make a crow laugh), the secretion of worms (silk?), even spun thread from gold approaching the fineness of the spider's web. As for color, natural hues are acceptable, but the human craze for variety wishes to pervert natural colors first to scarlet, then to rose, now to green, then to saffron, to violet, and to whatever mixture that confuses the eyes and surpasses the innate beauty of flowers.[63]

The luxury of form expresses itself either in the diversity of color or in the manner of composition. The former divides the garment between two, three, four or more parts and employs as many colors as in a kaleidoscopic picture. The manner of composition expresses a mental image by cutting, sewing, selecting, and separating—even to the point of creating tails (*caudandi*). Whereas nature distinguishes humans from brutes, the tail denied to humans by nature is now artificially produced in a garment. For this reason a bishop of Tournai preached that it ill befits Christian matrons to wear long trains by which they sweep the filth of pavements and roads.[64] In antiquity Ovid had grumbled that his mistress's gown touched the ground, but his reason for discontent was that it hid her ankle—hardly a complaint to attract notice from the theologian.[65] Excessive robes that trailed behind had been excoriated by moralists since the eleventh century, but the tail (*coe*) or train still remained in fashion in the twelfth century. At the end of the century the romanciers appear to have taken little notice.[66] After the prostitute Richeut gave birth to her son, she attends mass for her "churching" clad in a mantel consisting of a long *coë*. She outrages public decency not only by appearing in church but also by dragging her coat train in the dust on her return home (vv.469–86). The style was not, however, limited to disreputable society. The courtly and elegant lady of Jean Renart's *Lai de l'ombre* receives the amorous knight in a loose white *chainsse* with a train of over a yard (vv.314–17). As an accentuation of the distinctive element of the aristocratic costume, the *coe/cauda* continued to persist and to provoke outcry from the censors of public foibles.

Among his *questiones* Pierre the Chanter dealt with the extent to which a wife should adorn herself with cosmetics, jewelry, and clothes to please and retain her spouse's affection. The theologian sought to establish a compromise between the one extreme of the prostitute who incites lust and that of a wife who repels her husband and drives him into the embraces of another woman. It is sufficient for the wife to adorn herself so as not to displease her husband. This middle ground, however, is difficult to maintain.[67]

Jacques de Vitry also portrayed his saintly heroine Marie d'Oignies as seeking an equilibrium of dress. When she was a young girl, her parents attempted to dress her in charming clothes and adornments according to secular fashion, but she refused them, concurring naturally in her soul with the Apostle Peter's injunction (1 Pet. 3:2) to avoid hair braids, gold decoration, and stylish garments. Later, as a matron consecrated to God, she chose moderate clothes that affected neither squalor nor worldly taste. She fled both adornment and debasement, the one scenting of allurement, the other of self-glory. Although from an affluent family which had profited from twelfth-century commercial prosperity, she did not wear a chemise (*camisia*) next to her skin but a hair shirt which was called an *es-*

tamine. Her *bliaut* (*tunica*) was of white wool over which she wore a simple mantel (*pallium*) of the same color without fur trappings or fur lining. Like Pierre the Chanter, she understood that after the Fall the Lord had clothed the nakedness of the first parents not with costly vestments or artificial colors but with skin tunics. Content with these simple garments and warmed from within, she did not fear the winter's cold. In other words, she continued to dress according to her social status but adapted to theological counsels. Unable to resist an opportunity to preach, Jacques turned to his audience and contrasted Marie with contemporary women. "What do you say to this, you superfluous and pompous woman, who adorn your corpses with a multiplicity of garments and place tails on your clothes, thereby displaying yourself to be degenerate and bestial? Your garments will be eaten by moths and decay, but the vestments of this holy woman will be as redolent as saints' relics."[68] By her manner of dress Marie d'Oignies became a living sermon to the theologians' efforts not to abolish but to bring under discipline the excesses of aristocratic costume.

The Body Exposed

Ovid's half-light diffused over the human body suggested two directions to the poets. We have seen that certain Latin poets and most vernacular romanciers omitted the male form altogether and draped the female, leaving the genitals studiously concealed. Other clerics writing in Latin, however, adopted the Roman poet as an excuse to begin to uncover the body. In *Alda* Guillaume de Blois approached the heretofore unmentionable male organ. As Pyrrus imparts to the uninitiated Alda an elementary lesson in love, the girl cannot help but notice her partner's probing staff (*virga*) and bemuses over the tail (*cauda*) or swelling of the groin (*tumor inguinis*) whose stiffness forebodes pleasure. To her question of where can she procure this instrument, Pyrrus replies that a merchant was recently selling them in the market place at prices set by weight, but having little money he was personally limited in purchase power. You would have done better to have chosen pleasure over parsimony and bought the largest, is Alda's ready response.[69]

Among the vernacular writers, Jean Bodel was the first to adopt Guillaume's *demarche* toward the male body. When the wife of the merchant of Douai falls asleep in *Li sohaiz des vez,* disappointed by her husband's inattentiveness, she dreams that she is at an annual market where the normal wares of furs, cloth, and spices are replaced on the wagons, stalls, and in the houses with nothing other than balls (*coilles*) and pricks (*viz*). On sale at retail and wholesale prices, a good prick could be bought for thirty *sous*. A small one for delight might cost between eight and ten.

After carefully inspecting the merchandise, the wife selects one that is long and thick, both behind and in front, with an enormous glans. So large is the eye (*oil*=urethra) that it can accommodate a cherry. After agreeing on a price of fifty *sous*, the wife raises her palm to strike a bargain with the merchant and slaps her husband on the face, rudely arousing both from sleep.[70] The earliest of identified fabliau writers, Jean Bodel transformed Guillaume de Blois's theme into an extravagant fantasy and established within the genre a propensity to scrutinize male genitals.

The fantasy of abundance was embroidered in *Les quatres sohais Saint Martin* (The four wishes of Saint Martin), a proverbial tale of wish fulfillment, in which the peasant wife accepts the saint's boon in a manner surely incongruous to the latter. Her first wish is to have her husband's body loaded with pricks—each accompanied with balls—from his eyes, nose, head, arms, sides—front to back and head to foot. Each is to be extended and to possess an eye large enough to admit a bean, not soft or limp but square, large, black, white, and crimson. The man is transformed into a horny rascal. One prick is insufficient, she explains, since it was always soft as fur. Now I am rich in fine pricks (vv.92–134). This preoccupation with size was further developed in *Le fevre de Creil* in which the blacksmith, upon chancing to observe his apprentice Gautier relieving himself, cannot help but be impressed with the latter's endowment and thinks that this offers an opportunity to test his wife's fidelity. Fashioned by nature, the member in question is well built, a full fist in width, two in length, red as a Corbeil onion, fitted with balls, a tool that can bore any oblong hole round. Like that bought by the Douai wife, it also has a urethra so large that a Lombard bean could not impede the urine (vv.12–54).[71]

A robust physique, however, could also raise anxieties. In a story by the same name, a young fisherman from Pont-sur-Seine and his wife lie in bed conversing after a strenuous session of lovemaking. As she holds his ample prick in her hand—it was neither soft nor useless—the wife reaffirms her passion for her vigorous husband (vv.24–27). Despite her protestations he doubts how long she would abide him if he were so unfortunate as to lose his organ. To test this nagging suspicion he returns home one day with the detached genitals of a dead priest caught in his net, claiming that they are his own, severed by three knights who assaulted him. His worst fears are confirmed, because his wife leaves straightway, pausing only to collect her property. He retains her for a moment, however, by promising to share what remains of his money. When she searches his pants for the cash and finds instead a ready prick, she is persuaded to remain. Castration, as we have seen, was also the fableors' preferred punishment of peccant priests. The resulting mayhem afforded the authors ample opportunity for attending to male genitals. In *Aloul* (vv.343–52, 812–25) the priest survives two close calls. In the darkness of the stable an old servant nearly mistakes his balls for a sheep, and in the barn another servant armed with a knife is nearly persuaded that the priest is sausage or tripe suspended from the rafters. When the priest in *Le prestre crucefié* poses on a crucifix, he pays with his penis and testicles for his compounded impieties (vv.60–73).

Gautier, the blacksmith's apprentice, has attributes attractive to women other than his genitals. The author characterizes him as handsome and honest with broad hips, slender flanks, and shoulders thick and broad (vv.9–13). Whatever the potential appeal of these masculine assets, it is nonetheless clear that the fableors, unlike other contemporaries, were obsessed with those parts of the male body they frontally labeled "prick" and "balls." Defying the contemporary Ovidian school tradition to keep the male body out of sight and the aristocratic romances that clothed it in rich garments or protective armor, these writers displayed the male organs like meat on the butcher block accompanied by choruses of merriment.

Ovid's Corrina coyly undressed in the obscurity of nearly closed shutters. In high parody of this scene, the author of *De tribus puellis* turns up the lights. The fires of golden lamps illuminate the chamber with the sun's brightness. The girl uncovers herself, wishing to be seen naked, because her body is faultless. With no obstruction to vision the author proceeded to describe her beauty according to the conventional canon—snow-white skin, small breasts, flat stomach—but when he arrived at her flanks, once again he shifted to the Ovidian-romance tradition and averted his gaze. "I shall not tell you more, although I could talk about better things" (vv.247–63). The fabliaux challenged directly and bluntly this feigned modesty about female genitals.

Jean Bodel's incipient corpus was perhaps too limited to include an elaboration of the female body, but in his tale about peasants (*Barat*, v.357) he has already identified and distinguished the two feminine nether orifices in unadorned vernacular: cunt (*con*), and ass(hole) (*cul*). Although the two could be assimilated by synecdoche, their anatomical positions and functions were usually kept separate. This is the elaborated point of the *Trois meschines* in which a girl could not understand where to place her chamber pot. As her friend advises, "Your asshole is so close to your cunt that there is hardly a wiseman or a fool who can tell the difference. The one looks like an axe slice abutting a round hole" (vv.84–89). Not even the medical profession were accustomed to approaching the female so closely.

In an outrageous affront to both romance poets and theologians, the author of *Le con qui fu fez a la bresche* (The cunt that was dug with a shovel) rewrote the biblical story to account for the creation of the vagina. God made woman from Adam's rib according to orthodox theology and with a beautiful neck and face according to romance convention. When the devil inspects the lower parts of God's handiwork, however, he discovers that the Creator had installed only one opening at the end of the spine, thus forgetting the cunt, without which a woman is not worth a shallot. (This deduction was shared by André the Chaplain's woman from the higher nobility.)[72] God, therefore, delegates the devil to repair the defect which the latter performs by digging a deep ditch with a shovel. "May God never pardon anyone who speaks evil of women and their cunts," the author concluded, "because the latter are well constructed." Giving vent to aristocratic pretensions, the noble-born wife in *Berengier au long cul* (Berengier of the long ass) humiliates her peasant husband by raising her robe, turning her backside, and making him kiss her ass. (At this point the husband still believes her to be another knight.) As he peers into the crevice, it is the longest ass he has ever seen because the cunt and asshole appear to be joined (vv. 241–46). So common was the talk about female genitals that one fabliau, *Li jugement des cons* (The judgment on cunts), required three daughters, who sought marriages with boys of good family, to submit to a contest of riddles: Who is older, you or your cunt? With never a blush, each strove to outdo the others by their responses. The first replies that the cunt is older because it has a beard and I do not; the second that the cunt is younger because it does not have teeth and I do; and the third and winning entry that the cunt is younger because it has a hungry mouth and suckles at the breast, but I am weaned (vv. 118–53). Undoubtedly victory went to the third because a vagina that sucks and nourishes is preferable to one that bites.

Lest St. Martin's three remaining wishes be overlooked, the peasant husband retaliates by wishing as many cunts to bloom on his wife as pricks on him: two on her face, four on her brow—front, back, head to foot—of many kinds—straight, crooked, with and without hair, young, well-made, virginal, and bottomless. Now the peasant is as rich in cunts as his wife in pricks because each prick has its purse. Now the wife will be *bien coneüe,* that is, well-known/cunted/and screwed (vv. 141–91).[73] The fableors, however, were not as preoccupied with the size of female genitals as with the male. Only the harlot Hersent, made up to be a virgin, has the dimensions of a mare, a veritable ocean without coasts or soundings (*Richeut,* vv. 1280–81).

The unabashed goal of the fableors was to expose the male and female body to unobstructed view and to articulate its sex directly with fewest circumlocutions. Our examples have been chosen from those fabliaux where sexual themes predominate, but this is a mere sample of stories where the vocabulary of *vit, coilles, con,* and *cul* abounded. Jean Bodel's *Barat et Haimet,* for example, was basically a tale of two thieves, a peasant, and his wife in a struggle over the side of a ham, but during the contest the peasant's nether parts are uncovered when his breeches are stolen. Later the thief gains possession of the ham by disguising himself as the wife and proposing to touch the ham to her ass and cunt three times, presumably to cast a protective spell (vv.81–87, 354–59). Under these circumstances euphemism was pointless. This compulsive repetition of the vernacular lexicon of the sexual body is ample demonstration that the fableors took little notice of Augustine's theory of linguistic shame (*pudenda*) championed by the theologians. It further represents a pervasive scopophilia or the derivation of sexual pleasure from looking at nude bodies. Unlike the Ovidian and romance tradition, however, which radically distinguished between the stereotypical female body and the unobserved male body, the visual obsessions of the male fableaux authors were directed equally to men and women.

Despite the fixation on the body below the belt, when the fableors pictured aristocratic society they were not unaware of refined language, delicacies, and the erotic attraction of other parts of the female body that were valorized by Ovidian and romance literature. In *Guillaume au faucon,* for example, the noble and sensitive youth contemplates the body and face of the châtelain's wife in strictly romance terms beginning with her golden tresses and ending with her apple-like breasts (p.95). When the knight in the scarlet robe (*Chevalier a la robe vermeille*) finds his ladylove awaiting him naked on her bed he envisages her as beautiful, plump, and tender (vv.49–57). Such refined qualities were occasionally appropriated for other milieu as well. In a triangular intrigue among two money changers and a wife, the lover exhibits the wife's beauty to her husband without the husband recognizing her identity. Reversing the normal direction, he nonetheless intones the conventional canon of romance: from the feet to the breasts—firm and beautiful—and finally a white neck and throat (vv.94–99). As the butcher of Abbeville takes revenge on the priest, he discovers the latter's mistress naked, an occasion to admire the beauty of her white neck, chest, and breasts (vv.250–56). The head and upper torso, in which the breasts figure prominently, are also displayed according to romance convention on the girls seduced by the knight (*Prestre et le chevalier,* p.48) and the priest (*Prestre et Alison,* pp.10, 11). Not only in fabliaux involving aristocracy but also in other situations the ubiquitous cunt and ass could be conspicuous by their absence. The crudest fantasies and language were nonetheless reserved for the nonnoble merchants of Douai, the Norman peasants, blacksmiths and fishing folk of the Seine. Berengier of the long ass was not necessarily an apparent exception because this proud aristocratic woman avails herself of a *vilain* procedure to punish her cowardly peasant husband and to avenge the humiliation of *mésalliance.*

The fableors' scrutiny of naked genitalia, however, did not imply that they failed to notice the dress prominently featured in the romances. We recall that the earliest example of the genre inventoried the prostitute Richeut's outfit worn to church, and allusions to clothing lie scattered throughout the corpus. Whereas the garment formed an integral part of the sexual body in romance, by contrast, in the fabliau clothing scarcely impeded notice of the private parts. For that reason fabliaux couples were quick to shed their attire. The priest undresses the wife before he lies with her in Jean Bodel's *Vilain de Bailluel* (v.84). In the *Chevalier a la robe vermeille* the noble wife lies naked as she awaits her knightly lover. When he arrives attired in a new scarlet cloak, she orders him to disrobe immediately for more pleasant delight. That, in fact, he strips to the buff is confirmed by the narrator who discloses that unlike romance he removes his breeches and chemise as well (vv.52–68). The ubiquity of the bath amply attests the predilection for nudity in the fabliaux.

By employing *vilain* vocabulary about the sexual body the fableors were, in effect, not only ignoring Augustinian modesty but also proclaiming a linguistic challenge to the refinement of the clerical, Ovidian, and the romance traditions. This confrontation was perceptively enregistered in a fabliaux entitled *La damoisele qui ne pooit oïr parler de foutre* (The damoiselle who couldn't abide hearing the word "fuck"), whose popularity is demonstrated by four extant manuscripts and three different versions. Among the variations, a central story emerged: the daughter of a great baron (or of a rich nobleman or a rich peasant) is so refined that she is unable to hear dirty talk without fainting straight away. Her standards of linguistic propriety made it impossible for the father to retain laborers on the farm. At the instigation of the father, therefore, a young *vallet* (or a young cleric) is engaged to instruct her in the topography of the sexual body and its accompanying nomenclature, concluding, of course, with seduction. The audience was obviously treated to an erotic account in the prolonged journey across the sexual body guided by a linguistic atlas. As the girl slips her hand from the young man's chest down his body she asks the name of each point of interest, to which the young man replies with a euphemism. The journey is repeated on the girl's body with the girl now supplying the euphemism for each point the young man touches. By means of this child's game, the narrator was given opportunity to gloss the crude fabliaux vocabulary with metaphors: his prick becomes his *roncin* (horse), his shaggy balls become sacks of oats, or two marshals to tend the horse. When the journey is repeated on the girl's body, her firm breasts require a metaphor in only one version (sheep testicles). In the other two they are simply the fruit she carries on her bosom or simply her breasts, white and beautiful. But her navel becomes her pit (*noel=noyau*), her pubic mound a meadow, her cunt a fountain in the middle of a meadow, and her asshole her watchman or horns-man who guards the fountain and meadow.[74] If it is true that the euphemisms were not those of romance convention but rather metaphorical creations common to a child's imagination, they nonetheless serve the romance design of deflecting direct speech. The fact that the breasts were not glossed in two versions also recalled the romance tolerance of décolleté and the exposure of the bosom.

If the fableors were both acutely aware and overtly provocative of the romance tradition, their aristocratic opponents, who valued chaste speech, naturally reciprocated studied reticence. The Tristan legend, Marie de France, and Chrétien countenanced no *vilain* language in their revelations of love's mysteries. Only Jean Renart, ever attuned to his society, allowed a fabliau expression to slip into his romances, which otherwise vaunted courtly elegance. After Lïenor's triumphant vindication at Mainz which then cleared the way for the emperor to marry his true love, the latter asks his assembled barons whether he should await the feast of Ascension to hold the wedding. Since the high nobility were already gathered at Mainz, the duke of Saxony counsels the emperor to proceed with the ceremonies straightway. This advice only reinforces the emperor's own impatience to be united with his love, because, as he exclaims: "[T]he ass pulls stronger than rope" (*Ahi! plus tire cus que corde*, v.5300). Not only was *cus/cul* a key word in the fabliau lexicon that was banished from courtly romance, but the phrase itself, undoubtedly of proverbial origin, could also be found in *La damoisele qui ne pooit oïr parler de foutre (III)* (v.230).[75] By a verbal ejaculation uttered at the height of Conrad's excitement, Jean Renart returned fleeting but telling recognition of fabliau discourse.

Whether or not this momentary slip was deliberate, another writer imitated, if not parodied, the courtly style by composing an aristocratic lai devoted expressly and exclusively to the forbidden female organ and its vernacular nomenclature. As was the custom in Brittany long ago, the lai began, the finest members of the three orders (clerics, knights, and men of other trades) and their ladies, girls, and damoiselles gathered on the feast of Saint Pantelion to hold a contest as to who could write the best lai. After attending church, each recited a tale of courtly love or chivalric deeds to be judged by eight noble ladies, one of whom offered the final decision: Why, she asks, do good knights love to attend tournaments, adorn themselves in new clothes, and send jewels and rings to their lady loves? Why do they refrain from villainy and engage in courtship, kisses, and embraces? What is the great good for which all this is done? For only one thing: the desire for cunt (*l'entente du con*). Echoing André the Chaplain and *Le con qui fu fez a la bresche,* she explains: no woman, no matter how beautiful her face, would be worth a button to her friend or *dru* if she lost her cunt. The cunt,

114

therefore, is the appropriate subject for a new lai. The narrator concluded by raising a problem over how to entitle the lai. Most people, he averred, would prefer to call it the *Lai du lecheor* (the lai of the lecher). In order not to incur blame, he also will not use the right name. By implication, therefore, the correct title is the *Lai du con*.[76]

4

SEXUAL DESIRE

The Galenic physicians argued that sexual desire was primarily a function of the physiological processes of the body, yet in the chronology of sexual experience desire precedes coitus. For these reasons it seems appropriate to consider the subject at this point. I shall adopt an intentionally loose definition of desire as the emotional state surrounding intercourse that includes both appetite for and pleasure from the act. Like the ancient philosophers, the twelfth-century discourses considered appetite as one of the essential functions of the soul; like modern sexologists as well as ancient philosophers they also coupled appetite closely with pleasure.[1] Although my working definition of desire overlaps with the exalted emotion that is identified as love, it will nonetheless privilege the sexual and physical character over the idealized and spiritual emotion. Sexual desire was an important preoccupation—perhaps the most important concern—of all the five discourses except the fabliaux. Since each spokesman formulated a distinctive approach to the subject incorporating the legacy of his particular tradition, it will be strategically preferable to treat each voice separately throughout this chapter, except in the final section where they may be brought together on noncoital sexuality and the supremacy of desire.

Concupiscentia: The Theology of Desire

For almost a millennium the definition, analysis, and evaluation of sexual desire had been a central concern of the Church Fathers and theologians. In this process Augustine was of pivotal influence in formulating the terms of discussion for the Latin West. We have seen that his analysis was shaped both by his own sexual experiences and by the controversies over the subject that reverberated among post-Constantinian Christians. As he explored sexuality and marriage throughout his voluminous writings he deepened his understanding of sexual desire and its relation to the transmission of original sin.[2]

116

Augustine's reflections on sexual desire were rich in pertinent observations, enormously influential, but widely dispersed throughout his polemical treatises. It, therefore, became the task of the theologians at Laon in the early twelfth century, particularly of Anselme de Laon and Guillaume de Champeaux, to collect these scattered opinions and to distill from them coherent and systematic doctrine. After a half-century of elaboration, this process culminated in the *Glossa ordinaria* at Laon and the *Sentences* of Pierre the Lombard around 1154. The latter compilation, in turn, assembled the basic Augustinian materials on sexuality and original sin and presented the Church Father's theories in a more systematic form. As revealed in the Lombard, the theologians of the early twelfth century had dealt broadly with marriage in their collections, but they were also concerned with the theological implications of sexuality, particularly two major questions: (1) how sexuality was infected by concupiscence after the Fall, and (2) how original sin was then transmitted by sexuality through the human race.[3]

Against the encratic views of most Greek Church Fathers as well as contemporary Latin Christian writers, Augustine had argued that before the Fall the first humans in paradise were capable of sexual activity but without sexual desire. Recapitulating Augustine, the Lombard held that the first parents could command their genitals by rational will, just as one moves his foot or his hand to his mouth without the heat of lust, concupiscence, or even any craving of the flesh.[4] To summarize the central theological doctrine, the Fall into sin by the first humans was occasioned by pride, accompanied by disobedience to the divine commandment which, in turn, introduced original sin consisting of punishment, guilt, and a carnal fault. Its most concrete manifestation was *concupiscentia*. Under this scheme sexual desire, therefore, first appeared and originated in the Fall. The Lombard supported his definition of original sin by offering alternative terms: the tinder of sin or *concupiscentia,* also called the law of our members, the languor of nature (*languor naturae*), the despot in our members (*tyrannus*), or the law of the flesh (*lex carnis*).[5]

Implicit in *languor* and *tyrannus* is the element of disobedience in the sexual members. The Lombard neglected to develop the consequences of shame in his *Sentences,* but Augustine had explored them fully. Just as the first parents had disobeyed God, so their genitals began to recapitulate this insubordination by refusing to obey rational or volitional commands. Adam and Eve began to sense something new in their bodies. Their genitals, which had obeyed their commands before, were now in open rebellion. At times, a motion would appear as an unwanted intruder; at other times, it abandoned the lover against his wishes; it could arouse the mind but not the body. Augustine recaptured this loss of control in the experience of orgasm. Lust (*libido*) attacks the whole body from without and within. Joining and mixing with the body, it produces no greater physical pleasure (*voluptas*). When it reaches its extremity, the boundaries and awareness of thought are obliterated.[6] These new sensations induced the first parents to clothe themselves with fig leaves, to consider their genitals as shameful (*pudenda*), and to conceal these instincts which were no longer under control. To this day, couples refuse to copulate in public, hiding the generative act from their own children. Even brothels provide secrecy for their customers. Before the Fall sexuality could be discussed without obscenity; thereafter, it is no longer possible because the subject provokes indecent thoughts as the result of guilty feelings. Modesty and shame that presently inhibit speech are the most recent testimony to the power of concupiscence.[7]

The theologians had long been aware of the role of sight in engendering concupiscence. Commenting on Genesis 3:7 where Adam's and Eve's eyes were opened to the shame of nakedness after the Fall, Pierre the Chanter, for example, remarked that the eyes are linked to concupiscence and its knowledge. The eyes of children are closed to lust until puberty, but afterward these channels are open admitting the natural forces of concupiscence to flood through the members and to produce sensations of craving. Jesus confirmed the importance of vision in the Sermon on the Mount (Matt. 5:27) where he asserted that whoever looks on a woman with concupiscence has already committed adultery in his heart. This passage prompted the Chanter to distinguish between the first motion of sight and the subsequent intention to lust. It is the latter intent and not the initial sight that constitutes sin.[8]

Adopting the Augustinian analysis, Pierre the Lombard established a basic vocabulary for sexual desire among the theologians of the twelfth century. The two standard terms were *concupiscentia* and *libido* (lust), often combined as *libidinosa concupiscentia*. Occasionally the element of heat was added, as in *ardor libidinis* (ardor of lust), *fervor concupiscentiae* (fervor of concupiscence), or *fomes peccati* (kindling wood of sin), or the quality of craving, as in *pruritus* (itching) or *prava titillatio* (tickling). *Desiderium* (desire) itself was distinguished from *concupiscentia* as being the concrete manifestation of the latter. *Voluptas* (pleasure) bore negative associations, as, for example, in connection with prostitutes, but the more innocent connotation of *delectatio* (delight) was usually modified by "fleshly" (*carnis delectatio*) when it referred to sexuality. Because sexual desire was the direct consequence of the Fall, the standard theological vocabulary became thoroughly infused with negative connotations.[9]

Not only did sexual desire originate with the Fall, but, equally important, the resulting original sin was transmitted to the human race by sexual intercourse. Unlike the Pelagians who saw original sin as the imitation of

Adam's disobedience, Augustine had argued that original sin was biologically propagated. The Lombard accepted the fundamental propositions that concupiscence is present at every sexual act and conception and that the first parents genetically transmitted original sin to all posterity. The transmission takes place, moreover, not in the soul, but in the flesh which carries the fault (*vitium*) of concupiscence. This sexual transmission is strikingly emblemized by the rite of circumcision in the Old Testament. In obedience to God, Abraham submitted to the excision of his foreskin because original sin was transmitted through that member and in that member man had first sensed the guilt of disobedience. In the early twelfth century, Augustine's doctrine of the transmission of sin had been contested by rival theories from Anselm of Canterbury and Pierre Abélard. The Lombard admitted that the theologians had offered varied theories because the holy doctors of the church had spoken obscurely, but his acceptance of the Augustinian position assured its virtual preeminence over the second half of the century.[10]

The origin and transmission of sin were so important that they prompted numerous questions and discussions that were pursued by the Lombard and succeeding theologians like Pierre de Poitiers, Prévostin, and Stephen Langton, who were interested in speculative theology. Although Pierre the Chanter and his followers ignored such issues for the most part, they nonetheless accepted the solutions popularized in the Lombard's *Sentences*.[11] One topic, however, which drew the attention of all theologians from the start of the century was the role of marriage as the divinely instituted remedy for concupiscence. Against the Manicheans Augustine had written his *De bono conjugali* to affirm that marriage with its three concomitant goods of offspring, faith, and sacrament was instituted by God for the benefit of the human race. Including marriage among the seven sacraments of the church, Pierre the Lombard, in turn, noted that it had been established as a sacrament before sin, but after sin it became the divine remedy for carnal concupiscence.[12]

The central problem was how marriage remedied or excused the ills of sexual desire. The Lombard's treatment was not entirely clear and coherent, but he attempted to identify conditions under which concupiscence could be tolerated. He opened his discussion with the final causes of marriage originally formulated by Augustine. The first is the procreation of offspring according to the divine commandment in Genesis (1:28) to be fruitful and multiply. The second, according to the advice of the Apostle Paul (1 Cor. 7:2), is to avoid fornication (or incontinence, as phrased elsewhere). To this second he joined the Apostolic command (1 Cor. 7:3) to spouses to render to each other the marital debt (*debitum*). There are other final causes more or less valid for justifying marriages, as we shall have

119

occasion to see, but even the absence of the final cause (or the good) of marriage is not sufficient to destroy the matrimonial bond. The first cause, that of progeny, excuses sexual intercourse from guilt (*culpam*). We shall see that the motive of progeny ranked highest among all theologians for exonerating the sin of lust. The second class of avoiding fornication (or incontinence) and of rendering the marital debt do not excuse guilt but reduce it to a venial (*venialem*) level within marriage. Intercourse, even for the sake of satisfying concupiscence, is a venial sin if it is conducted within wedlock.[13]

After these conclusions which sought to mitigate the culpability of sexual desire, the Lombard introduced a statement from a Stoic philosopher identified as Sextus Pythagoricus: "Any exceedingly ardent lover (*omnis ardentior amator*) of his own wife is worse than an adulterer." Jerome who was the source of the quotation supplied further elaboration: "The wise man loves his wife with judgment not with affection. Let not the impulse of pleasure reign in him, nor the proclivity towards intercourse. Nothing is more foul than to love a wife as an adulteress." To this Jerome added a final dictum: "The generation of children is conceded in matrimony, but pleasures which are seized in the embraces of prostitutes are condemned in wives."[14] These apparent anathemas against passionate desire led to the question whether all fleshly delight (*delectatio carnis*) is sinful. On the authority of Gregory the Great some maintained that all carnal concupiscence and delight produced in intercourse are evil because they originated in sin. The Lombard countered that concupiscence is indeed evil because it is filthy, and the penalty of sin, but it is not always sin itself. Often a holy man, like Jesus himself, took fleshly delight in certain things, such as resting after work or eating when hungry. Such delight is not sinful unless it is immoderate. Similarly, where the goods of marriage are present, the delight of wedded intercourse can be cleared of sin.[15] Further into the discussion the Lombard appended a well-known passage from Augustine that arrived at similar conclusions: "What food is to the health of a man, intercourse is to the health of the race. Both are not without fleshly delight, which if modified, temperately restrained, and directed to natural use cannot be equated with lust. Illicit food for sustaining life is comparable to seeking offspring in fornication or adulterous intercourse. An immoderate appetite for licit food is equivalent to pardonable (*venialis*) intercourse in married partners."[16]

Although Pierre the Lombard did not succeed in purging his multifarious sources of ambiguity, he made an effort to reduce the contamination of guilt infecting the sexual desire of married couples. His line of reasoning, however, came under attack in the next generation from Huguccio of Pisa, the leading canonist of the Bolognese school. Although

Huguccio had sided with the Lombard and the French theologians in the debate over the substance of marriage (in favor of consent over copulation), he disagreed with the Parisian school over the nature of sexual desire. The canonist treated the subject in more contexts and in greater detail than his legal colleagues, but underlying the complexity of his discussion was a fundamental theme that kept reappearing: sexual desire is eradicably and irremediably sinful. Most simply stated, the delight (*delectatio*) that is felt in coitus from the emission of seed is basically pleasure (*voluptas*) accompanied by heat (*fervor*) and craving (*pruritus*). In an often repeated phrase intercourse within legitimate marriage is, therefore, impossible without sin, albeit a venial sin. (*Numquam coitus coniugalis potest exerceri sine peccato, saltem cum veniali.*) The Augustinian "final causes" of progeny, returning the marital debt and avoiding incontinence exonerate the act of conjugal coitus but do not eliminate the sinful element of sexual desire. Even a saint who has intercourse cannot escape sin. The greater the desire, the greater the sin; therefore, coitus with a beautiful woman is more dangerous than with an ugly one. Marriage belongs to many human activities that cannot be conducted free of guilt. When a husband is obligated to return the marital debt, he is, to be sure, held to sin by necessity, but in fact he is not held to sin, although he cannot do it without sin, just as one who has vowed to go to Saint-Jacques may not be able to accomplish the vow. Similarly, just as God commands to increase and multiply, he orders many mundane activities that cannot be performed without sin. Huguccio saw this reasoning as expressly opposing the French theologians Pierre Manducator and Pierre the Lombard who argued that coitus for the sake of progeny or rendering the marital debt was without sin and further charged that to oppose this view was heresy. In defense Huguccio distinguished his position, which imputed only venial sin to married intercourse, from that of the heretics which burdened it with mortal sin.[17]

As contemporaries to Huguccio, Pierre the Chanter and his circle renewed the debate with the canonist by pursuing the line of argument of the French school. Although not contributing directly to theological speculation on the origin of concupiscence and transmission of original sin, they did join in the discussion of marriage and sexual desire. Each member contributed in different and characteristic fashions. In his scriptural commentaries Pierre offered fragmentary insights into specific questions appended to the appropriate passages. Apparently arriving at the subject of marriage in the school debates at the end of his life, he died before his *questiones* could be written down. We have seen that his student Robert of Courson, nonetheless, incorporated the Chanter's opinions into his own *Summa,* noting that his master had participated in the lively disputations. As on other matters, Robert's *Summa* may be viewed as the last version of the *questiones* of

Pierre the Chanter's school. Robert himself contributed a lengthy discussion to a question popular among the theologians but now of heightened significance because of Huguccio's challenge: whether sexual intercourse (*carnale commercium*) can be accomplished without sin in marriage.[18] His own contribution was to explore virtue and merit according to the techniques of moral theology. Thomas of Chobham, in turn, recapitulated the discussion and organized the conclusions for the use of priests administering penance in the confessional. In the end all three contributed to a more practical analysis of sexual desire than that undertaken by the theologians of the Lombard's tradition.

To the question whether married intercourse can be performed without sin, Robert of Courson marshaled a long series of authoritative statements interlaced with complicated and involved arguments whose twists and turns can only be abbreviated and summarized here.[19] Since marriage was established both by natural law and divine command, its accomplishment must be presumed to be virtuous and meritorious, but it also contains patently sinful elements that relate to vanity rather than God. Throughout the argumentation, Robert's underlying concern was to assess and separate the positive and negative elements within the moral confusion of actual life. The problem is much like characterizing weather. If one part of the day is sunny and the rest is overcast, is the day to be called clear or cloudy? In a discussion comparable to Huguccio's, Robert assigned married intercourse to other meritorious activities like prayer, almsgiving, martyrdom, and preaching that contain a mixture of good and bad elements. One can preach, for example, for the glory of God and at the same time for the vain glory of personal reputation. An initial approach is to distinguish among three kinds of works represented by three eyes. One kind of work, called the simple eye, is done directly for God and is always meritorious. Another, the worthless eye, is done against God and is always reprehensible. The middle eye represents works under God, like marriage, that partly serve the world and children and partly God. The perfect should avoid such works, but according to Augustine it is sufficient for the imperfect that they do not perform them against God but under God, like plowing, sewing, eating, and drinking. A similar solution would divide such works among the categories of nature, grace, and guilt. Marriage for the sake of restraining lust (*libido*) is neither of grace nor of mortal sin but of nature because it is done for a good end.

Marriage for the goal of restraining pleasure is a case in point. Almost everyone admits that such activity involves guilt, not mortal but venial, because of the added factor of craving. Robert reported that his master the Chanter said that a distinction should be made between two things: the deed itself which is not a sin but of the class of good, not meritorious however, and that which adheres to it, the craving or twitching, which clings, not to the deed, but to the soul and prevents it from being meritorious by a venial stain. This stain is not really an action but semiaction because the twitching is only very venial. Another twofold distinction divides the deed between direct and indirect ends. The first is done directly for God without any intermediary. The second is done not directly for God in the first instance but to avoid incontinence, and only later referred to God. In a general sense, Robert concluded that knowing one's wife for restraining incontinence is done indirectly for God and, therefore, is a venial sin or a sin under God, but one that is excused from mortal guilt by the good of marriage.

Augustine had claimed that knowing one's wife for the sake of offspring and rendering the marital debt is no sin at all, but these goals cannot be accomplished without the lightest of venial sin (*sine aliquo veniali peccato levissimo*). Since there is a very slight blemish (*nevus modicissimus*), the Church Father must have used a figure of speech. Can such deeds be meritorious despite the specks of dust of venial sin? The Chanter was accustomed to assert that dust impeding contact with God does not obstruct the merit of the entire work. Although imperfect at the beginning, it is later related to God. Like the lancing of a boil, the pain might distract the patient from God, but the action is beneficial nonetheless. Although dust adhered to the feet of the Apostles, their preaching was nonetheless meritorious. As the Chanter argued during the lively debates of the last year of his life, such problems can be resolved by dividing all works into parts which can and cannot be related to God—those which are meritorious, and those which are venial sin. The two parts do not make a single action nor should they be joined under common terminology. That one can start off to church devoutly but later look at a woman in lust does not join the two parts in the same action.[20] To apply this solution to the problem at hand, if one knows his wife for the sake of offspring or the rendering of the marital debt, the first and the last parts are meritorious because they relate to God, but the middle, where all is absorbed in flesh, is venial sin. The same applies to other laudable activities such as praying and preaching. To respond to the first question—whether anything commanded by God cannot be accomplished without venial sin—Robert replied that this is true of returning the marital debt if one considers the deed as a single act, and this would also be true of preaching. Because of the human condition, therefore, Robert would initially concur with Huguccio that the commandments of the Lord can be scarcely fulfilled without venial sin.

The Lombard had attempted to reduce unqualified blame on sexual desire by introducing distinctions. Although concupiscence was evil, filthy, and bore the penalty of sin, it was not always a sin itself. In an analogous

manner the elaborate analyses of the Chanter and Courson sought to define, isolate, and thereby reduce the moral opprobrium against marital desire. Within their conceptional framework, sexual activity was equated to
praiseworthy activities like prayer, preaching, even martyrdom, which
were conducted for the sake of God, but in this sinful world could hardly
escape sinful contamination. By applying binary opposites they attempted
to find a middle ground between the unconditional extremes of merit and
sin in which they could apply a nuanced evaluation. The Chanter proposed
a distinction between the sexual act which was an *actio* and sexual desire as
a craving which was only a *quasi actio* but, more accurately, a stain that adhered to the soul. In this way desire was relegated to a passive experience,
while the sin itself was located in the active will. In support of his teacher,
Thomas of Chobham noted that when a holy man sleeps with his wife he
may feel a craving or fleshly pleasure. Since he does not apply his mind to it
nor is pleased by carnal delight, he sins in no way either mortally or venially, any more than if he had eaten sweet food.[21] According to the
Chanter and Courson, moreover, sexual desire occupied the least culpable
level of venial or pardonable sin—*venialissima, levissima, modicissima*—
mere dust in the Chanter's terminology.

Although framed in terms of concrete actions, Courson's involved discussion was written for theologians interested in the abstract nature of the
moral act. The Chanter and his students, however, were equally concerned with the practical consequences of their conclusions for the laity
who actually experienced sexual desire in matrimony. The Lombard had
collected opinions from Augustine and others and assembled them under
the category of the final cause of marriage. Since his organization was incomplete and at times confused, the Chanter and his colleagues sought to
introduce systematic classification into the Augustinian materials transmitted by the Lombard. Although each proposed slightly different classifications of sins incurred in marital intercourse, the schema were
nonetheless comparable. The Chanter offered two triadic divisions: one
according to the kind of intercourse, the other according to the weight of
sin. The first was divided among (1) carnal, when a man cannot abstain
from intercourse, which is mortal sin, unless it is excused by marriage, in
which case it becomes venial; (2) impetuous, that is, in a sacred place or
with a menstruating woman, both of which are mortal sins; and (3) conjugal, which is done for the sake of offspring and is always meritorious and
good. In the second organization marital intercourse can be (1) without sin
when rendering the conjugal debt, or for the sake of procreation to increase the worshipers of God; (2) venial, if done for avoiding fornication;
and (3) mortal (*criminale*), when done immoderately for the sake of fulfilling pleasure.[22] Courson adopted a fourfold schema that had become

classic by the early thirteenth century since it is also found in the canonist Huguccio: Augustine's doctrine can be resumed in four "causes:" (1) offspring, (2) rendering marital debt, (3) restraining incontinence, and (4) fulfilling lust. The first two are without sin, the third with venial sin, and the last with mortal sin.[23] Chobham, however, produced the most articulated outline for married intercourse: (1) licit, including generating offspring, returning the conjugal debt, and avoiding fornication (only the first two, however, are meritorious); (2) fragile, because of the weakness of incontinence, which is a venial sin, excused from mortal because of the honor of marriage; and (3) impetuous, a mortal sin, which is subdivided among (a) satiating one's lusts through meretricious blandishments, (b) abusing one's wife unnaturally, (c) violating the prohibited times, (d) forcing oneself on a pregnant wife, and (e) scandalously copulating in public view.[24] These classifications modified two views of the Lombard. Rendering the marital debt was now excused of venial sin, but the satisfying of concupiscence, a venial sin in the Lombard's scheme, now became mortal.

How did these classifications of marital intercourse relate to the underlying issue of concupiscence or desire which threatened all sexual activity with moral guilt? Huguccio had replied that they evaluated only the marital acts themselves but did not remove the fundamental and ever-present sin of *voluptas*. In the schema of the Chanter's circle, however, the merits of marriage did cancel both mortal and venial sin for the two major "causes" of offspring and rendering the marital debt. (In the case of the latter, as we shall see, only the demander not the responder is responsible for the guilt involved.) Courson and Chobham were unequivocal that no sin is incurred in these two causes; only the Chanter hesitated that although the entire act of coitus is not sin, a venial stain might adhere, as one might say, a venial sin. All agreed that intercourse for the purpose of restraining incontinence is a venial sin, also excused from mortal guilt by the good of marriage. (Only Chobham exonerated the cause of restraining fornication from all sin.) Against Huguccio, therefore, the Parisian theologians concluded that the two primary motivations for marital intercourse were cleared from all guilt implicated in concupiscence.

By eliminating or reducing the sinful effects of sexuality in the first three categories, the Chanter and his circle were then free to devote attention to the analysis of sexual desire called into question by the fourth "cause" of marriage, the fulfilling of desire (*causa libidinis explende*). With some hesitation all consigned this category to mortal sin[25] and cited the authority of Sextus Pythagoricus first quoted by Jerome and transmitted by the Lombard. In a brief scriptural comment and Chanter defined *voluptas* by the Lombard's attribute of immoderation and slightly altered Sextus Pythagoricus's text to "a vehement lover (*vehemens amator*) of his own wife is an adulterer." Elsewhere in his commentary he explored the limitless character of sexual orgasm: in the heat of desire (*libido*), which cannot be greater, the whole man is so absorbed that he can neither do nor think of anything else. One can say that mind and body become one flesh because the pleasure of the body totally captures and enslaves the mind. Like Augustine, Pierre stressed the servitude and loss of control found in orgasm as the essence of sexual desire.[26] Within the category of impetuous intercourse Chobham developed his teacher's treatment of immoderation. Citing Sextus's dictum (combining both the Lombard's and the Chanter's versions), he followed Jerome's suggestion that the vehement lover is one who treats his wife as an adulteress or prostitute. Such husbands, he continued, delight in the beauty of their wives, the sweetness of their flesh, and in adulterous or meretricious caresses. Day and night they use their wives as couches on which they pour out their lust in lascivious kisses and shameful embraces. Their women are not treated as wives but as objects of desire (*libinose*). These spouses whom they can have at will are had for pleasure. Since women should be judged on the same terms, the priest should instruct both husbands and wives to follow what is appropriate to matrimony, not the persuasions of prostitutes.[27]

Despite this detailed elaboration, these conclusions remained conventional. Robert of Courson, however, ended his discussion of the four "causes" with an original twist.[28] The common man (*vulgus*), he objected, does not pay attention to the theologians' fourfold scheme. By popular custom the laity approach their wives with the sole concerns that they are joined in wedlock and that they wish to copulate with each other, but certainly not with predetermined goals. How do we counsel them when they have sex neither for children, nor for rendering the marital debt, nor for restraining incontinence, but simply for the fourth "cause," that is, satiating their appetite? If Augustine declared that such sins made one mortally guilty by fulfilling lust, how did he understand lust? Courson replied that Augustine does not exclude ways of knowing one's wife other than the four. Although the first three are without mortal sin, beyond those three there is a fourth category that is also without mortal sin. In such circumstances is the simple layman (*aliquis simplex*), who is not obliged to know the legal subtleties but approaches his wife naively (*simpliciter*) desiring to use her as his own wife (*ad uxorem tanquam suam volens uti sua*) without thinking more about one goal than the other. It should not be concluded that the laity are thereby condemned for loving (*diligunt*) their wives too tenderly (*nimis tenere*) or for coming to them frequently. When Augustine says that they sin mortally by fulfilling their lust, he means against nature or by immoderate means. Immoderation is condemned even in licit matters. That is the correct understanding of Sextus's passage (here quoted in the Chanter's version and attributed to Fulgentius). Just as one who eats too much risks gluttony, so the vehement and immoderate lover of his wife incurs mortal guilt from too much intercourse. In this final conclusion, however, Courson reduced the penalty of having sex with one's wife for the sake of desire from a mortal to a venial sin. In effect, he concurred with the Chanter's Scriptural commentary that in natural uses there is either no guilt or venial sin, unless the immoderate pleasure of lust (*immoderata libidinis voluptas*) intervenes.[29]

By defining, isolating, and reducing the peccaminious elements in the marriage act, the Chanter's school endeavored to alleviate the oppressive burden imposed on the laity by the Augustinian tradition of concupiscence recently exacerbated by Huguccio's pessimistic interpretation. After all, marriage was uniquely the laity's business which was either blameless or infected with venial sin at most. Robert of Courson concluded his tortuous discussion of the moral nature of the marital act by simply asserting that if common and simple married couples refrained from excess in their sexual activities, they need not be overly concerned with the theologians' ratiocinations.

Delectatio: The Physiology of Desire

The *Prose Salernitan Questions,* we shall see, defined coitus as the natural union of man and woman, which not only emitted sperm and produced a fetus but was also accompanied by great delight (*operis multa comitante delectatione*). In ancient medicine the element of desire was accepted as given but seldom subjected to further analysis except as a pathological disorder. Caelius Aurelianus, for example, had noted that sexual appetite (*appetentia veneria*) was present in women but this desire of the mind was insufficient for conception without physiological receptivity. Among the three essential elements of spirit, humor, and appetite enumerated in Constantinus Africanus's manual on male coitus, the last arose from imaginary thoughts (*ex cogitacione fantastica ortus*). Except noting, as did Galen, that appetite was associated with the liver, Constantinus did not pursue the subject further. Guillaume de Conches's encyclopedia occasionally mentioned desire in women, but it was the *Prose Salernitan Questions* that devoted greatest attention to sexual desire.[30] Not content merely to treat Guillaume de Conche's hypotheses, the compilers formulated new questions, repeated them three or four times, and responded with different solutions. Within the realm of sexuality desire became the dominant preoccupation of *Prose Salernitan Questions*.

The medical doctors exploited the same range of Latin vocabulary as did the theologians. They acknowledged the theological coinage of *concupis-*

centia but preferred the more neutral terms of libido (*libido*) and desire (*desiderium*); the elements of heat (*calor luxurie*) and fleshly stimulation—itching (*prurigo*) and tickling (*titillatio*) entered into their analyses, but their word of choice was undoubtedly "delight" (*delectatio*). Unlike the negative connotations of theological concupiscence, the medical use of delight assigned an unequivocally positive quality to physical pleasure. It was even commuted to joy (*gaudium*) when love (*amor*) was defined as "nothing other than delight with joy" (*nichil aliud sit quam delectatio cum gaudio*).[31]

The physiologists were fully aware of the opinions of their theological colleagues in the schools. When one Salernitan collection posed the leading question—Why was there greater delight (*delectatio*) in intercourse than in other actions?—the reply was divided into theological and medical responses. The former explained it by concupiscence which was infused into the human race by the first parents and now gives pleasure to all human creatures. (We shall see that medical theory [*physica*] accounted for it by the concentration of nerves in different parts of the body.) Another collection went as far as to propose a medical/natural diagnosis (*secundum phisicam*) for the theological doctrine of the Fall that accounted for the origin of concupiscence. God had created Adam as a being temperate in all his faculties and placed him in a temperate paradise, as is evident from the perennial flowers in the garden of Eden. If the environment had not been temperate, God would have been at fault. Inhabiting a temperate body, an instrument that seeks equilibrium, Adam's soul heard the serpent's words through Eve, began to think on them, and became anxious. Too much thought and anxiety (*cogitatio* and *sollicitudo*) overheated this natural balance. His soul, now encased in an intemperate instrument, began to seek immoderate things, and through intemperate appetite he thereby fell into sin.[32] To the biblical account and its theological elaboration the doctors offered a medical alternative. Their resulting theories on desire likewise proposed alternatives to concupiscence that accounted for sexual desire in terms of physiology and psychology.

The fundamental question, original to and often repeated in the *Prose Salernitan Questions,* was, Why is there so much delight (*tanta delectatio*) in coitus? The responding analyses can be divided between the internal physiology arising from nature and psychological externals which derive from the soul. The former elements were framed by the general physiology of coitus, which, we shall see, consists of three factors: spirit, heat, and humors. Generated by the major organs, the humors or fluids (blood and semen) pass through the body and generate heat. After the blood has been transformed into semen, it is expelled by spirit.[33] According to one analysis, as the humors move they are purged of their impurities and bad traces. This purification is accompanied by moderate itching and tickling. When the semen is emitted into the vulva through the penis, the whole action of the body and intent of the mind converge on this single operation, producing such immoderate delight that nothing else can be desired or done. A certain master Johannes Ieiunus explained that because all members release these superfluities at the same time, great delight follows. Another response concentrated on the superfluity of sperm that accumulates in and afflicts the body during periods of sexual abstinence. When it is expelled in coitus, the result is the delight of release. But why does its expulsion bring more delight than other superfluities? The moderate heat and moisture of the sperm is transmitted through the nervous parts, such as the penis, which is a veritable tail of nerves. By stinging the nerve ends the heat produces tickling, itching, and great pleasure. A third response directed attention to the nervous system itself. Some parts of the body, such as the genitals, possess concentration of nerves. When they are agitated by the whole body, the delight is small, but when the sperm is emitted the whole body experiences delight. A final response focused on internal actions preceding intercourse by which spirit and heat work on members while they dissolve the pure blood. As the members impel, whiten, and expel the fluids, they are debilitated but do not sense the loss while intent on performing their actions. Once accomplished, however, they begin to rejoice with natural desire.[34]

In addition to the physiological basis, the *Prose Salernitan Questions* also paid attention to the psychological dimensions of sexual desire. The ancient Greeks, seconded by the Latin theologians, had attached great importance to the role of the eyes in the inception of desire. The doctors attempted to explain how vision was relevant. Not only are the interior movements of humors mediated through suitable bodily instruments but also through the external forces of the soul. Spirit is transmitted by the optic nerve from the eyes which comprehend and encompass the externals and then represent their form to the soul. In Neoplatonic terms, the harmonies of the heavens and the lost memories of former felicity are recalled and thereby made available to the inferior bodies. When these intentions of the soul reinforce the physiological action of the body, the resulting delight is so intense that nothing more can be wished or done.

Psychology also explains why sexual desire is greater in humans than in other animals. Even if one has never had intercourse, nonetheless from hearing about the pleasure one greatly desires coitus. Through reason, humans know the sweetness of intercourse and are aroused to the deed. Lacking reason, however, animals are not moved except at specific times (spring, for example) when nature incites the appetite.[35] The concurrence of the soul's facilities of sight, hearing, memory, and reason, therefore, heightens the physiological pleasures to make *delectatio* of intercourse the most intense of all sensations.

A closely related problem, entailing both physiology and psychology was to account for postcoital sadness. After coitus has been accomplished and the humors and spirits are transmitted to designated members—the male instrument delivering the seed, the female drawing it to the place of conception—humans feel sorry for having committed a transgression. Despite rendering the natural obligation to generation and sufficient food to the fetus, the other members feel empty and destitute of life-giving strength. Nature is deprived of food and the spirit impoverished of sustenance. Renouncing exterior and interior elements of human nature, remembering lost strength, and numbed of former delight, one regrets to have exposed the weakness of the flesh. It was even asserted that intercourse, twice repeated, weakens the body more than the loss of a pound of blood. The explanation followed that the extraction and whitening of sperm from pure blood diminishes the food and debilitates the other members that would have been nourished by blood. Although ejaculation produces momentary exhilaration, the sense of loss returns quickly. Yet, after these feelings of debility and regret, humans nonetheless return to intercourse repeatedly. The human body is subject to daily incommodities, but it still has the capacity to recover. Renewed food and drink restore the humors and revive lost spirits. Most important, the unquiet soul stimulates the mind, remembers former delights, revives the appetite, and excites the desire to repeat. In sum, three causes encourage repetition of intercourse: the physiological discharging of superfluities, the replenishment of the bodily parts, and psychological fulfillment of desire.[36]

A single component of sexual desire that develops out of proportion to the whole was to be considered a pathology or disease. If the craving (*pruritum*) for intercourse, for example, becomes uncontrollable, it is called satyriasis. Muscio and Caelius Aurelianus described this disorder as a painful itching of the genitals that affects both men and women. Seeking to relieve themselves with their hands, the afflicted have an insatiable desire accompanied by total loss of modesty. In addition, Muscio noted the condition of an enlarged clitoris in which the flesh becomes erect like a man's and seeks intercourse with shame.[37]

The *Prose Salernitan Questions* were largely unconcerned with pathology, but the Parisian compilation attributed to a master Alain did discuss the subject of maniacal lovers (*amatores manicos*) who were troubled by excessive imagination and thought. This phrase undoubtedly evoked the classical pathology of sexual desire, the *amor heroicus,* which possessed a long tradition extending back into antiquity. Discussed at length by both philosophers and medical authorities, including Hippocrates, it was transmitted to the medieval West through Arabic commentaries. Constantinus Africanus provided the standard text when he translated the Arabic treatise *Zād-al-musāfir* into Latin as the *Viaticum*. Not only was the *Viaticum* a standard authority at Paris throughout the twelfth century, but further interest in *amor heroicus* was exhibited in the French schools around the turn of the century. In addition to master Alain of the *Prose Salernitan Questions* a physician, master Gérard de Bourges, wrote a commentary to Constantinus's text at the request of Parisian colleagues. Although both treatments were founded on Avicenna's psychology in the *De anima* available in Latin since the mid-twelfth century, Gerard's commentary makes further use of Avicenna's *Liber canonis,* which dates it somewhat later than Alain's, perhaps in the third decade of the thirteenth century.[38]

Examined in these three treatises, the *amor heroicus* fitted into the vocabulary and analysis of sexual desire current in the Salernitan questions. Since its symptoms are the pathological aggravation of sexual desire in men, its causes can be divided between the physiological and the psychological. Constantinus defined it as: "The love (*amor*), which is also called *eros*, is a sickness (*morbus*) that touches the brain. It is great desire (*magnum desiderium*) accompanied by too much concupiscence (*concupiscentia*) and affliction of thinking (*afflictione cogitationum*). Certain philosophers say that *eros* is the noun chiefly signifying delight (*delectationis*)." Instead of *morbus* Gérard named it a *passio* (suffering), designated by the authorities as "a melancholic care" (*sollicitudo melancolica*). Both authors emphasized that since the body and soul are linked, the physiological and psychological factors interact with each other, but for the purpose of analysis they can be separated.

According to Constantinus the physical symptoms are sunken eyes, heavy, yellow eyelids, sleeplessness, and hard, abnormal pulse. To these Gérard added the dryness of the eyes and the lack of tears, except in fits of weeping for the object of desire. For Constantinus the psychological symptoms are excessive thoughts and worries (*cogitationes nimias, sollicitudines*), even to the point of depression (*profundatur*). Alain called them too much thinking and imagination (*nimiam cogitationem et imaginationem*). In addition Gérard specified the lack of emotional control and the inability to respond to conversation except when the subject is the beloved.

The causes of love sickness were complex. Physiologically, Constantinus attributed it to an excess of humors, particularly of black bile, a diagnosis with which Gérard concurred when he described it as melancholia resulting from an imbalance in the humoral complexion. For Constantinus the chief psychological cause was the contemplation of beauty. In Neoplatonic terms, when the soul looks upon a form similar to itself, it approaches madness in seeking fulfillment of pleasure. To both Alain and Gérard the psychological causes were the result of the brain's malfunction.

We recall that the *Prose Salernitan Questions* isolated the psychological components of sexual desire as vision, hearing, reason, and memory, but they did not extend their analysis further. Both Alain and Gérard, however, insisted on complex interactions between physiology and psychology. Alain maintained that the soul imitates the natural operations of the body in all of its actions, and vice versa. Glossing Constantinus, Gérard reiterated that the body follows the actions of the soul just as an artisan uses a tool, and the soul responds to the body according to its complexions. Both Alain and Gérard adopted the Arabic schema of the threefold psychological faculties (*vis, virtutes*) that was rooted in Galenic medicine and transmitted to the West in Avicenna's *De anima*. Although Avicenna had disagreed with Galen over the ultimate seat of "animal" faculties, he did accept Galen's conclusion that sensation and passions resided in the brain. (For Avicenna the heart had delegated these faculties to the brain.) Subject to variation, Avicenna's scheme accordingly located three ventricles in the brain that performed the cogitative functions of (1) collecting sensations/imagination, (2) reason/estimation, and (3) memory. Although lacking anatomical foundation, the distinction among the faculties of *imaginativa, cogitativa/extimativa,* and *memorialis* made sense in the processing of information through the brain.[39]

Following this tradition, Alain distinguished among three cells. The first is called *fantasica,* imagination, or the appetite of the soul. It can be likened to physical digestion, which is hot and dry. The second is the rational (*rationalis*) or the discernment (*discretio*) of things imagined. Being hot and moist, it is also likened to digestion because it distinguishes good from bad just as the natural faculty separates the pure from the impure. The third is memory in which things imagined and discerned are stored. Like the natural faculty of retention, it is cold and dry. These three cells thereby provide a physiological explanation for the origins of *amor heroicus.* The soul imitates the operations of the body through the instrument of the spirit. If the appetite of the soul is denied the thing is desires, it heats up and becomes drier, thereby vaporizing the humors and stimulating the appetite further. This sets in motion a self-generating cycle that threatens to destroy the subject. If this can happen in the sensory ventricle of imagination, how much more in the rational cell, the locus of understanding and discernment. For this reason lovers deprived of their desires become mad on account of an excess of imagination and thought in the first two ventricles.[40]

Gérard de Bourges attributed *amor heroicus* to the complex malfunctioning of the central ventricle or the estimative faculty. This faculty mistakenly judges a certain woman to be better, more noble, and more desirable than all others. It transmits this error of judgment to the imaginative faculty by commanding it to fix its attention on that person, which in turn orders the concupisible faculty to desire that person alone. (Gérard was unsure where to locate the concupisible faculty.) In the process the estimative faculty's malfunction heats up the central ventricle excessively and thereby draws off heat and spirit from the imaginative faculty's ventricle which becomes increasingly cold and dry, thus producing fixation and melancholic imbalance. Although Alain's and Gérard's explanations of *amor heroicus* differed in particulars, they both attributed the cause to an imbalance of heat in the cognitive ventricles of the brain. To this physiological etiology Gérard added a social dimension when he observed that the afflicted are called *heros* (heroes) or noblemen because their wealth and ease of life cause them to suffer more than others.[41]

Since master Alain was primarily concerned with the operation of the cognative faculties, his remedy for *amor heroicus* was merely to compensate the appetite to prevent destruction or severe damage to the ventricles. The cures prescribed by Constantinus and Gérard attempted to respond to both the physical and psychological causes. Because coitus serves to expel superfluities, Constantinus recommended therapeutic intercourse—especially with a person who is not loved—to purge excess black bile. Gérard further asserted that a complete cure requires this remedy to restore the humoral imbalance. Frequent intercourse and the exchange of numerous partners is most effective. In addition, Constantinus, seconded by Gérard, urged the salutary effects of temperate drinking of fragrant wine. Gérard also concurred with Constantinus that a temperate bath produces similar effects, particularly because it moistens the desiccated body. Along with wine and baths, Constantinus proposed the creation of an agreeable environment to assuage the pain. Fragrant and beautiful gardens with clear flowing waters, the pleasant company of handsome men or women, the conversation of dear friends, music, and the recitation of verses calm the suffering psyche. To these distractions Gérard added hunting and other sports. A final resort was the Ovidian remedy (here called the counsel of old women) of denigrating the object of one's desire by recalling, for example, her foul smell.

Although Gérard de Bourge's proposal of therapeutic intercourse (without benefit of wedlock) was highly questionable to the theologians, his commentary on *amor heroicus* was nonetheless read in the theological faculty at Paris at least by 1235 when Hugues de Saint-Cher quoted him directly.[42] Those of the Chanter's circle, however, were already aware of the medical problem at the turn of the century. Thomas of Chobham raised four cases of unhealthy love (*insanum amorem*) which were treated as sickness (*morbus*) not only of the soul but of the body as well in which the marrow swells, the veins are disturbed, and all bodily senses are debilitated. Such defects are cured both by spiritual correction and by medical prevention. Since the four lovers were clerics, bishops prescribed their remedies. In two cases the clerics were distracted by threatening their benefices with litigation or sending them off on business to Rome until they forgot their obsessions. In a third, the matron was cured of love for a priest through psychological effects of jealousy produced by the discovery of a ring falsified as a *gage d'amour* from her lover in the possession of another woman. In the final case, a cleric, incorrigibly possessed by insane love for an adulteress, was locked up in a cell with his mistress. Compelled to serve the demands of love day and night until exhausted up to the crest of his tonsure, he was not released until he swore an oath to renounce her embraces. Thomas justified this theologically dubious therapy as casting out Satan by satanic means, but the contemporary physicians might well have recognized it as therapeutic intercourse.[43]

Thus far the medical discussions of sexual desire assumed little difference between men and women, an attitude resulting from the Galenic anatomical hypothesis that both the female as well as the male body possess testicles and, most specifically, the Hippocratic-Galenic doctrine of the two seeds. According to these ancient theories it was axiomatic that since both man and woman must ejaculate semen to achieve conception, both must experience delight at the emission of their respective seeds. This axiom of the reciprocity of desire, however, underlay one gender difference that was raised by Guillaume de Conches and the *Prose Salernitan Questions*. Although a woman's complexion is moist and humid, she is more fervent in desire than man. The heat of female desire resembles wet wood, which catches fire less readily but burns longer and more strongly. Since the uterus of the woman is cold and the male semen hot and dry, the uterus rejoices to receive it. Whereas a man experiences pleasure only in the emission of his seed, a woman has a twofold delight (*duplex delectatio*), both in the emission of her seed and the reception of the man's. The anatomist master Nicholas analyzed the uterus's tissues. While men are quickly aroused and quickly recede, corresponding to the ignition of straw, the composition of the woman's uterus is more like iron, which warms more slowly but holds heat longer.[44] Both in intensity and duration the female sexual desire is stronger than that of the male.

In a versified discussion of the aphrodisiac *Diasatyrion*, Gilles de Corbeil embellished this clinical observation with hyperbole fueled by misogynistic fear of female sexuality. The attempt to satisfy the female organ is the height of stupidity. Like Tartarus and the ocean, the mouth of the vagina cannot be filled. It can be wearied but never satisfied by frequent intercourse. It is the Greek fire which burns inwardly but undying; it cannot be extinguished by art. The more one struggles to beat it out, the fiercer it burns and rages with the blast of desire.[45]

Another issue, raised and resolved by Guillaume de Conches and the Salernitan collections, involved prostitutes, whose sexuality the physicians found more immediately accessible to scrutiny than other women. Why do these women, although extremely active sexually (like the celebrated Richeut of the fabliaux) rarely conceive? The answer lies not only in the nature of their wombs but also in the factor of desire. Because they engage in intercourse only at a price and, therefore, with no pleasure, they rarely emit seed with which to conceive. The absence of female delight necessary for conception thereby ensures the prostitute's infertility.[46] Why is it possible, it then followed, that a woman who has been raped nonetheless conceives, since she neither experiences pleasure nor willingly consents? The solution lay in dividing the human will between the rational and natural, which are often at odds. What displeases the rational can please the natural or carnal will. Although rape cannot influence the will of reason, carnal delight can be stimulated. When a modicum of desire has been induced, a raped woman emits seed and conceives. Who can doubt that the woman emits seed when her children display her likeness and even her defects? As Guillaume de Conches specified, although the act might be repugnant at the beginning, it eventually becomes agreeable because of the vulnerability of concupiscent flesh.[47]

The physicians frequently considered a final question also unique to women: Why do women continue to desire intercourse after conception unlike other animals? This problem not only recalled theological arguments but also demanded the full scope of medical analysis, both physiological and psychological. As reported in the medical literature, the theologians had maintained that before the appearance of sin there was no delight in coitus except in procreating offspring. After the Fall concupiscence was enjoined on the first parents as punishment and flowed from Adam into all rational animals, including women, but not into brutish animals.[48] A pregnant woman's continued sexual desire is, therefore, the result of concupiscence and original sin. The medical/natural explanation (*physica ratio*), however, was twofold. Physiologically and anatomically, according to the first response, the mouth of the uterus is closed at conception, thus retaining blood and other superfluities. Since this aggravates the uterus, a desire arises to expel the fluids, which, as we have seen, is normally satisfied by intercourse. The anatomist master Nicholas rejected this explanation which had been transmitted by Constantinus Africanus. The uterus does not close immediately after impregnation, he asserted, but only gradually with the growth of the fetus as it presses on the inner mouth. There the sensitive nerves touch each other and, feeling nothing, seek the joy of fulfillment. Wishing to satisfy this appetite, women willingly receive the male sperm, which, however, cannot reach the womb. When the nerves which are cold and dry sense the sperm which is hot and moist, they are inflamed with fervent desire.[49]

A second explanation more apposite to that of the theologians was founded on psychological speculation. Humans share properties in common with other creatures—that of substance with stones, of life and sensation with trees, of movement with animals, and of rationality with angels—but by their memory of the past and their conjecture of the future humans are different from animals, who have knowledge only of the present. Remembering past delights, therefore, a woman desires to repeat them. Although it is difficult to sustain the heat of fire for long, the fetus increases the woman's heat. Seeking delights to which she has become accustomed, she burns with more fervent desire. Or to rephrase the psychological argument, since animals lack the faculties of imagination and memory, they are incapable of retaining the past delights of intercourse but repeat them only at fixed seasons prompted by natural appetite for procreation. As rational animals, possessing imagination and memory, humans continue to feel concupiscence for the great delight of intercourse. (The vernacular gloss to Ovid's *Ars amatoria* recapitulated this argument by distinguishing the sexual patterns of beasts from those of woman by the latter's faculties of reason and memory.) Or in a third formulation, unlike beasts which are driven by nature according to seasons, women have discernment by which they recognize the pleasure of coitus and desire it even when pregnant.[50] As in sexual desire itself, the psychological faculties of imagination, discernment, and memory unique to humans reinforce the physiological factors in female desire after conception and thereby distinguish women from animals.

The agreement among the *Prose Salernitan Questions* over the two seed doctrine which guaranteed sexual desire to women—or even superiority over men—was not to remain unchallenged for long. The *Quaternuli* of David de Dinant, which were condemned at Paris in 1210, contained Aristotle's physiological theories affirming not only that women were imperfect men, that men alone generated seed, but also that conception itself was not linked to female delight. Aristotle observed that women frequently conceive without accompanying pleasure in coitus. When women do experience delight in intercourse, it comes not from the emission of seed but from spirit and from friction. Their delight resembles that of children whose genitals are yet unformed. Women, like men, can find delight in coitus as they emit superfluities (not seed, however), but this does not occur to all women or at all times.[51]

Aristotle's theory was reinforced by Augustine. Not only does the woman passively receive the male seed and produce fruit in Augustine's agricultural imagery, but female desire is unnecessary for conception. Within this framework the Church Father interpreted the passage in Genesis 20 where God prevents the women of Abimelech from conceiving.

This effect is achieved by removing sexual desire, but significantly the masculine desire is removed not the feminine. Because of male seed and corresponding female passivity, Augustine believed that women can willfully engage in sexual intercourse but without desire to stimulate them, even when the man is present to excite them sexually.[52] By conjoining delight directly to the female seed and conception, the Salernitan questions had constructed a physiological need for orgasmic pleasure for women as well as men. By disconnecting female desire from reproduction, Augustine's and Aristotle's one-seed theory rendered delight accidental to female sexuality.

Passio: The Ovidian Tradition

On one level of fiction Ovid's erotic poetry was a narration of sexual conquest. When consummation is achieved, the outcome is described as the joys of Venus (*Veneris gaudia*), especially in the *Ars amatoria,* which was, after all, an instructional manual composed for achieving this very effect.[53] In the *Amores,* however, where his objective, Corinna, is married and of difficult access, the poet is rewarded at times with contented languor, seldom with joy, but often with frustration. Pierced by Cupid's darts, love becomes a wounded beast, or to use the universal metaphor, a raging fire.[54] As in the Apostle Paul (1 Cor. 7:9), the theologians, and the physicians, fire is Ovid's preferred imagery for sexual desire in the *Amores.* "What is permitted is uninteresting, what is not, burns more sharply."[55] Cupid is at times a tender boy easy to master in the more sanguine *Ars,* but he can also become a beast who puts up a fight. "We [lovers] burn with fire. . . . Wakeful nights bring loss of weight. . . . Care (*cura*) and pain (*dolor*) are the results of our great love. . . . " Because of this suffering, "let every lover be pale; this is his suitable color."[56] If sexual desire is equated with malefic concupiscence in the theological tradition and with physical delight in the medical, the Ovidians approached desire with ambivalence. Although ecstatic joy was the expected goal, it was often accompanied by severe suffering. Implicated in this mingling of joy and pain was the fundamentally adulterous nature of Ovid's desire. Since Corrina was married, Ovid was condemned to jealousy's torments.

As a product of the schools, André the Chaplain was not only a spokesman for Ovid in the twelfth century but also thoroughly imbued with the vocabulary and doctrines of his learned colleagues. In addition to summarizing theological and medical theories, however, he also turned in Book I to constructing a theory of *amor* in which desire (*cupido*) and suffering (*passio*) played leading roles—all under the inspiration of Ovid.

When the noble lady announces to the seducer of the higher nobility that she is already married, they turn to debate whether the love as defined by André can exist between husband and wife in marriage. Against the woman's contention that her spouse can be both husband and lover, the man defends the negative conclusion by evoking the three theological "causes" justifying matrimony. Beyond affection for offspring and rendering the marital debt, no other solace is permitted the married couple. Echoing Jerome, he affirmed that it is more harmful to seek pleasure in one's spouse than in others, because as apostolic law teaches, a vehement lover (*vehemens amator*) of his own wife is adjudged an adulterer. Not only has the extreme pronouncement of the Stoic philosopher Sextus Pythagoricus been elevated to apostolic authority, but the most radical implications of the theological arsenal have been extrapolated against the survival of love in marriage.[57]

In addition to the theological schema, the man of the higher nobility acknowledges and refutes an argument of legal origin. The woman had maintained that the affection of her spouse's whole heart was a love not incompatible with André's *amor*. Her opponent, however, immediately identifies this martial affection (*maritalis affectio*) with the legal concept that had been one of the constituent elements of matrimony in Roman law. Marital affection was a state of mind, involving liking, fondness, and comfort appropriate to wedded couples—qualities exhibited, for example, in the marriage of Joseph and Mary. The Roman-law concept was of particular interest to canon lawyers because it implied consent between partners, the crucial factor in the ecclesiastical definition of the conjugal bond. The higher nobleman, on the contrary, contends that such affection has no place in the lexicon of love because it lacks the immoderate, furtive, and concupiscent qualities essential to *amor*.[58] Completely ignored by the theologians, this fruitful concept was acknowledged—if only with passing recognition—in André's encyclopedic handbook.

Throughout the treatise André remained fully conscious of theological vocabulary (for example, *concupiscere, peccati fomes* etc.), but nowhere did he endorse his theological colleagues' efforts to analyze and exculpate some form of sexual desire.[59] In Book III, the violent palinode against his own definition of *amor*, the vehemence of his language excluded all accommodation. The acts of Venus are shameful and nefarious, producing only continual sorrow and denying heaven's rewards. In both Testaments God detests and punishes not only extramarital intercourse but also any kind of pleasure associated with sexuality. Transmuting the term *concupiscentia* to *luxuria*, he agreed with Huguccio that lust or pleasure of the flesh can only be sinful. If God is the source of chastity and modesty, the devil is the author of love and *luxuria*. All evils, all crime are consequences of love—so damnable that even between spouses it can scarcely be tolerated as venial sin without mortal guilt.[60] While it is true that André's definition of *amor* exceeded the scope of sexual desire, the latter is nonetheless condemned by implication with the former. Huguccio's sole qualification of venial sin is the closest that the Chaplain came to saving sexuality from total rejection in Book III.

André was sufficiently conversant with medical theory to quote from standard school treatises and turn them to his particular purposes.[61] This familiarity likewise informed his vocabulary on sexual desire. The neutral terms of *cupido* and *libido* were linked with the natural sexual drive shared with animals. By the instinct of desire, for example, all humans are naturally aroused with lust for persons of the opposite sex. Those who commingle their lust with every woman they see act like dogs or donkeys moved only by nature.[62] When focusing exclusively on human desire, André employed the standard medical term of *delectatio* (delight), alternating with *voluptas* (pleasure) as a synonym, but usually modified by adjectives denoting flesh or body (*carnis, carnalis, corporalis*) to make the physical connotation explicit. *Delectatio* was employed when he defined, in opposition to pure love, a mixed love (*mixtus amor*) that devotes every delight of the flesh to the final act of Venus. André had written the first part of this treatise to instruct his protégé on how to obtain all the pleasures of the body through love.[63] Although familiar with the physicians' terminology, André ignored the physiological analysis into spirit, heat, and humors. Only the quality of craving or itching may have been implied in the word *vexatur* (to be troubled).[64] Like most writers, however, he could not overlook the metaphor of fire. To enunciate incredulity over the possibility of pure love, the woman of the higher nobility declares that it is prodigious for anyone to be "placed in fire without being burned," an expression publicized by Pierre the Lombard.[65]

Closely associated with the physicians' notion of carnal delight was Ovid's expression of joy, but André took little notice of his ancient master's *gaudium*, preferring his own term of *solatium* (solace) for the pleasure of sexual intercourse. Thus love alone ministers the sweet solaces of delight and substitutes happy joys for the bonds of grief. In the radical repudiation of Book III theological values finally usurp the Ovidian terminology. The ancient joys of the flesh yield to eternal joys of heaven to which the momentary delights of the flesh must finally accede.[66] For André, therefore, *passio* or suffering became an important element in the definition of *amor*. Echoing the Latin poet—so many are the pangs we suffer in love—Ovid's medieval spokesman fashioned both a noun and a concept that was only adumbrated in the master.[67]

To quote André's celebrated definition: "*Amor* is a certain innate suffering (*innata passio*) that proceeds from sight of (*visione*) and immoderate thinking (*immoderata cogitatione*) about the appearance of someone of the other sex. It makes one wish above all else to obtain the embraces of the other and by the will of both to fulfill in these embraces all the commands of love." Evoking the analogy of fishing, he followed with an etymology: "The noun *amor* comes form the verb *amo* that means to catch or be caught. He who loves is caught on the line of desire and desires to catch the other on his hook (*hamo*) as well. Just as the experienced fisherman tries to catch fish on a barbed hook (*hami unco*), so the man caught by love tries to attract the other with enticing bait." Although André neglected physiology, he was willing to consider the psychological analyses current among the physicians. In the concluding statement to the first chapter, he formulated a summary definition of love that incorporates three factors prominent in contemporary medical discussion: "This [love] is therefore innate suffering (*passio innata*) from (1) vision (*ex visione*) and (2) thought (*cogitatione*) . . . and (3) it must be immoderate (*sed immoderata exigitur*)."[68]

The physicians had demonstrated how desire is stimulated through the eyes which mediate visual forms to the soul by transmitting spirit through the optic nerves. For André as well love begins with vision. Blindness, therefore, is an impediment to love because a blind man cannot supply the mind with visual objects necessary for thought. Although love acquired before blindness can survive, it cannot grow. The gaze of eyes, therefore, joins meditation and the sexual acts as means for perfecting love.[69] When the nobleman seeks to seduce a noblewoman, his initial request is to ask permission to look at her physically in order to assuage his torments. To the noblewoman, moreover, the bourgeois lover confesses that it is through sight that he has been wounded by love's arrows.[70] The vernacular commentary to the *Ars amatoria* likewise corroborated André's emphasis upon the eyes. Employing images reminiscent of Chrétien de Troyes, it compared love to the subtlety of sunlight. Just as light passes through a window and illuminates a room without damaging the glass, so love passes through the eyes and strikes the heart without the eyes feeling pain. We shall see that desire is revealed by a woman's eyes, particularly when she closes them in orgasmic ecstasy.[71]

Vision, however, is only a gateway into the mind where love as *passio* is truly generated. At this point André took advantage of the broad semantic spectrum of *passio* which signified not only suffering but also a mental activity, such as passion or emotion. "This *passio* is innate (*innata*)," he explained, "which can be demonstrated by the argument that it arises not from any action but solely from the thought which the mind conceives from what it sees. When a man sees a woman ready for love and formed to his choice, he immediately begins to lust for her in his heart. Thinking about her he burns with greater love and attains greater thought. As he thinks about her form, he desires to imagine his own acts, to search out the secrets of her body, and to take possession of each of her members. After full cognition has been achieved, love can no longer hold back, but proceeds immediately into action."[72] Despite the compulsion for physical expression, highest love is formed in the mind. As opposed to mixed love, pure love joins the hearts of two lovers in delightful affection. It consists of the mind's contemplation as well as the heart's affections. Although it may proceed through the steps of love, it omits the final solace. Just as the head is judged the most worthy part of the body, in which shape the Creator made humans in his image, likewise love of the upper part of the body is superior to the lower.[73] Summing up his love doctrine is epigraphic form, André included among his rules of love: (XXIV and XXX) "Every act of a lover is oriented toward the thoughts of his beloved," and "a true lover is occupied with the constant and unceasing imagining of his beloved."[74]

André's analysis of the mental operations of *amor* in fact resembled one theory in the *Prose Salernitan Questions* that explained the origins of sin through intemperance. After listening to the serpent and Eve, Adam began to think and become anxious about their words. Too much thought and worry heated up his natural balance and caused him to sin.[75] Although André's discussion of the mental components of love fitted into the physicians' physiology, his analysis was not as refined. He made little effort to distinguish between thinking (*cogitatio*) and imagination (*imaginatio*) and completely neglected the factor of memory.[76] This simplistic treatment contrasted with the more articulated theories of the doctors who distinguished reason, discretion, estimation, imagination, and memory, arranging them in hierarchy as they examined the origin and renewal of sexual delight and the reoccurrence of sexual desire among pregnant women. Whereas both André and the physicians were agreed on the importance of the psychological dimension, the doctors privileged it over physiology, but André neglected the physical etiology altogether.

Throughout André's discussion he repeatedly laid emphasis on the quality of immoderation (*immoderata cogitatio*).[77] Immoderate thoughts, in turn, lead to excessive sexual desire. Unlike marital affection, which is comfortably complacent, the affection of love is excessive and immoderate or, again, follows from an immoderate desire for fleshly delight.[78] As the higher nobleman defines it, "Love is none other than the excessive desire to obtain furtive, concealed and lascivious embraces"—indeed, approaching the passionate lover condemned by the theologians.[79] By continually repeating the term *immoderata*, André deliberately placed his concept of *amor* in opposition to the martial desire judged licit by contemporary theologians. From the Lombard through Courson we have seen that *immoderata* was the quality consistently condemned in sexual desire, to which

Sextus's *vehemens amator* had become the classic example. When André opposed his own theory in Book III, he returned the theological doctrine of moderation. Alluding to the biblical examples of Solomon and David, the Chaplain concluded that no matter how wise the man, once he has been seduced by Venus's deeds he loses all sense of proportion, all restraint against the lethal act and the will to moderate the movements of lust.[80]

One Salernitan question had observed that when the penis emits seed into the womb, the entire body works together with the soul to the accompaniment of such immoderate delight that one cannot wish anything else.[81] This rare use of the term *immoderate* was employed to explain why sexual intercourse produces so much delight; otherwise, immoderation was not associated with healthy sexuality. For the physicians genuine excess appeared in the pathology of *amor heroicus* which Constantinus Africanus characterized as the affliction of too much thinking, or by master Alain as too much thinking and imagination.[82] André's *amor*, therefore, appears to share psychological symptoms with the medical disorder. In particular, André noted that those afflicted by love are often inattentive to conversation, unless the beloved is mentioned, a symptom which Gérard de Bourges also noted. André's *amor*, moreover, was treated chiefly by aristocratic interlocutors. Gérard called *amor heroes* because *heroes* are noblemen who are susceptible because of riches and ease of life.[83] Except for sleeplessness, an observation derived from Ovid, André paid little attention to the physiological symptoms (sunken eyes, dryness, heavy pulse, etc.). He rejected Constantinus's unequivocal *morbus* (sickness) for the less extreme *passio* (suffering) which was later adopted by Gérard de Bourges as well.[84]

Like Ovid, André the Chaplain was fundamentally ambivalent about *amor* as *passio* (involving both thought and suffering). Although the bourgeois man can confidently assert that love is the origin and cause of all good, André himself provided only a brief chapter enumerating the benefits of love. Eliminating greed, endowing beauty, humility, and chastity, it enables humans to shine with virtue, but André devoted disproportionate attention to the ills of love.[85] Paleness, the hallmark of Ovid's lover, likewise characterizes André's woman when she catches sight of her beloved.[86] Like Ovid's, the Chaplain's *amor* is thoroughly infected with jealousy arising form the extramarital circumstances. Book III catalogued at least seventeen arguments against love, the last of which turned to physical disabilities. In the section where physicians were explicitly acknowledged, André argued that lovers lose strength through sexual intercourse, fail to receive nourishment from food and drink, and spend sleepless nights. Their life span is shortened, and they are increasingly susceptible to physical illness, premature senility, derangement and insanity.[87]

After a rapid catalogue of love's failings, André turned to an equally summary enumeration of female vices. As might be expected from conventional misogyny, he noted that all women are lustful (*luxuriosa*) without exception. No matter the social disparity, a woman will rut after a potent man, but no man, whatever his virility, will be able to satisfy a woman.[88] The Chaplain had discussed the sexual relations between men and women for two lengthy books without focusing directly on gender differences, but in these few lines he evoked the conventional topos of the insatiable woman for which the physicians' theory of twofold pleasure offered partial explanation and which, as we shall see, the fabliaux explored in *La dame qui aveine demandoit*.

Ovid, himself, had laid little emphasis on gender differences in his erotic poetry, but his thirteenth-century commentator added scattered observations. Citing the authority of Trotula, for example, he noted that women like to be propositioned, even forced to make love. In a series of glosses to Ovid's allusions to Byblis, Myrrha, Pasiphae, and other mythological figures, he demonstrated that feminine love is more tormented and uncontrolled than masculine.[89] When dealing with Ovid's observation that women conceal love better than men, the vernacular glossator added that female desire is like burning coals covered with ashes. They burn with greater heat, intensity, and duration than the more open passions of men. This explanation resembled the physicians' analogy of green wood. In place of the medical theory of the twofold delight, the commentator substituted Ovid's myth of the judgment of Tiresias as an explanatory device. Although the Latin poet apparently assumed that male and female desire were comparable in his erotic verse, in the *Metamorphoses* he recounted the dispute between Jupiter and Juno over who derived greater pleasure (*voluptas*) from sex, men or women. When the two deities failed to agree, they chose as arbitrator the wise man Tiresias who had observed the mating of serpents and had spent eight years of his life as a woman. Siding with his own sex, as was to be expected, he granted the decision to Jupiter who had contended that women have greater pleasure. Although Ovid's version was susceptible to nuanced and ambivalent interpretations, the thirteenth-century vernacular glossator simply affirmed that women are "hotter" (*plus chault*) than men.[90] The Ovidian commentator ignored the medical doctrine that women's humoral complexion was cold but nonetheless concurred with the conclusions of the specific theory of twofold female delight.

Joie et dolor: **Their Interplay in the Romance Tradition**

We shall see that romanciers consistently refused to name the sexual act explicitly but preferred to suggest its presence with words denoting pleasure. *Joie, delit, deduit,* and *solas,* the vernacular equivalents of Ovid's *gaudium,* the physicians' *delectatio,* and André's *solatium* became the standard terminology for intercourse. Like the medical treatises and the fabliaux, the romance tradition rooted sexuality in the linguistic soil of joy. Since these pleasurable qualities were emotions, they served to convey feelings of sexual desire. Unlike the physicians and fabliaux writers, however, the romance authors agreed with the Latin Ovidians that joy was accompanied by suffering. This affliction resulted not only from the adulterous frustrations of the Roman poet but also from a more elemental feeling which André the Chaplain codified as innate suffering. At the heart of human sexuality was an alternation between joy and suffering. By the mid-twelfth century the troubadour poets of southern France had formulated the basic vocabulary and literary conventions for expressing this polarity between *joi, deport,* and *solatz* on one hand, and *dolor, sofrir, mal, pena, trist,* and *afan* on the other. Planted at the center of human emotion, this alternation affected the realms of love and of sexual desire as well. The faculty of desire, including sexual desire, was articulated by a rich vocabulary in Provençal, including *talen, dezir, voluntat, enveja,* and their cognates.[91] With slight adjustments, the northern trouvères and romanciers adopted a lexicon and syntax for love and sexual desire that paralleled the troubadours. In the parlance of the northern *langue d'oil, joie et dolor* became the ubiquitous commonplace of the romance idiom.

The full spectrum of these emotions can be found in northern romance as early as Marie de France's lais. Her Anglo-Norman diction nourished a predilection for the term *talent* popular with the troubadours and fabliaux. Guigemar, for example, has no *talent* for women or girls (v.64); the queen levies the same charge against Lanval (vv.279–82).[92] Not only could Marie's lovers expect their desire to be rewarded with *pleisir* (*Laüstic,* v.48), *delit* (*Yonec,* v.220), and *joie* (*Yonec,* v.271; even for Tristan and Iseut, *Chevrefoil,* v.94), but they were also certain to suffer. The shaft of love wounds Guigemar more sorely than the huntsman's arrow (vv.380–84), bringing loss of color and sleep. The same arrow strikes Equitan (vv.54–64), and the same suffering afflicts Guilliadun after she sees Eliduc (vv.300–306). Sighs, trembling, paleness, fainting, and tears become the rituals of the *anguissuse / anguissusement* of Marie's lovers (for example, *Guigemar,* v.104).[93] Common to all discourses, love ignites with a spark and sets fire to the heart (*Lanval,* vv.117–19; *Guigemar,* vv. 390–91). While vision is usually responsible for starting the conflagration, it is the sole fuel for desire in *Laüstic* (vv.77–78).

The Tristan legend and its successors accorded similar treatment to these topoi. The unhappy fate of the celebrated lovers uncover both the agonies of adultery and the deep-seated tension between the joys and griefs of love. Enough has survived of the Anglo-Norman fragments of Thomas of Britain to demonstrate that this early version of the legend paid particular attention to the lovers' sufferings—exacerbated by their separation. Like André, Thomas wished to instruct his audience in love. Embellishing the story as an example (*essample*) to please lovers, he sought to offer comfort against change, injury, pain, grief, and all the tricks of love (p.163, vv.831–39). This programmatic statement is notable for its omission of pleasure. Although *joie, delit, deduit* occur in Thomas's verses, they are nearly always associated with bodily pleasures. Rarely enjoyed by the lovers, the joy is continually coupled with pain. While contemplating Iseut's image in the hall of statues, for example, Tristan recalls the delights of their great love but obsesses over the litany of their misery: travail (*travaus*), grief (*dolur*), pain (*paignes*), and torment (*ahans*, p.69, vv.1–4). During a brief and rare reunion, Tristan has pleasure with Iseut but only to console their grief (p.114, vv.721–23). Like the southern troubadours of Provence, their constant state of mind is that of grief, pain, anguish, and torment, the consequence of their inability to fulfill desire. Of all the romance authors, Thomas assembled the richest vocabulary and created the most developed sense of desire.

Again like André, Thomas proposed a judgment of love to his audience: consider this strange love among the four lovers. All have pain and grief; each lives in sadness, and none has pleasure from it. Although King Marc loves and desires (*aime et desire*) no one but Iseut and has the delight of her body, he suffers never-ending grief whether he wants to or not (*quel talent*) because another has her heart. Whereas the king has one torment, Iseut la Blonde has two. She has what she does not want (*ne volt*); cannot have what she does want. She cannot take delight in Marc's body because she does not want his heart. On the other hand, she desires (*desire*) and cannot love anyone but Tristan, but her husband forbids her to speak to him. Tristan likewise suffers from double pain and grief. He is married to Iseut aux Mains Blanches whom he does not love or desire (*ne amer ne volt*). Nor can he abandon her whatever his wish (*talent*). When he embraces her, he has little delight except for the sound of her name. He has grief for what he has, and more for what he does not have, the beautiful Queen Iseut, his *amie,* who is his life and death. Finally, there is Iseut aux Mains Blanches who desires (*desire*) her husband, has him but is not able to obtain delight from

him. She is in the opposite position from Marc. She desires to have pleasure by offering kisses and embraces, but Tristan cannot allow himself,
and she will not ask more.

Thomas confessed that he does not know who has the greater anguish
(*angoisse*) among the four and asks the lovers in his audience to make a
judgment: Who was better in love, or who had the greater pain without it
(pp.72–75, vv.71–151)? His four cases are, without doubt, asymmetrical,
each conditioned by differing circumstances, but within the differences
Thomas ignored gender distinction. In single grief the male Marc is paired
with the female Iseut aux Mains Blanches; in double, Iseut la Blonde with
Tristan. Despite the particular circumstances a symmetry is constructed
that undercuts the lines of gender. Although the surviving fragments allow more space to Tristan's agony, Iseut's pain is equally intense. She sighs
in her chamber for Tristan whom she desires so much (*tant desire*). She
thinks of nothing else in her heart except her love for Tristan (p.59,
vv.649–52).

Also like André's lovers, Tristan's and Iseut's suffering is accompanied
with intense cogitation, but Thomas, like the southern troubadours, situ-
ates these thoughts, not in the head but in the heart (*cuers*).[94] In her chamber Iseut thinks in her heart about her beloved (p.59, v.651). In the hall of
statues Tristan agonizes in his heart over Iseut's fidelity giving vent to
thoughts and reveries (p.69, vv.7–8), yet earlier he feels through his heart
that her heart remains true (p.36, vv.55–58). By designating the heart as
the seat of thinking and feeling, Thomas posited a fundamental distinction
between heart and body. Although Marc enjoys Iseut's body, he does not
have her *corage* (heart, p.72, v.85). Similarly, Iseut has Marc's body, but
does not want his heart (p.73, v.99). The dolorous separation of heart and
body, therefore, produces the unavoidable suffering of adulterous love.

After such pain and unfulfilled desire, death is the sole resolution.
Within the French corpus the death scene survived only in Thomas.
Tristan dies for both the grief and love of his *amie;* Iseut for pity of Tristan.
Arriving too late, she embraces her dead lover, kisses his face and mouth,
and, in turn, yields up her spirit. Thomas describes the last embrace of
physical love in the conventional posture of romance—she strains body to
body and mouth to mouth—but without the conventional reward of
romance—*joie et delit* (p.162, vv.809–19).

If Thomas laid stress on the lovers' anguish, Béroul viewed the legend
from the perspective of the magic potion that had initiated the tragedy.
Although the potion was technically effective for only three years, in
Béroul's fragment the entire story falls under its spell. Relieved of moral
responsibility because of the magic's force, the lovers are free to resort to
deception, trickery, and even perjury. In the opening scene they deliber-

ately misrepresent their situation to Marc who hides up a tree and over-hears their contrived conversation. In the penultimate episode of the or-deal Iseut swears her infamous equivocal oath (vv.4199–4213). Even the religious hermit recruited to reconcile the queen with the king asserts that it is necessary at times to lie a little to avoid shame (vv.2353–55). Although technically adulterers, both lovers protest throughout that their love is not a mere affair (*drüerie*, vv.33, 130), nor base love (vv.34, 57, 502, 4165), nor whoredom (vv.4166, 4194). Who can be in love for two or three years without discovery (vv.573–75)? Béroul disclaimed, but this appears to be precisely what the lovers have accomplished. After the potion wears off, Iseut formally renounces carnal relations (*la commune de mon cors*, v.2329), but the audience is permitted to doubt whether she will keep her word.

Protected from accountability, Tristan and Iseut suffer less than in Thomas. They flee from Marc into the forest, where they endure extreme physical and social deprivation, although neither feel the pain but rather share great happiness (vv.1784–87). Falling asleep in the wooded bower, they are not disturbed by thoughts but lie together in peace (vv.1829–31). The power of the potion so controlled their lives, Béroul affirmed, that each could say: Life is no burden (vv.2143–46). Love's agony, desire's un-fulfillment, and adultery's disjunction posed fewer problems in this ver-sion of the Tristan legend.

Chrétien de Troyes, who had offered his own version of the *Roi Marc et d'Ysalte la blonde*, now lost, wrote still another in his romance *Cligès* which so radically revised the legend that it may be considered a neo-Tristan or perhaps an anti-Tristan. Already in an early lyric Chrétien had taken a stand against Bérouls's *Tristan*. Addressing his lady in the troubadour manner, the poet avows that he never imbibed Tristan's poison; nonethe-less, his true heart and pure desire (*bone volentez*) produced a love more worthy because it was never forced upon him but entered freely through his eyes.[95] In *Cligès*, Chrétien adapted the Tristan themes to two genera-tions of couples. The first, Soredamor and Alexandre, are young like Tristan and Iseut but unmarried and, therefore, innocent of adultery. Soredamor, however, has disdained love for which insult *Amors* teaches her a lesson. Wounded with love's arrow, both she and Alexandre share all of the pangs suffered by Tristan and Iseut. The parallel with the legendary lovers is clearly conveyed by having them fall in love on shipboard, thereby permitting Chrétien opportunity to revive Thomas's celebrated pun (transmitted in Gottfried, vv.11, 989–12, 019) linking *la mers* (the sea), *la mer* (bitterness), and *l'amor* (love, vv.541–44). The legendary lexicon of suffering becomes their own: *dolonte, dolor, paine, mal, engoisse, soffert,* and the signs of love are further elaborated. Drawing on Ovidian and trou-badour precedents, Soredamor and Alexandre sigh, change color, turn

pale, tremble, and pass sleepless nights, effects that become classic in romance. Love heats a bath that both scalds and pleases Soredamor (vv.464–
67). For Alexandre it is a fire that sears the closer he approaches it; like
burning embers it conceals intense heat beneath ashes (vv.590–600). Alluding to the physicians' theories on lovesickness and perhaps to Béroul,
where the potion reigns, Alexandre protests that his madness has exceeded
the healing of potions, medicine, or even doctors (vv.623, 639–49). Like
Thomas's audience, Chrétien's would have had difficulty in deciding
which of the two lovers suffered more. Love imparts to them equally (*igau-
ment*), Chrétien declared, the gifts which are owed. He did it with equity
and right because both loved and desired (*covoite*) each other (vv.524–27.
Thus the one complains and then the other; one hides from the other; the
days go badly, the nights worse, so great is their pain (vv.1039–42).

Amor's arrow takes the form of the beloved's beauty and passes through
the eye to reach the heart. We have seen that eyes played an initial role
among theologians, physicians, and André, but it was perhaps Chrétien
who provided the most complex analysis.[96] It is the custom of all lovers,
Chrétien affirmed, to feed their eyes with mutual glances (vv.584–86).
Both Soredamor and Alexandre reproach their eyes bitterly for injury to
their hearts (vv.468–72, 684–96). Not only transparent glass through
which the beloved's image is received, the eyes are also reflective mirrors
to the heart (v.704) but, most important, active agents that war against the
heart. The heart, in turn, sits in the chest as a lighted candle in a lantern
(vv.708–10). The seat of thinking, it is also the source of desire. My heart
should not desire (*voloir*), Soredamor complains, that which makes me
suffer. It is desire itself that gives pain (vv.500–502). Observing their torments, Queen Guinièvre finally arranges an honorable marriage. Although heart and body are now united (vv.2304–6), Chrétien dwells little
on the lovers' happiness. Not wanting to waste words on ceremonies, he
limited their marriage to four lines, of which only one noted joy and pleasure (vv.2316–22).[97] Three months later Soredamor is pregnant with a
son, Cligès.

Cligès and Fenice replicate the experience of the first generation. Their
color changes; they turn pale, tremble, cannot eat or drink, lose sleep,
sense, and memory. They too suffer from *angresse, doloir, travaille,* and
painne. Reviving the heat metaphor, Chrétien asserted that he who wishes
to love must know fear, because without fear love is fire without heat
(vv.3847–56). In this second generation, however, the pain and sickness
has become sweet and the suffering a joy (vv.3042–44, 3073–74). *Amors*
tortures Fenice, but the torments are a delight (vv.4527–29). As with the
parents, love begins with the eyes and passes to the heart. Fenice places her
eyes and heart in him, and he promises her his heart, thus uniting two

hearts in one body. Chrétien explained this apparent paradox as the desire (*volonté*) of one passing to the other. Because they want one thing together it can be said that each has the other's heart, or they are like different persons singing in harmony (vv.2768–2805).

The second generation, however, experiences a kind of suffering not known to the first. Fenice and Cligès repeat the marital configuration of Iseut and Tristan. The former is the wife of the emperor/king (Alis or Marc), the latter his nephew. Although their love is formally adulterous, Fenice explicitly refuses on two occasions to follow Iseut's example to engage her heart intact to one while dividing her body between two leasers. In contrast, Fenice steadfastly will not separate heart from body (vv.3111–20). Her solution is to turn the magic potion of the Tristan legend against adultery. Whereas the potion is fatal in Thomas, in *Cligès* it brings happiness (v.3265). With one draught she drugs her husband, thereby shielding herself from the marital debt; with the other she feigns death to gain access to her lover. After the impostured funeral, the couple finally unite in the secret tower and taste the *joie, eise, deduire,* and *delit* that is their due. Like Béroul, Chrétien has used magic to absolve his lovers from the guilt of adultery. Despite appearances, Fenice has maintained an undivided union of heart and body. After Alis's death, Cligès legitimizes his desire for Fenice in public matrimony, thereby transforming his *amie* to his *dame* and confirming the union of heart and body (vv.6633–38).

Jean Renart's *Escoufle* also presents two generations of couples comparable to those in the Tristan legend and *Cligès*. The first consists of an arranged match between Count Richard and the lady of Genoa whom the emperor brings together and weds as befitted the high nobility. Dispatched in short order, the marriage is announced one week in advance; the pair enjoys a surfeit of love on their wedding day and on that night their *deduit,* thus promptly conceiving the lover of the next generation (vv.1736–53).[98]

From first days of infanthood their son Guillaume forms a second couple with Aelis, the emperor's daughter, who was also born on the same day. Jean distinguishes his precocious couple from two other child couples whose tormented love ended in tragedy. Guillaume's love was not like that of Piramus and Tisbé, a story first found in Ovid and expanded in a French version of the twelfth century.[99] Piramus had killed himself when he found Tisbé's bloody guimpel because he believed that she was killed by a lion. On better counsel, Jean advised, Piramus should have resisted this conclusion (vv.6360–79). Nor did Guillaume act like Tristan whose death was produced by the potion which Brangien gave him to drink. Taking Chrétien's stance against Béroul, therefore, Jean stressed that it was compulsion (*force: force voire!*) that led to the tragic dénouément (vv.6352–58).

Having rejected Tristan's example of this central point, Jean nonetheless retained the legendary pair as models for young love, comparing Guillaume and Aelis at every important turning point.

Raised together in the girl's nursery after the age of three, Guillaume and Aelis are even more precocious than Piramus and Tisbé. Within two years they have already learned the pleasure of the names *ami* and *amie* (vv.1981–89), but *Amors*, however, does not spare the children. As their eyes feed on each other, they experience the classic traits of anguish (*angoisse*), accompanied by sighs and sobs—which their glances cannot conceal (vv.1992–2003). With the emperor's announcement to marry the two, their suffering turns to joy. Like Cligès, Guillaume now calls his *amie* his *dame;* their conversations and their delights are no longer concealed but are enjoyed in the open (vv.2362–74).

Thereafter, alternations between grief and joy are set in motion. The reversal of the emperor's decision and separation provoke distress and deep cogitation. Unhappy, grieving, and miserable (*las, dolans, caitis*), Guillaume goes to bed that night to reflect on his lost joys and delights (*joie et delit*) (vv.3113–17, 3198–99). He regrets that he does not have Tristan's guile, experience, or astuteness to contrive occasions to come together in the forest or town (vv.3122–37). That night Aelis also laments their fate, and like André the Chaplain defines love (*aim*) as a hook (*haim*) that has caught them both (vv.3247–49). Their rendezvous in the garden and Aelis's chamber to plot an elopement transforms pain into great joy (vv.3544–45). Resuming kisses and embraces, Guillaume compares Aelis's beauty to the renowned Iseut's. No one can say that the queen was wise and beautiful except by hearsay and custom, but he has the testimony of his eyes and sight (vv.3450–59). Their elopement is filled with lovers' delights (*soulas, delis, deduis,* vv.4294). At the fountain near Toul, Aelis, like Iseut, bestows on her friend a ring by which she accords her body and love, for which Guillaume reciprocates his heart (vv.4488–99). When the buzzard steals the purse and ring, Guillaume contrasts his carelessness with Tristan's renowned courtesy, who kept the queen's ring for many years (vv.4616–21). The consequent separation revives all the sighs, tears, and suffering of *dolor* (vv.4750–55, 5164–69).

After years of fruitless wandering, the lovers' final reunion at Saint-Gilles restores their *joie et liece* (vv.7707). Those witnessing the event marvel at what *Amors* has done. Through the windows of their eyes their glances interlace one heart with the other. Not even Iseut and Tristan had known such a life (vv.7816–23). In an episode suggestive of the legendary tale, their beds were placed close to each other. Whereas Tristan made his passionate leap, Jean Renart refused to say what happened but observed that he who shivers before the fire willingly warms himself by drawing closer. With a little flip of the hip she could slip in next to him (vv.7864–

84). Since the troubadours and the Tristan legend, the romanciers had employed the fire metaphor for sexual desire as a raging, destructive force. Like one fabliau author, as we shall see, Jean Renart characterizes·it as a comforting, pleasant sensation. After the lovers have finally been reunited in bed, the legitimating marriage comes as an anticlimax; the *Escoufle*, like Chrétien's *Cligès*, wastes few verses on connubial bliss (vv.8329–33).

In the *Lai de l'ombre* Jean Renart returned to the Tristan legend, but this time more appropriately to recount a tale of adultery. Tristan remains the archtypical exemplar. The knight explicitly exceeds Tristan's skills at chess and fencing (vv.104–5), as Guillaume had implicitly done in *Escoufle* (vv.2018–33). Although Tristan feigned madness to gain access to Iseut, he did not endure a third of the knight's sufferings (vv.124–27). Both venture into love like Tristan putting out to sea without a mast (vv.456–57). The knight had had the pleasure of many ladies in his day but never ventured his service or homage. *Amors* (now a lady), who masters those under her dominion, wishes to exact tribute for this insolence (vv.112–19). Struck by an arrow fashioned from the lady's beauty, which lodges up to the feathers in his heart (vv.128–31), he is afflicted continually by the pains of *ahan, grant soufret, maus,* and *destroiz. Joie, solas,* and *delit* return only in his thoughts or at night when he dreams of her embraces. Awaking he reaches out to touch the body that causes him to burn (vv.144–84). His stratagem of casting a ring to her reflection in the well—a *cortoisie,* Jean affirmed, unsurpassed since Eve induced Adam to bite the apple (vv.918–21)—finally overcomes her resistance, and she reciprocally bestows her ring on him. Seated by the well, they feed on each other's kisses, nor do their eyes neglect their role; now it is time for hands to play the game of which both are the master. . . . presumably their bodies follow, although hers, at least, still belongs to another.

The *Roman de la rose,* Jean Renart's third story, tells of the love of Conrad, the young but powerful emperor, for Liënor, sister of Guillaume, the lowly knight of Dole. Arising from a description—albeit stereotypic, this love is severely tested when the seneschal claims to have taken the girl's virginity, but is finally consummated in marriage after Liënor succeeds in vindicating her virtue. The amatory progression is, therefore, from happy anticipation through painful testing to a jubilant conclusion. Jean Renart's innovation over his previous works was to insert into the narrative structure some forty-six songs appropriate for music (v.10). His purpose was not only to embellish the narrative or to establish a musical ambience but also to give lyrical voice to the feelings and motives of his principal characters. The songs, therefore, became the principal medium for expressing desire. Since they were excerpted from other authors, their message is subject to multiple layers of interpretation.[100]

Jean opened his romance with the image of Conrad as a gallant bachelor, the flower of chivalry. Unwilling to take his imperial duties seriously by finding a wife and producing heirs, he indulges his youth (v.136) and his wandering heart (v.3496) through amatory escapades exemplified by the spring hunt. The pleasures and solaces (vv.186–193) of these games are innocent of suffering or thought. He and his companions are not troubled with thinking, not even about their souls' safety (v.224). The hunt resounds to jubilant caroles or songs of dance:

> Main se leva bele Aeliz, (V.318)

with the recurring refrain:

> Dormez, jalous, et ge m'envoiserai. (V.321)

or again:

> Cui lairai ge mes amors,
> amie, s'a vos non? (Vv.536–33)

Bele Aeliz arises in the morning. . . . Sleep, you who are jealous; I shall amuse myself. . . . To whom would I give my love, *ma mie,* if not to you?

The emperor returns to one of his castles on the Rhine where he summons his jongleur Juglet to entertain him with a fine story. Juglet complies, not with a fabliau (*faule*) but with a wondrous tale about a knight from Champagne who loved a lady on the marches of Perthois. A possible allusion to the *Lai de l'ombre,* this story piques Conrad's interest for more, and thus Juglet sings the praises of the maiden of Dole. So enthralled is the emperor with this conventional portrait that he falls in love with the image, having never laid eyes on the girl. Lïenor's name itself becomes Love's spark to ignite the emperor's heart. "Blessed is the priest who christened her," Conrad exclaims; "he would become archbishop of Reims, if I were lord of France" (vv.788–800). Unlike the tradition culminating in Chrétien which situated love's inception in the eyes, Jean followed an alternate approach of the troubadours and Marie de France which caused men to fall in love from hearsay.[101] To give voice to this theme Jean introduces the first stanza of a well-known lyric from the Provençal poet Jaufré Rudel:

> Lors que li jor sont lonc en mai,
> m'est biaus doz chant d'oisel de lonc.
> Et quant me sui partiz de la,
> membre mi d'une amor de lonc.
> Vois de ça embruns et enclins
> si que chans ne flors d'aubespin
> ne mi val ne qu'ivers gelas. (Vv.1031–7)

When the days become long in May, I like the sweet song of the bird from afar. And when I have left there, I remember a distant love. I go from there deep in thought and bowed so that

152

neither song nor the flower of hawthorne is valued more by me than winter's frost.

Although its emplacement in the narrative is awkward, because this lyric is not sung by the emperor but by Guillaume and his company on their hurried journey from Dole to the imperial court, the verse nonetheless furnishes a classic formulation of the troubadour theme of distant love (*amor de lonh*) which was appropriate to the emperor in the sense that his own love, Lïenor, was still far removed. From the outset, Jaufré Rudel's lyric has been subjected to multiple readings, but one of the earliest found in the *vidas* or thirteenth-century biographies of the troubadours was that the poet has fallen in love with a lady without having seen her and, therefore, knows her only by reputation. Despite the richness of the lyric, Jean Renart inserted it at this place simply to evoke the traditional troubadour theme of the unseen and inaccessible.[102]

Smitten by love for this unseen woman, the emperor has no thoughts except for Lïenor which Jean articulates through a series of *grands chants courtois* sung by Conrad and those close to him. An initial stanza from a crusading song of the Châtelain de Couci provides Conrad with a voice to enunciate his newfound rejoicing and frankly carnal expectations. One fine morning, as sun streams into his bedroom, he opens the windows and intones:

> Li noviaus tens et mais [et violete]
> et roissignox me semont de chanter;
> et mes fins cuers me fet d'une amorete
> un doz present que ge n'os refuser.
> Or m'en doint Dex en tel honor monter,
> cele ou j'ai mis mon cuer et mon penser
> q'entre mes bras la tenisse nuete
> ainz q'alasse outremer. (Vv.923–30)[103]

The new season, the month of May, violets, and the nightingale all summon me to sing. My fine heart makes me a sweet present of love song which I dare not refuse. Would that God grant me the great honor to hold her naked in my arms, she in whom I have placed my heart and thoughts, before I depart overseas.

Echoing the troubadours, the *grands chants courtois* also mixed incipient joy with foreboding of grief. In a verse sung as a duet by Conrad and Juglet, Gace Brulé was among the first of the trouvères to lament the passing of flowers, greenery, birds, and fine weather and to fear the coming cold of winter:

> Et por ce chant, que nel puis oublier,
> la bon' amor dont Dex joie me doigne,
> car de li sont et vienent mi penser. (Vv.850–52)

That is why I sing, not able to forget the good love whose joy
God gives me, because from it arise and exist all my thoughts.

A stanza by Renaut de Beaujeu, a knight from Champagne, reinforced
these premonitions:

> Loial amor qui en fin cuer s'est mise
> n'en doit ja mes partir ne removoir
> que la dolor qui destraint et justise
> samble douçor quant l'en la puet avoir.
> . . . .
> por ce m'en lo quant plus me fet doloir. (Vv. 1456–59, 1469)

Loyal love which is placed in a fine heart should never go or
depart because the pain which grips and breaks it seems sweet
to those who can have it. . . . I am pleased with [love] when it
makes me suffer.

These notes of sadness nonetheless continue to find jubilant response in the
dance songs:[104]

> Aeliz main se leva.
> Bon jor ait qui mon cuer a! (Vv. 1579–80)

Aelis arises at dawn. May he have happiness who has my heart!

> C'est la jus en la praele,
> or ai bone amor novele!
> . . . .
> Bien doi joie avoir:
> Or ai bon'amor novele
> a mon voloir. (Vv. 1846–51)

Down in the meadow I have found a new love. I should be
joyous to have found a new love—all that I desire.

Within the repertory of *grands chants courtois* Conrad himself composes a
lyric:

> Ja fine amors ne sera sanz torment,
> que losengier en ont corrouz et ire.
> . . . .
> Je soufferrai les faus diz de la gent
> qui n'ont pooir, sanz plus, fors de mesdire
> de bone amor, . . . (Vv. 3188–89, 3192–94)

Fine love will never be without torment because it annoys and
angers the slanderers. . . . I suffer the falsehoods of men who
cannot prevent themselves from vilifying true love.

This stanza, in fact, predicts what will happen to Lïenor. In an aside Jean regretted that the emperor sang these lines because the seneschal heard them and misfortune resulted. After the seneschal has reported his alleged seduction of the maiden, Conrad descends through thought and grief (*pensis et dolanz*) into deep lamentation which he voices once more in the verses of the Châtelain de Couci:

> Por quel forfet ne por quel ochoison
> m'avez, Amors, si de vos esloignié
> que de vos n'ai secors ne garison
> ne ge ne truis qui de moi ait pitié? (Vv.3751–54)[105]

For what misdeed or for what reason, Love, have you so removed me from yourself that I have no help or healing from you, nor can I find anyone to take pity.

or in the line of the Vidame of Chartres:

> A ma dolor n'a mestier coverture. (V.4134)

It is impossible to hide my grief.

During the May celebrations at Mainz a minstrel from Châlons sings:

> Amours a non ciz maus qui me torment;
> mes n'est pas teuls com les autre genz l'ont,
> . . . .
> Et je di: "Las! mi mal, quant fineront?"
> Ne ja Jhesus fenir ne mes consente,
> s'aprés les mauls li bien gregnor s'en sont. (Vv.4587–93)

Love is the name of the disease that torments me, but it is not like love that other men suffer. . . . I exclaim, "When will my illness cease?" but Jesus will not allow it to happen unless after the illness the benefits are even greater.

Although engaged in imperial business, the emperor takes notice of the lines because they both diagnose his lovesickness and announce prophetically his future healing. Thus Conrad, whose amorous conquests have brought him only pleasure, has been obliged to learn to suffer. This mixture of joy and suffering was precisely the underlying theme of the *grands chants courtois* inspired by the troubadour lyric Jean Renart selected for the emperor to sing. Even the refrains of the dance caroles sung by the women intermingle sadness with joy.[106]

Like the male lovers in the *grands chants courtois* Conrad remains inactive throughout the narrative. This passivity is accentuated by his imperial dignity. Not having seen but only heard of his love, he is only free to approach her indirectly through her brother. When confronted with her alleged fall from virtue, he is powerless to react. The only true actor in the drama is Lïenor herself, who upon learning of the calumny sets about to vindicate her reputation and to make herself known to the emperor. Yet Jean Renart grants her only a minor voice in the lyric repertory. As Lïenor approaches the imperial court at Mainz, for example, she is in tears over her family's misfortune. Singers at the festivities cannot raise her spirits with song, not even the Auvergnat lyric, *Bele m'est la voiz altane* (vv.4653–59) (I love the celestial voice), which evokes the healing joys of the vernal leaf and bird.[107] Jean commented that if it were not for the seneschal she herself could have sung this *grand chant courtois*. The only songs that Jean did permit her were two *chansons de toile* sung in the company of her mother and the emperor's messenger at Dole. Before Lïenor herself sings, the stage is set by a *chanson de toile* sung by her mother, which replicates the two women's actual situation. A mother and her daughter, Aude, are seated at their needlework. Although seemingly tranquil, the room is charged with desire. The mother breaks the silence of Aude's thoughts for her lover Doon by advising her to forget Doon (vv.1159–66). In the next two *chansons* Lïenor sings of two maidens, Belle Aye and Belle Doe, both suffering from desire for absent lovers for whom they obstinately refuse to abandon hope (vv.1183–92, 1203–16). Although in one sense Lïenor is thereby resisting her mother's counsel, Belle Aye and Belle Doe do not faithfully represent her own position in the romance because their longing is reduced to passive waiting. The heroine's role is better articulated by the situation presented in still another *chanson de toile* sung further along in the narrative. Recalling the original scene of Lïenor and her mother, Belle Aiglentine sews with her mother but is absorbed by awareness that she has been made pregnant by Count Henri. When the mother discovers Aiglentine's preoccupation, she demands that her daughter confront Henri with her condition. Aiglentine travels straightway to the count, arouses him from bed, and asks him to marry her, a request he immediately accepts. The story concludes with a joyous wedding at which Aiglentine becomes both wife and countess. Each stanza ends with a refrain reiterating the heroine's direct action:

> Or orrez ja
> conment la bele Aiglentine esploita. (Vv.2238–39)

> Now hear what the Belle Aiglentine did.

Jean Renart assigns this *chanson* to a young Norman who performs it during the preparations for the tournament at Saint-Trond. Although Lïenor is not allowed to intone the verses herself, they undoubtedly fit her distinctive personality and action.[108]

In the end Lïenor foils the seneschal's plot, vindicates her honor, and introduces herself to the emperor. "Is it really you, my heart, *mon amie?*"

Conrad exclaims. "Have no doubt," she replies, "I am the belle Lïenor!" now linking her name, which heretofore the emperor knew only by hearsay, with her visual presence. Leaping to outstretched arms, the two cover themselves with embraces and kisses. A new song springs from Conrad's heart, not a melancholic *grand chant courtois* but a jubilant carole:

> Que demandez vos
> quant vos m'avez?
> que demandez vos
> dont ne m'avez vos?
> Ge ne demant rien
> se m'avez bien. (Vv.5106–11)

What do you ask, when you have me? What do you ask, am I not yours? I ask nothing, if you love me well.

The pain of frustrated longing is assuaged. Desire is transformed to a simple request reciprocally expressed between two hearts. The chorus of the assembled answer with the refrain:

> Tendez tuit voz mains a la flor d'esté,
> a la flor de liz,
> por Deu, tendez i! (Vv.5113–15)

Reach out your hand to summer's flower, to the lily. God, do it now!

They urge the lovers to follow the request with action. This was their *Te Deum,* Jean Renart concluded.

Only during the general rejoicing, when complex desire has finally been resolved to simple demand, did Jean Renart introduce the one *grand chant courtois* that named most directly and articulated most profoundly the nature of desire. A knight from Dammartin sings the first two stanzas of a Poitevin song which the audience surely recognized as the best-known *canso* of the renowned Provençal troubadour, Bernart de Ventadorn:

> Quant voi l'aloete moder
> de goi ses ales contre el rai,
> que s'oblie et lesse cader
> par la douçor q'el cor li vai,
> ensi grant envie m'est pris
> de ce qu voi. . . .
> Miravile est que n'is de sens
> ne coir dont desier non fon.
>
> Ha! las! Tant cuidoie savoir
> d'amor, et point n'en sai!
> Pas onc d'amar no pou tenir

celi dont ja prou nen avrai.
Tol mei lou cor et tol meismes
et soi meesme et tol le mon,
et por tant el ne m'oste rent
fors desier et cor volon. (Vv.5212–27)[109]

When I see the lark moving its wings of joy against the rays of the sun, until by the sweetness which goes to his heart, he forgets himself and lets himself fall, a great desire [envie] seizes me at this sight. It is a marvel that I do not leave my senses or that my heart should not melt from desire [desier].

Hélas, I thought I knew so much about love and I know nothing. I am not able to keep myself from loving her from whom I shall obtain nothing. She keeps all, my body, my heart; she and everyone leave nothing else except desire [desier] and a languishing heart [cor volon].

As the wedding preparations are quickly moved ahead to satisfy the impatient emperor, Conrad once again sings dance lyrics:

C'est la gieus, en mi les prez, (v.5440)

Down there is the meadow . . .

with the repeated line:

J'ai amors a ma volenté
teles com ge voel. (Vv.5444–45)

I have all the love I want, such as I desire.

Amidst celebration, Jean Renart has again reintroduced the *grand chant courtois*, this time in a masterpiece of troubadour lyricism. Since Bernart de Ventadorn cannot obtain his lady, all that is left is the desire of his languishing heart (*cor volon*), here denominated by the Provençal/French lexicon of *dezirer/desirer* and *enveya/envie*. To capture the oscillations of his heart Bernart envisages the familiar flight of the lark. Inhabiting high grass, the lark must catapult himself vertically into the air. When he reaches a great height, he plummets suddenly downward to his nest, singing all the time. So the poet's desire soars in joy and losing awareness plunges in self-forgetfulness. Centuries later Goethe's celebrated lyric replicated the sensation as *himmelhoch jauchzend / zum Tode betrübt*. To accentuate this alternation, Jean Renart juxtaposed the *dolor* of the *grand chant courtois* with the *joie* of the carole. In contrast to the troubadour's suffering of unrequited *desier*, the emperor is now filled with the jubilant satisfaction of simple *volente* and *voel*.

On the wedding day Conrad honors his promise to make Lïenor both his *amie* and his wife and, therefore, queen and lady of the Empire (vv.3016–19). That night in a fine bed and in the arms of his *amie* the emperor enjoys the happiness (*siecle*) and pleasure (*deduit*) that befits consummation (*dou sorplus qu'il i covint*). To suggest to his audience the measure of Conrad's happiness, Jean Renart recalled the joys of a score of fictional lovers, of whom he named Tristan and Lanval (vv.5507–15). Once again the legendary Tristan and Iseut were evoked, not the tormented adulterers of Thomas of Britain but the youthful lovers who inspire Guillaume and Aelis in *Escoufle*. If one knew that moment of happiness (*aasier*) when Tristan loved Iseut the most as he embraced, kissed, and received love's recompense (*sorplus*), one would have means of comparison. When his audience also recalled the *Lai de Lanval*, they had still another comparison. In Marie de France's version the young knight Lanval loves an enchanted lady, the virtual creation of his most daring fantasies. She is richer than the emperor Octavian and fairer than the summer's rose or lily. The pair pass the afternoon on a bed whose linen was as valued as a castle. Bestowing both her love and body (v.133), the lady's greatest desire (*desir*, v.130) is to serve her knight. She promises Lanval that he would not want anything (*ne vudra mes*, v.136) since she would satisfy his desire (*a fere tut vostre talent*, vv.137, 168) both now and in the future. Jean Renart brought Conrad's night to a close by concluding that the emperor's happiness far exceeded these lovers. Like Tristan and Lanval, the male Conrad takes his pleasure of the female Lïenor; yet like Queen Iseut whose beauty drew the young Tristan, and the magical lady who summoned Lanval, in the last analysis it was not Conrad but Lïenor who is the true actor in the romance and transforms desire into joy.

Talent: The Fabliaux

The men and women of the fabliaux were so engrossed in coupling that they appear to have had little inclination to express or to reflect upon accompanying emotion. Within their lexicon their characteristic expression was the crude, direct, and unambiguous term *foutre* (fuck), but they also shared with romanciers the euphemisms of *joie* (joy), *deliz* (delight), *deduit* (delight), and *solaz* (solace). These appeared not only in fabliaux that dealt with the aristocracy but also in authors like Jean Bodel who portrayed the lower levels of society.[110] By making abundant use of a vocabulary that evoked pleasurable feelings, the fabliaux writers, like their romance colleagues and the physicians, thereby attributed a positive quality to sexual desire. The desire for sex was, therefore, assumed, by implication, to be an agreeable experience.

On rare occasions, when the fabliaux evoked desire as distinct from the sexual act, their accustomed vocabulary consisted of broad and neutral terms like *talent* and *volenté*. *Talent* ranges from desire to simple wish or will; *volenté* from passion to volition. In common with the Latin terms *libido, cupido,* or *desiderium,* both French words imply a natural appetite akin to hunger and thirst. As the prostitute Mabel and the trickster Boivin maneuver to defraud each other, for example, Mabel declares that it is foolish for a man to endure *talent* for a woman too long; it is like trying to go hungry. Boivin replies that in the seven years after his wife's death he has lost all *talant* (vv.244–49). When the valet David finally seduces the prudish daughter, he does his good (*boen*) and his desire (*talant*) which did not diminish after four times (*Damoisele qui ne pooit oïr (II)*, vv.205–7). This last usage approximated the sense of *volenté* or will, when, for example, Jean Bodel's cleric does his will (*fetes mes volentez*) with Gombert's daughter (v.63) or when the lady has her will (*ot bien sa volenté*) with the obliging young man who calls himself *le foteor* (p.314). Women are portrayed as sharing libidinous urges as well. The lady who made a confession about her sexual life admits that she had had her *talent* with her servants, protesting that woman are of such nature that they have such needs (*Le chevalier qui fist sa fame,* vv.131, 151–52). The young fisherman from Pont-sur-Seine likewise recognizes that a young well-fed wife normally desires (*vodroit*) his frequent attention (*Pescheor,* vv.21–22).[111] As for the wife with the insatiable appetite (*Dame qui aveine demandoit,* p.322), she knows what women by nature do to have what they desire (*ara en cure*) and what pleases them the most.

Since sexual desire is natural, it is not normally threatening or destructive. The fableors make use of the ubiquitous fire-metaphor, but it is not raging or out of control—except in the case of the insatiable wife (*Dame qui aveine demandoit,* p.326). When Gombert's wife, for example, mistakes the second cleric for her husband, she notices that whereas he used to be old and tired, this night he is warm (*eschaufez,* vv.121–22). When David goes to bed with the prudish girl, he approaches her just as a peasant curls up before the fire in the middle of the house (*Damoisele qui ne pooit oïr (II),* vv.120–23). The heat of desire is a warming, comforting sensation.

Most noteworthy about sexual desire in the fabliaux is the absence of profound suffering and cogitation so prominent in the Ovidian and romance tradition, as we have seen. The copyist of Jean Bodel's fabliaux extended oblique recognition to this tradition in the story of the merchant of Douai. Although the couple had long enjoyed what canonists would have recognized as marital affection (*Que li uns ot l'autre mout chier*), that night fatique and neglect provokes in his wife disturbing thoughts and desires (*voloir et la pansee*) which she tries to dismiss before falling asleep in anger and boredom (*par ire et par anui,* vv.62–70).[112] Her dreams, we remember, however, succumb to the most extravagant of sexual fantasies. The scribe transformed the title from *Li sohaiz des vez* (The dream of pricks) to *li sohaiz desvez* (The insane desire) which is as close as the fabliaux came to the symptoms of lovesickness. Whatever the illness, however, it is easily cured by the husband awakening to his duties, and the two quickly recover their conjugal health (*La nuit furent mout bien ensanble*). If fabliaux lovers were seldom troubled by thoughts, neither were they wounded through their eyes. The two clerics, to be sure, cannot keep their eyes off Gombert's wife and daughter, whom they covet (vv.12–15), but sight is rarely the source of pain that it became for André the Chaplain and the romances. Only when dealing with the aristocracy do fableors recognize love as innate suffering prompted by vision and accompanied by immoderate thinking. At this extreme, the young hero in *Guillaume au faucon* is tormented by all of the classic symptoms befitting a lover schooled by André the Chaplain or imitating the celebrated love of the legendary Tristan, but in the fabliaux the innumerable clerics, townsmen, and peasants, along with their wives, daughters, and mistresses are quite innocent to this agony.

The Supremacy of Desire: Noncoital Sexuality and the Desire for God

Throughout this chapter sexual desire has been taken to include the complex of emotions surrounding coitus. We shall see that not only the physiological effects of food and drink can enhance desire but also the mental activities and physical gestures involved in erotic foreplay. Throughout these preliminaries, however, coitus may not always be accomplished. Lovers may stop short at any stage of lovemaking, thus rendering enhanced desire as an end in itself. The lexicon and images of sexual desire, moreover, may also be transferred from physical coitus to other objectives. During the Middle Ages the goal that was most commonly acknowledged was the love and possession of God, the most laudable of all human activities. The practice of noncoital sexuality and the love of God, therefore, were two different ways of proclaiming the supremacy of desire itself.

Most powerful in stimulating sexual desire were those gestures that were usually summarized as kissing and embracing. All five discourses took notice of these gestures but assigned them widely diverging value. Since the theologians were not inclined to explore the details about activities that inflamed concupiscence, they usually avoided discussing foreplay and treated it only in a negative context. Recalling a story from Jerome's *Life of Paul the Hermit,* for example, Pierre the Chanter cited a youth who was forced to endure sexual blandishments calculated to induce him to

161

commit idolatry. Bound in golden chains and placed in a garden of delights, he was approached by a beautiful woman who attempted to arouse him with kisses and caresses (*deosculans et palpans*), but the boy bit off his tongue and spat blood into the mouth of the seductress. In a similar mood Thomas of Chobham restricted his discussion of lascivious kisses (*oscula lasciva*) and shameful embraces (*turpes amplexus*) to the context of a husband and a wife engaged in impetuous intercourse who perform meretricious actions day and night solely for the purpose of satisfying sexual desire.[113]

The physicians who debated the physiological and psychological origins of sexual desire in the *Prose Salernitan Questions* ignored these actions as being of little medical interest. Only in the context of medicaments and aphrodisiacs did Constantinus Africanus offer a brief list of techniques that might increase desire. These consisted of writing of love, kissing the breasts, holding hands, sucking the tongue, looking at the face, and murmuring sighs.[114]

The fableors likewise sustained little interest in techniques preparatory to intercourse. Throughout the recitations of frenetic sexuality, to be sure, many couples, both married and unmarried, engage in foreplay. Jean Bodel's merchant of Douai is greeted with embraces and kisses from his wife (*Sohaiz*, vv.21). In the darkness of the peasant household Bodel's cleric slides into bed with the daughter and embraces and kisses her before having his will and delight (*Gombert*, vv.77–81). Such techniques were the stock-in-trade of the prostitutes Mabel (*Boivin*, vv.133–34) and Richeut (vv.739–40). For all this embracing and kissing, however, the language of description is limited to the stereotypical *acolé et baisié*.[115] Only the fisherman from Pont-sur-Seine protrudes his tongue (*a besier et a langueter*, v.184). When the knight who possessed the gift of eliciting words from female genitals was joined in bed by the servant girl, he pretends to make love with embraces, kisses on the mouth and face, touching her breasts, and placing his hand on her cunt, but this was only to gain access to her organ and to make it perform audibly (vv.413–17).

There is little doubt that the final stage of intercourse preoccupied the fabliaux. When the bourgeois youth finally beds his neighbor's daughter in *Auberee*, for example, "he embraces, kisses and assuages her. The one draws himself close to the other, and they play the game for which they came together" (vv.404–8). Frequently all foreplay is omitted in the rush to join bodies. In full view of Jean Bodel's peasant from Bailluel, the priest undresses the peasant's wife and then falls upon her (vv.84–87). In similar circumstances the priest of *Le prestre ki abevete* flips the wife onto the bed, hoists her skirts, and does that thing that all women love (p.56). In these circumstances speed served to hold the observer's attention, but other fabliaux omitted preliminaries as well.[116] The butcher of Abbeville climbs into bed with the priest's servant after offering a bribe but no other persuasion (vv.227–29). When the apprentice to the blacksmith of Creil displays his spectacular endowments, the wife responds by pulling up her dress and readying herself immediately (vv.133–45). During the protracted seduction in *La damoisele qui ne pooit oïr* where the young man descends the girl's body, exploring, naming, and touching, even he forgets to kiss and embrace before watering his horse at the fountain.

As the ancient authority on the art of love, Ovid presented himself as the specialist on foreplay. Although restrained in describing love's final act, he suffered few inhibitions in recounting preparatory techniques, particularly those allegedly of personal experience which he detailed in the *Amores*. Even here he preferred to represent them as fantasies rather than deeds. On the celebrated summer afternoon with his mistress he was content to describe her body.[117] The delights of foreplay were reserved for flights of imagination on four other occasions: in jealous agony over the public caresses Corinna's husband bestowed at a banquet, when transforming himself into a ring to accompany Corrina's finger as it ventured under her dress, when in despair over a bout with impotence, and when chiding a mistress for unfaithfulness.[118] *Amor* shapes a thousand ways for making love, he boasted, but, in fact, they consisted of a handful of repeated procedures: embraces with the arms, pressing of thighs and feet, caressing of breasts and particularly the nipples under clothing, whispering words and moans of delight, but most especially exploring the mouth with the tongue (*osculaque inseruit cupida luctantia lingua*). The poet returned to this last delight time and again.[119]

When the poet codified his experiences in the *Ars amatoria,* he continued to boast of a thousand ways to make love,[120] but he suppressed the details in favor of generalized precepts. Only at the close of Books II and III does he report two specific examples.[121] In the first, he alludes to the secret insinuation of hands and fingers, as he closes the door on the lovers; in the second, all that reaches the reader is the girl's posture on the couch accompanied by soft *voces,* joyous murmurs, and suggestive words.

The clerics who rewrote Ovid for the schools combined the poet's expertise in foreplay in the *Amores* with the fabliaux's obsession for consummation. When Pyrrus gives lessons to the uninstructed Alda, Guillaume de Blois has the pair gaze into each other's eyes, hold each other in their arms, and then kiss—biting and sucking their lips and tying their tongues in knots—before he turns to lower maneuvers (vv.421–64). After the narrator of the *De tribus puellis* finishes his meal of poultry thighs with the girl of his fantasies, they repair quickly to bed where he exalts in the splendor of her body—as Ovid admired Corinna, lavishes her with kisses, uncovers her breasts and thighs (more tender than the poultry)—but, like Ovid, draws the curtain at this climactic point (vv. 271–300).

While the Latin comedies drew inspiration from the *Amores,* other scholars had long followed the *Ars amatoria* which sought to reduce the amatory experience to a series of rules. Ovid offered no fixed canon but suggested that the answers would come in numbers and stages (*per numeros uenient ista gradusque suos* I, v. 482). Contemporary to Ovid himself, Horace had suggested that Venus's nectar consisted of five parts (*Carmina* I.13, vv. 15–16). The late antique scholiasts Porphyrio and Donatus adopted this number and coined the classic "Five lines of love" (*Quinque lineae amoris*): sight, speech, touch, kiss, and consummation (*visu, alloquio, tactu, osculo, concubitu [or coitu]*). In all probability, Abelard echoed this tradition when he described his delights with Heloise. Abandoning scholarship for love, their kisses were more numerous than learning, their hands found breasts more quickly than books, and their eyes reflected love more than the Scriptures. Furthermore, he boasted, they omitted no step (*gradus*), and if love could imagine anything untried, they added it.[122] By the late twelfth century, therefore, the five steps of love had become a common-place appearing not only in the Latin love poetry of the schools, rhetorical handbooks, but even in biblical commentaries, preachers' manuals, guides to confessors, and synodical statutes.[123]

With all this contemporary acknowledgment, it is not surprising that André the Chaplain's handbook also cited the steps of love, which were reduced to four and altered slightly. The townsman explains to the towns-woman that the steps of love (*gradus in amore*) had been set at four since antiquity: the first consists in giving hope, the second in granting kisses, the third in the enjoyment of embraces, and the last in the yielding of the whole person.[124] Hope replaces sight and talk, which were implicitly as-sumed because sight was essential to André's definition of *amor,* and fur-ther insistence on speech was pointless in a treatise that recorded interminable conversations. Beyond this classification, however, André offered no further details about foreplay.

What was innovative about André's use of the ancient convention in the Latin tradition was the distinct possibility of omitting the last step of con-summation. Whatever Ovid's reticence about enunciating intercourse, he left little doubt that this was the assured goal of his poetry and instruction—an attitude to which his twelfth-century epigones and the fableors took few exceptions. In André's recorded conversations, however, the sugges-tions arose on more than one occasion that the last step was not obligatory. The townsman's protracted casuistry of the four stages allows, in passing, that the woman can withdraw from an affair after the third stage. The man of the higher nobility likewise permits this recourse to women of the same class.[125] By introducing the concept of pure love (*amor purus*) as opposed to mixed (*amor mixtus*) or consummated love, the man of the higher nobility elevates this possibility to a preference. André's celebrated *amor purus* unites the hearts of two lovers with the affection of love (*dilectionis*). It begins in the contemplation of the mind and heart, proceeds through kisses on the mouth, embraces with the arms and even innocent contact with a nude lover (*verecundum amantis nudae contactum*), but omits the last solace.[126] This argument may simply be a sophistic ploy to seduce the lady, but André nonetheless presents it as a viable, if not preferable, alternative to coitus. Since the man of higher nobility reveals himself to be a cleric, it is conceivable that pure love offered further advantages to the clerical order by circumventing technical restrictions on sexuality.

The argument for pure love was also congruous with the concept of love by the higher parts proposed by the man of the higher nobility in opposition to love by the lower regions. Expressing deep skepticism over the former possibility, the lady of the higher nobility argues that the total effect of love can only be attained through the goal to which all lovers move. Without it they are thought to have nothing more than foreplay (*amoris . . . preludia*).[127] At the conclusion to the *Ars amatoria* Ovid had termed his amatory exercises a magnificent game or play (*Lusus habet finem:* III, v.809). André used the same word when he referred to sporting (*lusit*) with courtesans or servants in the grass,[128] but in the previous passage he coined a new word for the amatory vocabulary, foreplay (*preludia*), and thereby encapsulated the essence of Ovid's erotic tradition.

André the Chaplain's stages of erotic foreplay were undoubtedly derived from the Latin tradition, but his notions about pure love may have been inspired by the vernacular tradition of the southern troubadours. It is questionable that by the mid-twelfth century the Provençal poets had systematized the steps of love-play to the degree found in the *Quinque lineae*,[129] but the essential components nonetheless surfaced in their writings as can be seen from Bernart de Ventadorn whose lyrics were most accessible to the northern romanciers. The poet is pleased to behold his lady's mouth, eyes, brow, hands and arms as well as the rest (no.35:vv.19–22).[130] Although speaking only from belief, he knows that the body under her clothing is fine, beautiful, and white (no.8:vv.33–40). The more he sees her, the more he is overcome by love and desire (no.5:vv.19–21). Much of his lyrical production conveys declarations of love (no. 5:vv.17, 18, for example) and consists of a monologue with his lady (in which she remains silent). She should not be surprised if he asks her for kisses (*baya*) and embraces (*acola,* no.7:vv.41–45). He will die of desire if she does not permit caresses (*manei*), kisses, and the closeness of her body, white round and smooth (no.36:vv.30–36). On different occasions Bernart imagines himself in her chamber removing her shoes, enlaced in her arms, and even lying together breast to breast (no. 26:vv. 29–35, no. 27:vv. 41–45, no. 28:vv. 33–40), but it is never clear that coitus was expected. To love her sexually (*per drudaria*), he declares, is not fitting (no. 25:vv. 49–50). He has always wanted one woman from whom he has never had pleasure (*jauzimen*, no. 30:vv. 6–7). The most he can ask of his lady is that the day she gives him her love with a kiss, she should think about offering the rest (*del plus*, no. 13:vv. 16–18). The opaqueness of troubadour language and the pervasiveness of stereotypes have generated controversy among modern critics as to the physical sensuality implied.[131] To what extent the troubadours sang about consummation may never be determined, but there seems to be little doubt that their verses bear a potent erotic charge. Since the ladies of Jaufré Rudel were distant and those of Bernart de Ventadorn were variously resistant, they were assuredly of difficult access. With access to their beloved restricted, the poets were left with little more than desire (*dezirer*) and a languishing heart (*cor volon*, no. 43:v. 16) in Bernart's famous line. Or in another passage, love which enamors the heart imparts not pleasure but longing and desire (no. 3:vv. 25–28).

The vernacular romances written for the aristocracy of northern France were fully apprised of the ancient Latin tradition of the *Quinque linea amoris*. In Marie de France's *Guigemar*, for example, the lovers talk, kiss, and embrace; Marie hopes that they will have the *surplus* which others are accustomed to enjoy (vv. 531–34). In Chrétien's *Cligès* the emperor Alis, drugged in his sleep, dreams that he holds, kisses, speaks to, sees, and embraces his bride Fenice (vv. 3316–21) without ever enjoying any delight. We have already seen the importance of sight to initiation of love in *Cligès*. Since lovers were forever engaged in conversation, it was unnecessary to insist on speech. Like the fabliaux, embracing and kissing (*d'acoler et de baisier*) became the code words for physical expression of love. Erec holds and kisses Enide on their wedding night (vv. 2041–47); Cligès and Fenice embrace and kiss when they are finally united in the hideaway tower (v. 6255); in *Escoufle* the empress bestows a hug and a kiss on her husband in bed as she persuades him to agree to her plot against Guillaume (v. 2872); Guillaume and Aelis kiss and embrace in the garden before planning their elopement (v. 3549), a habit that they indulge throughout their flight (v. 4325); the lady of Montpellier embraces and kisses the count of Toulouse when she is assured of his love (v. 5847); upon recognizing his belle Lïenor the emperor Conrad leaps to her arms and covers her eyes and face with a hundred kisses (vv. 5098–5101), and on his wedding competes with Tristan and Lanval in the pleasures of kisses and embraces (v. 5509). Like the fabliaux, these physical gestures were so conventionalized that the authors were rarely inclined to elaborate. Only Jean Renart sought to rival

Ovid's *Amores,* the latter's twelfth-century imitators, or the fabliaux. After picnicking near a fountain, Guillaume and Aelis take time for the solaces of embraces and kisses:

> Por ce que li baisiers li plaise,
> Ele oevre si sa bele bouche
> Que l'une langue a l'autre touche
> Malgré les dens blans et serrés
> K'amors lor a si desserrés
> Que li uns ne puet l'autre mordre.
> Bien doit si dous baisiers amordre
> .II. amans quant il sont ensamble. (Vv.4336–43)

Because the kiss is pleasing to her, she opens her beautiful mouth in such a way that one tongue touches the other. In spite of the white and closely ranged teeth for love has so opened them that the one can not bite the other. Well should a sweet kiss unite two lovers when they are together.

What separated these romances from the fabliaux and linked them with Ovid was their steadfast reluctance to name the fifth stage directly. Avoiding the fabliaux's *vilain* vulgarity and the vernacular equivalents of Latin clinical vocabulary, the romance writers resolutely masqued intercourse with euphemisms of pleasure. Like the southern troubadours, *joie, delit, deduit, solaz,* and *sorplus* constitute their vocabulary of coitus. This delicacy of expression leads to a further question, whether the northern romanciers considered André the Chaplain's doctrine of pure love (with its troubadour antecedents) a plausible alternative. Marie de France appears to have furnished the clearest examples of such behavior. In *Laustic,* for example, the lovers are reduced to communicating through sight and words between adjacent houses. In *Eliduc,* although the hero talks with, kisses, and embraces the princess Guilliadun (vv.471–72), Marie asserted that their lovemaking (*drüerie*) is limited to courting, speaking, and the exchange of gifts to avoid all appearance of foolishness, frivolity, or shame (vv.575–80). Applied to married couples, however—Alexandre and Soredamor, Cligès and Fenice, the count Richard and the lady of Genoa, the emperor and empress, and Conrad and Lïenor—the question of pure love was both superfluous and antithetical to the aim of reproduction expected of such unions. Nor did Jean Renart allow much doubt over the objectives of Conrad's amatory escapades at the hunt despite the omission of foreplay (vv.277–83).

Among young unmarried couples, however, whose amorous inexperience is recounted at length, the romanciers appear to have exercised deliberate ambiguity. In the *Graal,* for example, Perceval's mother instructs the young *nice* on the boundaries of lovemaking permitted to a knight aspiring to courtesy. He is allowed a kiss but absolutely forbidden the culmination (*soreplus*, L. vv.544–47; R. vv.546–49). Combining irony with incongruity, Perceval manipulates these limits. On the first encounter with the damoiselle of the tent, he insists that, in fact, he has respected his mother's advice, but the girl's *ami* has serious doubts. "Who takes a kiss and doesn't do more (*plus*)?" (L. vv.691–764, 3842–47, 3883–88; R. vv.691–765, 3860–65, 3901–6). On the second with Blancheflor the girl joins him in bed almost naked where they spend the night embracing and kissing, arm in arm, mouth to mouth. Although it was indeed a night of solace (*solaz*), the audience cannot be certain to what extent the youth has obeyed his mother (L. vv.1980–2067, R. vv.1982–2069).

Jean Renart also played upon the youth of Guillaume and Aelis to mask their sexual experiences. The emperor wishes to marry the children who have shared the nursery since infancy. When he learns that they are accustomed to lie together the whole night (v.2821), he insists on their separation. In protest Guillaume declares that if he kissed Aelis's eyes and mouth, if his hand dared to pass beneath her Syrian gown, if he felt her nude body, he did not do it to her shame or loss but because she was promised as his wife (vv.3026–47). Similar thoughts occur to Aelis as she arises naked from her bed that night and fantasizes on Guillaume's fine hands that had touched her stomach, hips, and body in every way (vv.3280–89). During the couple's flight Jean was not clear as to the limits of the exploratory kisses enjoyed during the idyllic *dejeuner en herbe*. At their final reunion at Saint-Gilles Jean placed their beds next to each other but refused to tell what happened thereafter (vv.7864–84). From the opening scene in the nursery throughout the entire narrative the audience would have difficulty in determining whether or at what point the young pair consummated their love before their nuptial night.

Through inexperienced couples Chrétien and Jean rehearsed the traditional steps of love—looking, talking, kissing, embracing, even caressing naked bodies—yet stopped short of the final act. In effect, their young pairs are made to appear to practice the pure love that André the Chaplain advocated. Following Marie de France, Jean Renart even suggested that such love is appropriate to adults as well. At Saint-Gilles the count, although the lover of the lady of Montpellier, was accustomed to frequent the chamber of the maidens where he reclined with them to eat his fruit by the fire and to take his pleasure after dinner. There Aelis, still separated from Guillaume, knew how to make him comfortable and to settle his head by endearment in her lap. She is described in deshabillé, and he is shown repeatedly to be in a state of undress, even naked (vv.7021–7105). The language, ambience, gestures, and emphasis on undress suggest the conventions of love, but once again it is noncoital, because at Guillaume's arrival the author was careful to explain that Aelis has never seen a man who pleased her so much since she lost her young lover (vv.7406–9). By masking coitus behind euphemisms of joy and through scenes of pure love, both Chrétien and Jean suggested that foreplay might become an end in itself. Using Ovid's techniques they, therefore, subverted the master's final goal, and by privileging the enhancement of desire over coitus, like the southern troubadours, they elevated desire itself to a supreme goal. Although coital love still predominated in their romances, its omission nonetheless remained a viable alternative.

* * *

An alternative to the frustrations of this noncoital eroticism was the proposal to satisfy desire by transferring the object from a sexual partner to a supremely transcendent goal, that of the love and possession of God. The principal literary medium for this transposition and sublimation was the Hebrew love poetry collected in the Old Testament under the title of the *Song of Songs* (*Cantum cantorum*). This was an epithalamium, a nuptial song, whose actors consisted of a bridegroom, bride, and their respective companions. In the Latin text of the Vulgate sensual imagery was conveyed in erotic vocabulary articulating the body: *os* (mouth), *labia* (lips), *genae* (cheeks), *ubera/mammae* (breasts), and *femur/crura* (thighs), *osculetur* (kisses), *amplexabitur* (embraces), and sexual desire, *amore langueo*. From the third century when the Greek Church Father Origen wrote a commentary which was later reworked into Latin and transmitted by Jerome and Rufinus, the poetry was endowed with a spiritual interpretation in which the literal sensuality was transmuted into totally different meanings. By the late twelfth century the spiritual readings had divided into three major traditions. A mystical interpretation, exemplified by Origen and later by Bernard de Clairvaux, understood the bridegroom and bride to stand for God/Christ, and the soul. An ecclesiological reading, such as proposed by Robert of Tombelaine and the *Glossa ordinaria,* read the poem as the love between God/Christ and the church, whereas Rupert of Deutz proposed a Marian interpretation which saw the pair as Christ and Mary. As the most glossed book of Scripture, the *Song of Songs* inspired hundreds of commentaries which explored these themes, often interweaving them in the same commentary.[132]

Pierre the Chanter's program to gloss the entire Bible included a substantial commentary to the work. By including fragments of phrases and expanding on particular points, his preface paraphrased the standard introduction found in the *Glossa ordinaria.*[133] He provided an *accessus ad auctores* when he noted the author, the material and the mode of treatment (*modus agendi*). Salomon, began Peter following the *Glossa ordinaria,* composed three works: *Proverbs* involving morals or ethics for beginners, *Ecclesiastices* treating the physical nature of things for the proficient, and finally the *Song of Songs* dealing with the divine figures of theology for the mature and perfect, those who attain the love and peace of God alone.[134] It is especially important that those who read the last work are perfect in knowledge and strong in faith lest the lubricity of an immature mind convert the text into fleshy concupiscence. For this reason the Chanter acknowledged the Hebrew tradition that reserved the study of the *Song of Songs* for those over thirty years of age.[135] The book is entitled *cantica* both in the singular and plural because it contains three songs or stages through which the faithful make their way to spiritual perfection; for example, through the song of abandoning sin as Moses left Egypt, through that of practicing good works as Moses wandered in the desert, and through that of consummating and perfecting virtue like David's epithalamium of the husband and wife. The work contains four sets of actors: the bridegroom and his companions who help him retain the beloved, and the bride and her young girls who are still tender in faith but ready to imitate the bride. Echoing Origen and the *Glossa ordinaria,* Pierre exhorted those who are spiritual to hear the erotic words (*verba amatoria*) sung spiritually and to learn how to transfer the soul's motion and the flame of natural love to better things.[136] The goal of the work is the love of God (*finis est delectio dei*). Pierre concluded his preface by resuming his erotic doctrine found elsewhere. Among four kinds of love are: the highest love, the *amor divinus vel etherus,* that of God and neighbor; and its direct opposite, sexual lust (*venereus libidinosus*) which is diabolical and damnable. In between are two forms which can be tolerated if exercised under God and with measure but are detestable if immoderate and against God. These are worldly love (*mundalis*) and carnal love (*carnalis*), that is, love of one's own flesh and family.[137]

The Chanter situated his commentary in the exegetical universe of the *Song of Songs* by aligning it with the ecclesiological interpretation of the *Glossa ordinaria* which, in turn, was inspired by Robert of Tombelaine. The material of the work consists of the bridegroom and bride, that is, the head and members, or Christ and the church. In contrast to the *Glossa ordinaria* which termed the material *theoretica,* Pierre was more specific, calling Solomon a theologian (*theologus*).[138] The Chanter's most distinctive trait was to turn the *Song of Songs* into an elaborate allegory on preaching and teaching that followed the parts of the sexual body. "Let him kiss me with the kiss of his mouth" (1:1), for example, represents the mouth of the father, of Scriptures, and of preaching. Teeth stand for the expositors of Scriptures, lips for the preachers. The neck, breasts, and joining of the thighs also recall preachers, as well as the sixty queens who ruled themselves and generated progeny. At the same time breasts stand for teachers who impart the nourishment of knowledge.[139] By invoking these academic functions his commentary appears to have been directed to his theological students for whom teaching and preaching were principal activities.

Despite these ulterior goals the erotic imagery nonetheless remained imbedded in the scriptural text. The three songs signify being loved, being desired, and being possessed.[140] The final stage is to rest in the arms and embrace of the bridegroom. Exceeding all other levels in dignity, it represents the consummation of husband and wife in David's epithalamium.[141] The mode of treatment is to show by what sort of desire (*quali desiderio*) the members adhere to the head and strive to please him and with what affection (*quali affectione*) praising, admonishing, and comforting the bridegroom loves the church.[142] All elements were available for commuting the sexual desire of Scripture to the spiritual desire of God, proposed by the mystical interpretation, but Pierre the Chanter was not chiefly interested in the spiritual union between God and the soul. If Bernard de Clairvaux had used the passionate cry for a kiss to express the soul's desire, Peter's exposition of the passage merely catalogued the categories of kisses but omitted the factor of spiritual yearning.[143] On the key passage "for I languish with love" (*quia amore langueo*, 2:5) the Chanter commented that its spiritual sense is the bridegroom's love for the church. Quoting Ovid, he noted that all lovers turn white which is their appropriate color.[144] With little doubt his commitment to the ecclesiological tradition decisively overshadowed the spiritual sublimation of sexual desire, the alternative exegesis.

If Pierre the Chanter appeared to have been indifferent to spiritual desire in his commentary to the *Song of Songs,* the ancient tradition initiated by Origen and revitalized by Bernard de Clairvaux was again renewed by the saintly Marie d'Oignies and circulated in her biography by Pierre's disciple, Jacques de Vitry. Since the imagery and vocabulary of the *Song* widely pervaded religious circles, it not surprising that it resurfaces powerfully in Jacques's account of Marie's life. Among the holy women the preacher found in the diocese of Liège were matrons who, having known sexual feelings in married life, now desired a heavenly spouse alone. There were others who languished for years in bed by reason of their desire (*prae desiderio languerent*), having no other cause for their infirmity than their souls' longing (*desiderio animae*) for which they cried out "support me with flowers and surround me with apples for I languish in love" (*Song,* 2:5). Still others were so seized with spiritual intoxication that they passed entire days in utter silence "while the king was on his couch" (*Song,* 1:11). Above all these women was Marie d'Oignies who was comforted by angelic songs in contrast to miserable and fatuous women who—undoubtedly like Jean Renart's audience—fueled the fires of lust with lascivious *chansons*. Having eaten nothing on her deathbed for forty days, Marie approached the blessed passage with desire and joyfulness of mind (*cum desiderio et mentis hilaritate*).[145] Present at Oignies, Jacques reported her last days in detail. As the end approached, she became impatient, consumed with violent desire (*rapta vehementi desiderio*) for the embraces (*amplexaretur*) of her lord. She heard his voice calling, "Come my beloved (*amica*), my bride (*sponsa*), my dove, and you will be crowned" (*Song*, 4:8). After drawing up her testament, she began to sing and await the nuptial day in high elation. This glorious day, a day of rejoicing and exultation (*dies nuptialis, dies gaudii et exultationis*), came finally on Sunday, 23 June 1213.[146] No greater contrast can be imagined than between Iseut dying of unfulfilled desire in the arms of her dead lover and Marie joyfully welcoming death as access to the embraces of her spiritual spouse. The commutation of sexual longing into spiritual desire transformed vocabulary as well. *Voluptas*, the pejorative rendering of sexual pleasure in Latin, now was made fit for spiritual ecstasy. Concluding Marie's *Vita*, Jacques expostulated on her repose in heaven where, aflame with divine voluptuousness (*torrens divinae voluptatis*), she fulfills and satisfies all in the spirit of full liberty.[147]

5

COITUS

All discussion of the act of coitus proceeded directly from consideration of the sexual body. The *Prose Salernitan Questions* proposed a physiological definition that separated the function into three component parts: "Coitus consists of the union of a man and woman by the action of a voluntary and natural conjunction resulting in the emission of sperm, and the procreation of a fetus, the entire act accompanied by great delight."[1] Accordingly we can divide the process into three chapters, although each cannot be isolated completely. In addition to delight (*delectatio*) which has been treated in the preceding chapter, we have physical union (*commixtio, coniunctio*) to the point of ejaculation, and procreation (*procreatio*) to the point of birth.

Myths of Origins: Poets and Theologians

Both pagan and Christian cosmologies had sought to situate coitus in myths of origins. In terms analogous to the Genesis story of creation, Ovid had evoked the beginning of the world when order appeared within the primal confusion producing stars, earth, and waters. Sky was placed over earth; land was separated from waters; beasts roamed the forests, birds the air, fish the sea, and the human race wandered alone in the fields. Endowed with animal strength and rude bodies, humans claimed the forest as their home, grass as their food, and leaves as their couch. In these bestial surroundings, seductive voluptuousness entered to soften their harsh souls. A woman and a man found themselves together in the same place. No teacher taught them what to do there, but the goddess Venus enabled the sweet act without instruction. Like birds, fish, deer, serpents—indeed all beasts—humans began to couple. The thirteenth-century vernacular gloss opined that this passage demonstrated that sexual intercourse was neither sinful nor artificial but thoroughly natural. All those who engage in sex master its functions under nature's law. For Ovid, however, these primeval settings accounted not only for the origins of coitus but also for the great discrepancy between the brutish beginnings of sexuality and its present refinement, thanks to the civilizing art taught by Ovid and poets like him.[2]

Universally read in the Middle Ages, the biblical account of creation performed a comparable service for Christians. Having brought forth the heavens, seas, and earth populated with animals, God created Adam and Eve, placed them in an earthly paradise, and provided them with instructions, among the most important to be fruitful and multiply. Unfortunately, the first humans chose to disobey God and fell into sin, thus forsaking paradise and introducing concupiscence, pain, sickness, and death into the world. Contrary to the preponderance of patristic opinion, which directly attributed the origin of the sexual act to the consequences of the Fall, Augustine had envisaged Adam and Eve as capable of engaging in intercourse without sin or shame in paradise before the Fall. (In fact, however, the first parents did not exercise this potential option.) The sexual organs of the first parents completely obeyed their volition according to the dictates of reason, much like hands and feet. Concentrating on physiology, Augustine demonstrated not only that the bony structures of hands, feet, and fingers obey the will but even the pliant muscles of the mouth and face, corresponding to the tissues of the genitals. Although Pierre the Lombard reported in his day some curiosity over the mechanics of this prelapsarian sexuality, he summarized Augustine's propositions with less detail.[3] Pierre the Chanter, followed by Robert of Courson and Thomas of Chobam, concurred entirely with the Augustinian-Lombardian conclusions and adopted the image of the "finger touching finger" as the gesture of sinless coitus among the first humans.[4]

We have seen that after Adam and Eve's rebellion and Fall, concupiscence entirely infected the sexual act which resulted in shameful disobedience of the genital organs. The uncontrolled passion of intercourse, therefore, was emblematic of the first parents' disobedience to their creator.[5] Like Ovid, the theologians divided sexuality into a primal and a present state but with reversed evaluation. Whereas the primal state was bestial for the poet, it was pristinely pure for the theologians. Whereas the present age had registered progress through the poets' instruction of refined love, for the theologians the irrational passion of concupiscence now thoroughly corrupted sexuality.

The physicians, who studied natural physiology and occasionally compared human with animal behavior, provided reinforcement to Ovid's naturalistic framework. The theologians, however, envisaged human sexuality as restricted to the divinely ordained sacrament of marriage for which they defined precise goals. We have seen that several formulations of these goals were available to the Parisian theologians at the turn of the century. When Robert of Courson summed up the Chanter's teaching, he distinguished between two causes for the divine institution of matrimony: the first is situated in sinless paradise where coitus was without stain, conception without ardor, and birth without pain; the second is outside paradise for the remedy and restraint of sin guided by licit motives. The first was designed to increase nature, the second to inhibit vice. Matrimony, therefore, is subject to natural law and natural regulations which produce all creatures. This explicit recognition of the naturalness of coitus within marriage recalled an ancient tradition formulated by Isidore of Seville in the seventh century and preserved in the opening chapters of Gratian's *Decretum* in the twelfth.[6] It suggested a potential rapprochement between theology and natural science, but his reconciliation was not realized in the Chanter's circle.

The Physiology of Coitus

The authoritative text on sexual intercourse was the *De coitu* composed by Constantinus Africanus at Salerno in the eleventh century. At the beginning of the twelfth century and in northern France, Guillaume de Conches introduced modification that served as a point of departure for the physiological discussions of the *Prose Salernitan Questions* at the end of the century. In effect, Constantinus's monograph was limited chiefly to male sexuality and the final goal of ejaculation by the penis. The physicians of England and northern France who contributed to the *Prose Salernitan Questions* inherited this masculine orientation, reinforced by the Galenic emphasis on the male body as normative to the female. Until the moment of conception, the treatment of female sexuality was subordinated and related by analogy to male concerns. The phallic imagery for coitus of foot, hand, and finger proposed by Augustine and adopted by the theologians further corroborated this masculine image.

Constantinus had analyzed male intercourse as consisting of three factors: appetite originating from the liver, spirit from the heart, and humor from the brain. Guillaume de Conches, followed by the *Prose Salernitan Questions,* adopted the triune division but changed the factors. The three necessary elements were semen which is emitted, heat which warms the body and propels the semen, and spirit which raises the penis and finally expels the semen. The semen—to summarize an involved process to which we shall return in the next chapter—results from humor generated by the liver and transmitted through vessels to nourish the body, combined with humor from the brain which is led through veins past the ears to the kidneys and thence to the testicles where it is whitened and transformed into sperm. Animal force kindles natural heat which moves the blood in the liver and by moving generates warmth. As the vessels gather the materials, they are prepared and liquified by heat because heat dissolves, but coldness congeals. The liver refines and thins a kind of vapor which then passes to the heart. From the heart the arteries convey this spirit to the penis which becomes extended and rigid like a bag better to perform the ejection of semen. If one of the elements is lacking, the operations fails. Like Constantinus, the *Prose Salernitan Questions* assumed that the basic paradigm in both males and females is masculine since the last stage, the erection of the penis, is unique to the male.[7]

Among the four standard complexions (sanguine, phlegmatic, choleric and melancholic) the choleric (hot and dry) is most resistant to sexual activity, but the sanguine (hot and moist) is most suited.[8] Within this traditional framework, the *Prose Salernitan Questions* noted individual variations, citing cases from their own circle of colleagues. The choleric, for example, have little appetite and sexual capability, as was master Reginaldus de Omine. Master Hugo de Mapenore, however, had small appetite but great capacity, whereas master Philippus Rufus Cornubiensis possessed the contrary attributes. Master Johannes Burgensis and especially master Willelmus Chers were fortunate to be endowed with capabilities commensurate to their appetites. As to variations among women, the *Questions* were best informed on the complexions of prostitutes. Although women are by nature colder than men, some are, in fact, hotter than some men, and like men their appetite for intercourse varies according to complexions and individual characteristics. Some, for example, are cold and moist at the beginning and feel little delight. After prolonged intercourse, however, friction generates heat, the humors are dissolved, and the woman is able to pay her natural debt. Others are stirred only by signs and confections, but once stirred they cool off easily. They seek only quick coitus and reject any other. Still others have emissions that feel colder than ice but which are discovered to be ungenuine. An infusion of the hottest sperm is necessary to reduce coldness and revive the humors. Because this kind of lover offers a performance more amicable and consonant to female nature, women reward him with soft and pleasant pledges and entice him with embraces. Other men who lack these pleasure-giving skills they avoid as tiresome.[9]

The annual seasons correspond analogously to the four basic complexions: the heat and aridity of summer are choleric, the cold and dryness of autumn are melancholic, and winter's cold and humidity are phlegmatic. The temperate heat and humidity of spring, however, correspond to the sanguine disposition and are most suitable for sex. Frequent activity in hot summer is harmful because it extinguishes the natural heat. Combined with dryness, it absorbs the body's natural humidity and dries it out. Autumn's dryness produces the same effect. Occasional intercourse can be safely performed in winter, because of abundant moisture, but if indulged in frequently it is harmful. The optimal season is, therefore, spring.[10]

In addition to the physicians, the church authorities also proposed a calendar of seasons appropriate for sexual activity. Developing a suggestion from the Apostle Paul (1 Cor. 7:5) that certain times are more appropriate for prayer than for sex, the compilers of penitentials in the early Middle Ages constructed elaborate calendars for regulating the sexuality of married Christians.[11] Subject to great variation, certain features were nonetheless common throughout Western Christendom from the sixth to the eleventh centuries. Churchmen forbade coitus on Wednesdays, Fridays, Sundays, and perhaps on Saturdays (at least Saturday night) throughout the year. More restrictive, each of the three principal church feasts—Christmas, Easter, and Pentecost—was accompanied by long periods of Lent, lasting forty days or more, when sexual intercourse was likewise forbidden. These Lenten periods of abnegation preceded Christmas and Easter but normally followed Pentecost. Since Easter and Pentecost were moveable feasts in the spring (Easter from 22 March to 25 April and Pentecost from 10 May to 13 June), long Lenten seasons of abstinence moved back and forth from winter into summer and encroached on the season the physicians most recommended for intercourse. In addition, other major church feast days (Saint John the Baptist, 24 June, for example) were also interdicted. After churchmen deducted all the days consecrated to prayer and abstinence, those available for conjugal rights to a scrupulously observant couple amounted to, at most, ninety-three each year.[12]

By the twelfth century, however, these draconian restrictions had been allowed to lapse. Already in the eleventh century the long Lenten seasons were broken up or in the case of Pentecost had disappeared, and the weekly restrictions were no longer enforced. At the mid-twelfth century Gratian and Pierre the Lombard remembered only Christmas, Rogations days (three days before Ascension), and other unspecified *reliquae festivitates*.[13] Thomas of Chobham summarized current opinion among the Chanter's circle by recalling the general principle of abstention during the major festivities but limited his examples to the single days of Christmas, Good Friday, Easter, Pentecost, and the Assumption of the Virgin Mary.[14] Following a more established tradition in canon law, he noticed that marriages could not be celebrated during the Lenten seasons of Christmas and Easter.[15]

In the light of current policy to minimize calendar restrictions, it is of interest that Robert of Courson raised the difficult situation of a wife who seeks intercourse with her husband on Easter or Good Friday, the most sacred of the church feasts. The extremity of this case brought to mind the teaching of contemporary "semiheretics" who proposed that five days of each week be forbidden to sexual intercourse: not only Thursday, Friday, and Sunday, the days on which Christ was captured, executed, and resurrected, but also Tuesdays and Saturdays dedicated to the memory of All Souls and the Virgin Mary as well as other feast days. Robert objected that since nearly the entire week thereby was denied to conjugal activity, the institution of marriage itself was at risk. Apparently Cathar sympathizers with an antipathy toward matrimony were attempting to revive the weekly restrictions of the early penitentials. Warning women against the persuasive sermons of these "semiheretical" preachers, Courson subordinated, as we shall see, all sexual abstinence for the holy seasons to the mutual consent of both spouses.[16] One partner's potential veto thereby permitted married couples to escape the rigor of the holy days.

The writers of aristocratic romances likewise noticed the annual seasons appropriate to sexual activity. Although rarely concerned with precise dating, most authors set the loves of their heroes in the world of eternal spring in which the cold and inclemency of fall and winter rarely intrude. As a rule, the story opens in the *tans novel* of April and May when all nature begins afresh. Chrétien, for example, began the *Graal* in the Gaste Forest with the trees flowering, the bushes budding, the meadows green, and the birds singing (L., R. vv.69–76). He counted the revolving years by the reappearance of April and May just as the Capetians began the royal calendar on Easter (L. v.6012, R. v.6220).[17] Pentecost (Whitsun) provides the date for Arthur's court at Carduel (which opens the *Lion*, vv.1–6), Erec and Enide's marriage (v.1878), and Guillaume's and Aelis's coronation at Rome (*Escoufle*, v.8885). Rivalin meets Blancheflor in the blossom time of May in Gottfried von Stassburg's *Tristan* (vv.536–45). Just as Jean Renart was exacting about geography, he was also precise on internal dating. Guillaume and Aelis began their elopement during the *doucors du tans* of May (v.3274), and in the *Roman* Conrad intones his new love for Lïenor with the Châtelain de Coucy's "Le nouviaus tens et mais" (v.923). Lïenor's calumny, vindication, ordeal, and marriage are all packed into the last week of April and the first days of May when the May Day festivities begin at Mainz.[18] Her impatient bridegroom cannot wait Ascension to hold the wedding (vv.5287–89). Most action, including sexual activity and marriage, therefore begins during the spring season as recommended by medical authority, but it also falls within a period relatively unencumbered on the ecclesiastical calendar. Even according to the most severe restrictions, 23 April was the latest day of the Easter Lent, and the Lent of Pentecost never began before 11 May. The month of May, the exuberant and sunny season of romance dalliance, was usually free of the gloomy shadows cast by ecclesiastical abstinence.

Despite medical warning, the summer's heat does not seem to have inhibited sexual activity in the romances, but ambivalence and suspicion of danger nonetheless lingers. The illicit love of Tristan and Iseut occurs during the summer on their flight into the forest. When King Marc discovers them asleep in the wooded bower in Béroul's version, they are lightly clothed and lying apart because of the heat (vv.1774–76, 1794). Chrétien's reworking of the legend also places Cligès and Fenice naked and asleep in the heat of their garden where they likewise are discovered (vv.6262–6366). Although Jean Renart's youthful lovers take flight in the spring, by the time they reach Toul in Lorraine the days have become hot. It is Aelis's siesta by the fountain during the heat that provides the buzzard an occasion to steal the ring and separate the couple. Whatever the physiological disadvantages, however, heat rarely diminishes amorous ardor. In our sample, however, winter is remarkable for its rare appearance. Only in the *Graal* is winter suggested when Perceval becomes lost in revery as he contemplates a visage formed by blood drops on the snow (L. vv.4175–80, R. vv.4195–98). Only once does Jean Renart allude to a cold season when the count of Saint-Gilles visits his mistress at Montpellier and is entertained by the fire in the ladies' chamber.

On the other hand, the abundance of sexual energy discharged in the fabliaux shifted attention away from the seasonal conditions prescribed by the physicians or the churchmen. Occasional details suggest that clement weather propitious for sex was generally assumed. In *Chevalier qui fist parler*, for example, the squire Huet can steal the clothes of the three maidens because it is summer and they are swimming in a pool (vv.112–25). In *Meunier*, when the wife steps out naked into courtyard to relieve herself, it is understood that it is not dead winter (p.90). Only *Aloul* seemed to follow romance convention by specifying that the priest espies the unclothed wife on a beautiful morning in April (vv.40–44). Otherwise, the fableors' audiences were given to understand that anytime was a good time for making love.

In addition to the influence of humors and seasons, Guillaume de Conches and the *Prose Salernitan Questions* considered the effects of food, drink, and sleep. Since antiquity the schools of medicine were agreed on the close connection between eating (dietetics) and sexuality.[19] According to prevailing views in the twelfth century, humors originating in all parts of the body generate the sperm in both sexes. Chief among these is blood which the liver produces from the nutrition of food and drink transmitted by the stomach. The violent expulsion of sperm by both man and woman in intercourse draws nutrients away from other organs of the body, resulting in feelings of postcoital debilitation. Renewed infusions of food and drink, however, generate new humors, restore the humoral balance among the organs, and replenish the supply of sperm. Since Constantinus Africanus believed that semen was produced by moisture, spirit, and heat, those foods which were moist, gaseous, and warming were most conducive to generating semen and stimulating coitus. He appended an extensive discussion of foods, like chickpeas, and drinks, like extract of ginger, that brought about these results as well as other foods and beverages that dried out and diminished the supply of sperm. At one point in his discussion, Constantinus concluded that men are most sexually robust and endowed with sperm if their testicles are temperately hot and moist, if they copulate during spring, and if they drink plenty of wine.[20]

Largely unconcerned with therapeutics, the *Prose Salernitan Questions* devoted little attention to the subject of aphrodisiacs, anaphrodisiacs, and their attendant claims. The earlier treatises of Constantinus (*Liber de coitu*) and the *Liber minor de coitu* had ended with chapters which detailed the properties of foods, potions, unguents, and medicines that increased or diminished sexual activity. With poetic embellishment, Gilles de Corbeil extolled the virtues of the aphrodisiac *Diasatryrion* and recommended it especially for revitalizing moribund marriages. Mixed with other ingredients, however, it can also be a depressant, useful for safeguarding chastity.[21]

On a practical level, Constantinus also discussed the effect of external conditions on coitus. The best time is when the body is temperate, that is, neither satiated nor hungry, neither cold nor hot, neither dry nor humid. If moderation is unobtainable, heat is preferred to cold, feast to famine, and before sleep rather than after. The last condition allows the woman quiet and rest to conceive. Intercourse in the middle of the night is harmful because food is half-digested; in the morning before eating is also inadvisable because food is completely digested and the body weakened. Guillaume de Conches and the *Prose Salernitan Questions* did not agree entirely. Sex immediately after meals is harmful because it draws off from the stomach the heat necessary to digest food. Intercourse performed after long fasting or vigorous exercise also depletes the body of strength. The optimal condition is after sleep when digestion is completed.[22]

Since Ovid was a member of the affluent and well-fed Roman aristocracy, he gave little thought to the effects of food on seduction. For him banquets were worthy of mention not for nutritive value but for opportunities to meet the object of prey. Indifferent to food, he nonetheless enthusiastically recommended the properties of wine. The festive day calls for sex (*Venerem*), song and undiluted wine (*merum*), he exalted in his *Amores*. In the more didactic *Ars amatoria* he urged attendance at banquets where both wine and conquest abound and where *Amor* enlists Bacchus's assistance. In a celebrated passage, he proclaimed: "Wine prepares the spirits and makes them ready for the heat of passion. Care flees when drowned in strong wine. Laughter arises . . . and grief and anxiety disappear from the wrinkled brow. Often girls bewitch the minds of youths, and Venus working through wine becomes the fire in fire." Only in the cold second thoughts of the *Remedia amoris* did Ovid remember to caution: "Wines indeed prepare the mind for Venus, unless you take too much, for then the heart is numbed and drowned in strong drink." Although Ovid's vernacular interpeter agreed that wine stimulated lust, he was more concerned about the disabilities of drunkenness.[23]

In the aristocratic setting of the romances, wedding banquets provided splendid occasions for describing eating and drinking. The banquet traditionally took place after the church service and before the bridal couple were led to the nuptial chamber. At Pentecost King Arthur hosted a regal feast for Erec and Enide at which he commanded his pantlers, cooks, and butlers to distribute an abundance of bread, wine, and venison (vv.2006–14). At Arthur's feast for Alexandre and Soredamors at Windsor, Chrétien will not waste words on the festivities, but we can rest assured, he averred, that the feasting was abundant (*Cligès*, vv.2312–22); nor will he stop for details on the wedding of Alis to Fenice, except to include the evening supper which was essential to the plot because it was there that the emperor was drugged with the magic potion (vv.3200–3208). Conrad's climactic marriage to the belle Lïenor at Mainz, however, offered Jean Renart a fitting occasion to describe the setting of tables, the serving of the great nobility, singing, entertainment, and the bewildering variety of meats and wines (*Roman*, vv.5449–58). Wedding feasts were public celebrations whose chief purpose was to provide the host—King Arthur or the Emperor Conrad—opportunity to display power and largesse, not to sustain the bridal couple for the wedding night.

Within the aristocratic literature of the twelfth century, attitudes toward the effects of food and drink on sexuality ranged from indifference to disgust. Comparatively well fed like Ovid's Roman, the aristocratic hero is less interested in the enticements of the table than of the bed. As Chrétien's innocent Perceval experiments with love's delights, he eats with great appetite, not before but after his amatory escapades with the damoiselle of the tent (L. vv.732–51, 3863–65; R. vv.734–55, 3881–83). Having defeated Blancheflor's arch enemy, he returns to the girl's chamber for refreshment and rest, but the young knight prefers kisses, embraces, and sweet words to drinking and eating (L. vv.2352–60; R. vv.2354–62). When the young Lanval passes an afternoon with the lady of his fantasies, he first spends it in bed before repairing to a supper interlarded with kisses

(vv. 153–88). During the hunt Conrad and his young companions likewise lay siege to the ladies before they celebrate with a sumptuous lunch consisting of minutely described patés, venison, cheeses from the Clermont valley and Moselle wines (vv. 367–78). If these knights and ladies were mindful of medical advice, they seem to be following the prescriptions of the *Prose Salernitan Questions* to avoid sex on a full stomach and to restore the bodily humors lost from lovemaking.

Those who write for aristocratic society in the twelfth century, however, thought of love not only as joy and pleasure but also as grief and pain—discomfort that made eating and drinking difficult if not impossible. With few exceptions, André the Chaplain neglected food in his handbook. Defining love as innate suffering, he emphasized the debilitative effects of intercourse observed by physicians, noting that lovers not only lose sleep, which diminishes appetite, but also fail to nourish their bodies with food and drink, which depletes physical strength.[24] Amplifying the theme of suffering, Thomas of Britain rendered Tristan and Iseut virtually seasick, a condition that expunged all mention of food or drink. Chrétien's lovers in *Cligès* repeat the symptoms. On shipboard Alexandre and Soredamor feed only on the glances of eyes (vv. 584–86). When Cligès leaves for Brittany, Fenice is no longer able to eat or drink (vv. 4336–45). According to romance, therefore, a violent distaste for food and drink is the risk that all aristocrats run when they fall in love.

Against this aristocratic stance, Pierre the Chanter returned to Ovid and the medical theories by arguing that food and wine are not indifferent to nor excluded by desire but, on the contrary, enhance, indeed exacerbate, the sexual drive. The Garden of Eden established the ur-paradigm where Adam and Eve ate the forbidden fruit before falling into sin and introducing concupiscence into the world. Commenting on the Genesis passage, Pierre revived Gregory the Great's gloss that explained that although the first parents were tempted by vain glory and avarice, the first vice was gluttony when they ate the forbidden food.[25] In the *Verbum abbreviatum* Pierre placed the treatment of sexual vice immediately after the chapter on gluttony because of direct causation. When Proverbs (30:15) says that the leech has two daughters, crying out, "Give, give," this refers to the maw of the stomach and unfulfilled lust. Craving gluttony calls out to the hand, "Give, give"; the distended stomach calls out to the genitals, "give, give." Many kinds of illicit lust are born of gluttony: simple fornication, adultery, incest, and the sodomites' most shameful vice. The explanation is simply anatomical: the stomach and the genitals are close to each other (*Vicina enim sunt venter et genitalia*). Gluttony was further linked to drunkenness. Like the former, inebriation distends the stomach, inflames the flesh, feeds and warms lust, as the infamous shame of Lot and Noah demonstrated. These direct connections are further confirmed by the classical poets, among them Ovid's celebrated verses on wine, which the Chanter repeated in full. To encapsulate the linkage among food, drink, and sexuality, Pierre quoted Terence's line which was the common coinage of all clerical schoolboys: "Without Ceres and Bacchus, Venus shivers in the cold.[26]

The clerics who rewrote Ovid for the schools also concurred with Terence's epigram. When the narrator of the *De tribus puellis* finally gains access to the chamber of the maiden, dinner is already prepared with smoking meats and full goblets. Although the youth is too excited to eat, his hostess insists that he taste the tender thighs of a dove and drink from her cup in anticipation of pleasures to follow (vv. 188–216). Thus fortified, they pass a night that rivals Ovid's most vivid fantasies.

Even more than the Latin comedies, the fabliaux concurred with Pierre the Chanter over the connections among food, drink, and sexuality. Although the aristocracy are rarely seen eating in the fabliaux, the authors were thoroughly engaged with the bourgeoisie, peasants, clerics, and the demimonde at table.[27] Whatever their marital status or particular condition, the diners share the intent to prepare themselves for love's exertions. When Jean Bodel's merchant from Douai returns home, his wife welcomes him warmly in hopes that she might obtain what she has missed for three months. Seating him by the fire, she serves meat and fish accompanied by wines from Auxerre and Soissons. We do not forget that the wine was unfortunately too abundant, and the good woman was forced to pass the night alone with her dreams (vv. 20–46). The restorative properties of food were openly acknowledged in *Le vallet aus douze fames* which introduced a young Norman who boasts that it would take at least twelve wives to satisfy him. Six months of marriage with one, however, reduces him to skin and bone from a barrage of lovemaking day and night. When he finally concedes his foolishness, she resuscitates him with baths, grooming, and ample quantities of food and drink according to the doctors' prescriptions (vv. 140–49).

The prevalent couple at table in the fabliaux, however, consisted of a matron and a clerical lover, usually the local priest. Again, Jean Bodel offered an early paradigm in his *Vilain de Bailluel* where the peasant's wife is introduced in the midst of baking a capon and cake and pouring out wine for an anticipated visit of the priest (vv. 13–19). Thereafter we witness a virtual parade of priests sneaking into peasant or bourgeois houses where they are entertained sometimes in the bath, but invariably at table before joining their hostess in bed. When the pair is surprised by the husband, as in the *Borgoise d'Orliens,* the townswoman locks her spouse out of the house and has him beaten by servants while she offers cakes and wines of

Auvergne to a clerical student before "holding council" until dawn (vv.262–72).[28] Prostitutes as well, like Richeut (vv.1256–60) and Mabel (*Boivin de Provins,* vv.176–85) set their tables to lure customers; in the masculine counterpart of *Le foteor,* the gigolo and the wife first take a bath and drink wine together (vv.280–88). This abundance of food and drink may well have stimulated the humors necessary for sex according to Constantinus Africanus, but according to the more recent opinion of the *Prose Salernitan Questions* sex so soon after eating is bad for the digestion. In the misogynistic diatribe with which André the Chaplain concluded Book III of his *De amore,* he identified a species of women who secretly invite companions to tables in hidden places where they eat at unaccustomed hours.[29] André imputed this behavior to the enslavement of Eve's belly, but Pierre the Chanter and the fabliaux audiences might well have suspected other motivation.

Although most romance writers were reluctant to establish direct causation between food and sexual desire, Jean Renart was less inhibited. When the empress in *Escoufle* conspires to persuade the emperor to abandon his plans to marry his daughter to Guillaume, she assuages his anger by taking him to bed. A chamberlain serves raw and cooked fruit and wine before the wife applies kisses, embraces, and endearing words that accomplish her purpose (vv.2861–75). As the young lovers flee north from Rome, they too combine the pleasures of food and love. After reserving lodging each evening, they refill their bottles with cold or young wine and procure provisions for the next day: cakes, wrapped patés, cold meat, and roasted chicken. The next day they travel until prime, choose a fountain en route, partake of a lunch, and give themselves over to embraces, kisses, and *solas,* and *deduit* for which the days seem short and nightfall comes quickly (vv.4296–4331).

Chastity

Guillaume de Conches and the *Prose Salernitan Questions* attended to specific questions involving the physiology and function of intercourse, but Constantinus Africanus's comprehensive treatise on coitus not only treated a broad range of dysfunctions and therapy but also sought to situate sexuality within the general framework of good health for men, a concern that had long preoccupied ancient physicians. Constantinus reported that although Epicurus had pronounced sexual activity as harmful, Galen had included it with exercise, baths, food, drink, and sleep as conducive to healthful living. If practiced with care, moreover, it had therapeutic value for the sluggish and infirm. Because coitus tends to dry out the body, for example, it is particularly beneficial to those suffering from an overabundance of phlegm. It also purges superfluous vapors, thus quieting, cooling, and aiding the body. For the same reason it is useful for calming melancholia, dementia, and concupiscent love, provided that one lies with someone other than the one desired. Galen had warned that excessive coitus not only drains away seed but also vital spirit through the arteries, inducing debility, even death. Those who engage less live longer as demonstrated by domesticated animals and eunuchs. Despite the dangers of excess, Constantinus nonetheless agreed with Galen that moderate sex under favorable conditions was conducive to healthful living for males.[30]

The role of sexual intercourse in women's health also prompted debate among the ancient physicians. As early as the Hippocratic corpus, but reinforced by Galen, physicians had proposed that reproduction is essential to female nature. Since the uterus is the organ that defines women, intercourse is not only necessary for conception but also to keep the uterus properly moistened. If it dries out, it begins to move and to cause further disorders. Sexual activity and pregnancy are, therefore, essential to female health. Against this tradition Soranus of Ephesus argued that women are not fundamentally different from men. Although the female functions of conception, parturition, and lactation may be subject to pathologies specific to the respective organs, women do not have diseases that are peculiarly feminine. Apart from reproduction and its attendant problems, the woman's physical constitution is equivalent to man's. Intercourse, moreover, is harmful to both men and women because the body is made ill by desire and the debilitations of excreting seed. By comparing the health of neutered animals and continent humans, Soranus concluded that perpetual virginity is the most healthful of states. While menstruation and pregnancy are useful for perpetuating the human race, these functions are particularly dangerous to the childbearer. Virginity, which safeguards women from the latter, is, therefore, of special benefit.[31]

The conclusions of Soranus's defense of virginity were transmitted to the Latin West by the abbreviated summaries of Muscio and Caelius Aurelianus. Caelius noted that neutered animals are stronger and that women who remain virgins because of law or religion are less subject to sickness. Omitting the obvious dangers of pregnancy, Caelius nonetheless stated that virginity is the most salutary state for both men and women, although intercourse is necessary for the propagation of the human race.[32] Despite its survival in the translations of Muscio and Caelius, Soranus's advocacy of virginity had little influence on the school of Salerno and its followers in the twelfth century. The gynecological treatises of Johannes Platearius and the *De curis mulierum* from the Trotula corpus, for example, assumed the Galenic appraisal of the benefits of intercourse for women. According to *Cum auctor* the peculiar affliction of the "suffocated womb" threatens widows and nubile virgins because they cannot discharge excess sperm through normal intercourse.[33] These Galenic propositions which Constantinus Africanus transmitted to the *Prose Salernitan Questions* reinforced a context in the late twelfth century in which physicians considered sexual intercourse to be essential to the health of both men and women.

Summoning up his medical learning, André the Chaplain also entered the debate over the healthfulness of sexual intercourse. Among the plethora of arguments marshaled against sexuality and women in Book III of *De amore* was a series of medical theorems. Venereal activity debilitates the body, decreases the appetite for food and drink, and takes away sleep— all essential to good health. Loss of sleep further affects the mind and induces madness. It provokes poor digestions and fevers and shortens life span. André could even remember reading in a medical treatise that intercourse prompts premature senility. He attributed the theory of sleep to Johannicius's *Isagoge,* the standard manual on medicine, but it actually derived from Guillaume de Conches and was repeated in the *Prose Salernitan Questions*. Except perhaps for the risk of senility, all charges levied against coitus from medical literature were drawn from examples of immoderate intercourse and were distorted to apply to sexuality in general. André could find little in contemporary Salernitan medicine to support his extreme position.[34]

The prevailing rationale in support of chastity, therefore, was drawn not from current medical theory but from religion. Since the early Middle Ages the chief advocates of sexual continence were the monks whose writings and personal example extolled the superiority of perpetual virginity. We have seen, however, that by the beginning of the twelfth century the new monastic orders accepted only adults who could be sexually experienced, and that by the end of the twelfth century contemporary monks and nuns had composed few treatises on virginity. Apparently they had also ignored the surviving Soranic medical treatises that offered a physiological defense to their position. Equally significant, the contemporary theologians of the secular clergy, although personally obligated to chastity if they aspired to holy orders, likewise took little interest in the claims for virginity. Pierre the Chanter, for example, openly admired the charismatic abbot Bernard de Clairvaux and the Cistercian order of monks, but neither his *Verbum abbreviatum* contained a chapter on the monastic virtue of chastity nor did his biblical commentaries and *questiones* dwell on the issue.[35] Only in the alphabetical and comprehensive compilation of *distinctiones,* entitled the *Summa Abel,* did he turn to the traditional rationale for monastic virtue. Just as marriage replenishes the earth, virginity populates heaven. It excels martyrdom because, although the latter can be obtained in a moment, the former is achieved only through prolonged distress and struggle. Concluding with significant qualifications, he maintained that chastity concerns the body but is of no value without accompanying attitudes of charity and humility of heart. Humble marriage is better than proud virginity![36] In a similar vein, Thomas of Chobham discussed cases of nuns and lay virgins whose chastity had been secretly violated and noted that virginity itself is not a spiritual virtue. A righteous woman, for example, who marries and loses virginity in the conjugal bed, loses her virtue in no way but retains the moral goodness she formerly possessed, since what was virginal modesty now becomes wedded modesty and will eventually become widowed modesty. Virginity, therefore, is only accidental to the fundamental virtue of modesty. Gilles de Corbeil sought to illustrate the theologians' teaching with a personal example. He knew of a canon who led an angelic life of absolute chastity for thirty years, but at the price of inordinate pride. On his deathbed, however, when sham dissolves before truth, he called his brothers and friends to his side and asked forgiveness for arrogant vainglory. Although he had despised their carnal pleasures as befitting pigs, he would have done better to have sacrificed his virtue to Corinna than to have so engorged his virginity. Not that he recommended debauchery as a remedy for self-satisfaction, Gilles hastened to add, but simply to highlight the perils of pride.[37]

If the Chanter and his disciples neglected to emphasize the excellence of chastity, they were nonetheless destined to produce a new champion for the monastic virtue among their number. We have seen that as preachers from the Chanter's circle dispersed throughout the Lowlands, Jacques de Vitry discovered the remarkable personality of Marie d'Oignies in the region of Liège. Although married at age fourteen, Marie's precocious sanctity, exhibited in her childhood preference for clothing, continued into the early years of her married life. To chastise her body and keep it under subjection, she passed most of the night working with her hands and praying. What remained she spent hidden at the foot of her bed with little sleep. Although she did not have power over her own body according to Christian marriage, she cruelly girded herself with a rough rope hidden under her chemise. Such austerity, Jacques commented, it not to be commended widely, because of the canonical principle that the actions of grace are the privilege of a few and not the common precept for all. It is not surprising, however, that she did not live long in the wedded state. The Lord heard her sighs and supplications and inspired her husband Jean to agree to mutual chastity. Imitating her example, he became her companion in the angelic calling and pursuit of holy religion.[38] Throughout her life she so disciplined her flesh that for years she never experienced the first promptings of lust. During the protracted period of fasting, however, when a dear friend pressed her hand in a gesture of spiritual affection, but with no shameful thought, he immediately felt the first movements of desire from proximity to a woman. Although she was unconscious of it, he heard a celestial voice exclaim, "Do not touch me" (*Noli tangere me*). At first not understanding the pertinence of this well-known scriptural phrase, he soon realized that God was safeguarding the chastity of his friend. As portrayed in the *Vita, Marie* d'Oignies finished her days as an exemplary witness to the virtue of sexual continence—not the ancient virginity of the nun or monk consecrated at birth, but the chastity of the *mulier sancta* of new monasticism who voluntarily enlisted in this rank after marriage.

Sexual Modesty

The descriptive modes for treating the sexual act followed directly from the representations of the sexual body, ranging, as we have seen, from extreme reticence to graphic explicitness. Although theologians like Robert of Courson conceded that coitus belonged to the natural world by divine creation, they nonetheless subscribed to the Augustinian tradition that sexual intercourse was so thoroughly contaminated with concupiscence that it was entirely infused with shame. To this theological repugnance the medical doctors took open exception. In response to a disciple's suggestion that the subject matter of coitus was not decent, Guillaume de Conches had replied sharply that nothing natural is shameful but rather the gift of creation. Only hypocrites and ranters avoid the subject, fearing vocabulary more than the reality. The riposte was preserved verbatim in the Salernitan questions.[39] As for terminology, the doctors avoided direct and obscene speech, such as *futuo* (fuck), or even metaphors, such as *caedo* (strike) or *fodio* (dig), to choose a vocabulary based on metonymy. *Coitus* (coming together), *coniunctio, commixtio* (joining), *concubitus* (sleeping), and the coupling of *Venus* (the goddess of love) with *opus* (work) and *actio* (deed), plus their verb equivalents, constituted the semantic field for intercourse. Despite the accusation of fearing words, the theologians, in fact, employed a vocabulary comparable to that of the physicians, adding perhaps *copulatio* (joining) and substituting *carnalis* (fleshly) for the pagan *venereus*. Biblical passages such as "Adam knew his wife Eve" (Gen. 4:1) reinforced the classical use of *cognoscere* as carnal knowledge. The one theological contribution to the Latin sexual vocabulary, however, was *debitum* (debt) occurring in the unique scriptural passage of I Corinthians 7:3: "The husband renders to the wife her due (*debitum*) and the wife to the husband." This Latin word stock became the clinical and learned vocabulary current in the schools for the sexual act.[40]

Besides this clinical approach, Ovid contributed a coy modesty to the Latin vocabulary of the schools. Just as the self-proclaimed master of love

188

declined to name the sexual body directly, so also the sexual act. During the often considered summer afternoon with Corinna in the *Amores,* not only does the poet stop short of describing her full nakedness (*singula quid referam?*), but as he clasps her to himself, he exclaims, "Who does not know the rest?" (*cetera quis nescit?*). As for the vagina, *cetera* becomes the euphemism for coitus. Again in the *Ars amatoria,* when the seducer finally joins his mistress in bed, the poet's muse must remain outside the closed doors while words and fingers continue their work.[41] A genius of indirection when dealing with the verbal permutations of sexuality, Ovid's closest approach to direct discourse is to join the love goddess to assorted neutral nouns (*Veneris . . . lascivia, gaudia, conubia, furtiuae, modus, sensum, munus*). Only in the *Ars* when referring to beasts will he use the clinical *coit*—but the maiden averts her eyes—or the unvarnished *concubitus* in the *Remedia,* when he seeks to generate repulsion against one's mistress.[42]

Ovid's epigones in the Latin schools, however, began to take leave of their master. We have seen that the poets were less inhibited in expressing the sexual act and that André the Chaplain preferred a clinical approach reminiscent of the learned physicians and theologians. Although the royal chaplain showed little concern with the details of the sexual body (except perhaps to experiment with metaphorical conceits), he was prepared to discuss intercourse openly and directly. Of interest here, his precise and unambiguous vocabulary for coitus included not only *opera Veneris/actus Veneris,* shared with Ovid and the medical authorities, but also, more important, a preference for *solatium/solatia* (solace, consolation). This euphemism with a broad range of meanings found few sexual antecedents in Ovid's amatory poems, nor was it common among twelfth-century Latin writers, but its French equivalent was shared by the vernacular gloss to the *Ars amatoria* and, most important, by contemporary vernacular poets. By this route *solas* joined the stock of indirect expressions for the sexual act.[43]

If the Latin school authors were not inclined to follow Ovid's path of indirection, his true successors in the twelfth century were the romance poets. Although they felt perfectly at liberty to garnish their narrations with innumerable embraces and kisses (*d'acoler et de baisier*), they resorted to a whole spectrum of circumlocutions for depicting the coital act itself. The most graphic were the earliest in the Tristan legend. In Béroul Iseut swears that no man has entered her thighs (v.4205), and Gottfried von Strassburg notes that Blancheflor was able to raise the mettle of the wounded Rivalin in order to conceive Tristan (vv.1302–25). Chrétien is satisfied to employ the bed to evoke intercourse as, for example, on the wedding night of Erec and Enide (vv.2017–18), of the Emperor Alis and Fenice (*Cligès,* vv.3287–92), and during Perceval's amorous adventures (for example, L. v.2052, R. v.2054). For Jean Renart the bed likewise signified the consummation of the marriages of Count Richard and the lady of Genoa (*Escoufle*, vv.1747–49) and of Conrad and Lïenor (*Roman*, vv.5503–5). Jean also can be as coy as Ovid as to whether the young Guillaume and Aelis have had intercourse when their beds were placed next to each other (*Escoufle*, vv.7876–84). In like fashion in the *Lai de l'ombre* Jean takes leave of the two lovers at the well as they begin to kiss and caress (vv.942–55). Less ambiguous is the manner in which the emperor and his gallants receive the ladies on the hunt: "The knights await them, extending their arms and hands to draw them under the covers. Only he who has fought in such battles can know their pleasure" (*Roman*, vv.211–15). Physical coitus was still robed in the metaphors of fire and battle.

Announced in the Tristan legend, the loss of a maiden's virginity became another standard metonymy for representing intercourse. In Gottfried's version Iseut has given herself to Tristan on board ship, but King Mark, duped on his wedding night by Iseut's servant Brangane, drinks the customary toast to having taken Iseut's maidenhead (vv.12, 631–646). On her wedding night Chrétien's Enide loses the title of maiden and awakes the next day a new *dame* (vv.2053–54), whereas Fenice is mistakenly called a *dame* because she remains a virgin during her wedding night (*Cligès*, v.5180–82). In this tradition Jean Renart situated the title-episode of his *Roman de la rose*. To disqualify Lïenor the seneschal has gone to lengths to impugn her virginity (*pucelage*, v.3586)—to the point of disclosing the intimate rose on her thigh. The central question of her virginity is repeatedly raised throughout the episode. For her part, when Lïenor has vindicated her honor she can finally reassert publicly: "I am the virgin (*pucele*) of the rose!" (v.5040).

Within these stock framing devices of bed and virginity the vocabulary denoting coitus also became increasingly conventionalized. Echoing the physicians, Thomas called Tristan's purported union with Iseut aux Mains Blanches a natural act (*naturel fait*, p.54, v.518) or work (*ovre*, p.54, v.523 = *opera*). La commune (vv.1193, 2329, 3773, 4163) is Béroul's characteristic expression for sexual congress. Chrétien had a penchant for biblical terminology, for example, when Erec and Enide render their marital debt to each other on their wedding night (*lor droit randent a chascun manbre*, v.2036 = *reddere debitum*), or when Fenice protests that the Emperor has not known her as Adam knew (*conut*=*cognoscere*) his wife (*Cligès*, vv.5178–79). Throughout the romance corpus, however, words like *joie*, *delit*, *deduit* (joy, pleasure), *solaz* (solace, consolation), and *soreplus* (surplus, the rest) became the accepted terminology for the sexual act, although they were frequently used with other connotations as well. By exploiting this word-stock they merely followed the example of the southern troubadours for whom *gaug*, *jauzimen*, *jauzi*, *joie*, and *solatz* served to designate physical consummation.[44] Among innumerable examples that can be furnished in northern romance: Erec and Enide have *la joie et le delit* in their marriage bed (v.2017), as do Cligès and Fenice in their tower garden (v.6332). What Jean Renart's newly wedded couples, Richard and the lady of Genoa, and Conrad and Liënor, do in bed is called *deduit* (*Escoufle,* v.1749 bis; *Roman,* v.5503).[45] Within the broad semantic range of *solaz* are numerous examples of sexual activity corresponding to André the Chaplain's *solatium.* When Chrétien's Perceval and Blancheflor lie in bed, arm in arm, and mouth to mouth, they have a night of *solaz* (L. vv.2062–65, R. vv.2064–67), although it is never resolved whether intercourse has actually been performed. The coronation of Guillaume and Aelis at Rome in *Escoufle* brings knights and maidens together in new loves in which there is *solas* and *deduit* (v.9025). In the *Roman* Jean has never seen men with so much *solaz* as at the return of the knights to the tents (v.195), the same *solaz* that the count of Luxembourg enjoys with his ladylove (v.325).

After Marie de France's Guigemar succeeds in convincing the lady of the sincerity of his intentions, she finally grants him her love. As the two are at their ease, lying together, conversing, often kissing and embracing, Marie added this comment: "I hope that this was accompanied by that *surplus* to which others are accustomed to do," vv.527–34). The use of the word *surplus* (surplus, the rest) to suggest intercourse was further elaborated by Chrétien de Troyes as he narrated the adventures of his neophyte knight, Perceval. The unknown extent to which the youth's erotic experiences had progressed allowed the author to assume his most Ovidian of stances. When Perceval departs to seek his chivalric fortune, his mother offers him advice on how to treat damsels and ladies: "If you come to their aid, you may also court them. You may kiss a maiden, if she consents, but I forbid you to go further" (*le soreplus vos an desfant,* L. v.545, R. v.548). What the mother intimates by *soreplus,* Ovid had suggested by *cetera* (the rest). Whether or not Perceval obeys his mother when he spends a night of *solaz* with Blancheflor may remain open, but it is clear that when the young man meets his first maiden in distress, although he does force a kiss he refrains from going further. Many episodes later, however, the maiden's *ami* and protector is not convinced. "No one will believe that he kissed her without going further (*sanz fere plus*)," he complains. "One thing leads to another. . . . A woman who abandons her mouth gives the *soreplus* easily" (L. vv.3839–46, R. vv.3858–60). This was, in fact, Ovid's clear doctrine: "He who takes kisses but not the rest (*cetera*), is worthy to lose that which was also given him."[46] Although Perceval protests, "There was no more, and I did nothing more" (L. v.3888, R. v.3906), he comes up against the force of Ovidian tradition embedded in the romances. As Jean Renart joined Conrad with Liënor on their wedding night, his language clearly resonated the tradition prepared by Marie and Chrétien: "When Tristan loved Iseut and could take pleasure by embracing, kissing, and the surplus that accompanied it (*sorplus qu'il covint*), . . . then you can be sure that one would not be able to compare their happiness easily to this" (*Roman*, vv.5507–15).

Within the romance context, therefore, the lexicon of *joie, delit, deduit, solaz*, and *soreplus* could scarcely occur unequivocally. On one extreme, these words evoked the nuptial night when a child was conceived; on the other, it could be regarded as a mere dalliance or flirtation. Between these limits was a whole range of possibilities epitomized by Perceval's ambiguous behavior. In addition, as we have seen, they connoted the accompanying emotional experience of desire. All such indeterminacy was well chosen, however, because equivocation lay at the heart of romance sexuality. "The most choice and delightful pleasure is that which the story keeps silent from us and hides," affirms Queen Guenièvre after her night with Lancelot (*Charette*, vv.4682–84).

Sexual Techniques

Finding words to denote the sexual act led to the question of how far the authors would go in describing the erotic techniques of coitus. And since they invariably assumed that the performers were heterosexual couples, they approached implicitly, if not explicitly, the fundamental questions of gender: What roles were assigned to men and women? Who initiated intercourse? These were not issues to which the romanciers willingly responded, because of their nearly complete reticence in sexual matters. Nor were the theologians inclined to explore the intimate details of an activity on which they shared profound ambivalence, but they were custodians of one fundamental principle of far-reaching significance in the coital relations of married Christians. In discussing matrimony in I Corinthians 7, Paul the Apostle had defined intercourse as a *debitum*, that is, a debt, right, or obligation owed by one spouse to the other: "The husband renders to his wife her due (*debitum*) and similarly the wife to the husband" (v.3). The obligation, moreover, was absolutely reciprocal, "because the wife does not have power over her body, but the husband, and the husband over his body, but the wife" (v.4). The fundamental mutuality was further underscored in the formulation of the two phrases. In the first the wife appears first as the demander whom the husband has the obligation to satisfy. In the second the husband is presented first as having rights over the wife's body, thus reversing the order. Pierre the Chanter glossed this passage by encapsulating its significance. Following the Lombard, he declared: "In this the man and woman are equal, even though the husband's lordship over the wife is not thereby eliminated." In other words, despite the normal hierarchy of husband over wife, in sexual relations spouses are completely equal.[47]

It was easier, however, to proclaim the broad principle of sexual reciprocity than to enforce it within the complexities of practice. Full compliance opened a Pandora's box of casuistic conundrums. If one spouse demands an immoral sexual act, is the other obligated to respond? What if a wife asks for her conjugal rights during a sacred season? What if a husband demands a sodomistic practice from his wife? The canonists Gratian had raised the case of holy seasons, following the suggestion of the Apostle that couples could separate for periods of prayer (I Cor. 7:5), but concluded that such abstinence was legitimate only with the mutual consent of the spouses.[48] Without exploring the variety of practical problems involved, the succeeding Decretists strengthened the principle of sexual reciprocity. Distinguishing spontaneous intercourse from coerced, Rufinus declared that a husband who is forced to return the conjugal debt does not sin, not even venially.[49] For Huguccio, moreover, refusing to respond to the marital debt is itself a mortal sin. A husband, therefore, is faced with a moral perplexity between this mortal sin and the venial sin involved in the sexual delight or craving of coitus. He advised the husband to attempt to elude the wife's request by offering excuses of time, place, or future compliance, but if she persists he can satisfy her demands without any sin. (This was the one case when Huguccio rendered sexual intercourse blameless.)[50] The *Glossa ordinaria* to the *Decretum* of Johannes Teutonicus concluded that it may be a sin to ask for one's marital rights, but no one sins in responding to the conjugal obligations.[51]

Among the theologians, Robert of Courson likewise followed the Apostle's suggestion and Gratian's example. He turned his attention to the specific example of holy seasons, as we have seen, and formulated the problem in extreme terms. Does a man sin by having intercourse with his wife on holy festivals, even if she requests it on Easter or Good Friday? Couples may refrain from marital embraces out of reverence for the holy seasons according to the Apostle, but only by mutual consent. If one or the other, however, seeks the conjugal debt by word or even by sign and the spouse is capable of compliance, he or she cannot refuse.[52] This unequivocal formulation reinforced the Pauline principle of reciprocity, which, in turn, imputed strict gender equality, at least in the privileged realm of sexual relations. The principle also implied a division of moral responsibility. Only the demander was guilty of an immoral act, not the responder, thus splitting in half the guilt for questionable sex. In his brief comment, Pierre the Chanter had suggested that sin was removed because marital intercourse, when returning the debt, is without sin to one from whom it is requested.[53] Although the obligation to respond is entirely mutual, it is nonetheless noteworthy that the woman is the initiator in most of the cases posed by the canonists and theologians.

If the conjugal obligation is joined to the observation that women are the usual petitioners, and reinforced by medical theory, that women's sexual appetites exceed those of men, we have precisely the situation that was exploited in the fabliau, *La dame qui aveine demanoit pour Morel sa provende avoir* (The lady who asked for Dobbin to be fed his oats). This lady and a *vallet* loved each other with great abandon of heart and body. Even after marriage each continues, according to the biblical command, to love the other equally as one is loyally obligated (p.319). More than Tristan and Iseut, they make love without cease, day and night, in bed and on the ground. To contrive a more seemly way to summon her partner, the lady invents the courteous euphemism, "Let Dobbin have his oats." Dobbin's hunger, however, persists unabated by the week, day, hour. . . . Unable to extinguish the devouring flame—like Gilles de Corbeil's Greek fire—the husband falls sick, his bones drained of their marrow. After a short convalescence revives him, the wife recalls him once more to his duty (*devoir*). Reduced to desperation at this point, the *vallet* turns his backside to her lap and discharges his bowels. "Here, take the bran; the barn has been emptied of oats." Thereafter the wife accepts what she can have without forcing the rest, whereas the husband serves her as he can whenever he pleases. "I do not say," interposed the narrator, "at her wish but at the will of her husband." The moral for the married, he concluded, "is to do it in measure whenever you see the time and place" (p.329). Fully comprehending the terms and implications of the theological principle, the fableor, not without malicious humor, uncovered the latent conflict between the unqualified marital obligation between spouses and the female reputation for sexual voracity. Contrary to theological teaching, however, his conclusion was to subordinate the wife's appetite to the husband's will.

Like the theologians, the physicians were less interested in specific sexual techniques than in general principles of human behavior and physiology. Only the *Liber minor de coitu,* which concentrated on therapeutics, considered the question of coital positions. The safest and most natural is the man lying prone on a supine woman with her head raised for greater pleasure. If the woman, however, assumes the male position, performs from either side, or sits, the man risks abscess of the loins, eruptions in the bladder and penis, and hernia.[54] We have seen that it was axiomatic in twelfth-century physiology that sexual desire was necessary for emitting sperm. Since the *Prose Salernitan Questions* remained faithful to the Galenic doctrine of the two seeds, both men and women had to experience desire to produce seed and bring about conception. Although the Salernitans had also argued that feminine desire could exceed masculine, conception none-theless required reciprocity between men and women; both partners had to garner sufficient desire to emit their respective speed. Implicit in the theory, therefore, was the simultaneous emission of both seeds. The *Prose Salernitan Questions* did not treat this assumption in their discussion of conception, but they did note the advantages of simultaneous climaxes in coitus as they dealt with the variety of female complexions discovered among prostitutes. After discussing how women with cold and moist complexions needed to be warned by vigorous lovemaking, the discussion then turned to coital techniques. If the duties of both partners are exercised and completed at the same time (*simul*) so that neither anticipates or delays the climax (*celebratio*), then such great delight follows that sex is repeatedly and frequently sought. Because prostitutes find so much pleasure in men experienced in these techniques, they embrace them more ardently and fervently than others.[55]

Ovid pulled the shades whenever he approached carnal consummation directly, but his obsession with sex nonetheless encouraged him to flirt with the subject obliquely. Censoring his mistress for blatantly revealing her love life at the end of the *Amores,* he thereby fabricated an excuse for revealing her techniques: thigh over thigh, tongue thrust into red lips, with words, sounds, and the shaking of the bed, these are the thousand ways of making love. Once she is reclothed, however, modesty once again effaces the obscene business.[56] The episode of his impotency allowed him further warrant to reminisce about happier occasions. What joys does he not imagine, what positions (*modos*) does he not conjure up in his mind? Such imaginary exercises prompted counting: twice with a blonde, three times with others he could name, but Corrina made him perform nine times on one short night![57]

When the poet finally brings the lovers to bed at the end of Book II of the *Ars amatoria,* the locked door to their chamber does not entirely exclude his coaching them in erotic techniques. As they murmur endearments, the left hand should not be idle nor the fingers unable to find those parts where Cupid secretly thrusts his darts. Most important, the pleasure of love should not be hurried but gradually encouraged by slow delays. Once you have found the place which makes women rejoice, do not let shame keep you from touching it; you will know from the gleam of her eyes and her sweet sighs. Do not unfurl your sails to leave her behind; finish the line at the same time (*simul*). Pleasure is fullest when a man and women lie equally (*pariter*) vanquished.[58]

As the thirteenth-century translator opened Ovid's text to a lay audience, he both rendered the poetic figures of the Latin into concrete terms and developed them in the commentary. The places where women love to be touched, for example, were glossed as the cunt (*con*) and the breasts (*mamelles*). When Ovid referred to Achilles's exhaustion from battle, thereby unable to make love except with his hands, the commentary continued that such techniques are against nature. The man wishing to sin less would better have the woman mount on top. In all events, the lover should not hurry but slow down and stop when he has found the female locus of pleasure. As to signals from the eyes and accompanying words, the woman will appear almost to faint and close her eyes as if she were dead. Her orgasmic pleasure will shorten her breath. If she can normally shout *harou* six times she will be able to utter it no more than twice, so great will be her delight. Like a mad dog she will bite her lover on the mouth or neck. Again, as Ovid had insisted, try to finish together if you can, because, as the *chanson* says, "the game is good and beautiful when love comes together (*vient d'ambedeux*)." One should only make love when there is sufficient time and leisure.[59]

Until Ovid's manual on lovemaking was translated into French in the early thirteenth century, it was not directly accessible to the laity but remained the possession of the school clerics skilled in Latin, but with little need for such instruction. As early as the last quarter of the twelfth century, however, the fabliau *Richeut* recognized Ovid's pretensions in erotic techniques and situated him in the competition between laity and clerics. The competition was enacted in the rivalry between the prostitute Richeut (for the laity) and her son Samson, who had benefited from a school education (vv.557–619). When they discuss how love is best taught, Samson vaunts his book learning, but Richeut claims that her experiential knowledge (*us*) gives her the advantage (vv.694–710). More precisely, Richeut believes that she can better instruct Samson on the art of love (*l'art d'aimer*) than Samson can learn from Ovid (vv.747–50). The curriculum of this learning is not revealed, but the mother judges that book learning (*escriture*) reduces control whereas she can teach him how to fall into and out of love more quickly (vv.699–703). So defined, this love lore was undoubtedly broader than Ovid's specific recommendations for simultaneous orgasms, but we shall see that Richeut, Samson, and the fableors themselves nonetheless displayed impressive experience in sexual technique.[60]

In unexpected ways Ovid's doctrine of simultaneous orgasm found widespread agreement among the discourses of the turn of the century. Not only did his vernacular translator concur with and further develop his technique, but the physicians of the *Prose Salernitan Questions* saw the advantage of simultaneous arousal and completion for heating the humors and overcoming the natural resistance of the cold and moist female complexion. More remarkable, despite the theologians' distrust of intercourse infected by concupiscence, the Pauline doctrine of mutual obligation between husband and wife in sexual matters could offer little objection to reciprocal lovemaking.

Although Ovid couched his sexual techniques in poetic figures, these intimations nonetheless encouraged his twelfth-century imitators to test the master's self-imposed constraints. The *De tribus puellis* not only satirized Ovid's summer afternoon by brashly expatiating on the mistress's body but also detailed erotic techniques. As they enter the bed, she covers her lover with thousands of kisses, joins flanks and stomach to his, offers breasts and thighs for caresses until the two bodies converge to play their parts, at which point the narrator stops with the Ovidian, "What shall I do? I can tell what we did, if shame did not forbid. . . . Did it turn out well? Only Love and Venus know all" (vv.269–300). Moreover, as Pyrrus imparts instruction in love to Alda, Guillaume de Blois further explicated erotic techniques. With their arms the lovers embrace and with their tongues explore their mouths. After a surfeit of kisses, Pyrrus takes the rest (*cetera*) with a swelling and rigid penis. To ensure that they have mastered the lesson they repeat it, and to outperform Ovid they continue ten times. The education lasts seven days and nights in this manner (vv.449–81, 515–16).

André the Chaplain assigned the discussion of sexual intercourse to interlocutors of the highest nobility. Prior to revealing that he is a cleric, the man raises a distinction between pure and mixed or composite love. We have seen that the former originates as an affection in the lovers' hearts and minds, and is expressed by kisses and embraces, but omits the final solace. By contrast, mixed love culminates in the ultimate deed of love (*in extremo Veneris opere*). Although the man approves of both forms, he has undoubtedly introduced the former as compatible with his clerical status, but the woman remains incredulous as to whether restraint is possible, arguing that it is judged monstrous if one is placed in a fire but is not burned. Later in the conversation she, in turn, introduces the proverbial distinction between a woman's upper and lower halves. The man immediately elects the upper, condemning the lower as bestial, because it subjects the body to indecent positions, fit only for prostitutes. Although eventually agreeing with the man, the woman argues initially that whatever solaces alleviate men's cares originate from the lower half. In language recalling the *Lai du lecheor,* the lady goes as far as to maintain that no matter how beautiful a woman, if she is found useless in coitus, she will be rejected by all. Just as a building's foundations are deemed more worthy than the walls, so women are judged by their lower parts. When asked to decide between these two positions, André himself, the diligent researcher of love, equivocated. Both pure and mixed love proceed from the heart's affection but are expressed in different ways.[61]

As the Latin Ovidians approached coital techniques or discussed the legitimacy of intercourse, they retained the linguistic probity of their preceptor. The comedies never yield to coarse speech, and André himself maintained a clinical, learned vocabulary. The closest a Latin writer came to verbal obscenity is when the servant Fodius puns upon his own name as he swears to Babio that he has not "dug" (*fodit*) the latter's wife.[62] The Latin writers of the Ovidian tradition, therefore, sided with the theologians, doctors, and romance writers in erecting a barrier against vulgar speech about coitus.

The fableors were well acquainted with these restraints, particularly in those stories treating the noble classes which imitated the romance language of *fin' amors*. During the absence of the husband in *Le chevalier a la robe vermeille*, for example, the lady invites her knight to bed to have more pleasant *deliz*. With formulaic indirection the author will not speak of their *joie* and *solaz*, because those who understand know what it is. Both enjoyed the *deduit* that lovers have when they play together (vv.62–77). These standard romance terms were adopted in many fabliaux ranging from the refined and sensitive *Guillaume au faucon* to the more coarse Jean Bodel. In the latter's *Sohaiz* the exhausted merchant forgets his wife's *delit* (v.44), and the cleric in *Gombert* embraces, kisses, and has his *deliz* with the peasant's daughter (v.81).[63]

Despite familiarity with romance convention the linguistic barrier crumbled in the fabliaux. Just as Pyrrus teaches Alda the techniques of love in the Latin poem, so the young man of the *Damoisele qui ne pooit oïr* not only teaches the prudish maiden to name the body's parts but, most directly, to tolerate the word fuck (*foutre*, v.8). From Jean Bodel's earliest fabliau and thereafter *foutre* became the word of choice to designate sexual intercourse. "I have just fucked the host's daughter," the one cleric reports to his companion while they share Gombert's hospitality (v.152). Other comparable terms such as *culeter* (to cunt), *estre vertoillie* (to be skewered), *arecier* (to get it up), *locier* (to move in and out), and *feru et heurté* (to bump and batter) surface along with numerous circumlocutions, but *foutre* joined *vit* (prick), *coilles* (balls), *con* (cunt), and *cul* (asshole) as the standard sexual lexicon of the fabliaux.[64]

The three versions of the *Damoisele qui ne pooit . . .* recorded this transition from euphemism to direct speech. In two versions the young men pasture their roncins (horses) and make them drink at the fountain up to their heads (I, vv.105–6; III, v.210). (We remember that even the sexually insatiable wife can only bring herself to ask her husband to feed Dobbin his oats.) In a third version, however, David drops the metaphorical conceit and "puts his prick into her cunt to do his good and desire" (II, vv.204–5). One of the versions concluded with a comment on the transition:

By this example I wish to demonstrate that women are not too proud to say *foutre* out loud if they fuck all the same. . . . Certain people speak of it who exalt the word, because there is a great difference between doing and saying, but ass [still] pulls harder than rope. I say this on account of the *vilain*'s daughter who was converted as soon as she had the young man's horse drink at her fountain. (III, vv.223–36)

The explanation is simple enough: only those who are sexually experienced can speak of the act directly, but apparently this included most of the fableors' audiences, because graphic descriptions of this nature abound. In the *Le fevre de Creeil,* for example, as the well-endowed apprentice makes love to the blacksmith's wife, it was to be expected that the author will not spare the details: "The prick is as rigid as a pole. Probing to find a place, it is ready to thrust in" (vv.143–45). In *Boivin de Provins* the hero takes the prostitute Ysane by pricking her cunt with the end of his cock and going up to the balls (vv.278–81). Jean Bodel's cleric avers that he has drilled a hole in the cask of Gombert's daughter (v.155).

After Jean Bodel's priest undresses the wife of Bailluel, the two fall on each other, he above, she below (vv.86–87). When the fabliaux make coital positions explicit, the woman supine and the man prone seems to be the most common practice, also suggested by the metaphor of riding horseback. This preference agreed with the medical opinion that this posture was most healthful and with the canonist judgment that it was most virtuous.[65] As was to be expected, the prostitutes introduced variety into their *métier.* Although professional girls could make a little money on their backs (v.14), when Richeut sets about to become pregnant she endures pushing and pulling from above and below until she succeeds (vv.149–51). Not to be excelled by his mother, Samson does it backward and forward. Placing the women on their backs, he draws their knees up to their chests. He enters from the side, forward, and the rear. He takes them sitting (*à brachet*), doggy-like (*à pissechien*) and bending forward (*à estupons*)—if you will excuse my speech—the narrator interposed (vv.936, 945–53). As the *vallet* is pressed by his insatiable wife, he too must perform forward and backward, up and down (p.324), until exhausted. Under less demanding conditions the ever-active cleric in Bodel's *Gombert* nonetheless brags that he has taken the vilain's daughter from behind and the side (v.154). Among the theologians, Pierre de Poitiers was most explicit about coital positions. Not only did he repeat Augustine's condemnation of extravaginal intercourse as being against nature, but he included the canine (*canino more*) and female superior positions as well. According to the martyr Methodius, the last enormity had provoked God to punish the world by flood. In Thomas of Chobham's comprehensive taxonomy, *impetuosus* coitus included acts against nature, which, in turn, envisaged not only masturbation, intercourse with beasts and the same gender, but also with women in those members not made for coitus, as we have seen.[66] Thus defined, these proscriptions would have eliminated oral and anal sex, but would not have pronounced on the vaginal variations reported by Pierre de Poitiers and the fabliaux. The fableors, for their part, appear to have avoided such "unnatural" practices and limited all sexuality to the genitals. When the aristocratic Berengier forces her peasant husband to kiss her ass, for example, genital action is not involved; her purpose is to avenge social outrage.[67]

The frenetic sexual activity of the fabliaux inevitably called for numerical accounting. The physicians had asserted that coitus repeated twice produces the same sensation as the loss of a pound of blood.[68] The second cleric in Jean Bodel's *Gombert*, however, claims that he performed three times with the wife (v.117), David four with the prudish girl (*Damoisele qui ne poit . . .* II, v.207), but the cleric in the *Meunier,* always in competition with Bodel, boasts of seven with the miller's daughter (p.92). In one night of lodging at the priest's house, the voracious knight performs five times with the virgin niece, three to four with the concubine, and demands equal accommodation from the host (pp.68, 81, 82). Only the priest in *Prestre et Alison* matches Ovid's record of nine (p.21). Invoking his analysis of coitus, Thomas of Chobham might have objected that such feats exceed the requirements of conception and dangerously indulge concupiscence with meretricious and adulterous habits.[69] If, however, he considered the implications of the Pauline principle of reciprocal obligations between spouses, he might have been forced to concede that married couples could not be denied these exertions.

Nonconsensual Coitus: From Seduction to Rape

Among the five discourses, mutual consent between a man and a woman was undoubtedly the optimal norm governing sexual relations. We have seen that the canonists and theologians considered consent to be the irreducible foundation for marriage, which further guaranteed reciprocal access to the spouse's body. Included in the physicians' definition of coitus was a union that was natural and voluntary (*naturali ac voluntaria . . . actione*).[70] Ovid had assumed mutual interest between lovers both in the erotic fantasies of his *Amores* and in the precepts of his *Ars.* The interminable arguments between the male and female interlocutors in André the Chaplain likewise proceeded from the promise of mutual consent. Marie de Champagne's definition of noble love rendered it axiomatic that love be bestowed freely without constraint.[71] Nor could absence of consent be easily detected between the heroes and heroines of the romances or between the men and women of the fabliaux. Although consent was the ideal in individual cases, closer scrutiny of the couplings might reveal ambiguity over total reciprocity. Some element of coercion was always possible. Placed on a continuum, coercion could range, on one side, from seduction by a partner benefiting from age, experience, authority, or particular circumstance through varying degrees of physical force and end, on the other, with brutal rape. Because superior strength was frequently masculine, rape was usually perpetrated by men, but a social dimension was added when a man's physical power was reinforced by membership in a dominant class that bestowed authority over women of inferior status.

Incidents of seduction where a woman or a man attempted to profit from an advantage to have intercourse with an unwilling partner occur rarely in the five discourses. Among the theologians, Robert of Courson imagined the situation in which a prostitute employs enticing fraud to seduce an adolescent boy.[72] Among the amatory adventures narrated by Chrétien, Lancelot encounters and successfully resists the beautiful Demoiselle Amoureuse who demands sex in payment for hospitality (*Charette*, vv.931–1280). Among the hundreds of couplings in the fabliaux, the case of the young girl who could not abide the word "fuck" might be considered a seduction by the linguistically knowledgeable young man, but the girl nonetheless appears to be most willing to learn both words and deed.[73] Although other examples of seduction can undoubtedly be found in the five discourses, they are not prominent. The notable exception to this relative lack of concern was the *pastourelle*.[74] This genre of contemporary poetry was centered on the theme of a knight who rides through the countryside and discovers a solitary shepherdess (hence the title) whom he attempts to seduce by deceit, gifts, money, force, or other persuasions. With antecedents in Latin and Provençal poetry, the genre flourished in Old French from northern France at the end of the twelfth and throughout the thirteenth century. Among hundreds of extant examples were two fragments inserted into Jean Renart's *Roman* and two complete poems attributed to Jean Bodel. In Jean Bodel's *Contre le douz tans novel,* a knight comes across a shepherdess playing a flute while he enjoys a spring canter through the countryside near Cassel in Flanders. Seeking her love, he offers better adornment and attire than her shepherd suitor can provide. She refuses his proposal and declares her fidelity to a shepherd whom she plans to marry once the churches have been reopened. (Apparently an interdict had been levied in the region because of hostilities between the Flemish and French.)[75] Not all knights obtain their designs, as seen in this case, but the potential seduction of lower-class women was the pervasive theme of the *pastourelles*.

The employment of overpowering physical force distinguishes rape from seduction, as can be seen in the legal definition offered by Philippe de Beaumanoir in his *Coutumes de Beauvaisis* dating from the second half of the thirteenth century: "*Femme efforcier.* . . . Forcing a woman is when one has carnal knowledge of a woman against the will of that woman and despite the fact that she does everything in her power to resist him." The Latin equivalent *raptus*, current in Roman and canon law, included not only the sexual rape but also the abduction of the woman.[76] All five discourses as well as the *pastourelles* attested the ubiquity of rape. Although the canonists had treated the subject at length in their commentaries, Thomas of Chobham limited discussion to the rape of unmarried women. The heinous character of the crime is underscored by the death penalty demanded both in Scripture and in Roman law.[77] Pierre the Chanter drew upon Jerome's *Life of Paul the Hermit* to cite the case of an adolescent boy who was bound and forced to submit to the caresses of a beautiful woman.[78] Jacques de Vitry evoked the contemporary and more realistic atrocities perpetrated by Brabançon soldiers at the siege of Liège in 1212. To escape rape many beguines threw themselves into the river or cesspools, preferring death to the corruption of their chastity.[79] Guillaume de Conches and the physicians of the *Prose Salernitan Questions* took cognizance of the subject when they considered pregnancy incurred after rape.[80]

The threat of rape was ever present throughout the romance genre, even in the Tristan legend, which was centered on the mutual passion between the two lovers. In Béroul's version, Iseut is condemned to gang rape by a hundred lepers (vv.1155–1234). Throughout Chrétien's romances, rape appeared in numerous guises not only as a crime to be punished but also as a phenomenon to be expected in aristocratic society, even to be aestheticized, that is, to be rendered inoffensive to chivalric sensibilities. As Erec, for example, sets out on a series of adventures to prove that marriage has not debilitated his prowess, he uses his wife Enide as bait for rape to attract villainous champions with whom to battle. As a neophyte, Perceval was repeatedly instructed that it was the unquestioned duty of all knights to come to the rescue of maidens in distress (*pucele desconselliee*, L. vv.531–36, 1653–60; R. vv.533–38, 1656–65). These included demoiselles and ladies in danger of abduction and rape, whose importunities absorbed the energies of Chrétien's heroes Yvain, Gauvain, and Lancelot. At one point, Lancelot's great dilemma is how to choose between addressing the long-term *raptus* of Queen Guenièvre and the immediate rape of the Demoiselle Amoureuse (vv.1096–1125). Throughout the narrative of *Cligès*, essentially a story devoted outwardly to marriage, Fenice is abducted no less than four times. Perceval forces at least twenty kisses on the unwilling demoiselle of the tent and takes her ring. The girl's knight questions not only

202

whether Perceval stopped with a kiss but whether the deed was really rape: "Whatever woman offers her mouth readily gives up the rest . . . she is too much a coward to accord it; but wants him to take it with force" (*que a force li face*, L. vv.3845–46, 3857; R. vv.3860–61, 3875).[81]

In contrast to the scores of rapes or potential rapes in the romances, the phenomenon occurred with remarkable rarity in the fabliaux.[82] With an abundance of sexually active women it appears as if rape had become pointless. In Jean Bodel's *Gombert* (followed by *Meunier*), neither of the two peasant women is prepared to accommodate the clerics, but the daughter is bribed with a simulated ring, and the wife mistakes the intruder for her husband. The lecherous monk of *Segretain moine* succeeds only in forcing a kiss upon the wife (p.219). Within our corpus, the closest a fabliau came to depicting rape, or at least nonconsensual coitus, was *Le prestre et le chevalier* in which the avaricious priest literally sells the bodies of his unwilling niece and concubine to the knight. Led to the knight pale and weeping, the virgin niece returns to her uncle in pain and raging grief. Equally resisting, the concubine vents her subsequent fury against the priest. When it becomes the priest's turn to be violated, however, he evokes the language of the romance and poses "as a man in distress" (*fait comme .i. hons desconseilliés*, p.84), escaping humiliation only at the cost of emptying his purse.

Among the numerous rape scenes Chrétien de Troyes presented in his romances, the most striking but also the most ambiguous was that of the Demoiselle Amoureuse in the *Charette* to which the poet devoted over three hundred lines of verse (vv.931–1280). The scene unfolded in three distinct sequences. As Lancelot pursues his quest to rescue the abducted Queen Guenièvre, he meets a lovely maiden who refuses him hospitality unless he consents to sleep with her. When the knight agrees with great reluctance, the girl takes him into her empty house and then proceeds to stage her own rape by knights of her household, whom she calls off after Lancelot appears to have succeeded in protecting her. In the final sequence the girl leads the hero by the hand to the bed. As they lie there for some time, both clad in their chemises but without touching each other, the girl finally accepts the sincerity of Lancelot's fidelity to the queen and lets him sleep in peace. Not only is the attempted rape—depicted in rude detail—itself a fabrication, but the brutal scene is embedded in the broader framework of an unsuccessful seduction of a male by a female. As Lancelot prepares to enter the bed, he himself feels raped, or at least coerced by his promise: "Is this not force? It is as good as such" (*Donc est ce force? Autant le vaut*, v.1209). This ironic and complex treatment of rape could have served multiple purposes, among which was the entertainment of the men in Chrétien's audience as they contemplated a girl stripped to the waist while the hero debates at length with himself as to whether he should come to her rescue.[83]

Jean Renart's use of rape in the *Roman de la rose* conveyed still another set of ambiguities. In the contest between Lïenor and the seneschal—the former to become the emperor's wife, the latter to obstruct her ambition—both fabricate lies. The seneschal claims that he has seduced the girl: "I have had her virginity" (*qu'il a eü son pucelage,* v.3586), he tells the emperor, and he proves his charge by imparting details about the rose on her thigh. This version is passed from the emperor to Guillaume and from Guillaume to his nephew. For her part Lïenor also constructs a falsehood: "One day . . . your seneschal came by chance to the place where I sewed and did me harm and outrage by taking my virginity (*qu'il me toli mon pucelage*). He then took my belt, purse, and clasp" (vv.4778–87), which Lïenor had planted on the person of the seneschal to give credence to her accusation. In his subsequent denials the seneschal merely repeats Lïenor's charge word for word (vv.4808–11), but when required to formulate an oath in preparation for the ordeal, he clarifies that the accusation is specifically rape: "I deny that I have ever seen, shamed or harmed her, nor did I force her virginity" (*ne ne forçai son pucelage,* v.4920). Thus Jean presented his audience with a confrontation indeed familiar to the world of litigation. The man's story is seduction; the woman's is rape. As in Chrétien rape was once again linked with seduction, and fabrication played a leading role in the narrative. One final characteristic established the context for both rapes: the alleged victim was represented as entirely alone.

Since the romances were limited to the world of the aristocracy, the rapes represented therein involved noble women abused by men of the same social station, no matter how ignoble their conduct. Ever sensitive to social differences, however, André the Chaplain devoted a chapter to the love of peasant women by aristocratic men in which social domination reinforced masculine physical force. Distinguished from the townspeople (*plebeii*) and rooted to the soil, peasants (*agricultores*) are bestial by nature and, therefore, impervious to the teachings of cultured love. To the aristocratic man foolishly attracted to a peasant woman, André offered brief instructions: do not forget to compliment her; find an opportune spot; and do quickly what you want, even with violent embraces. To penetrate her rude exterior requires at least a modicum of compulsion (*modicae coactionis*).[84] In short, a peasant woman is fair game for rape. Implicit in this conclusion was the premise that as an inferior member of society she has no recourse against her aristocratic master.

Jean Bodel's second *pastourelle*, *L'autrier quant chevauchoie,* like many *pastourelles,* puts André's precepts into practice. As the knight-narrator is riding along a pine grove one day, he comes upon Marion, a pretty shepherdess, tending sheep with her dog. To her despair, a wolf runs off with one of her flock. Since it is unnecessary for the knight to praise her beauty or offer gifts, as in Bodel's other story, he proposes to retrieve her sheep if she would leave Robin, her shepherd *ami*. Not only does the girl accept with alacrity, but she offers both herself and her virginity for the service. As the knight returns with the sheep to collect his reward, the girl calls out to Robin for help, now protesting that she has pledged her faith to the shepherd. To punish this treachery, the knight dismounts in a fallow field and with short dispatch does his will (*fis en ma volenté*, v.65) until he has had his fill. When Robin finally arrives in response to her cries, he accuses her of willingly playing sexual games (*kau jeu de pic-en-pance*, v.74) with the knight and thereby betraying her faith to him.[85]

In nearly one out of five of the extant French *pastourelles* the knight's seduction of the shepherdess ended in rape, as in Jean Bodel's present example.[86] Even if the seduction did not entail physical violence or was unsuccessful, as in Bodel's *Contre le douz tans novel*, the threat of rape remained the ultimate sanction to accomplishing the knight's desires, if flattery, promises, gifts, and money were ineffective. As in the romances, that the shepherdess was alone was the essential clue to the situation. A necessary condition of the profession, solitude was implicit in Bodel's first example and explicitly stated in the second: "She tends sheep alone without a companion" (*seule senz compaignon*, vv.5–6). Even the fragment in Jean Renart's *Roman* was also explicit that the girl was with her sheep but without companions (vv.4576–78). No matter the final dénouement, the context of isolation offered foreboding of rape. Although never overtly voiced, moreover, the social disparity between the knight and shepherdess reinforced the knight's strength over his victim. Because of aristocratic domination the peasants are unable or unwilling to protect their *amies*. Although the helplessness of peasant women suggests an element of social realism, it did not exclude an equally important veneer of male fantasy. Shepherdesses may have been as stinking, coarse, and bestial to courtly society as the flocks with which they cohabited, but they are invariably portrayed with qualities of noble demoiselles. In *Contre le douz tans* she has a bright visage with the complexion of a rose; in *L'autrier* she is pretty with blond hair; her face, mouth and chin are fit to behold; and her neck gleamed white (v.17). Blondness and paleness were the least bucolic and most aristocratic attributes of feminine beauty. Her speech throughout, moreover, employs the grammar and vocabulary of courtly French. In effect, therefore, the contemptible peasant has been thoroughly sanitized to make her fit for masculine aristocratic desire.

6

CHILDREN

The Physiology of Reproduction: From Conception to Birth

"Desiring that the species of animals should not perish but endure permanently," opened Constantinus Africanus's monograph *De coitu*, "the Creator ordained that it be renewed through coitus and generation and therefore not fall into total extinction." Coitus, in other words, was divinely constituted mechanism for continuing the work of creation. We recall that the *Prose Salernitan Questions* declared that the procreation of the fetus (*fetus procreatio*) was the consequence of the emission of sperm after the natural and voluntary union of a man and woman.[1] In the physiological literature, therefore, children were assumed to be the intended result of sexual union. Drawing upon Guillaume de Conches and the Salernitan anatomists, the *Prose Salernitan Questions* summarized and elaborated with only slight variations the ancient medical theories that explained the process of reproduction.

We have seen that the *Questions* adopted the theory of pangenesis to account for the origin of sperm, unreservedly accepted the Hippocratic-Galenic doctrine of the two seeds, and ignored Aristotle's doctrine of the unique male seed. Arguments for the two positions were drawn from observations of genetic inheritance. Not only does pangenesis explain the reproduction of the different parts of the body, but the two seeds account for why a child inherits traits from both its parents. Who can doubt that the mother's sperm is present at conception when her children resemble her, even to the point of her defects? If a father, to take another example, has an incurable gout in one member, his son will have a similar infirmity in the same member. The child of a blind man, on the other hand, will not lack eyes, nor will the mutilation of feet, ears, or noses be inherited in children, because nature flees imperfections and works to perfect each in its kind. Parents pass on the materials of bone, flesh, and nerves which are perfected in their offspring. In response to the question, From which of the parents will the fetus inherit? the answer depends on three conditions: (1) when the two sperm are in conflict, no fetus is produced, or if one does result, it assumes an entirely different form; (2) when one sperm is superior to the other, the fetus resembles the stronger party; and (3) when the two are in temperate accord, the fetus resembles both. Parents' sperm may transmit both superficial and deep-seated traits simultaneously, which complicates the possible resulting combinations.[2]

In accordance with Hippocratic–Galenic tradition a woman requires the convergence of male and female sperm to conceive. The Salernitan anatomists and physiologists formulated the image of minting coins as the apt expression for conception. The human figure is stamped in the manner of currency (*ad modum monete*) in the mint of conception (*in monetam conceptionis*). This takes place in the uterus whose fibrous interior is designed to retain the semen and whose structure, as we have seen, is divided into seven cells. The number of cells limits the number of children to whom a woman can give birth at one time. They are arranged within the uterus three on the right, three on the left; and one in the middle. Within this context the *Prose Salernitan Questions* reported two principal theories on how gender is determined within the womb. In the first, if more male than female sperm is deposited on the right side, a boy results. More female than male on the left produces a girl. Equal amounts in the middle result in a hermaphrodite, but if the fetus leans more to the right than the left, it will be a boy. If, however, more female sperm is found on the right, the result is a virago; a corresponding excess of male sperm on the left produces an effeminate boy. A second theory explained that sperm on the right side of the uterus is heated by the nearby liver, thus producing hotter blood required for a man, whereas the colder left side results in the cold female complexion.[3] The gynecological treatise *Cum auctor* employed the distinction between right and left sides to advise how to determine the sex of the fetus before birth. A drop of blood drawn from the right side of the mother is placed in spring water. If it sinks, the fetus is a boy; if not, a girl. Hippocrates was quoted as saying that a boy endows his mother with good coloring and a large right breast, but a girl fetus is indicated by pallor and a large left breast.[4]

Unknown either to Galen or Constantinus, the anatomical curiosity of the seven-celled uterus appears to have surfaced in the West at the beginning of the twelfth century in the Latin translations of the pseudo-Galen *De spermate,* probably of Byzantine origin. It combined ancient numerological speculation with medical theories involving the elements of right/ left and hot/cold to account for congenital hermaphroditism and multiple births. It is strange, however, that although the twelfth-century proponents claimed that births are thereby limited to seven at one time, no one remarked on the frequency of multiple parturitions. Only Constantinus, who envisaged a bicameral uterus, discussed evidence for multiple births which extended to quintuplets.[5]

The *Prose Salernitan Questions* outlined two schema for the embryological development of the fetus. In the first, taken directly from Guillaume de Conches, the embryo is surrounded and protected by a small sack. By the seventh day drops of blood appear on the surface of the sack, sinking into the liquid of conception in the third week. In the fourth week the liquid begins to coagulate into solids of a consistency somewhere between flesh and blood. By the seventh formative powers begin to confer a human figure on the material, followed by the assimilative powers of coldness and dryness that produce bones. Coldness and moisture produce phlegm and lungs; heat and dryness, cholera and the heart; heat and humidity, blood and the liver. Then appear the rounding forces that shape the hands, nose, and the like. After the members have been assimilated and shaped, a subtle air courses through the arteries and confers motion and life. Motion begins between the seventieth and ninetieth day depending on the ultimate time of birth. Physicians affirmed that if there is not sufficient vital motion before the seventh month, a child born at that time will die. The eighth and ninth months provide a period of rest and nourishment before the final birth.[6]

In the second schema if the sperm of man and woman are cold when they join, they dissolve; if hot, they dry up; but if equal in temperature, the woman conceives, envelopes the semen, and attaches it to the uterus by a root through which it is nourished. Thereafter the *Prose Salernitan Questions* considered the development of the fetus month by month, each assigned to the power of a celestial planet. (1) Saturn's coldness congeals the sperm like a nut without form and structure. (2) Jupiter's heat and humidity produce spirit, muscle, and roundness. (3) Mars's heat and dryness divide the thighs and arms from the sides and form the neck and head. (4) The heat and dryness of the sun produce the heart and liver, into which the soul is infused and begins to move. (5) Venus's coldness and moisture complete the interior complexion, the intestines, fingers, toes, ears, nose, mouth, and genitals. (The penis is formed and the vagina [*pudicus circulus*] is bored through.) (6) With heat and humidity Mercury forms the eyes, eyebrows, eyelids, hair, and nails. (7) The cold and humid moon finishes the fat and skin and fills the diverse vessels with fluids. Since the fetus is complete at this point, it strives to exit, but the vagina (*natura*) attempts to retain it. If the vagina is weak, it exits, but if the uterus is stronger, it remains. (8) Saturn adds strength while the fetus rests and is comforted in the womb. And finally (9) Jupiter's heat and moisture fortifies it for exit. The *Prose Salernitan Questions* paid little attention to the operation of birth, but

Guillaume de Conches explained that because the fetus is accustomed to heat and moisture, its first sound is a cry of pain as it encounters the cold and dry world. For that reason nurses often place it in a warm bath. The first human voice, therefore, is that of grief.[7]

Female menstruation nurtures the fetus in the uterus. The menstrua are the superfluous contents of the woman's body that are drawn to the uterus and expelled by spirit and heat for general health. According to widely accepted imagery, just as the flower precedes the fruit of a tree, so the menstrua precedes the fetus. (In polite speech, therefore, they are called flowers.) The term *menstrua* derives from the monthly (*mense*) action of the new moon which purges the female body as it waxes and wanes. Since women are of cold complexions and are unable to cook all the food in their stomachs, the remaining superfluities are expelled each month. After conception, however, heat arises from the fetus, the food is better digested, and the superfluities are reduced, becoming food for the fetus. When the sperm enters the uterus, its mouth closes to protect conception, thereby terminating menstruation. Within the enclosed uterus the fetus is linked to the mother by nerves in the umbilical cord, like an apple stem to a tree. Blood passes along this conduit from the liver to the fetus. Part of the menstrual blood is diverted to the breasts where it is converted into milk for subsequent feeding of the baby.[8]

The medical details of conception and birth elicited only passing notice from the contemporary theologians and literary authors. Pierre the Chanter, as we have seen, fully accepted the Galenic doctrine of the two seeds in his commentary to the Psalms where he distinguished the primary meaning of conception as the union of the seed of a man and a woman in the uterus. In glossing the verse "in the time of ten months I was coagulated in the blood of my mother from the seed of man" (Wisdom 7:2), he demonstrated a passing acquaintance with current physiological and embryological theories. The difference between the sexes is seen in the white sperm of the male and the blood red of the female. When they are mixed together, a body proceeds to form until it becomes animated at birth, a process which takes from seven to nine months. In the tenth it is said to be perfect, alive and healthy born.[9]

The few scenes recorded in the fabliaux and the romances also skirt the subject with few details, but in contrast to the theologians they appear, for the most part, to suggest the single-seed theory. When the prostitute Richeut, for example, decided to become pregnant by any available man, she is said to have reaped where she had not sewn. The male child that fills her belly, therefore, is not her seed (*germe*) but that of whoever was the father (vv.396–402). (It may also be noted that the baby enters the world crying louder than a magpie, but is comforted by a nurse who picks him up and baths him according to the doctors' prescription [vv.413–61].) The wife in *L'enfant qui fu remis au soleil* claims that she conceived by swallowing a snowflake during her husband's absence, an explanation that fails to convince her spouse (vv.32–36).

Although Marie de France's lais recounted an unusual number of births, the author is satisfied merely to indicate the event, perhaps because most were conceived illicitly.[10] Gottfried's version of *Tristan*, however, asserted that Blancheflor received the hero directly from Rivalin (vv.1324–34). In *Cligès*, moreover, Chrétien said specifically that in three months after the wedding Soredamor finds herself full of Alexandre's seed (*semance, grainne*) which she carries to term. The seed germinates into fruit producing a beautiful child (vv.2336–44). When the lady of Genoa gives birth to a son in Jean Renart's *Escoufle,* the seed (*semance*) of her fine womb falls to earth (vv.1752–57). Unlike the contemporary theologians, the vernacular writers employed the agricultural metaphor of the seed that suggested a single seed in accordance with Aristotle's views and against Galenic contemporary opinion that two seeds were required. In *Richeut* and *Cligès* the seed came specifically from the man. Only Jean Renart designated it as from the mother's womb, which appears to be the closest the romance authors came to recognizing the Hippocratic-Galenic theory of the female sperm.

The Natalist Policy of Churchmen

That reproduction is a physiological consequence of coitus was indisputable. To what extent reproduction is the exclusive goal of coitus was open to question. The Old Testament text in which God commanded Adam and Eve to be fertile (*prh*), increase (*rbh*), and fill the earth (Gen. 1:28) massively reinforced the priority of reproduction in ecclesiastical tradition. The New Testament writers relatively neglected this mandate, which bore incalculable consequences for the development of Judaism. More concerned with the immanent return of Christ (the parousia), they envisaged marriage and coitus less in terms of reproduction than as a means to avoid fornication and immorality. The Greek Fathers of the early church were likewise less concerned with reproduction than with the ideals of virginity and celibacy. Entirely the consequence of the Fall and sin, sexuality and reproduction were not imaginable in the primal paradise. The Latin Fathers, however, were susceptible to the Old Testament tradition, further buttressed by Stoic philosophers who argued that reproduction was the sole rationale for sexual activity. Most important was Augustine's opinion which was formulated to meet Manichean opposition to marriage and reproduction. After sustained discussion, he decided not only that God's command to increase and multiply was delivered to the first parents before the Fall, but also that it remained in effect after sin entered the world. In a statement that was subsequently of greatest influence in the Latin church, Augustine defined progeny (*proles*) as the first of three essential goods (*bona*) for marriage and, therefore, for sexuality. (The remaining two are faith and the sacrament.)[11]

In the twelfth century the Augustinian doctrine was preserved in Gratian's authoritative collection for the canonists and Pierre the Lombard's for the theologians.[12] Pierre the Chanter summarized Augustine's conclusions in his commentary to the Genesis passage: God ordered the first parents to fill the earth with their offspring's posterity, a command that could only be accomplished with sexual union. In refutation of the Manicheans, therefore, God instituted the marriage of man and woman in paradise so that a husband could know his wife for the procreation of progeny. To sum up the theological tradition, Robert of Courson rehearsed two Augustinian schema that defended the divine establishment of marriage. The first was the three goods of matrimony in which progeny raised for the worship of God was first and foremost. The second, as we have seen, was the four "final causes" of marriage, of which two are without sin. The second of these consists of returning the marital debt and involves only coitus, but the first is the "cause of progeny" (*causa prolis*) which subordinates coitus to reproduction. Once again in the hierarchy of theological values, the reproduction of children was the primary justification for intercourse.[13]

This emphasis on procreative sexuality found ritualistic articulation in the contemporary rites for blessing the nuptial chamber which preceded the development of the marriage liturgy itself. It is significant that the earliest evidence of ecclesiastical intervention into marriage occurred in sixth-century Gaul, not in connection with the family's wedding ceremony but in the blessing of nuptial chamber. In northern France in the twelfth century, the ordo of Evreux instructed the priest on blessing the chamber at night when the spouses come to bed, adding a benediction over their bodies and invoking the protection of the angel Raphael. Another contemporary benediction prayed that they live in God's love, grow old, and increase (*multiplicentur*), thus echoing the Genesis commandment. Another blessed the young people and their seed (*semina*).[14] It is not surprising, therefore, that these benedictions could have been confused with popular fertility rites. Pierre the Chanter noticed that church palls were used for adorning nuptial chambers or robing pregnant women. Even when such vestments were not consecrated, they should not be put to mundane use because they were originally assigned to the church.[15] It is apparent, therefore, that popular imagination could distinguish only with difficulty between the licit ecclesiastical benediction of the nuptial chamber and fertility practices that borrowed church paraphernalia to serve as quasi-charms.

The churchmen's unanimous verdict that procreation was the final and least objectionable goal of sexuality yielded the corollary that all means to prevent conception and birth were forbidden. Contraception and abortion, therefore, were unequivocally condemned as being unnatural and murderous. Since the age of the Church Fathers and throughout the early Middle Ages penitentialists, canonists, and theologians elaborated a set of proscriptions and rationale whose arguments were epitomized by statements from Augustine which Gratian and Pierre the Lombard collected for the attention of the twelfth-century schools. The centerpiece was Augustine's dictum, identified as *Aliquando,* that forbade poisons of sterility (*sterilitatis venena*) which extinguish the fetus in the womb. Applying Augustine's statement to contraception or to abortion either in the early or late phases, the influential Huguccio resumed contemporary canonist opinion by concluding that such potions destroyed the principal good of marriage.[16]

Robert of Courson omitted consideration of contraception and abortion—perhaps because of this unanimity among churchmen—but in treating conditional marriages, he affirmed in passing that a marriage contracted on the promise of preventing future children through poisons of sterility was not valid. Pierre the Chanter, however, defended the universal prohibition against contraception in his characteristic manner by explicitly concentrating on a difficult moral dilemma, that of therapeutic contraception. Like the author of the gynecological treatise *Cum auctor,* he recognized that parturition could be life-threatening to women. Through many childbirths, for example, a wife had ruptured her umbilical cord. Although the physicians had warned that another birth would certainly result in death, her husband demanded his conjugal rights. Pierre decided that just as a starving person is not required to relinquish his last piece of bread during a devastating famine, the woman is not required to submit to her husband. Church authorities should prevent her husband from pressing his demands. Although debilitated by the infirmity, she is still youthful enough to conceive. Pierre, moreover, refused to approve those who advised that she uses poisons of sterility to prevent conception, because by these means she is guilty of homicide of her own children.[17] Thomas of Chobham offered a survey of birth-control practices in a chapter devoted to women who kill their offspring, a theme inspired by Augustine's equation of contraception and abortion to murder. Among the five enumerated, the first pertained to contraception and the second to abortion. Those who search for sterility through potions or incantations are obstructing the propagation of the human race. Some women use them to conceal the consequences of their sexual indulgence while others, as the Chanter had noted, do so to avoid the trauma of birth. It is a lesser sin, however, to extinguish an unformed being than a child whose body is infused with a soul. Reporting on particular techniques, which, we shall see, were prescribed by physicians, Chobham condemned all forms of abortion as homicide.[18]

Included among the prohibitions against nonprocreative sexuality were not only artificial and external means of contraception and abortion but also other practices such as oral and anal intercourse and coitus interruptus. Augustine proscribed the first two as misuse of members not made for that purpose. Both Gratian and Pierre the Lombard, however, collected his summary opinion, the dictum *Adulterii malum,* in such an obscure place that it attracted little comment from the canonists and theologians. We remember, however, that Pierre the Chanter had raised the case of a wife whom the husband forced to submit to extravaginal sex and concluded that it was equivalent to sodomy. The biblical example of Onan (Gen. 38:7–10), moreover, who spilled his seed on the ground to avoid conception, appears to refer to coitus interruptus. (This was the literal interpretation of the passage in the authoritative *Glossa ordinaria.*) Onan's deed was likewise included among sodomistic practices in Pierre's comprehensive chapter against homosexuality in the *Verbum abbreviatum.* Like sodomy, it was a form of nonprocreative sexuality which Augustine had condemned as homicide.[19]

Restraints on Fecundity

If ecclesiastical doctrine was uncompromisingly natalist, it nonetheless placed remarkably severe restraints on fertility by interdicting coitus during lengthy periods of time that were carefully specified. During the early Middle Ages the penitentials not only enjoined continence during particular days of the week and the holy seasons, as we have seen, but also according to the physiological rhythm of the female body. Subject to diverse definitions, coitus was forbidden during periods of menstruation, pregnancy, postpartum, and occasionally lactation. If all the calendar and physiological periods were observed by a scrupulous couple, the days available for procreation were reduced to only forty-four to fifty-seven a year. Churchmen in the early Middle Ages were evidently little aware of or concerned with the demographic effects of their theory.[20]

By the twelfth century, however, the number of holy days was reduced, as we have seen, and less attention was paid to the restrictions based on feminine physiology. After summarizing the sacred seasons, Thomas of Chobham mentioned menstruation, pregnancy, and postpartum (*in puerperio*) but without offering precise details or extended discussion. Children conceived during menstruation risk leprosy; husbands who approach their wives during the last stages of pregnancy may provoke abortions; and postpartum flux contaminates more dangerously than menstrual fluids. If the wife fears for the husband's continence imposed by her pregnancy, she may go to church for purification as soon after birth as she feels ready, so that she can render the marital debt.[21] Beyond periods of abstinence mandated by ecclesiastical sanctions, churchmen did recognize one voluntary restraint on fecundity that was legitimate. While acknowledging the reciprocal sexual demands on married couples, the Apostle Paul had also urged spouses to agree to periods of mutual abstinence for prayer (1 Cor. 7:5). Mutually agreed upon continence, therefore, remained the only approved method of birth control.

Although the prohibitions were universal toward women, individual canonists and theologians could hesitate about their application to men. The canonist Huguccio, for example, whose sexual morality was extremely rigorous, reported with approval the practice of *coitus/amplexus reservatus* by which the husband unites with his wife to render the conjugal debt but refrains from ejaculation. Huguccio may have countenanced this form of birth control because he believed, as we have seen, that without ejaculation there is neither *voluptas* nor sin. Only the absence of male ejaculation distinguished this technique from *coitus interruptus* which the biblical example of Onan condemned. Pierre the Chanter cited another case of a libidinous man who cooled down his genitals with herbs or potions so that he was no longer capable of procreating. One opinion judged this recourse to be without sin as long as the man refrained from physical mutilation. Another opinion, however, could not distinguish between the sin of castration and that of obliterating natural potency by whatever means.[22] Although the Chanter did not decide between the two answers in this unfinished *questio,* one possible mitigating factor was that illicit contraception was obviated by an anaphrodisiac which licitly repressed sexual desire.

With one oblique exception, the *Prose Salernitan Questions* followed the lead of Guillaume de Conches and avoided discussing the subjects of abortion and contraception. Like Constantinus Africanus in the eleventh century, they often took a stance independent of their theological and canonist colleagues, but apparently in these areas they respected the ecclesiastical natalist policy. Constantinus himself had omitted the chapter on abortion in his Latin translation, the *Viaticum* (Zād al-musāfir), but had nonetheless included a section on contraception in the *Pantegni.* Entitled "concerning those who do not wish to procreate" (*De generare nolentibus*), it briefly treated magic amulets to protect women for whom conception was medically hazardous. Contrary to Constantinus's custom, this particular chapter was not a translation from Arabic sources but original to his treatise. A faithful Galenian, he felt that sexuality was central to female well-being which, in turn, required consideration of contraception. By the third decade of the thirteenth century, Avicenna's *Canon* transmitted to the Latin West a much larger selection of ancient and Arabic prescriptions and techniques for inducing abortions and preventing conception.[23]

At the turn of the twelfth and thirteenth centuries, however, the Salernitan gynecological treatises made available ancient lore on these subjects, but the learned physicians of Northwest Europe may also have informed themselves from the Latin adaptations of Soranus's *Gynecology*. Muscio merely noted Soranus's preference for contraception over abortion and recommended the latter procedure only for medical reasons. It was specifically forbidden to adulteresses or those seeking gain. Caelius Aurelianus, however, followed his ancient predecessor closely. Contraceptive remedies should be clearly distinguished from abortion which destroys a conception already made. Of interest to medieval readers, Caelius recalled the controversy among ancient authorities over abortion. Although Hippocrates had generally forbidden abortive medicines, in his book on the *Nature of the Child* he did prescribe for discretionary cases in which a woman lost her fetus by jumping and striking her buttocks with her feet (the so-called Lacedaemonian leap). (Thomas of Chobham reported a related procedure by which a woman jumps three times from a bench. On the third leap the fetus falls out enveloped in a small membrane.) Agreeing with opinions reported in Muscio, other authorities prohibited abortive medicines altogether because the function of medicine is to save rather than to threaten life. Still others withheld abortions in cases of adultery and the vain desire to preserve feminine beauty but allowed them when the uterus is too small, unable to perform its function, its mouth is infected with scrofulus, or similar impediments that might threaten death. Since it is safer to inhibit than to destroy conception, contraceptive means are preferable and should be considered first.

Pregnancy can be prevented through numerous procedures: avoiding times most suitable for conception; at the moment before the man ejaculates, the woman withdraws, arises, distends her body, sits, sneezes, and drinks something cold; anointing the mouth of the uterus with rancid oil or honey; placing fine wool at the entrance before intercourse; and employing suppositories to close the uterus's mouth to prevent the seed from reaching the base before the moment of conception. Then followed a long list of contraceptive remedies and potions. To effect an abortion the woman should reverse the prescribed procedures for caring for the fetus thirty days after conception. Other abortive techniques included walking with energetic movements; carting by draft animals; treatment of the uterus with sweet and hot oil; anointing the whole body, rubbing the pubis, the stomach, and loins strenuously; daily baths in water not too hot, but lingering in the tub while drinking wine and eating pungent foods; and finally the administering of a variety of abortive medicaments. For contraceptive devices the *Cum auctor* suggested that the woman wear on her bare skin the uterus of a nanny goat that had never conceived, or wear the testicles of a male weasel bound to her side in a goose skin, or, perhaps most simply, taste a jet stone (*lapis gagates*).[24]

Although Guillaume de Conches and the *Prose Salernitan Questions* virtually ignored contraception and abortion, they did turn their attention to a problem that churchmen considered legitimate, that of sterility in married couples. In their opinion two fundamental conditions adversely affect fertility: the lack of sexual desire, and physiological disorders. How can it happen, they queried, that women cohabit legally and with great delight with their husbands alone but do not conceive? Since the problem is not desire, the difficulties are physiological arising either from the wife's womb or from the quality of the sperm of the woman, man, or both. Agreeing with *Cum auctor,* they noted that a woman's uterus can have too much fat obstructing the lower mouth and preventing semen from reaching the place of conception. It can be constricted also by too much dryness, or its interior smeared with viscous humors. The retentive force of the uterus can be deficient, allowing the expulsive force to prevail, or the muscles can be too soft to hold the seed. When there is no defect in the uterus, the fault can be attributed to the quality of the sperm. If it is too cold, it congeals; if too hot, it dries out; if too humid, it dissipates; if too dry and hard, it refuses to assimilate. Male sperm can be too thin, and men with cold and dry testicles rarely generate. It was emphasized throughout that sterility is due to multiple causes in both men and women that impede the assimilation of the sperm necessary for reproduction. To determine which partner was at fault the *Cum auctor* offered a ready test. The urine of the man and woman were to be placed in separate jars containing bran and left for nine days. Whichever putrefied and bred worms indicated sterility. If neither partner failed the test, then the treatise went on to suggest remedies of the same nature as those for contraception.[25]

In the *De philosophia* Guillaume de Conches had suggested that female sterility could also be caused by too much intercourse. This led Guillaume and the *Prose Salernitan Questions* to consider the observation that prostitutes were often infertile. Why do prostitutes, who frequently have intercourse, infrequently conceive? Not only do these women lack sexual desire in their customary business, as we have seen, but their reproductive anatomy is also defective. Because of repeated coitus prostitutes suffer from obstructed uteruses. The fibrous lining of their wombs which should retain the semen is covered over and becomes smooth as marble. After the semen is discharged, but before it can be incorporated, it is spoiled, destroyed, and loses capacity to produce offspring.[26]

These medical discussions shared a widespread perception that prostitutes rarely or almost never conceive, a belief that also found expression in the fabliau *Richeut*. At the height of her career the prostitute Richeut has as yet no offspring. To obtain a child to blackmail her rich clients, she not only copulates with every available customer, but she also drinks a special herb, mandrake with *elebore* (vv. 126–27, 144–48). This concoction is apparently deemed necessary to produce pregnancy, thus acknowledging her previous infertility. If prostitutes were perceived to be normally sterile, they thereby offered a means of birth control and an outlet for male indulgence in nonreproductive sex. We remember that twelfth-century churchmen disapproved of prostitution because of extramarital sexuality but did not explicitly acknowledge its contraceptive function. The necessary elements were nonetheless available for considering prostitution as such. Augustine had recognized the practice in his widely read *De bono conjugali* when he declared that sex that exceeded the needs of procreation was only a venial sin with a wife but a mortal sin with a prostitute. He had further observed in the *De nuptiis et concupiscentia* that when one man lies with multiple women many children are born (as befitted the ancient Hebrew patriarchs), but when multiple men have intercourse with one woman, the objective is not progeny but the fulfillment of lust, because few children result. Concluding that such women are not wives but harlots, he gave explicit recognition to the contraceptive role of prostitution.[27]

One final observation on the female physiological nature also bore contraceptive consequences. We have seen that the physicians felt obliged to explain why women, unlike animals, continued to feel desire after they become pregnant. The physicians were interested in the scientific ramifications of the question, but the theologians were ever quick to detect its relevance to illicit contraception. In listing the various kinds of *impetuosus* intercourse, Thomas of Chobham included coitus with a woman approaching birth. Ignoring the physicians' opinion that such intercourse was naturally desired by the wife, he charged the husband with wanting nothing other than to fulfill his own lust.[28] Not only did such action risk an abortion, but the ultimate purpose was clearly contraceptive.

The churchmen's preoccupation with fecundity contrasted starkly with a pronounced lack of interest in children among the Latin Ovidian authors, the fabliaux, and, to a lesser degree, the romances. We may safely assume that all medieval writers needed little reminding that they were the fruit of their parents' sexuality and that their own activity could likewise produce children, as Abélard and Heloise knew to their regret. Despite these assumptions, little sexual activity recounted in literature resulted in children both within and without marriage. In contrast to the ecclesiastical stance, therefore, the linkage between intercourse and reproduction was scarcely acknowledged within literature.

Ovid initiated the attitude for literature. Although the *Amores* chronicled numerous couplings with his mistress as well as with other passing fancies, only once does he record a pregnancy. This occurs when Corrina maladroitly attempts to abort a child, who the poet presumes to be his own. In terror Ovid invokes the pantheon of deities responsible for childbirth to save his mistress from immanent death. Expressing no particular regret over the fate of his putative fetus, he devotes a second stanza to decry the evils of abortion. "If this ancient recourse had pleased mothers in the past, the human race would have long been extinct. . . . Where would you [Corinna] yourself have been if your mother had tried it?" In the *Ars amatoria,* his handbook for lovers, however, Ovid preferred to remain silent on the consequences of sexual activity. Even when mythologizing on the origins of sexuality, the first humans couple like beasts but without mention of reproduction. The only direct allusion to offspring involves cosmetics. "Childbirths shorten the flower of youth," he warns girls. "Continued harvesting ages the fields."[29]

Those who wrote in this tradition in the twelfth century equally ignored the consequences of pregnancy throughout the numerous amatory escapades. It is true that Alda's and Pyrrus's week-long tryst renders Guillaume de Blois's heroine pregnant, thus requiring matrimony, but this is the sole example among the Latin comedies (*Alda,* vv.515, 527–28, 552, 566). Although the clerical André the Chaplain is quite aware of the church doctrine on progeny, the subject of reproduction is remarkably absent throughout the entire encyclopedic compendium. Even the violent palinode of Book III, the most ecclesiastically oriented of his treatise, considers the goals of progeny only tangentially.[30] More attention, we have seen, was devoted to the distinction between mixed and pure love, the latter which proceeds through the erotic stages but omits the final solace.[31] As a cleric himself, André may have preferred pure love because it was appropriate to his celibate status and avoided the disadvantages of paternity. The techniques of pure love recalled the contraceptive effects of Huguccio's *amplexus reservatus.* André's allusions to nonprocreative practices, therefore, befitted his reticence to acknowledge the reproductive effects of his erotic doctrine and confirmed his allegiance to Ovid.

The fabliaux accentuated this reticence over progeny. Despite hundreds of recorded copulations, remarkably few offspring followed. Children, to be sure, are included in the *mise en scène* of peasant households. In Jean Bodel's *Gombert* (vv.22, 88–89, 96–97, followed by *Meunier* [p.91]), for example, the baby's crib serves as a channel marker to aid the navigation of the two clerics as they exchange places under cover of darkness. In the *Povre clerc* the *vilain*'s customary absence is explained by his habitual trip to the mill to fetch flour for his children (p.195), and in *Prestre qui fu mis* the cobbler's three-year-old daughter reveals the wife's affair with the priest (p.25). These children, who serve the needs of adulterous plots, are presumably born within legitimate marriage whatever the doubts over their putative fathers. Only in *Prestre et le chevalier* was a causal relation made explicit between coitus and reproduction and this, significantly, under conditions that heaped ridicule on causation. The knight threatens the priest that "he will be fucked, and if God pleases, he will become pregnant" (p.86).

André the Chaplain had remarked that if God condoned the act of fornication, there would be no reason to institute marriage, because God's people could increase more rapidly through fornication and other extramarital activity than through matrimony.[32] The fabliaux, however, did not recognize such reasoning, because the innumerable tales of fornication and adultery resulted in very few children. In addition to Richeut's determined efforts to produce a child out of wedlock, the sole exception was *L'enfant qui fut remis au soleil,* in which a wife conceives a son by her lover during the protracted absence of her merchant husband and explains her impregnation, as we have seen, by a snowflake (vv.17–18, 33–36). (This fabliau circulated in both Latin and vernacular versions.) A rare glimpse into the precarious position of a priest's concubine is afforded in the *Bouchier* where the servant girl questions the legitimacy of the children (vv.365–67).

This perception of low fecundity continued into romance literature. Throughout the romance corpus of the Tristan legend and Chrétien, children are rare and many prominent couples sterile. Tristan's, Iseut's, and Marc's triangular love, for example, produces no progeny. Fenice's magic potions are not only contraceptive with Alis, but no offspring is recorded in her marriage to Cligès nor in Erec's and Enide's as well. We shall see that only Jean Renart's couples of high lineage are fertile. As the supreme model of chivalric society, however, Arthur's and Guenièvre's union remains irremediably barren.[33]

The single and important exception to this general sterility in the romance genre dominated by men was the one author who was female. In four out of twelve of her lais, Marie de France envisaged sexual activity as explicitly resulting in children. Although the marriage between the rich man and his wife in *Yonec* is barren (vv.19–20, 37–38), the two wedded couples in *Le fresne* (vv.9–11, 65–67) each produce a set of twins, but the fertility is beclouded by the general suspicion that twins are the result of two men and, therefore, adulterous (vv.39–42). (This belief is, however,

219

quite innocent of current medical opinion on multiple births.) What is particularly noteworthy in Marie is that the numerous extramarital liaisons are equally fertile. The spurious offspring of the peccant wife and knight in *Bisclavret* are born with deformed noses (vv.312–14), but the equally adulterous fruit of the young wife and the knight is the hero Yonec (vv.325–27), who eventually succeeds to his father's ring and sword and slays his mother's husband (vv.414–24, 531–42). Milun and a baron's daughter, both unmarried, likewise produce a son, who is reunited with his biological parents at the end of the tale (vv.53–54). In the meantime the newborn child is confided to Milun's sister in Northumbria. The long journey to deliver the child to the aunt afforded Marie opportunity to embroider details on infant care. As the company travels from town to town they stop seven times a day to change, bathe, and give the child over to a wet nurse (vv.109–14). (Only Jean Renart approximated this interest in infants when he described how nurses fed and bathed Guillaume during his first three years [*Escoufle,* vv.1786–1805].) As a woman, Marie was acutely aware of the biological consequences of her sexuality and appeared to be the sole romance author who is able to recognize the full implications of intercourse on reproduction, even when beyond the bonds of matrimony.[34]

The Politics of Lineage: The Romances

In the theologians' schema, the goals of marriage consisted not only of procreation, the rendering of the marital debt, the avoidance of fornication, and the diffusion of charity, but also of admittedly political purposes. Robert of Courson summed up the Lombard, the *Glossa ordinaria,* and his own teacher the Chanter, when he listed the reconciliation of enemies and the confirmation of peace and treaties as the fourth and fifth "final causes" of marriage.[35] The deployment of dynastic marriages to confirm and buttress diplomatic agreements was so entrenched within royalty and the aristocracy that contemporary examples abound. Louis VII, for example, gave two daughters from his first wife Eleanor to the counts of Troyes and Blois and two daughters from his second wife to the heirs of his Angevin arch rivals, young King Henry and Count Richard. To ratify the treaty of Le Goulet (1200), Philip Augustus wedded his son Louis to Blanche de Castile, the niece of his English antagonist, King John. In 1212 Otto of Brunswick espoused the widow of Philip of Swabia, his rival for the imperial crown, after the latter's assassination. To underscore the negative effects of the reverse principle, André the Chaplain noted that illicit love could break marriages, inflame wars, and dissolve treaties of peace.[36] In all likelihood he had in mind the hostilities that broke out after Henry of Anjou married Eleanor of Aquitaine, recently divorced from Louis VII.

Undoubtedly marriage rendered the most potent political service by establishing lineage—the reproduction of heirs to perpetuate a family's landed domain, political authority, and future prestige. By the birth of Philip Augustus in 1165, the Capetians had produced seven male heirs in unbroken succession since 987, thus establishing beyond all doubt their dynastic right to the French kingdom. As the royal apologists were quick to point out at the time, the Capetian achievement contrasted with the difficulties of the Anglo-Normans and the failure of the German Salians to establish hereditary rights over their respective realms.[37]

Pierre the Chanter, however, was not as convinced of the merits of dynasticism which could result in the imposition of immature or wicked princes on the people. His preference lay with the ecclesiastical principle of election that prevailed currently in the German Empire.[38] Nor were the romance authors fully persuaded of the superiority of succession from father to son. Gottfried von Strassburg has Marc, King of England and Cornwall, renounce marriage and heirs from his body in favor of his nephew Tristan whose chivalric qualities had already been demonstrated (vv. 4446–88). Alis, the Greek emperor, in Chrétien's version of the Tristan legend also promises not to marry, nor to produce an heir, so that his nephew, the valiant Cligès, can succeed to the throne (vv. 2530–37, 3141–51). For his part King Arthur, the supreme paragon of chivalric royalty, never grows old (or older), has no children, makes no move to designate his nephew Gauvain in his place, and gives no thought to the succession of his kingdom.

Among the romances, however, other forces surfaced which favor the hereditary principle. Counselors urge Gottfried's King Marc to take a wife with whom he can beget an heir, either son or daughter. The king finally agrees to marry Iseut to avert civil war (vv. 8350–60). Although Alis's decision to marry Fenice and disinherit Cligès is motivated by treachery (vv. 2615–20), the wife is nonetheless of royal blood, as in the preceding case: Iseut la Blonde is a royal Irish princess; Fenice, the daughter of a German emperor. In Jean Renart, however, the problem of political succession has become acute. In *Escoufle* the emperor has no son, only a daughter; in the *Roman* the emperor Conrad is content to remain a bachelor with little concern for heirs. In both romances, therefore, a crisis has arisen over succession fully comparable to that of the contemporary German Empire after the death of Henry VI in 1197—a crisis which preoccupied Jean's patrons: Baudouin, count of Hainaut; Hugues, bishop of Liège; and Otto of Brunswick, the Welf candidate to the disputed imperial throne. Following the precedent of the Tristan legend, the great barons of the empire urge a dynastic solution in both stories. In the one they want the emperor's daughter to take a husband; in the other they want the emperor himself to marry to ensure political stability through legitimate heirs. In both romances, however, a conflict emerges over the choice of spouses. In both, moreover, the barons propose the French king or his daughter, that is, spouses of comparable royal lineage. (King Louis VII had complained that he was plagued with a surfeit of daughters.) In defiance the emperor in *Escoufle* wants his daughter Aelis to marry Guillaume, the son of the count of Montivilliers, and in the *Roman* Conrad sets his heart on Liénor, daughter of a lowly knight from Dole.[39] As Aelis crouches on the windowsill about to leap into elopement, her doubts over the contemplated *mésalliance* are expressed in terms of a debate between *amors* on one side and *sens* and *raison* on the other (vv.3884–3963). The latter represent the claims of imperial *linage* about to be reduced to concubinage in nearly the same terms as those of Tisbé who questions her love for Piramus.[40] In *Escoufle,* moreover, the emperor proposes a marriage between two children, a contemporary practice which ecclesiastics tolerate—Thomas of Chobham admitted—because advantageous noble alliances guarantee peace and accompanying benefits to the church.[41] Although the conflict over *mésalliance* produces dramatic tension, both the imperial and baronial parties concur that the solution remains that of the Capetians founded on lineage and dynastic right.

The need to preserve landed domain, political authority, and family honor through the bonds of lineage pertained equally to the nobility, but only Marie de France articulated these concerns for the strata below royalty. In *Yonec,* for example, the lord of the rich Breton seigneurie of *Carwent* marries in search of heirs, but unsuccessfully (vv.13–20); in *Le fresne* vassals reproach a knight for dallying with a mistress and not wedding a noblewoman who could produce children to whom his land and inheritance would pass (vv.313–24). The other romanciers, however, restrict their discussion to kings and assume that counts, barons, castellans, and knights will follow the royal example. In the mixed society of the fabliaux, however, we have seen that aristocratic personages are acutely disturbed by *mésalliance* which threatens lineage. Berengier, the daughter of an impoverished châtelain, humiliates her base-born husband because he has cheapened her lineage (vv.24–27, 33–34, 55–60). In the *Jugemenz des cons,* marriage to a particular suitor is recognized as benefiting the family's lineage (vv.33–37). Fear of social disparity descended even to the rich bourgeois and poor neighbors in *Auberee* (vv.40–47). By acknowledging lineage's importance in imitation of royalty, therefore, the nobility found renewed incentive to accept the churchmen's natalist policy. Aristocratic wealth, power, and privilege were best secured by passing these advantages on to one's children. Pierre the Chanter, however, had specified that marriage is instituted to produce children to be raised in the faith (*ut reli-*

giose educetur). A contemporary but unedited theological treatise pursued the theme that such marriages are not to secure possessions with heirs but to bequeath offspring on earth to serve God.[42]

Lineage also depends on the institution of marriage to guarantee the legitimacy of offspring. The sixth "final cause" of marriage, Robert of Courson continued, is the discernment to identify children (*discernendorum discretio*). Following Augustine's argument, he asserted that without matrimony no one could know how to distinguish an heir from a nonheir or one's own from spurious children. If free sexual intercourse is permitted to everyone, there will be no more discernment among humans than among animals. Whoever observes that one's mother has been available to another's lust would not be able to know who is one's father and, therefore, be incapable of fulfilling the divine commandment to honor one's parents. Children born of our wives—declared André the Chaplain, extending the discussion— bring solace because we can recognize them as legitimate offspring. Those born of fornication, however, offer no consolation to the father because they are denied inheritance. For these reasons human law enjoins abstinence on widows during the period of mourning to avoid confusion of blood and the mixing of lineage. In a related case, Courson raised the problem of a prince who, thinking that he had wedded the daughter of an emperor, had actually married her handmaiden. The spurious sons of this union later overthrew the kingdom.[43] Lineage, therefore, required the vigilance of legitimate matrimony. With characteristic perception Marie de France's lai *Yonec* evoked a countervening successorial nightmare for aristocratic society. In essence she portrayed the quandary of a lord, who, unable to father his own heir, is contested by a knight-lover who impregnates the wife in the guise of a hawk. The story concludes with the son of the adulterous union killing the lord and claiming the lord's inheritance for himself.[44]

Although the writers of romance were little concerned with the physiological tie between sexuality and fecundity in general, the specific demands of lineage on aristocratic society nonetheless encouraged them to pay close attention to the ecclesiastical program of marriage and progeny for these purposes. It was entirely in the interest of noble families to produce children to perpetuate lineage, but born within matrimony to assure legitimacy. Although Tristan, Rivalin's and Blancheflor's love child, was conceived out of wedlock during the father's convalescence, the Breton lord Rual li Fontenant urges the couple to marry publicly in a church in the sight of priests and laymen and to pronounce their vows according to Christian rite before the child is born (Gottfried, vv. 1304–34, 1628–34). In Chrétien's version, Alexandre and Soredamor are solemnly wed at Windsor three months before Cligès is conceived (vv. 2315–19, 2336–39). In

Jean Renart's *Escoufle* after the emperor and empress hold a magnificent wedding for Count Richard and the lady of Genoa, the bride conceives and brings to term a boy on the same day that the empress gives birth to a girl (vv.1715–17, 1738–67).

The respect accorded to the ecclesiastical program is best seen in the frequency with which romanciers enact the blessing of the nuptial chamber. In *Erec at Enide,* for example, archbishops and bishops are present that night when the young couple come together with joy and delight in their chamber and bed (vv.2017–20). Although the wedding night of Alis and Fenice in *Cligès* is a farce, a great number of bishops and abbots bless the matrimonial bed with signs of the cross (vv.3287–92) before the emperor, thoroughly drugged, passes the night with his bride. Jean Renart was equally careful to include the ceremonies in his romances, but the celebrations of Conrad's and Lïenor's marriage are conflated with the imperial coronation at Mainz. If the nuptial chamber was blessed, it was lost in the confusion of the *grant feste* that evening. Officiating at the coronation during the day, the archbishop of Cologne nonetheless remains in town that night (*Roman,* vv.5372–81, 5479–5515). Whatever the ambiguity at Mainz, Jean left no doubt about Count Richard's marriage to the lady of Genoa at Rome. The empress leads the two to their bed, while a bishop sprinkles incense and blesses with priestly expertise (*Escoufle,* vv.1739–47). Given this massive sacerdotal intervention, the conception of a future emperor was assured. Writers in the Ovidian and fabliau tradition might retreat from the consequences of sexual fecundity, but when upholding the demands of lineage, the authors of romance could only accede to the ecclesiastical doctrine of progeny. Priests were heartily welcomed to the aristocratic connubial chamber.

CONCLUSIONS
SEXUALITY, GENDER, AND HISTORY

Sexuality

For page after page we have been listening to what a few men (and an occasional woman) say about a biological function that most men and women perform with regularity. What conclusions can we draw from this minuscule sample of testimony concerning universal human behavior? It is clear that around the year 1200 in northern France churchmen considered themselves to be the spokesmen best qualified and most authoritative to speak about sexuality. For over a millennium the subject preoccupied the religious leadership of Western Europe. When Augustine, the influential Church Father, for example, recounted his personal search for God in his *Confessions,* his adolescent sexual habits raised the first obstacle to his quest only to be last to be resolved before his soul could rest in peace with its Creator. When he turned to an exhaustive critique of classical civilization in his monumental *City of God,* the first Roman tradition that he challenged—the rape and suicide of Lucretia—implicated sexuality. "If she is an adulteress, why is she praised? If chaste, why is she killed?"[1] From late antiquity into the early Middle Ages, the dominant discourse on sexuality was that of the Church Fathers followed by monks speaking about virginity in Latin. At the same time authors of penitentials created a disciplinary regime regulating the sexual behavior of lay men and women.

Since the eleventh-century canon lawyers and theologians formulated theorems which Gratian codified in the *Decretum* in the 1140s and Pierre the Lombard in the *Sententiae* in the 1150s. They defined the universal instinct of sexual desire as concupiscence and attributed it to the Fall of the first humans into sin. Thoroughly corrupted by evil, it was transmitted throughout the human race as a venereal disease affixed to original sin. To remedy this congenital infection God instituted holy matrimony to constitute the exclusive domain for sexual relations. Thus defined, marriage was inalterably heterosexual, monogamous, exogamous, indissoluble, and primarily intended for procreation. All sexual activity outside of matrimony was proscribed as iniquitous fornication or adultery. Celibacy, originally enjoined upon monks and nuns, was extended to the secular clergy as well and descended through holy orders to the rank of subdeacon. Restricted within the boundaries of matrimony, sexual relations came under churchmen's undivided legal jurisdiction. Having tolerated aberrant behavior from the French nobility and royalty in the past, the papacy, now in the person of Innocent III, decided to make a decisive case of Philip Augustus's scheme to disabuse himself of his queen. To impose the church's authority he placed the royal domain under interdict in 1200. The Lateran Council of 1215 established the mechanism to supervise the sexual lives of lay men and women throughout Latin Christendom by decreeing that all the faithful of both sexes confess their sins to a priest and submit to penance at least once a year.[2] Thus was instituted a universal technology for disciplining sexual behavior that sought to enforce the hegemony of ecclesiastical discourse over human sexuality.

What is noteworthy about the four other discourses around 1200 was the extent to which they refused to submit to the churchmen's discourse. Even the contemporary theologian Pierre the Chanter and his circle attempted to reduce the excesses of the traditional doctrine by suggesting that the essence of concupiscence was immoderation. If sexual appetites could be moderated, they could be tolerated more readily, and ordinary lay men and women who were innocent of theological subtleties were to be left undisturbed. Although the physicians of the *Prose Salernitan Questions* acknowledged the distinctive doctrines of their learned colleagues, they preferred to offer alternative medical-natural explanations. Sexual delight arises as the result of physiological processes involving humors and nerves or of the psychological factors of sight, reason, and memory. The royal chaplain André, however, studiously disregarded the moderating efforts of his theological colleagues by equating love with extremes, and he exaggerated the theories of his medical colleagues to show the inherent harmfulness of sex. Following his master Ovid, he offered an ambivalent assessment of sexuality as involving both joy and suffering. The romance authors who directly addressed aristocratic lay people likewise equated love with alternations between delight and sorrow, but resolutely ignored the theological notion of concupiscence. Performing for broader audiences of lesser nobility and townspeople, the fableors overlooked both suffering and concupiscence and declared sexual experience to be uncomplicated pleasure. Because the two vernacular voices which were expressly directed to preponderantly lay audiences were consistently inattentive to the foundational tenet of theological discourse, the resulting silence was deafening.

Although a chaplain informed by theological education, André was nonetheless singularly unconcerned with the positive role of marriage in sex, but the fableors and romanciers fully recognized the ubiquity of the institution of matrimony and its particular suitability for rearing children. In four romances of Chrétien and two of Jean Renart the principal lovers are satisfactorily wedded by the end of each narrative. In conformity to the ecclesiastical regime, all of the marriages in the romances and fabliaux are monogamous and exogamous. Unlike the habits of contemporary French kings and nobility, no husband attempted to separate himself from an undesirable wife and to acquire a new spouse by legal means. The closest example of divorce among the discourses was Marie de France's case of King Equitan who attempts to murder his seneschal and to marry the latter's wife. Also markedly dissimilar to contemporary aristocratic practice, no marriages occur between cousins or other relatives within the prohibited degrees of consanguinity established by the church. In stark contrast to the churchmen's program, however, the three discourses refused to concede that matrimony is the exclusive forum for sexual relations. Unmarried couples, particularly youthful partners, fornicate frequently and without apology. Ovid's personal recommendation of adultery in the *Amores* and *Ars amatoria* prepared the way for the axiom repeatedly urged by André that marriage is intrinsically incompatible with true love. The archexemplary triangle of Tristan, Iseut, and Marc inspired other adulterous situations within romance literature, and over half of the fabliaux in our corpus narrated tales of marital infidelity throughout all levels of society except the highest, which was omitted. Undefiled matrimony, the churchmen's answer to the depravity of sex, had failed to win unequivocal support in the lay discourses.[3]

The procreation of children was one of two unproblematical goals which the theologians assigned to the institution of marriage. The physicians were careful to elaborate the physiological theories of how children were conceived. Although they were aware of ancient techniques of contraception and abortion, they did not contribute to the discussion, most likely in deference to the strident ecclesiastical opposition. Unlike authors in the nineteenth century, for whom virtually every sexual union was followed by conception—especially if it was extramarital, the Ovidians, fableors, and romanciers were relatively unconcerned with the procreative consequences of sexuality. (The sole exception here was Marie de France.) Scores of couples join without engendering children, particularly in the fabliaux where the abundance of sexual activity is singularly contrasted with the partners' infertility. In the romances, however, whenever an aristocratic family's future is threatened, the procreative function of marriage comes to the fore. The contemporary royalty and aristocracy realized the advantages of family lineage for assembling, safeguarding, and perpetuating the lands and honors on which their economic resources and political authority were founded. For the same reason Marie de France's nobility and Jean Renart's emperors seek wives to conceive children and to perpetuate families. The ecclesiastical definition of monogamous and exclusive matrimony guaranteed the authenticity of their progeny, and the priestly blessing of the nuptial chamber enhanced their fertility. Whenever royalty and aristocracy are concerned with lineage they welcome the churchmen's matrimonial program.

Since the eleventh century, church reformers had attempted to reduce the sexual activity of an increasing number of clergy. but Pierre the Chanter and his colleagues at Paris questioned the thrust of this program. Fearing that the restrictions might be unenforceable among the numerous lower clergy and encourage more undesirable abuses, they attempted without success to limit the celibacy requirement to the rank of deacon, allowing subdeacons and clerics in minor orders to marry legitimately and raise families. The policy of reducing restrictions applied only to the male clergy; Jacques de Vitry publicized Marie d'Oignies's example of the *mulier religiosa* to recruit married women for sexual renunciation and the more perfect life of chastity. Whereas abstinence was to be restricted to monks and the higher orders, it was to be extended among women. If the romance authors took virtually no notice of the sexual comportment of the clergy, the physicians, Ovidians, and fableors were uninhibited in publicizing the vigor of their erotic energy. In a parenthetical passage, the *Prose Salernitan Questions* noted the sexual proclivities and capacities of a group of identified clerics, one of whom became a bishop. André the Chaplain acknowledged the clerical lover with approval even to the point of rationalizing his need for sexual outlet, but the fableors gleefully recounted the amatory adventures of the young and predatory cleric as well as the mature parish priest who frequents the home of the bourgeois or peasant woman in her husband's absence. These four discourses apparently agreed with the Chanter that the program to enforce clerical celibacy was increasingly a failure, but the clerical behavior recounted—comprising adultery as well as fornication—far exceeded the bounds permitted by the most indulgent churchmen.

Within the cacophony of divergent voices the theologians were unable to assert hegemony, but this did not prevent concurrence at particular points. The theologians, for example, shared with the physicians a technical and clinical vocabulary in Latin to describe the sexual body and its activities. André was likewise familiar with these locutions, but he also employed an Ovidian lexicon that concealed the body with euphemisms, refined the articulation of the sexual act, and shifted attention to erotic foreplay. Drawing on a complementary word stock from the southern troubadours, the northern romanciers translated the Ovidian lexicon into the vernacular, sustained the tonality of the Roman poet, and retained the emphasis on foreplay. By contrast, the fableors challenged this courtliness, unleashed a *vilain* vocabulary that directly and crudely named the body and the sexual act, and in the frenzy to copulate took little heed of preliminaries. In effect, therefore, the two languages of our five discourses minted three lexicons of sexuality: a Latin clinical vocabulary shared by the theologians, physicians, and André; a set of refined locutions in Latin and French shared by the Ovidians and the romances; and a coarse idiom exclusively enunciated in French by the fableors.

Despite differing perspectives, the theologians and fableors nonetheless were able to agree on specific analyses. Lamenting the fundamentally extramarital nature of the prostitute's profession, the theologians likewise drew attention to the pervasive features of greed and deception with which the fabliaux concurred fully and offered abundant corroboration. When the theologians, moreover, attributed sexual stimulation to the process of eating and drinking (because of the proximity of the stomach to the genitals), they articulated a bourgeois and peasant practice richly illustrated in the fabliaux. On numerous occasions a matron is pictured entertaining her lover at table before the two retire to bed. On the other hand, the physicians outlined a more complex relationship between food, drink, and intercourse. Concerned that sexual activity depleted physical energy, they counseled sex before eating and warned of the dangers of making love on a full stomach. It appears as though writers addressing the aristocracy were better informed on the current school medicine, because the romances present lovers who prefer to eat after their amorous exertions. Overshadowing these minor congruences, all the spokesmen (and Marie de France) unequivocally agreed on one common conviction: in accordance with traditional Hebraic-Christian antipathy, they judged all homoerotic relations to be the most reprehensible of sexual behavior.

Gender

Because of a universal presumption of heterosexuality, the issue of gender was implicit in all five discourses. With only the exceptions of the two Maries, the five discourses originated from indisputably male voices. The exceptions, however, did not diverge markedly from the masculine conclusions about sexuality but simply offered different emphases on specific points. Since Marie d'Oignies was limited to her native vernacular, her words and deeds were mediated in Latin by her theological mentor Jacques de Vitry. Jacques had paid particular attention to the piety expressed by different groups of women in the Liégeois diocese, among whom Marie was exemplary. If her alimentary practices articulated a spirituality that was uniquely feminine, her consuming desire for chastity did not differ greatly from the male monastic orders.[4] As we have seen, what was gender-specific to the movement of *mulieres religiose* was that her contemporary promoters were urging her example of sexual abstinence upon married females at the time they were urging the reduction of celibacy for clerical males. As far as can be determined, Marie de France, for her part, spoke in her own and, therefore, feminine voice with delicacy and subtlety, but her attitudes about the sexual body, desire, and act were not noticeably different from contemporary romances composed by males. Perhaps she was more absorbed with extramarital liaisons than was Chrétien and Jean Renart, but certainly not less than the Tristan legend and the fabliaux. She did, however, appear to concur with the precocious Heloise and Marie, countess of Champagne (as reported by André), on the coercive constraints of matrimony, a perception that was not lost on aristocratic wives subject to patriarchal marriages. Most important, she was the most acutely aware of the reproductive consequences of sexuality among the lay discourses. In four out of her twelve lais children are the direct result of extramarital as well as marital activity. Her contrast with male romanciers and fableors on this point may surely be ascribed to a personal sensitivity to the unique feminine function.

Given the condition that the five principal voices were uttered by males, they too constructed an implicit gender of sexuality. Endemic to their discussion was a pervasively assumed asymmetry which placed men on top over a broad continuum of relationships ranging from the masculine determination of marriage partners to the emblematic coital position of man-prone-woman-supine. Important to this male-skewed asymmetry were the anatomical and physiological propositions inherited from antiquity. Aristotle and Galen had postulated a fundamental homology between the male and female bodies, the former turned outward, the latter inward. This essential similarity assumed the normative and superior role of the masculine body. Coitus was envisaged solely in terms of the male need to ejaculate seed. For this reason Augustine was accustomed to employ phallic imagery when he envisaged the sexual act as the movement of the foot, hand, or finger. Articulating a primordial theory of shame, he envisaged the erection of the penis as the most apposite expression of uncontrolled concupiscence. Because of masculine predominance only the man emits sperm in Aristotle's view, seconded by the Old Testament and Augustine, who likened the man to a farmer sewing by hand. While the Hippocratic tradition had postulated a second, female seed, Galen had argued that it was weaker and contributed less than the male. According to the latter, the woman also needed to feel some kind of desire to emit seed, but Aristotle's one-seed doctrine, again with Augustine's concurrence, eliminated the requirement of female desire for conception. Although a woman might experience desire in particular circumstances, it was accidental to the ultimate process of conception. As an inferior being, a woman was essentially receptive and passive to the man whose active role rendered him the child's true and only progenitor.

As to gynecology, the twelfth-century physicians inherited doctrines from two traditions that bore nuanced conclusions for gender. The Hippocratic-Galenic held that although sexuality can be abused through excess, moderate intercourse is essential to the general health of both males and females. Since the uterus is unique to the woman and defines her nature, its normal function in coitus and conception is important for female well-being. The gynecologist Soranus, however, refused to accept the womb as defining female nature. Reproduction was, therefore, accidental, not essential, for female health; intercourse was intrinsically harmful to women; and virginity is the most wholesome and preferable state.

Although the authors of the *Prose Salernitan Questions* had access to these ancient gynecological disputes and probably preferred the Hippocratic-Galenic position, they did not choose to advance the discussion with their own contributions. Along with other twelfth-century spokesmen they were more inclined to search for gender symmetry in sexual relations.[5] Unlike Aristotle and Galen, they neglected to stress the homologies between male and female anatomies with the important exception of the testicles by which both men and women produce sperm. The twelfth-century physicians openly rejected the one-seed doctrine of Aristotle, although it appears to have survived in vernacular literature. Not only was the two-seed theory asserted in its place, but the Galenic qualification of weak female sperm was ignored for the implicit assumption of equality between the two. Despite Augustine's authority, Pierre the Chanter accepted the contemporary position of his medical colleagues. The physicians retained the male model of ejaculation for coitus undoubtedly because it was equally necessary for the woman to emit sperm. The basic reciprocity was emblematized, however, by the Chanter's school when it transformed Augustine's coital image of the single finger for that of finger-touching-finger. Both men and women must, therefore, experience sexual desire to effect union, to emit seed, and to conceive. Although the physicians were relatively unconcerned with sexual techniques, they did recognize the advantage of partners arriving at simultaneous climaxes, advice which Ovid and his followers had endorsed enthusiastically when they counseled lovers not to hurry but to attain orgasm together.

The fundamental reciprocity of sexual relations received unexpected reinforcement from the theologians who generally hesitated to inquire into the details of matters tainted with concupiscence. The ecclesiastical axiom that marriage was constituted only through the mutual consent of both partners through *verba de presenti* further set into effect the Pauline corollary of the marital debt.[6] Since Apostolic authority held that the husband and wife did not possess his or her own body but that of the spouse, neither partner could deny the marital debt when sought by the other, thus creating unconditional sexual symmetry within Christian marriage. Rendering the marital debt was the second of two unproblematical goals of marriage. Pierre the Lombard and Pierre the Chanter underscored the principle that, unlike other relations in which the husband has dominance over the wife, sexual relations constituted a special and privileged realm of gender equality.

Echoes of this sexual reciprocity which the physicians, Ovidians, and theologians generated in Latin discourse may also be heard in the vernacular. In the fabliaux it would be difficult to distinguish by gender the intensity of desire for each other among the hundreds of men and women who couple with abandon. Scopophilic interest in bodily protrusions and orifices is, moreover, distributed equally with the equipment of both sexes openly displayed. We remember that when the Norman wife petitioned the good St. Martin to transform her spouse into a veritable porcupine of phalluses, the husband reciprocated with a wish that she be fitted with as many purses. The romanciers, however, were more concerned with pleasure and suffering, but Thomas of Britain could not distinguish between the sufferings of his celebrated lovers, paring the genders reciprocally. Chrétien matched his pairs of young lovers with mutual desire for each other as well. Since the antique *Bildungsroman* of Daphnis and Chloe, the exploration of nascent sexuality between youthful couples has been the locus classicus for expressing the reciprocity of desire.[7] Chrétien had experimented tentatively with Perceval, but Jean Renart contributed his fully articulated version in the mutual love of Guillaume and Aelis in *Escoufle,* further advanced by Conrad and Lïenor in the *Roman.* The years surrounding 1200, therefore, were a moment of unprecedented gender equilibrium within the discourses of sexuality.

The achievement of pronounced gender reciprocity served only to highlight other asymmetries on a lesser scale. Certainly, masculine domination persisted in numerous forms, among them the relentless male gaze. When the canon of Ovidian and romance decorum shielded the masculine body from view, but privileged the female breasts and those attributes perceived when clothed, gender was indeed distinguished and the male viewer's perspective valorized. The prevalence of the brutal act of female rape is, of course, the epitome of male domination. Although the theologians and

Chrétien could think of cases of nonconsensual intercourse forced upon boys and men, most examples occurred with women, often with peasants subjected both to male strength and social superiority. The aristocratic *pastourelle* devoted an entire literary genre to this ultimate act of engendered-sexual asymmetry.

It was also conceivable that gender asymmetry could incline to the female side. In addition to the medical theory of the two seeds and the recognition of variations among individual sexual complexions, the physicians also asserted that women, unlike men, enjoy a twofold delight both on the emission of their own sperm and on the reception of the male. This observation accorded with the moral of Ovid's story about Tiresias who demonstrated to Jupiter's satisfaction that women derive greater pleasure from sex than men. The perception of greater female desire directly led to the traditional misogynistic fear that women can never be satiated. The Ovidian André and the vernacular commentary to the *Ars amatoria* alluded to this apprehension, but it received most vivid expression in the fabliau *La dame qui aveine demandoit pour Morel sa provende avoir,* where the wife drains the husband of his sexual marrow until he is reduced to a repugnant response to regain control. The fabliaux likewise reechoed this misogynistic interpretation by picturing the wife but not the husband as the usual adulterer. In theological casuistry it was likewise the woman who is characteristically cited as the initiator or petitioner of sexual transgression.

Gender asymmetry skewed by greater female desire, however, also could be viewed in a positive light. Romance heroines were rarely reduced to abject passivity. The numerous women in Marie de France's lais are aware of their social vulnerability, defend themselves astutely, and often assume the initiative in their *rapports* with their lovers.[8] The leading example among our romances is the belle Lïenor of Jean Renart's *Roman de la rose.* After the seneschal's calumny, Conrad himself is unable to react. Inhibited by imperial dignity, he cannot move directly but must resign himself to the inactivity articulated in the *grands chants courtois.* Lïenor, however, is mobilized into action. She marshals her resources, journeys to Mainz, plots a stratagem, dresses for the confrontation, arrives at court, unmasks the seneschal, and reveals herself to Conrad. Announcing herself as the "maiden of the rose," she becomes both the primary actor and the title character of the *Roman.* In this spectacular progress feminine desire is crowned with a climactic reward.

The search for gender symmetry among the five discourses, however, encountered a serious obstacle from the recovery of Aristotle's natural and metaphysical writings in the Latin West. The Stagirite's characteristic notions on males and females first surfaced at Paris in the treatises of David de Dinant around 1200. The *Liber canonis* of Avicenna endowed them with further reinforcement during the second quarter of the thirteenth century. Aristotelian anatomical theories revived the homologies between men and women latent in Galenic anatomy. The Parisian *Anatomia vivorum,* which was written in the second decade, spelled out the similarities and concluded with the ancient paradigm that the male was normative to the female. David de Dinant revived the characteristic Aristotelian doctrines that only the male emits sperm, that the female merely contributes menstrual blood to nourish the embryo, and that women require no desire to conceive, because, in the notorious epigram, "the woman is essentially an imperfect male, just as is a boy." This physiology merely corroborated Aristotle's underlying metaphysical assumptions that the male is the efficient cause conferring form; the female the material cause contributing only matter; the former active, the latter passive. Since its formulation in the fourth century B.C.E., the Greek philosopher was incalculably influential in shaping gender theories in Western thought. The Parisian theologians reacted against the reappearance of his natural theories and metaphysics with sharp hostility on different fronts in 1210 and 1215. However they assessed his theories of gender, they objected to the pervasive naturalism of his metaphysics, but by mid-century the Greek philosopher's naturalism was accommodated with Christian theology largely through the efforts of scholastics, most notably Albertus Magnus and Thomas Aquinas. At the same time, Averoës accepted Aristotle's natural science among the Arabs and Maimonides among the Jews. Rehabilitated by the scholastics, Aristotle's gender theory was institutionalized at the university of Paris and throughout the educated world of Western Europe. Precisely how his specific notions on gender became established in the universities and affected other discourses has yet to be explored. Since the thirteenth century was a complex era of conflicting intellectual currents, it deserves study in its own right, but at this point there appears little doubt that the Aristotelian reemergence endowed doctrines of masculine superiority with potent scientific rationale.[9] Viewed in this light, the Hippocratic-Galenic theories of the two seeds which the *Prose Salernitan Questions* endorsed and the four other discourses nurtured, rendered the years around 1200 as a privileged moment of gender symmetry in Western thought before the deluge of Aristotelianism.

History: A Postlude

As we have listened to multiple voices talking about sexuality and have juxtaposed and compared them on different subjects, we have heard them interact, at times agreeing with, disagreeing with, ignoring, and influencing each other. Up to this point I have limited this study to an exercise in intertextuality. My firmest conclusions, therefore, result from the purely verbal engagement of one discourse with another. Beyond the verbal interplay, however, what does all this talk tell us about social behavior? About what people actually did in northern France around 1200? How can we pass from the text to the contextual realm of sexual behavior? These questions need not concern the literary critic, but they stubbornly refuse to decamp from the center of the historian's task. They remain particularly intractable because the very phenomenon is universal, but at the same time highly diversified, deeply private, and probably markedly different from our own despite whatever physiology or psychology we share with our distant ancestors. To contemplate employing these five discourses for historical purposes necessitates a number of assumptions or hypotheses. These assumptions are difficult to test—nor can we be assured that they are capable of demonstration—but they should be made explicit to clarify our task.

Modern literary critics often accept the implicit essentialistic assumption that literature consists of texts possessing aesthetic merit that can be read with pleasure over time. From this premise critics may further assume an identity between their own reading and that of the medieval audience. Because literature is timeless, critics merely constitute the most recent cohort of a text's audience and share at least a common core of appreciation with the contemporary listeners and readers.[10] Historians, however, who deal with both texts and society are encouraged to pay particular attention to the contemporary audience. We have seen that each of our five discourses was addressed to discrete, if occasionally overlapping, listening and reading publics. While the authors' intended message may appear accessible to us, we have less guidance as to the audience's reception. As I have said, I found myself laughing at the fabliaux: But did the thirteenth-century audience share my sense of humor? Hans Robert Jauss and like-minded critics have devised a series of techniques for assessing audience response (*Rezeptionsästhetik*) that promises to respond to the historian's needs. They propose to identify the audience of a particular text/discourse, delineate the "horizons of expectations" or how that audience's literary experience enabled them to understand and judge the work, and finally to measure the "aesthetic distance" between the expectations and the work and thereby assess the audience's response. In the triangle of author, work, and public, the public does not passively receive the author's work but actively attempts to understand the text in terms of its own literary experience.[11] When confined within sparse materials and a limited time span, however, I found it difficult to apply these techniques. My chief recourse was to determine how one writer understood a previous author, or, more specifically, how a spokesman understood the tradition in which he was working. The results have not suggested a profound receptivity. When, for example, Pierre the Lombard or Pierre the Chanter read Augustine's theory of concupiscence, they reformulated an argument less refined than revealed in the fifth-century debate between the Church Father and Julian of Eclanum. Nor did the *Prose Salernitan Questions* perceive the nuances of Galen's doctrine of the double sperm when he criticized Aristotle's single-seed theory. Although the twelfth-century physicians did not possess direct access to Galen's writings, their discussion of sexual physiology was not as full as their major source, Constantinus Africanus, as his, in turn, was a reduction of Galen.[12] When Jean Renart described an enameled cup which Count Richard offered to the church of the Holy Sepulchre (*Escoufle,* vv.576–616), he provided the most extensive reading of the Tristan legend from the next generation, but his interpretation merely recounted the chief narrative features.[13] In a similar mode, his evocation of Marie de France's *Lanval* (*Roman,* vv.5507–15) served only to evoke Conrad's and Lïenor's sexual bliss, certainly not a sophisticated appreciation of Marie's delicate lai. André the Chaplain's appropriation of Ovid obscured the urbanity and polish of the ancient master.

From these examples of receptivity we may ask the more fundamental and difficult question: How did the contemporary audiences, in fact, receive the spokesmen themselves? The problem has not been addressed directly and sustainedly for our five voices, but the above examples suggest a preliminary and partial answer. Whatever the interpretive capabilities of the diverse audiences, they did understand the texts on the surface or literal level. This was the point of entry into all texts. With little doubt students of medicine understood the *Salernitan Questions* at this level, and theological students, as well as most clerics, were trained to read both the *questiones* and the Bible *ad litteram.* Pierre the Chanter's acknowledgment of André the Chaplain's overarching framework of *ad cautelam* suggests that at least theological clerics could have read the Chaplain at face value. In a similar fashion, the audiences for Jean Bodel and Jean Renart could follow and appreciate the narratives of the fabliaux and the romances, just as Jean Renart himself followed the Tristan story. In sum, the contemporary audiences of our five voices could and did understand the literal interpretation, which I have attempted to explicate in this study. The question remains to what depths could and did these audiences extend their interpretations beyond this point of entry. Theological students were expressly trained in multiple interpretations of the Scriptures. Numerous clerics undoubtedly possessed the rhetorical formation to appreciate the irony and humor of André's convolutions, and knights and ladies must have responded to the sheer beauty—involving nuance, imbrication, and complexity—of the lyric verses with which Jean Renart embellished his *Roman de la rose.* To what extent and whether they heard these texts as modern critics do is a task yet to be demonstrated. We can nonetheless credit medieval audiences with impressive hermeneutical sophistication as long as we remember that their multiple readings included, not among the least, the surface interpretation.

Although we have assumed that contemporary audiences understood the surface interpretation, it nonetheless remains hazardous to accept the further hypothesis that literary texts provide unobstructed reflections of sexual behavior. We must be prepared that they remain colored by convention, irony, humor, and other deflections that contemporary audiences appreciated but are less imperceptible to us at the literal level. To compensate for the opaqueness of texts we may posit three additional assumptions. In the first place, if—as I have attempted to do in this study—we read each spokesman in conjunction with his discursive tradition, we may be better able to detect and thereby take into account the conventional and stereotypical which he inherited. This is the closest I come to reader response. To see Pierre the Chanter in terms of Pierre the Lombard and Augustine, for example, helps us to recognize the direction from which his argument developed. To read Jean Renart in the context of the Tristan legend offers us a "horizon of expectation" for Jean's public. Second, if discourse is not perfectly reflective of society, we may nonetheless assume that it acts upon social behavior. It can be argued, for example, that although the twelfth-century romances did not portray the practices involved in contemporary tournaments with full accuracy, they nevertheless proposed ideals for conducting these pastimes that eventually shaped actual aristocratic behavior. Here literary texts actually molded and directed social practice.[14] Some discourses were assuredly more active and hegemonic than others. We have seen that although theologians claimed supreme jurisdiction over sexual matters, their influence on the other discourses was sporadic and selective. Conversely, although they may not have influenced behavior to the extent of their claims, their voice was not completely without effect as churchmen sought to enforce their proscriptions by interdicting the royal domain and enjoining penance on the faithful. The other discourses may have acted on their respective audiences in comparable ways: the physicians and Ovidians on clerics in the schools and courts; the romances enunciating courtly ideals for kings, barons, and their entourages of knights and ladies; and the fabliaux entertaining but also proposing suggestions to the lesser aristocracy and townspeople. While these discourses did not perfectly mirror their public, they still exercised an impact in varying degrees. We may surmise that actual sexual behavior operated not too far beneath the surface of their discursive proscriptions. In the third place, moreover, if no discourse is absolutely determinative, then multiple voices are more revealing than single. When compared and juxtaposed, they extend their reach, encompass the subject, and point to a center where presumably lies social reality. More precisely, if sex is not self-evident but conditioned by religion, medicine, and literature, these discourses tend to circumscribe the terrain of the historical phenomenon. Recognizing their deficiencies, we are reduced to accepting the conclusion that multiple discourses remain the best available evidence for sexual behavior in the twelfth century.

From its beginnings sexology, or the modern study of sexual behavior, has relied heavily on discursive evidence. At the turn of the nineteenth century, Richard von Krafft-Ebing, Havelock Ellis, and Sigmund Freud collected hundreds of case histories reporting sexual experiences. While Freud compiled them from therapeutic sessions with patients, Krafft-Ebing and Ellis encouraged their subjects to write them down as autobiographic testimony, which they published. In the 1940s and 1950s, Alfred Kinsey and his associates conducted interviews with over 18,000 males and nearly 6,000 females and recorded their experiences on detailed questionnaires. Freud's and Kinsey's personal contact with the subjects allowed the investigators to monitor and validate the evidence. Ellis and Kinsey, moreover, often compared their results against animal behavior, but the primary technique was simply to record and interpret human discourse on sexuality. Their interpretation of the evidence was admittedly shaped by theoretical premises, the composition of samples, their varied interests in pathology, and other biases, but the verbal testimony of men and women relating their personal experiences was their consistent access to sexual behavior. It was not until the 1950s and 1960s that William Masters and Virginia Johnson passed from talk to direct observation of the sexual act. First employing prostitutes (like the medieval physicians), the investigators eventually extended their study to some 700 men and women (800 in their second study) whom they measured and photographed; they checked blood pressure, pulse, and ventilation to examine under clinical conditions the physiology of sex as it was being performed. Even within this "laboratory experimentation," however, they continued to be preoccupied with psychological factors, most particularly the importance of communicating sexual feelings accomplished only through words. Although modern sexologists have developed numerous techniques of observation and control which are totally unavailable to the historian of sexuality in the distant past, it is still noteworthy how much of the study of human sex in any age depends upon the evidence of discourse.[15]

APPENDIX 1

ROBERT OF COURSON, *SUMMA* [XLII, 31, 32]

MS, Paris, BN lat. 14524, fols. 154ra–155vb
Excerpts published in Müller, *Paradiesesehe* 153–61.

[154ra] [31] Post hec queritur utrum possit compleri carnale commercium sine peccato. Quod videtur quia matrimonium est de iure naturali et a domino institutum, et quandoque fuit preceptum sicut egredientibus de archa. Ergo impletio eius sicut cuiuslibet alii precepti in casu meritoria est quod probatur auctoritate Augustini qui dicit quod quatuor de causis cognoscitur uxor, scilicet causa prolis, vel causa reddendi debiti, vel causa incontinentie refrenande, vel causa libidinis explende. Duos priores modi, ut idem testatur Augustinus, nullius sunt criminis sed tercius semper habet culpam tamen venialem, sed quartus semper culpam mortalem. Sic ergo duo sunt modi cognoscendi uxorem sine omni culpa.

Item isti tres [154rb] commixtionis carnalis fines scilicet propter prolem suscipiendam, propter debitum reddendum, propter incontinentiam refrenandam sunt boni et ipsum contrahere est bonum et deo beneplacitum et contrahentes sunt in caritate. Ergo si contrahant ex caritate et dirigant intentiones eorum ad quemcumque istorum trium finium merentur in carnali commixtione. Nam ab initio talis operis habeant bonam intentionem et eam dirigebant ad bonum usque ad finem; ergo merentur hoc faciendo.

Item omne opus cuiuscumque virtutis meritorium est; ergo omne opus prudentie meritorium est. Sed qui cognoscit uxorem suam ne labatur in aliam prudenter agit quia prudenter timetur quod accidere potest; ergo sic meretur.

Item quilibet debet esse carior sibi quam alteri, sed aliquis precavens alteri ne alius ruat in fornicationem meretur; ergo in precavendos sibi propter idem meretur quod probo per simile. Ecce aliquis proficiscens in expeditionem fert secum victualia ne compellatur rapere aliena; ergo voluntas huius est bona. Et omnis talis voluntas est arbor bona, sed si arbor est bona omnes fructus ex ea sunt boni. Ergo cum ex tali voluntate procedat iste fructus scilicet refrigerantio in proprio vase ne rapiat aliena [ei] meritorius est. Sed dicit aliquis quod nullum tale opus meritorium est quia in aliqua parte eius homo efficitur totus caro, sed et caro et sanguis regnum dei non possidebunt.

Sed contra. Si tale opus non est meritorium quia habet aliquam partem que non refertur ad deum, pari ratione totalis alia oratio vel elemosina vel martirium vel predicatio vel quodcumque aliud opus cuius alia pars non refertur ad deum non est meritorium. Ergo si predicas et pulverem contrahis in aliqua parte predicatonis vel si martirium pateris et acerbitas pene te non permittat meditari ad deum in aliqua sui parte, vel si oras et aliqua musca irruat ut vana sit aliqua pars orationis, nec sic mereris. Ergo ad hoc quod aliqua oratione vel tali opere merear oportet quod in singulis sillabis vel litteris animus meus moveatur ad deum. Ergo si decanto ex penitentia mihi in[154va]iuncta psalterium et in aliqua parte, non refero animum ad deum teneor iterare totum vel redimere, et hoc videtur efficacius proposse probare per simile. Nam si una pars diei fuerit clara et alia obscura, non dicetur tota dies clara nec tota obscura. Item si claritas est tantum in principio diei et totum residuum sit obscurum, non possumus dicere quod claritas prime partis reflectatur ad sequentes partes ut ex illa dicantur clare. Pari ratione, si prima pars orationis vel predicationis est devota et relique non sunt [ms: sint] devote, non possumus dicere quod devotio prime partis sit deambulatoria ad sequentes ut illas faciat devotas. Nec devotio ultime partis potest esse retrograda ad precedentes ut illas faciat devotas. Nam hec argumentatio neccesaria est huius partis. Nulla devotio est determinata illa que subest vanitati; ergo hec pars non est devota.

Item necessaria est hec argumentatio hoc subest devotioni; ergo est devotum, pari ratione hec est neccesaria. Hoc subest vanitati; ergo est vanum. Sed constat quod in predicando et orando et cognoscendo uxorem est invenire aliquam partem que subest vanitati, scilicet illa in qua non refertur animus operantis ad deum. Ergo illa pars non est meritoria sed est veniale peccatum quia est vanitati subiectum. Ergo opus constans ex illa parte et aliis partibus non est meritorium. Nichil enim constat ex peccato veniale et actione meritoria, et ad idem facit illa auctoritas [Gratian, *Decretum*, C.32, q.2, c.4; Lombard, *Sententiarum* 4.32.3]: Vir sanctus ut propheta cum cognoscit uxorem non adest presentia spiritus sancti. Unde david [Psalm 50:7]: *In peccatis concepit me mater mea*. Ex dictis ergo habetur quod non potest expleri carnale commercium sine peccato.

Sed contra. Hoc est preceptum et institutum a domino. Ergo aliquid est preceptum a domino quod sine peccato non potest expleri. Ergo nemo potest hoc implere quin peccet; ergo non videtur esse preceptum a domino.

Solutio. Credimus esse distinguenda tria genera operum, tria genera oculorum. Quedem enim sunt opera que fiunt propter deum directa, et illa semper sunt meritoria que fiunt oculo simplici. Alia contra deum, et illa semper demeritoria que fiunt oculo nequam. Alia sub deo que fiunt o[154vb]culo medio ut opera coniugatorum qui partim serviunt mundo et liberis et deo, sed deum omnibus proponunt, et talia prout sepius non faciunt perfecti nisi meritorie quia possunt illa referre non directe ad deum, et tunc non sunt meritoria quia non omnibus que facit perfectus, et si in se bona sunt, meretur. Imperfectus autem, dicit augustinus, facit illa sepe nichil merendo. Sufficit enim ei ut illa que facit sint sub deo et non contra deum, cuiusmodi sunt arare, seminare, ma[n]ducare, et bibere.

Sed contra. Nulla sunt opera que non sunt nature vel gratie vel culpe, et hec non sunt gratie quia non sunt meritoria nec culpe quia non sunt peccata mortalia. Ergo sunt nature et fiunt propter bonum; ergo cum condiuntur caritate, meritorie fiunt; ergo iste meritorie cognoscit propter refrenandum [*ms:* reservandam] libidinem.

Fere omnes dicunt quod talia opera in cognoscendo uxorem propter voluptatem reprimendam sunt venalia propter pruritum adiunctum, et secundum hoc talia opera sunt culpe, scilicet venialis, non mortalis. Magister noster cantor dicit quod duo sunt ibi distinguenda, scilicet opus ipsum quod non est peccatum sed de genere bonorum, non tamen meritorium, et aliud ei adherens, scilicet pruritus sive vellicatio quedam que non operi sed anime adheret, et illa macula venialis est que impedit ne illud opus sit meritorium. Et quod sic sit distinguendum, probatur quod per primum hominem qui si cognoscere vellet uxorem suam in primo statu non plus pruriret caro quam si digitus digitum tangeret. Sed cum idem tactus ipse sit modo inter virum et mulierem et propter originale superadditum sit, illud veniale. Patet quod modo sicut ibi illa duo diversa quia motus in primo homine non fuit pruribilis sed in nobis est pruribilis.

Sed contra. Illa macula adherens est peccatum; ergo est actio; ergo cuicumque inest illa, macula agit illa. Sed quicumque illa agit, agit totali ratione; ergo simul duobus motibus movetur quod concedit magister cantor. Tamen dicit quod nescit se scire quid sit [in] genere illa vellicatio que venialissima est, non plene concedens quod sit actio sed quia actio per predicta patent solutiones premissorum.

Nam hoc moveri ad refrenandum [*ms:* reservandam] voluptatem in propria uxore ne deterius contingat, non [155ra] est ex prudentia quia tunc ex caritate esset. Potest tamen dici quod origine est ex prudentia, sed quia non directe propter deum fit non est ex caritate, scilicet, in formatione quia tunc esset meritorius motus, et dicuntur ex virtutibus esse dupliciter ut hec propositio exnotet originem vel in formationem. Omnis et solus motus meritorius est ex caritate in formatione, sed omnis ille est ex illa origine qui directe et originaliter et primo loco procedit ex illa. Quilibet debet esse carior sibi quam alteri, sed in precavendo alteri ne ruat in fornicationem meretur; ergo et in precavendo sibi propter idem meretur. Non sequitur quia motus alterius non sunt in sua potestate quos reprimat sicut motus proprii quos reprimere potest.

Dicimus itaque quod duplex finis est distinguendus: unus directus et alius indirectus. Directus finis est in opere quando illud fit directe et nullo medio propter deum. Finis indirectus quando opus omni primo loco nec directe fit propter deum, sed primo loco fit propter [in]commodum vitandum quod postea refertur ad deum. Unde hec locutio multiplex est. Iste qui cognoscit uxorem causa incontinencie refrendande facit hoc opus propter deum. Nam si propter notet primum finem, falsa est; si secundum, vera est. In primo sensu talis argumentatio neccessaria est. Iste facit hoc opus propter deum, ergo meretur. In secundo sensu nichil valet. Unde dicimus generaliter quod quicumque cognoscit uxorem suam propter incontinentiam refrenandam, facit opus quod est veniale peccatum et peccat sub deo, sed bonum coniugii excusat illud opus ne sit peccatum mortale.

Sed cum dicit augustinus [*De bono coniugali,* 7] quod duo predicti modi cognoscendi uxorem, scilicet causa prolis et causa reddendi debiti, nullius sint criminis, tamen expleri non possunt illi modi sine aliquo veniali peccato levissimo; tamen et quia aliquis nevus venialis peccati modicissimus illis se ingerit, dicit augustinus quod illi modi nullius sunt criminis eo tropo loquendi quo dicitur nil habuerit codrus. De hoc autem quod queritur utrum aut redditio debiti aut predicatio aut perpessio martirii aut oratio possit esse meriti quamvis pulvis venialis peccati se ingerat. Dicere solet cantor [155rb] quod talis pulvis venialis peccati vel modica retardatio motus ad deum, non impedit quin totale opus sit meritorium. Si ab inicio fuerit inchoatum et similiter relatum ad deum sicut incisio pedis fistulanti que fit in caritate et ex caritate meritoria est quamvis in alia parte acerbitas pene retardet animum pacientis ne moveatur ad deum. Sic et eodem modo dicunt fere omnes de predicatione, de oratione, et de elemosine largitione, et de quacumque alia actione que fit in caritate scilicet quod talia nichilominus sint meritoria, licet alia particula talium operum non referantur ad deum quia quamvis pulvis adheserit pedibus apostolorum nichilominus predicatio eorum fuit meritoria.

Hec est trita solutio plurimorum. Plenius tamen et verius potest solvi sicut asseruit predictus cantor magister noster in extremo anno vite sue cum vivacius de hiis disputatum est quod scilicet in omnibus talibus operibus successivis distinguendum est inter particulas que referantur ad deum et illas que non referantur ad deum. De omnibus illis particulis que ad deum referuntur dicit quod sint meritorie. De illis vero que non referuntur ad deum sed subsunt vanitati vel carnali delectationi dicit quod venialia sunt peccata. Et quia ex peccato et opere meritorio non constat aliquid, dicimus quod ex illis particulis que sunt meritorie et ex illis que sunt peccata non fit una actio nec copulantur ad communem terminum sicut accidit de illa actione eundi ad ecclesiam quam iste incipit propter bonum et de subsequenti actione qua videt mulierem ad concupiscendum eam ex qua et prima non fit una actio. Immo oportet necessario quod aliquid interveniat ne copulentur ad faciendum unum. Nichil enim potest constare ex virtute et vicio vel ex merito et demerito.

Ex iam dictis patet solutio premissorum. Nam si aliquis cognoscit uxorem causa prolis vel causa reddendi debiti, prime particule redditionis debiti et ultime in quibus movetur ad deum sunt meritorie. Medie vero in quibus totus absorbetur a carne et totus fit [155va] caro sunt peccata venialia. Unde non concedimus quod totali illo opere mereatur iste vel demereatur quia ex illis particulis non fit unum totale opus. Simili modo dicimus de oratione quod ille partes que subsunt devotioni devote sunt, que aut subsunt vanitati vane sunt. Sed in hoc est differentia quod quamvis animus orantis in illis partibus non referatur ad deum sed rapiatur ad iniustas vanitates, tamen virtus insita orationi facit eam in aliquo valere oranti quamvis in illa parte nichil mereatur cum non moveatur ad deum et ut musce vanitatum fedant, ita aliquas partes orationum. Ille redimende sunt vel reiterande ab illo qui ex voto vel ex iniuncta sibi penitentia tenetur orationes illas devote deo reddere, et tamen non peccat quamvis in omni sillaba non ferat animum ad deum, cum hoc nemo possit facere. Unde periculosum est ex voto vel ex penitentia teneri ad solutionem huiusmodi orationi. Simili modo dicimus de predicatione scilicet quod ille partes predicationis que referuntur ad deum sunt meritorie. Sed ille quibus pulvis vane glorie se admiscet venalia sunt peccata. Et quamvis diceremus quod una actio esset ex partibus meritoriis et ex indiferentibus vel venialibus actionibus, non diceremus tamen quod huiusmodi actio totalis esset meritoria, sed diceremus quod una pars eius esset meritoria et alia non.

Unde ad hoc quod primo quesitum est, scilicet, utrum aliquid sit preceptum a deo quod non possit expleri sine peccato veniali, dicimus hoc esse verum de redditione debiti, si dicamus unam esse actionem ex omnibus particularibus actionibus que fiunt in redditione debiti sicut predicare vel aliquamdiu vivere est in preceptum a domino, et tamen hoc vix contingit adimpleri sine veniali peccato.

Sed adhuc obicitur de premissa auctoritate augustini qua proponitur quod non sunt nisi quatuor modi cognoscendi uxorem. Nam vulgus nullum illorum quatuor modorum attendit; immo de quadam consuetudine vulgari accedunt laici ad uxores suas non attendentes [155vb] nisi hoc quod coniuncti sunt in matrimonio vel quia unus appetit copulari alteri non attendens aliquem determinate finem. Quid ergo dicemus de talibus?

Constat quod neque commiscentur causa prolis, neque causa reddendi debiti, neque causa refrenande luxurie incontinentie, ergo secundum augustinum: omnes taliter coeuntes peccant mortaliter. Item si vir saturatur de eo quod suum est implendo appetitum suum, quomodo peccat mortaliter cum augustinus dicat quod qui cognoscit uxorem pro explenda libidine peccat mortaliter? Quid appellat augustinus explere libidinem? An peccabit vir in festivis diebus vel noctibus si cognoscat uxorem, et si uxor petat instanter in die pasche vel passionis dominice, debet ei denegare debitum, cum dicat ioel propheta [2:16] ut tempore ieiunii *egrediatur sponsus de cubili suo et sponsa de thalamo suo?* Numquid credendum est semihereticis quibusdam qui dicunt quod in .v. feria non debet accedere vir ad uxorem quia in vespera eius captus est dominus, nec in sexta feria quia in illa passus est, nec in sabbato quia in illa est sollemnitas gloriose virginis, nec in die dominica quia in illa resurrexit dominus, nec in secunda feria quia tunc celebratur pro animabus, nec in aliquibus festivis diebus, et sic fere totam ab usu matrimonii excipiunt septimanam, et sic oblique totum nituntur destruere matrimonium.

Solutio. Dicimus quod augustinus non negat plures esse modos cognoscendi uxorem quam predictos quatuor. Primi tres modi sunt sine peccato mortali, et preter illos tres potest esse quartus sine mortali peccato, scilicet, cum simplex aliquis, qui non tenetur scire apices iuris accedit ad uxorem, scilicet, simpliciter, non tenendo magis ad hunc quam ad illum finem, sed accedit ad uxorem tanquam ad suam volens uti sua. Non enim iudicandum est laicos ideo damnandos esse quia nimis tenere diligunt uxores suas vel quia frequenter accedunt ad eas, sed secundum augustinum tunc peccant mortaliter cum eis utuntur ad explendam libidinem, sed quocumque modo sive contra naturam sive quocumque alio modo sit immoderate, scilicet, ut immoderatus sit excessus qui damnatur etiam in li[156ra]citis, unde fulgentius. [Cf. below p. 299n.14]: *Vehemens amator uxoris adulter est.* Sicut enim in nimio esu incurrit aliquis castrimargiam, ita in nimio coitu contrahat vehemens et immoderatus amator uxoris ex nimio coitu mortalem maculam.

[32] De temporibus coeundi dicimus quod ad tempus debent cessare ab amplexibus sed non nisi de mutuo consensu pro reverentia dierum festivorum, ut secundum apostolum [I Cor. 7:5] qui habent uxores sint quasi non habentes *ut vacent orationibus.* Sed tamen si alteruter instanter petat debitum vel voce vel signis, si relicus est ydoneus vel potest reddere, non potest ei quod suum est negare iuxta illud apostoli [I Cor. 7:4]: *Vir non habet potestatem sui corporis sed muleri* et econverso. Unde si vir pro reverentia festivitatis vult ab amplexibus cessare et mulier ei consentiat, bonum est. Si autem illa dissentiat et debitum petat, non est in potestate viri negare, quia si ipse negaret et illa propter eius defectum laberetur in adulte-

rium, peccatum illius viro imputaretur. Unde non sunt audiendi predicti semiheretici qui predicant in contrarium et in caveis et in scriptis occulte detrahunt matrimonio seducentes mulierculas honeratas peccatis per dulces et adulatoriusos sermones. Cum hec de omnibus dubitabilibus de matrimonio dicta sufficiant.

◦◦◦

APPENDIX 2
PIERRE THE CHANTER, *VERBUM ABBREVIATUM* (LONG VERSION)

MSS. Vatican, Reg. lat. 106, fols. 153rb–154va.
Paris, Mazarine, 772, fols. 43vb–43va.

Cf. (Short Version) PL 205:333–35; trans. in Boswell, *Christianity, Social Tolerance*, 375–78.

Contra sodomiticam turpitudinem XLVI

Peccatum cuiuslibet libidinis parit ociositas et habundantia panis et saturitas vini. Et maxime illam ignominiosam libidinem Sodomorum et Gomorreorum quam redarguens Moyes. In fine Genesis ait [13:13]: *Homines sodomite autem pessimi erant et peccatores coram domino nimis.* Item [18:20–21]: *Clamor Sodomorum et Gomorreorum multiplicatus est et peccatum eorum agravatum est nimis. Descendam* inquit dominus *et videbo utrum clamorem qui venit ad me opere conpleverint.* Glosa: *Novitas tante et tam inaudite turpitudinis quasi ammirationem et dubitationem parit in audiente. Unde dominus quasi admirans et dubitans super tanto scelere introducitur loquens sic: Descendam et videbo. Incredibile enim videtur homines tantum flagitium perpetrasse.* Nota quod cum dominus tantum fetorem non possit sustinere cogitur de empireo descendere ut in tales animadvertat. Item nota etiam hoc quod cum minora sunt peccata, ministris utitur deus. Cum vero gravia, ipse punit ut hoc peccatum Sodomorum, peccatum homicidii, peccatum superbie, et huiusmodi. Hinc est quod ait *descendam et videbo* etc. quasi diceret etiam me qui *scrutor renes et corda* [Jer. 17:10]. Reddunt isti stupidum pre nimia et insolita specie libidinis. Item. Super hunc locum Gregorius: *Peccatum in voce est culpa* [ms:quando] *est in actione* [*Glossa ordinaria*] sed occultum vel cum tenui nota. In clamore est quando est in evidentia et frequentia ut hoc peccatum et peccatum homicidii. De quibus dominus [Rom. 12:19]: *Mihi vindicta et ego retribuam,* vel peccatum in clamore est quando est in libertate cum manifesta sceleris perpetratione. De duobus igitur peccatis tantum maximis et paribus, homicidio scilicet et vicio sodomitico, legitur clamor ad dominum ascendisse de terra. Nec mirum si de his preceteris legitur dominus conqueri. Ideo scilicet quod *masculam et feminam creavit* [Gen. 1:27] ad multiplicandos homines, sed quos dominus constuit et astruit creando et nature modo procreandi dando homicide et sodomite quantum in eis est hos perimunt et destruunt abeuntes post carnem alteram. Et ut hostes precipui et adversarii dei et generis humani adversus naturam militant. Quasi si dicerent deo: tu homines creasti ut multiplicarentur, nos vero operam dabimus ut opus tuum minuatur et destruatur. Item. Cum dominus penam pro aliis peccatis infligendam differat pro hoc pacientiam et bonitatem sibi innatam videtur exuisse, non expectans diu sodomitas, sed eos magis puniens temporaliter igne celitus misso consummaturus, tandem penam eorum per ignem gehenne.

Item. Isti qui hoc laborant vicio androgei fiunt nunc agentes nunc pacientes. Quia utrumque usurpant officium quia habentes orificium. Quod ne liceret cum dominus virum plasmasset de limo terre in agro damasceno, formaturus mulierem de costa eius in paradiso? Ne crederet eos quis androgeos preocupans formationem mulieris ait [Gen. 1:27]: *masculum et feminam creavit eos* quasi non erat consortium viri ad virum vel mulieris ad mulierem sed tantum viri ad mulierem et converso. Item. Propter ignominiam istam quam inferunt creatori et nature permittit dominus fetus nasci corruptos et andregeos qui nec plene viri nec plene femine sunt. Unde ecclesia homini androgeo, id est, habenti instrumentum utriusque sexus aptum, scilicet, ad agendum et paciendum, optionem eligendi indulget in quo velit sexu permanere. Quo vero instrumento magis calescit, quove magis est infirmus, permittit ei uti. Si magis calescit ut vir, permittit eum ducere. Si vero calescit magis ut mulier permittit eum nubere. Si autem in illo instrumento defecerit, numquam conceditur ei usus reliqui sed perpetuo continebit ut sic vicium illud extirpetur. Et nullatenus agentis et pacientis officium sequens vestigia alternitatis vicii sodomitici a deo detestabilis posse convenire uni et eidem persone credatur.

Item. Patet criminis huius atrocitas in pene inflictione quia *pluit dominus sulphur et ignem super Sodomam* [Gen. 19:24] et finitimas civitates per quod notari voluit et fetorem et ardorem peccati. Et quasi ad tales puniendos qui nec angelis parcere volebant, ignem gehenne prevenit, non expectans generalis incendii cathaclismum ut hic pena inchoata in eternis consummaretur suppliciis. Et pentapolim *subvertit et omnem circa regionem et universos habitatores urbium et cuncta terra virencia* [Gen. 19:25], Loth solo cum familia liberato ministerio angelorum. In cuius persona quidam sic loquitur ad deum:

> Hostes nature deus ictu fulminis ure
> Qui maris in crure perdunt germen geniture.

Item alius:

Intereant et eant ad tartara non redituri
Qui teneros pueros pro coniuge sunt habituri.

Item. Hanc ignominisiosam libidem suggillat apostolus ad Romanos sic dicens [Rom. 1:23–28]: quia *immutaverunt* ydolatre scilicet *gloriam incorruptibilis dei in similitudinem ymaginis corruptibilis hominis et volucrum et quadrupedum et serpentium. Tradidit illos deus in desideria cordis eorum* scilicet *in inmundiciam; ut contumeliis afficiant corpora sua in semetipsis quia commutaverunt veritatem in mendacium et servierunt creature pocius quam creatori. Propter hoc inquam tradidit illos deus in passiones ignominie; nam femine eorum immutaverunt naturalem usum in eum usum qui est contra naturam. Similiter et masculi relicto naturali usu femine exarserunt in desideriis suis invicem masculi in masculos turpitudinem operantes et mercedem quam oportuit erroris sui in semetipsos recipientes. Et sicut non probaverunt deum habere in noticia tradidit illos deus in reprobum sensum ut faciant ea que non conveniunt* etc. Item ad [1] Corinthios [6:9–10]: *Nolite errare neque fornicarii neque ydolis servientes neque adulteri neque molles neque masculorum concubitores neque fures neque avari neque ebriosi neque maledici neque rapaces regnum dei possidebunt.* Item ad Thimotheum I [1:9]: *Iusto non est lex posita sed iniustis, contaminatis, fornicariis, masculorum concubitoribus, plagiariis, mendacibus et periuriis* etc. Item ad Colossenses [3:5]: *Mortificate ergo* etc. Item Petrus in epistola II [2 Pet. 4]. Item. Epistola Jude [7]: *Sicut Sodoma et Gomorra et finitime civitates modo simili ex fornicate* quasi extra modo vel supra quam credi queat fornicate *et abeuntes post carnem alteram* scilicet que est masculus cum masculo, altera scilicet a naturali dei institutione maris et femine ad multiplicationem generis humani in cultu dei perseveraturi; viri enim et uxoris est una caro; *facte sunt exemplum ignis eterni penam sustinentes.* Item. In Levitico [18:22]: *Non conmisceberis cum masculo coitu femineo quia abhominatio est* etc. Item. Coitum etiam masculi cum masculo pari pena punit ut coitum hominis cum bruto, scilicet morte. Unde in eodem [20:13]: *Qui dormierit cum masculo coitu femineo uterque operatus est scelus vel nephas morte moriantur: sanguinis eorum super eos.* Sed nunc quomodo abierunt hec in dissuetudinem ut que graviter punit dominus, intacta relinquat ecclesia, et que leviter punit, ipsa gravissime puniat? Timendum ne hoc ex avaricia procedat. Illud vero ex refrigerio caritatis omittat. Item. Iudicum in medio vicium hoc suggillatur et transfoditur.

Item. Hii destructores hominum, qui scilicet sodomitico vicio laborant, similes sunt Onan filio Jude, cui cum preciperet pater ut accederet ad uxorem fratris sui causa sobolem suscitande, introiens ad eam semen fundebat in terram nolens suscitare semen fratri. Et ideo percussus est a domino eo quod rem detestabilem faceret ut legitur in Genesi [38]. Item. Hii ut ait Ysaias [1:9–10] sunt quasi Sodoma, id est, *muti a laude dei,* et Gomorra, id est, *asperi enormitate peccatorum* [*Interlin. Gloss*]. Sodoma enim muta interpretatur; Gomorra autem exasperans dicitur. Item. Iosue [6:26]: *Maledictus vir coram domino qui suscitaverit et edificaverit Ierico civitatem. In primogenito suo fundamenta illius qui iaciat et in novissimo liberorum portas eius ponat.* Multo magis maledictus est qui suscitat cineres Sodome, id est, peccatum sodomorum perdens sic primogenitum et novissimum filiorum fidem, scilicet, que est quasi primogenita et humilitatem que est in fine omnium neccessaria amittet.

Et sicut uxor Loth mutabitur in statuam salis [Gen. 19:26], lapideus enim erit, et carens omni sensu spirituali sicut statua salis que in se sensum non habet. Alios tamen sentire facit et condit ne per similem culpam similem incurrant penam. In quo etiam notandum quod solo respectu ad sodomam uxor Loth conversa est in statuam salis, quasi diceret dominus: Nolo ut huius criminis aliqua sit memoria, aliquis respectus, aliquod vestigium pro enormitate ipsius [cf. Luke 17:32]. Item. Etiam pro enormitate et in detestatione huius criminis dominus a deo offensus est terre illi ut converteret Pentapolim in lacum fetidum in mare scilicet mortuum versa est tota regio Pentapolis ut non vivat piscis vel avis in eo. Naves etiam homines vivos continentes non sustinet. Arbores, ut legitur, in terra illa nascuntur ferentes poma pulchra exterius usque ad maturitatem perducta sed ad levem horum tactum in cinerem fetidum et favillam rediguntur. Item Ioel hoc vicium dampnat dicens [3:3] *Et posuerunt in prostibulum puerum et puellam vendiderunt pro vino ut biberent.* Item Ysaias [66:16–17]: *Multiplicabuntur interfecti a domino qui sanctificabantur et mundos se putabant in ortis* etc. Super quem locum invenitur in Glosa: *Quiddam ineffabile ignominiosum abhominabile ad usque turpitudinis detestationem.*

Item huiusmodi homines patici et enervati sunt masculi illi quos pharao iubet necari. Immo quos iubet effeminari et ad abusus suos reservari qui se masculos converterunt in feminas abutentes coitu femineo. Item. Hii irritatores sunt Sardanapalli qui vir corruptior fuit omni muliere. Hii tales non tantum muti sed etiam ceci efficiuntur percussi a domino aorisia nec ostium Loth, id est sacre scripture, possunt invenire palpantes in meridie ut videntes non videant et intelligentes non intelligant. Item Ieremias in fine Trenorum super omnem planctum et dolorem ruine urbis et captivitatis ad cumulum omnium miseriarum populi sui hanc quasi villissimam ignominiam adicit planctum scilicet et gemitum super vicio sodomitico habitum dicens [5:13]: *Adolescentibus impudice abusi sunt et pueri in ligno corruerunt* quasi vicium istud gentilium solet esse proprium ad nostrates hodie. Proh dolor usque traductum.

APPENDIX 3

PIERRE THE CHANTER, *QUESTIONES*

MS. Munich, Clm 5426, fol. 163rb.

De arte amandi

Omnis scientia est a deo, sed ars amandi est scientia. Ergo est a deo. Ergo est bona. Ergo eius usus bonus est. Si enim eius usus esset malus, ipsa esset mala, quod dici non posset cum sit a deo. Nullum enim malum a deo est.

Respondeo: Dicimus quod ipsa ars, et precepta que ibi ponuntur, bona est in se.

Sed nil prodest que non ledere possit. Idem, verbi gratia: *Precipio* [*sic*] *quod amare cupis* [*sic*], *reperire labora* (Ovid, *Ars amatoria* I, v.35). *Elige cui dicas "Tu michi sola places"* (I, v.42).

Ratione. Istud preceptum servandum est in modo vite eligendo et in multis aliis. Similiter, si precipit colloqui cum mulieribus et talia, dico quod hec omnia in bono possunt fieri. Ipsa etiam accio qua quis commiscet se meretrici in eo quod actio bona est et a deo et omnis proprietas predicamentalis. Posset enim alia eadem actio in essentia esse meritoria. Si ipsa esset coniugata et ipse mediante illa actione redderet debitum, non peccaret.

Ars igitur amatoria bona est in se, sed nos abutimur ea et convertimus ad peiorem usum. Tamen dicit magister quod ipsa ars est bona, tamen eius usus est malus. Nec sequitur regulam dyale[c]ticorum in hoc: non enim cuiuslibet boni usus est bonus, ut venenum bonum est quia a deo, et tamen eius usus malus. Ergo ille qui docet artem amatoriam, nonne utitur ea et peccat mortaliter?

Dicimus quod non utitur ea sed tradit eam. Ille autem qui per eam corrumpit mulieres, utitur ea. Doctor vero tradit eam, non ad usum, sed ad cautelam.

TABLE 1. FABLIAUX CONTAINING SEXUALLY ACTIVE CHARACTERS CLASSIFIED BY SOCIAL GROUP

	Clerical	Vilain/Peasant	Bourgeois/Merchant
Jean Bodel	Gombert c Vilain p	Barat Gombert Vilain	Sohaiz
Others	Aloul p Borgoise c Bouchier p Chevalier qui fist 　parler p Chevaliers, des deus 　clercs c Cuvier c Dam. qui ne pooit 　(III) c Estormi p Meunier c Perdris p Pescheor p Povre clerc c Prestre crucefie p Prestre et Alison p Prestre et la dame p Prestre et le chevalier p Prestre ki abevete p Prestre qui fu mis p Putains c Richeut p Segretain moine 　(monk)	Aloul Crote Dam. qui ne pooit (III) Jouglet Perdris Prestre ki abevete Quatres sohais	Auberee Berengier Boivin Borgoise Bouchier Cuvier Dame qui aveine 　demandoit Deus changeors Enfant qui fu remis Estormi Jugement des cons Meunier Pescheor Povre clerc Prestre et la dame Richeut Saineresse Segretain moine
Total	23	10	19

Note: c = cleric; p = priest; total no. fabliaux = 50. *continued*

TABLE 1 *continued*

Craftsmen	Knights	*Mésalliance*
Fevre	Aloul	Aloul
Prestre crucefie	Berengier	Auberee
Prestre qui fu mis	Chevalier a la robe	Berengier
	Chevalier qui fist parler	Dame escolliee
	Chevalier qui fist sa fame	Dam. qui ne pooit (I)
		Jouglet
	Chevalier qui recovra	Jugement des cons
	Dame escolliee	Prestre ki abevete
	Dam. qui ne pooit (I)	
	Dam. qui ne pooit (II)	
	Foteor	
	Guillaume au faucon	
	Jouglet	
	Jugement des cons	
	Prestre et le chevalier	
	Prestre ki abevete	
	Putains	
	Richeut	
	Tresces (II)	
	Trois dames	
	Vallet aus douze fames	
Total 3	20	8

TABLE 2. FABLIAUX CONTAINING SEXUAL ENCOUNTERS CLASSIFIED BY ECCLESIASTICAL
CATEGORIES

	Marital Sex	Adultery	Clerical Adultery
Jean Bodel	Sohaiz	Gombert	Gombert
		Vilain	Vilain
Others	Chevalier a la robe	Auberee	Aloul
	Crote	Berengier	Borgoise
	Dame escolliee	Chevalier a la robe	Cuvier
	Dame qui aveine	Chevalier qui fist sa	Estormi
	demandoit	fame	Perdris
	Dam. qui ne pooit (I)	Chevalier qui recovra	Pescheor
	Guillaume au faucon	Deus changeors	Povre clerc
	Jouglet	Enfant qui fus remis	Prestre crucefie
	Jugement des cons	Fevre	Prestre et la dame
	Pescheor	Foteor	Prestre ki abevete
	Quatre sohais	Guillaume au faucon	Prestre qui fu mis
	Vallet aus douze fames	Meunier	Segretain moine
		Saineresse	
		Treces (II)	
		Trois meschines	
Totals	12	16	14

	Fornication	Clerical Fornication	Clerical Concubinage
		Gombert	
	Bouchier	Chevaliers, des deus	Bouchier
	Dame qui aveine	clercs	Chevalier qui fist
	demandoit	Meunier	parler
	Dam. qui ne pooit (II)	Prestre et Alison	Prestre et le chevalier
	Dam. qui ne pooit (III)		
	Prestre et chevalier		
Totals	5	4	3

	Prostitution
	Boivin
	Foteor
	Putains
	Prestre et Alison
	Richeut
Total	5

Note: Total no. fabliaux = 50.

SHORT TITLES

Texts
(F=Fabliaux)

Abelard and Heloise, *Letters*

 Ed. J. T. Muckle, *Mediaeval Studies* 12 (1950), 163–213; 15 (1953), 47–94.

 Trans. Betty Radice, *The Letters of Abelard and Heloise* (Harmondsworth, Middlesex, 1974).

Aloul (F)

 Ed. NRCF, 3:20–44.

 Trans. Eichman and DuVal, *French Fabliaux*, 1:163–201.

Anatomia magistri Nicolai

 Ed. Franz Redeker, *Anatomia magistri Nicolai phisici und ihr Verhältnis zur Anatomia Choponis und Richardi* (Leipzig, 1917).

 Trans. Corner, *Anatomical Texts*, 67–86.

Anatomia Richardi Salernitani

 Ed. Ignaz Schwarz, *Die medizinischen Handscriften der königlichen Universitätsbibliothek in Würzburg* (Würzburg, 1907).

Anatomia vivorum

 Ed. Robert Töply, *Anatomia Richardi Anglici* (Vienna, 1902).

 Trans. Corner, *Anatomical Texts*, 87–110.

Andreas Capellanus, *De amore*

 Ed. and trans. P. G. Walsh, *Andreas Capellanus on Love* (London, 1982).

Arnoul d'Orléans, *Lidia*

 Ed. and trans. Edmond Lackenbacher, in Cohen, *La "comédie" latine*, 1:226–46.

 Trans. Elliot, *Seven Medieval Latin Comedies*, 126–46.

Art (*L'*)

 L'art d'amours: Traduction et commentaire de l'"Ars amatoria" d'Ovide.

 Ed. Bruno Roy, (Leiden, 1974).

 Trans. Lawrence B. Blonquist, *L'art d'amours* (*The Art of Love*), Garland Library of Medieval Literataure, Series A, 32 (New York, 1987).

Auberee, [by Jehans] (F)

 Ed. NRCF, 1:296–312.

 Trans. Brians, *Bawdy Tales* 70–81.

Augustine, *De bono coniugali*
Ed. PL, 40:373–96, and J. Zycha, Corpus scriptorum ecclesiasticorum latinorum 41 (Vienna, 1900).
Trans. Charles T. Wilcox, in *Saint Augustine, Treatises on Marriage and Other Subjects,* ed. Roy J. Deferrari, The Fathers of the Church (New York, 1955), 9–51.
Augustine, *De civitate dei*
Eds. PL, 41:13–804, and Corpus christianorum, Series Latina, 47–48 (Turnholt, 1955).
Trans. Henry Betteson, *The City of God against the Pagans* (Harmondsworth, Middlesex, 1972).
Augustine, *De Genesi ad litteram*
Ed. PL, 34:245–86, and J. Zycha, Corpus scriptorum ecclesiasticorum latinorum 28.1 (Vienna, 1894).
Trans. John Hammond Taylor, *The Literal Meaning of Genesis,* 2 vols., Ancient Christian Writers 41, 42 (New York, 1981, 1982).
Augustine, *De nuptiis et concupiscentia*
Ed. PL, 44:413–74, and C. F. Urba and J. Zycha, Corpus scriptorum ecclesiasticorum latinorum 42 (Vienna, 1902), 209–319.
Trans. F.-J. Thonnard, E. Bleuzen, and A. C. De Veer, *Oeuvres de Saint Augustine,* Bibliothèque Augustinienne 23 (Paris, 1974), 32–289.
Avicenna, *Liber canonis*
Ed. (Milan, 1473).
Berengier (F)
Berengier au long cul (*I*), by Guerin
Ed. NRCF 4:270–77.
Trans. DuVal and Eichman, *Cuckolds,* 51–58.
Berger et Petit, *Contes à rire*
R. Berger and A. Petit, *Contes à rire du nord de la France,* Trésors littéraire médiévaux du nord de la France (La Ferté-Milon, 1987).
Béroul, *Tristan*
Béroul, *Le roman de Tristan*
Ed. Ernest Muret and L. M. Defourques, Les classiques français du moyen âge (Paris 1947).
Trans. Alan S. Fredrick, *The Romance of Tristan by Beroul* (Harmondsworth, Middlesex, 1970)
Boivin (F)
Boivin de Provins, by Boivin de Provins
Ed. NRCF 2:96–105.
Trans. Eichman and DuVal, *French Fabliaux,* 1:62–79.
Borgoise (F)
La Borgoise d'Orliens
Ed. NRCF, 3:366–74.
Trans. Eichman and DuVal, *French Fabliaux,* 2:26–35.
Bouchier (F)
Le bouchier d'Abeville, by Huistace d'Amiens

Ed. NRCF, 3:322–35.

Trans. Eichman and DuVal, *French Fabliaux*, 2:2–25.

Brians, *Bawdy Tales*

Paul Brians, *Bawdy Tales from the Courts of Medieval France* (New York, 1972).

Caelius Aurelianus

Ed. Miriam F. Drabkin and Israel E. Drabkin, *Gynaecia: Fragments of a Latin Version of Soranus' Gynaecia from a Thirteenth Century Manuscript*, Supplements to the Bulletin of the History of Medicine 13 (Baltimore, 1951).

Chanter, *Summa*

Pierre the Chanter, *Summa de sacramentis et animae consiliis*, 5 vols.

Ed. Jean-Albert Dugauquier, Analecta mediaevalia Namurcensia, 4, 7, 11, 16, 21 (Louvain, 1954–67).

Chanter, *Verbum abbreviatum*

Pierre the Chanter, *Verbum abbreviatum*

Ed. (Short version), PL, 205:23–554.

MS. (Long version), Vatican, Reg. Lat. 106.

Chevalier a la robe (F)

Le chevalier a la robe vermeille

Ed. NRCF, 2:300–8.

Trans. Eichman and DuVal, *French Fabliaux*, 1:149–61.

Chevalier qui fist parler (F)

Le chevalier qui fist parler les cons, by Garin.

Ed. NRCF, 3:158–73

Trans. Harrison, *Gallic Salt*, 216–55; Hellman and O'Gorman, *Fabliaux*, 105–21.

Chevalier qui fist sa fame (F)

Le chevalier qui fist sa fame confesse.

Ed. NRCF, 4:236–43.

Trans. Eichman and DuVal, *French Fabliaux*, 2:94–105.

Chevalier qui recovra (F)

Le chevalier qui recovra l'amor de sa dame.

Ed. MR 6:138–46.

Trans. Hellman and O'Gorman, *Fabliaux*, 45–50.

Chevaliers, des deus clercs (F)

Des chevaliers, des deus clercs, et les villains

Ed. and trans. Eichman and DuVal, *French Fabliaux*, 2:192–95.

Chobham, *Summa confessorum*

Thomas of Chobham, *Summa confessorum.*

Ed. F. Broomfield, Analecta mediaevalia Namurcensia 25 (Louvain, 1968).

Chobham, *Summa de arte praedicandi*

Thomas de Chobham, *Summa de arte praedicandi.*

Ed. Franco Morenzoni, Corpus christianorum, Continuatio mediaevalis 82 (Turnholt, 1988).

Chrétien, *Charette* [*Lancelot*]

Chrétien de Troyes, *Le chevalier de la charrette.*

Ed. Mario Roques, *Les romans de Chrétien de Troyes: 3,* Les classiques français du moyen âge (Paris 1958).

Trans. William W. Kibler, *Arthurian Romances* (Harmondsworth, Middlesex, 1991), 207–94.

Chrétien, *Cligès*

Chrétien de Troyes, *Cligès.*

Ed. Alexandre Micha, *Les romans de Chrétien de Troyes: 2,* Les classiques français du moyen âge (Paris, 1957).

Trans. William W. Kibler, *Arthurian Romances* (Harmondsworth, Middlesex, 1991), 123–205.

Chrétien, *Erec*

Chrétien de Troyes, *Erec et Enide.*

Ed. Mario Roques, *Les romans de Chrétien de Troyes: 1,* Les classiques français du moyen âge (Paris, 1970).

Trans. Carleton W. Carroll, in William Kibler, *Arthurian Romances* (Harmondsworth, Middlesex, 1991), 37–122.

Chrétien, *Graal*

Chrétien de Troyes, *Le conte du graal.*

Ed. L. = Félix Lecoy, *Les romans de Chrétien de Troyes: 5,* 2 vols., Les classiques français du moyen âge (Paris, 1972, 1975).

Ed. R. = William Roach, *Le roman de Perceval ou le conte du graal,* Textes littéraires français (Geneva, 1956).

Trans. William W. Kibler, *Arthurian Romances* (Harmondsworth, Middlesex, 1991), 381–494.

Chrétien, *Lion* [*Yvain*]

Chrétien de Troyes, *Le chevalier au lion.*

Ed. Mario Roques, *Les romans de Chrétien de Troyes: 4,* Les classiques françaises au moyen âge (Paris, 1982).

Trans. William W. Kibler, *Arthurian Romances* (Harmondsworth, Middlesex, 1991), 295–380.

Cohen, *La "comédie" latine*

Gustave Cohen, *La "comédie latine en France au XIIe siècle,* 2 vols., Collection latine du moyen âge (Paris 1931).

Con qui fu fez (F)

Du con qui fu fez a la bresche.

Ed. NRCF, 4:19–21.

Trans. Eichman and Duval, *French Fabliaux,* 2:44–47.

Constantinus, *De coitu*

Constantinus Africanus, *Liber de coitu: El tratado de andrologia.*

Ed. Enrique Montero Cartelle, Monografias de la Universidad de Santiago de Compostella 77 (Santiago de Compostella, 1983).

Trans. Paul Delany, "Constantinus Africanus, *De Coitu:* A Translation," *Chaucer Review* 4 (1969), 55–65.

Constantinus, *De genecia*

Ed. Monica H. Green, "The *De genecia* Attributed to Constantine the African," *Speculum* 62 (1987), 312–23.

Corner, *Anatomical Texts*
George W. Corner, *Anatomical Texts of the Earlier Middle Ages* (Washington, 1927).
Courson, *Summa*
Robert of Courson, *Summa*. MS Paris BN lat. 14524.
Crote (La) (F)
Ed. NRCF 6:31–32.
Trans. Eichman and DuVal, *French Fabliaux*, 2:260–63.
Cum auctor
Ed. Monica H. Green (unpublished) (Numbers refer to sections.)
Cuvier (Le) (F)
Ed. NRCF, 5:141–44.
Trans. Eichman and DuVal, *French Fabliaux*, 2:142–49.
Dame escolliee (La) (F)
Ed. MR, 6:95–116.
Trans. Brians, *Bawdy Tales*, 24–36.
Dame qui aveine demandoit (F)
La dame qui aveine demandoit pour Morel sa provende avoir
Ed. MR, 1:318–29.
Trans. Nora Scott, *Fabliaux des XIIIᵉ et XIVᵉ siècles* (Paris, 1977), 176–80.
Damoisele qui ne pooit oïr (I) (F)
La damoisele qui ne pooit oïr parler de foutre (I).
Ed. NRCF, 4:80–83.
Damsoisele qui ne pooit oïr (II) (F)
La damoisele qui ne pooit oïr parler de foutre (II).
Ed. NRCF, 4:84–89.
Damoisele qui ne pooit oïr (III) (F)
La damoisele qui ne pooit oïr parler de foutre (III).
Ed. NRCF, 4:65–79 (MS D)
David de Dinant, *Quaternuli*
Ed. Marian Kurdzialek, *Davidis de Dinanto quaternulorum fragmenta*, Studia mediewistyczne 3 (Warsaw, 1963).
Deus changeors (Les) (F)
Ed. NRCF, 5:275–82.
Trans. Eichman and DuVal, *French Fabliaux*, 2:196–207.
Digesta
Ed. T. Mommsen, *Corpus iuris civilis* (Berlin, 1920), 1.
Dronke, *Medieval Latin*
Peter Dronke, *Medieval Latin and the Rise of European Love-Lyric*, 2 vols., 2d ed. (Oxford, 1968).
DuVal and Eichman, *Cuckolds*
John DuVal and Raymond Eichman, *Cuckolds, Clerics, and Countrymen: Medieval French Fabliaux* (Fayetteville, Ark., 1982).
Eichman and DuVal, *French Fabliaux*
Raymond Eichman and John DuVal, *The French Fabliau: B.N. MS. 837*, 2 vols. (New York, 1984).

Elliot, *Seven Medieval Latin Comedies*
 Alison Goddard Elliot, trans., Garland Library of Medieval Literature, Series B,
 20 (New York, 1984).
Enfant qui fus remis (F)
 L'enfant qui fu remis au soleil
 Ed. NRCF, 5:218–21.
 Trans. Eichman and DuVal. *French Fabliaux*, 2:174–81.
Estormi, [by Hues Piaucele] (F)
 Ed. NRCF, 1:13–28.
 Trans. Eichmann and DuVal, *French Fabliaux*, 1:2–27.
Faral, *Les arts poétiques*
 Les arts poétiques du XIIe et du XIIIe siècle, Bibliothéque de l'Ecole des Hautes-
 Etudes, Sciences historiques et philologiques 238 (Paris, 1924).
Fevre (F)
 Le fevre de Creeil.
 Ed. NRCF, 5:78–82.
 Trans. Eichman and DuVal, *French Fabliaux*, 2:134–41.
Flameborough, *Liber poenitentialis*
 Robert of Flamborough, *Liber poenitentialis.*
 Ed. J. J. Francis Firth, Pontifical Institute of Medieval Studies, Studies and Texts
 18 (Toronto, 1971).
Foteor (Le) (F)
 Ed. NRCF, 6:66–75.
Geoffroi de Vinsauf, *Documentum*
 Geoffroi de Vinsauf, *Documentum de modo et arte dictandi et versificandi.*
 Ed. Faral, *Les arts poétiques,* 265–320.
 Trans. Roger P. Parr, Medieval Philosophical Texts in Translation 17 (Mar-
 quette, Wis., 1968).
Geoffroi de Vinsauf, *Poetria nova*
 Ed. Faral, *Les arts poétiques,* 197–262.
 Trans. Margaret F. Nims, *Poetria nova* (Toronto, 1967).
Gottfried von Strassburg, *Tristan*
 Gottfried von Strassburg, *Tristan und Isolde.*
 Ed. Friedrich Ranke, *Tristan und Isold,* 12th ed. (Zürich, 1967).
 Trans. A. T. Hatto, *Tristan* (London, 1960), 37–297.
Gratian, *Decretum*
 Ed. A. Friedberg, *Corpus iuris canonici* (Leipzig, 1879), 1. C. = *Causa in Pars se-*
 cunda, c. = *capitulum,* D. = *Distinctio in Pars prima* and *De Poen., De Poen. = De*
 Poenitentia.
Guillaume au faucon (F)
 Ed. MR, 2:92–113.
 Trans. DuVal and Eichman, *Cuckcolds,* 87–104.
Guillaume de Blois, *Alda*
 Ed. and trans. Marcel Wintzweiller, in Cohen, *La "comédie" latine,* 2:105–51.
 Trans. Elliot, *Seven Medieval Latin Comedies,* 104–25.

Guillaume de Conches, *Dragmaticon*
  Ed. (Strassburg, 1567).
Guillaume de Conches, *De philosophia mundi*
  Ed. PL, 172:87–94.
Harrison, *Gallic Salt*
  Robert Harison, *Gallic Salt: Eighteen Fabliaux* (Berkeley, Calif., 1974).
Hellman and O'Gorman, *Fabliaux*
  Robert Hellman and Richard O'Gorman, *Fabliaux: Ribald Tales from the Old French* (New York, 1965).
Isagoge Iohannicii
  Isagoge Joannitii ad tegni Galiegni.
  Ed. *Articella* (Venice, 1487).
Jacques de Vitry, *VMO*
  Jacques de Vitry, *Vita Marie Oigniacensis.*
  Ed. D. Papebroch, *Acta sanctorum* (Paris and Rome, 1867), June 5:547–72.
Jean Bodel, *Barat* (F)
  Barat et Haimet.
  Eds. NRCF, 2:62–75; Nardin, 119–48.
  Trans. Berget and Petit, *Contes à rire,* 39–47.
Jean Bodel, *Gombert* (F)
  Gombert et les deus clers.
  Ed. NRCF, 4:296–300, Nardin 85–94.
  Trans. Berget et Petit, *Contes à rire,* 25–28.
Jean Bodel, *Sohaiz* (F)
  Le sohaiz des vez
  Eds. NRCF, 6:267–72, Nardin, 99–107.
  Trans. Berget and Petit, *Contes à rire,* 31–34.
Jean Bodel, *Vilain* (F)
  Le vilain de Bailluel
  Ed. NRCF, 5:246–49, Nardin, 77–84.
  Trans. Berger and Petit, *Contes à rire,* 21–23; Harrison, *Gallic Salt,* 390–97.
Jean Renart, *Escoufle*
  Ed. Franklin Sweetser, Textes littéraire françaises (Geneva, 1974).
  Trans. Alexandre Micha, *L'escoufle: Roman d'aventures,* Traductions des classiques français du moyen âge 48 (Paris, 1992).
Jean Renart, *Le lai de l'ombre*
  Ed. Félix Lecoy, Les classiques français du moyen âge (Paris, 1979).
  Trans. Norma Lorre Goodrich, *The Ways of Love: Eleven Romances of Medieval France* (Boston, 1964), 253–74.
Jean Renart, *Roman*
  Le roman de la rose ou de Guillaume de Dole.
  Ed. Félix Lecoy, Les classiques français du moyen âge (Paris, 1979).
  Trans. Jean Dufournet, Jacques Kooijman, René Menage, and Christine Tronc, *Guillaume de Dole ou le roman de la rose,* Traductions des classiques français du moyen âge, (Paris, 1979).

Jouglet [by Colin Malet] (F)
    Ed. NRCF, 2:204–14
    Trans. Eichman and DuVal, *French Fabliaux*, 1:118–35.
Jugement des cons (Le) (F)
    Ed. NRCF, 4:29–33.
    Trans. Eichman and DuVal, *French Fabliaux*, 2:48–55.
Liber minor de coitu
    Ed. Enrique Montero Cartelle (Valladolid, 1987).
Lombard, *Sententiarum*
    Pierre the Lombard, *Sententiae in IV libris distinctae.* 2 vols.
    Ed. PL, 192:519–962, and Q=[Quarrachi], Spicilegium Bonaventurianum 4, 5
    (Rome, 1971, 1981).
Mansi
    J. D. Mansi, *Sacorum conciliorum nova et amplissima collectio,* 31 vols. (Florence and
    Venice, 1759–93).
Marie de France, *Lais*
    Ed. Alfred Ewert, Blackwell's French Texts (Oxford, 1976).
    Trans. Robert Hanning and Joan Ferrante, *The Lais of Marie de France* (New
    York, 1978).
Mathieu de Vendôme, *Ars versificatoria*
    Eds. Faral, *Les arts poétiques,* 109–93, and Franco Munari, *Opera* 3, Storia e let-
    teratura 171 (Rome, 1988).
    Trans. Aubrey E. Gaylon, *The Art of Versification* (Ames, Ia., 1980).
Meunier (F)
    Le meunier et les deus clers.
    Ed. MR, 5:83–94.
    Hellman and O'Gorman, *Fabliaux,* 51–58.
MGH SS
    Monumenta Germaniae historica, Scriptores
MR
    Anatole de Montaiglon and Gaston Raynaud, *Recueil général et complet des fabliaux
    des XIIIe et XIVe siècles,* 6 vols. (Paris 1872, reprint New York, 1964).
Muscio
    Muscio, *Gynaecia.*
    Ed. Valentino Rose, *Sorani Gynaeciorum vetus translatio latina* (Leipzig, 1882), 1–
    168.
Nardin
    Pierre Nardin, *Jean Bodel: Fabliaux* (Paris, 1965).
NRCF
    Ed. Willem Noomen and Nico Van den Boogaard, *Nouveau recueil complet des
    fabliaux,* 6 vols. (Assen, 1983–).
Nuncio sagaci (De)
    Ed. and trans. Alphonse Dain, in Cohen, *La "comédie" latine,* 2:140–165.
Ovid, *Amores*
    Ed. E. J. Kenney, *Amores, Medicamina faciei femineae, Ars amatoria, Remedia amoris*
    (Oxford, 1961), 5–100.

Trans. Peter Green, *The Erotic Poems* (Harmondsworth, Middlesex, 1982), 85–165.

Ovid, *Ars amatoria*

Ed. E. J. Kenney, *Amores, Medicamina faciei femineae, Ars amatoria, Remedia amoris* (Oxford, 1961), 113–200.

Trans. Peter Green, *The Erotic Poems* (Harmondsworth, Middlesex, 1982), 166–238.

Ovid, *Remedia*

Remedia amoris.

Ed. E. J. Kenney, *Amores, Medicamina faciei femineae, Ars amatoria, Remedia amoris* (Oxford, 1961), 205–37.

Trans. Peter Green, *The Erotic Poems* (Harmondsworth, Middlesex, 1982), 239–63.

Paden, *Medieval Pastourelle*

Ed. and trans. William D. Paden, Garland Library of Medieval Literature, Series A, 35, 2 vols. (New York, 1987).

Perdris (Les) (F)

Ed. NRCF, 4:8–12.

Trans. Eichman and Duval, *French Fabliaux,* 2:36–43.

Pescheor (F)

Le pescheor de Pont seur Saine

Ed. NRCF, 4:124–29.

Trans. Eichman and DuVal, *French Fabliaux,* 2:68–77.

Pierre de Poitiers, *Summa de confessione*

Pierre de Poitiers, [*Summa de confessione*] *Compilatio praesens*

Ed. Jean Longère, Corpus Christianorum, Continuatio mediaevalis 51 (Turnholt, 1980).

PL

Patrologiae cursus completus . . . series latina, 221 vols. Ed. J. P. Migne (Paris, 1857–1903).

Povre clerc (Le) (F)

Ed. MR, 5:192–200.

Hellman and O'Gorman, *Fabliaux,* 129–34.

Prestre crucefié (Le) (F)

Ed. NRCF, 4:104–6.

Trans. Eichman and DuVal, *French Fabliaux,* 2:62–67.

Prestre et Alison (Le), [by Guillaume le Normand] (F)

Ed. MR, 2:8–23.

Prestre et la dame (Le) (F)

Ed. MR, 2:235–41.

Trans. Larry D. Benson and Theodore M. Andersson, *The Literary Context of Chaucer's Fabliaux: Texts and Translations* (Indianopolis, 1971), 328–37.

Prestre et le chevalier (Le), [by Milon d'Amiens] (F)

Ed. MR, 2:46–91.

Prestre ki abevete (Le) (F)

Ed. MR, 3:54–57.

Trans. DuVal and Eichman, *Cuckolds*, 43–46.
Prestre qui fui mis (F)
  Le prestre qui fui mis au lardier, by Baillet.
  Ed. MR, 2:24–30.
  Trans. Harrison, *Gallic Salt*, 290–305.
Prose Salernitan Questions
  Ed. Brian Lawn, *The Prose Salernitan Questions*, Auctores Britannici Medii Aevi 5 (Oxford, 1979).
Putains (F)
  Les putains et les lecheors.
  Ed. NRCF, 6:151–53.
Quatres sohais (F)
  Les quatres sohais Saint Martin.
  Ed. NRCF, 4:211–16.
  Trans. Harrison, *Gallic Salt*, 176–95.
RHF
  Recueil des historiens des Gaules et de la France, 24 vols. (Paris, 1734–1904).
Richeut (F)
  Ed. Philippe Vernay, Romanica Helvetica 103 (Berne, 1988).
  Trans. Donald Eugene Ker, "The Twelfth-Century French Poem *Richeut*," (Ph.D. diss., Ohio State University 1976), 186–238.
Saineresse (*La*) (F)
  Ed. NRCF, 4:309–12.
  Trans. Eichman and DuVal, *French Fabliaux*, 2:106–11.
Segretain moine (*Le*) (F)
  Ed. MR, 5:215–42.
  Trans. Harrison, *Gallic Salt*, 86–137.
Soranus, *Gynecology*
  Trans. Owsei Temkin (Baltimore, 1956).
Statuts synodaux français
  Ed. Odette Pontal, *Les statuts synodaux français du XIIIe siècle* 1, Collection de documents inédits sur l'histoire de France, Section de philologie et d'histoire jusqu'à 1610, Série-in-8⁰ 9 (Paris, 1971).
Thomas, *Tristan*
  Thomas de Bretagne, *Le roman de Tristan.*
  Ed. Bartina H. Wind, *Les fragments de roman de Tristan*, Textes littéraires français (Geneva, 1960).
  Trans. A. T. Hatto, *Tristan* (Harmondsworth, Middlesex, 1960), 301–53.
Tresces (*Les*) (*II*) (F)
  Ed. NRCF, 6:248–58.
  Trans. DuVal and Eichman, *Cuckolds*, 63–76.
Tribus puellis (*De*)
  Ed. and trans. Paul Maury, in Cohen, *La "comédie" latine*, 2:231–42.
  Trans. Elliot, *Seven Medieval Latin Comedies*, 147–58.
Trois dames (F)
  Les trois dames qui trouverent l'anel (*I*), by Haisiau.

Ed. NRCF, 2:229–36.
Trans. Eichman and DuVal, *French Fabliaux*, 1:136–47.
Trois meschines (Les) (F)
Ed. NRCF, 4:223–26.
Trans. Eichman and DuVal, *French Fabliaux*, 2:89–93.
Vallet aus douze fames (Le) (F)
Ed. NRCF, 4:146–150.
Trans. Eichman and DuVal, *French Fabliaux*, 2:78–87.

Studies

Allen, *Concept of Women*
　Prudence Allen, *The Concept of Women: The Aristotelian Revolution 750 BC–AD 1250* (Montréal, 1985).
Baldwin, *Government of Philip Augustus*
　John W. Baldwin, *The Government of Philip Augustus: Foundations of French Royal Power in the Middle Ages* (Berkeley, Calif., 1986).
Baldwin, *Masters, Princes, and Merchants*
　John W. Baldwin, *Masters, Princes, and Merchants: The Social Views of Peter the Chanter and His Circle*, 2 vols. (Princeton, 1970).
Boswell, *Christianity, Social Tolerance*
　John Boswell, *Christianity, Social Tolerance, and Homosexuality: Gay People in Western Europe from the Beginning of the Christian Era to the Fourteenth Century* (Chicago, 1980).
Brundage, *Law, Sex*
　James A. Brundage, *Law, Sex, and Christian Society in Medieval Europe* (Chicago, 1987).
Burgess, *Marie de France*
　Glyn S. Burgess, *Le Lais of Marie de France: Text and Context* (Athens, Ga., 1987).
Duby, *Medieval Marriage*
　Georges Duby, *Medieval Marriage: Two Models from Twelfth-Century France*, trans. Elborg Forster, The Johns Hopkins Symposia in Comparative History (Baltimore, 1978).
Gravdahl, *Ravishing Maidens*
　Kathryn Gravdahl, *Ravishing Maidens: Writing Rape in Medieval French Literature and Law*, New Cultural Studies Series (Philadelphia, 1991).
Flandrin, *Uns temps*
　Jean-Louis Flandrin, *Un temps pour embrasser: Aux origines de la morale sexuelle occidentale (VIᵉ-XIᵉ siècle* (Paris, 1983).
Green, "Transmission"
　Monica H. Green, "The Transmission of Ancient Theories of Female Physiology and Disease through the Early Middle Ages" (Ph.D. diss., Princeton University, 1985).
Jacquart and Thomasset, *Sexualité et savoir médical*
　Danielle Jacquart and Claude Thomasset, *Sexualité et savoir médical au moyen âge*, Les chemins de l'histoire (Paris, 1985).

Trans. Matthew Adamson, *Sexuality and Medicine in the Middle Ages* (Cambridge, 1988).

Karnein, *De Amore*

Alfred Karnein, *"De Amore" in volksprachlicher Literatur: Untersuchungen zur Andreas-Capellanus-Rezeption in Mittelalter und Renaissance,* Germanische-Romanische Monatsschrift, 4 (Heidelberg, 1985).

Müller, *Paradiesesehe*

Michael Müller, *Die Lehre des Hl. Augustinus von der Paradiesesehe und ihre Auswicklung in der Sexualethik des 12. und 13. Jahrhunderts bis Thomas von Aquin,* Studien zur Geschichte der katholischen Moraltheologie 1 (Regensburg, 1954).

Muscatine, *Old French Fabliaux*

Charles Muscatine, *The Old French Fabliaux* (New Haven, 1986).

Noonan, *Contraception*

John T. Noonan, Jr., *Contraception: A History of Its Treatment by the Catholic Theologians and Canonists* (Cambridge, Mass., 1965).

Nykrog, *Fabliaux*

Per Nykrog, *Les fabliaux: Nouvelle édition,* Publications romanes et françaises 123 (Geneva, 1973).

Rousselle, *Porneia*

Aline Rousselle, *Porneia: De la maîtrise du corps à la privation sensorielle* (Paris, 1983).

Trans. Felica Pheasant, *Porneia: On Desire and the Body in Antiquity* (Oxford, 1988).

Schnell, *Andreas Capellanus*

Rüdiger Schnell, *Andreas Capellanus: Zur Rezeption des römischen und kanonischen Rechts in De Amore,* Münstersche Mittelalter-Schriften 46 (Munich, 1982).

Vieillard, *Gilles de Corbeil*

C. Vieillard, *Gilles de Corbeil: Essai sur la société médicale et religieuse au XIIᵉ siècle* (Paris, 1909).

Wack, *Lovesickness*

Mary Frances Wack, *Lovesickness in the Middle Ages: The Viaticum and Its Commentaries* (Philadelphia, 1990).

Zeimentz, *Ehe*

Hans Zeimentz, *Ehe nach der Lehre der Früscholastik,* Moraltheologische Studien, Historische Abteilung 1 (Düsseldorf, 1973).

NOTES

Introduction

1. Baldwin, *Government of Philip Augustus*, 82–87.

2. All published in Paris in the series Bibliothèque des histoires." English trans. Robert Hurley, *The History of Sexuality, 1: An Introduction* (New York, 1978); *2: The Use of Pleasure* (New York, 1985); *3: The Care of Self* (New York, 1986). For the revised program see Foucault, *The Use of Pleasure*, 12. Didier Eribon (*Michel Foucault [1926–84]* [Paris, 1989], 286–93, 339–47) has chronicled the composition of these volumes.

3. Rousselle, *Porneia* is an important treatment of medical discourse on sexuality in antiquity.

4. Peter Brown, *The Body and Society: Men, Women, and Sexual Renunciation in Early Christianity* (New York, 1988).

5. Elaine Pagels's, *Adam, Eve, and the Serpent* (New York, 1988) is a comparable essay on Christian attitudes toward sexuality in late antiquity.

6. For a short introduction to the immense subject of "courtly love" see Roger Boase and Dianne Bornstein, in *Dictionary of Medieval History* (New York, 1983), 3:667–74. For the origins of the term see David Hult, "Gaston Paris and the Invention of 'Courtly Love,'" *Medievalism and the Modernist Temper*, ed. R. Howard Bloch and Stephen G. Nichols (in press).

7. The fullest study of the sexual significance of the troubadours remains René Nelli, *L'erotique des troubadours*, 2 vols. (Paris, 1963). Moshé Lazar (*Amours courtois et fin'amors dans la littérature du XIIᵉ siècle*, Bibliothèque français et romane, Série C: Etudes littéraires 8 [Paris, 1964]) and Charles Caproux (*Joy d'amor [Jeu et joie d'amour]* [Montpellier, 1965]) have argued for the sexual nature of "courtly love."

8. For some examples: R. Howard Bloch, *The Scandal of the Fabliaux* (Chicago, 1986); Alexandre Leupin, *Barbarolexis: Medieval Writing and Sexuality*, trans. Kate M. Cooper (Cambridge, Mass., 1989); and Lawrence D. Kritzman, *The Rhetoric of Sexuality and the Literature of the French Renaissance* (Cambridge, 1991).

9. In the series Chemins de l'histoire (Paris). English trans. Matthew Adamson, *Sexuality and Medicine in the Middle Ages* (Cambridge, 1988). Thomas Laqueur

(*Making Sex: Body and Gender from the Greeks to Freud* [Cambridge, Mass., 1990]) treats medical and anatomical discourse for the entire span of Western European history.

10. Brundage, *Law, Sex* (Chicago). Pierre J. Payer (*Sex and the Penitentials: The Development of a Sexual Code, 550–1150* [Toronto, 1984]) limits its scope to the early penitential system.

11. Vern L. Bullough has pioneered in the study of medieval sexuality in numerous essays and specialized articles. See, for example, his collection in *Sex, Society, and History* (New York, 1976). For examples of historians' treatments of marriage and family see Georges Duby, *Medieval Marriage; Le chevalier, la femme, et le prêtre* (Paris, 1983), trans. Barbara Bray, *The Knight, the Lady, and the Priest* (New York, 1983); and Christopher N. L. Brooke, *The Medieval Idea of Marriage* (Oxford, 1989). Two comprehensive bibliographies of the historical studies are Michael M. Sheehan and Jacqueline Murray, *Domestic Society in Medieval Europe: A Select Bibliography* (Toronto 1990); and Joyce E. Salisbury, *Medieval Sexuality: A Research Guide*, Garland Medieval Bibliographies (New York, 1990).

12. Boswell, *Christianity, Social Tolerance* (Chicago). See also Michael Goodich, *The Unmentionable Vice: Homosexuality in the Later Medieval Period* (Santa Barbara, 1979).

13. Leah L. Otis, *Prostitution in Medieval Society: The History of an Urban Institution in Languedoc* (Chicago, 1985). With a similar focus Jacques Rossiaud (*La prostitution médiévale* [Paris, 1988]) concentrates on the Rhône valley in the fifteenth century.

14. With the exception of the female troubadour or *trobairitz* in southern France. See the recent studies of Meg Bogin, *The Women Troubadours* (London, 1976) and *The Voice of the Trobaritz: Perspectives on the Woman Troubadours*, ed. William D. Padden (Philadelphia, 1989).

15. For recent examples of the history of women see Shulamith Shahar, *The Fourth Estate: A History of Women in the Middle Ages*, trans. Chaya Galai (London, 1983); Penny Schine Gold, *The Lady and the Virgin: Image, Attitude and Experience in Twelfth-Century France* (Chicago, 1985); and R. Howard Bloch, *Medieval Misogyny and the Invention of Western Romantic Love* (Chicago, 1991). *Histoire des femmes, 2: Le moyen âge*, ed. Georges Duby, Michelle Perrot, and Christiane Klapisch-Zuber (Paris, 1991), trans. Arthur Goldhammer, *History of Women in the West, 2: Silences of the Middle Ages* (Cambridge, Mass., 1992), has a chapter by Claude Thomasset on female sexuality which summarizes his earlier work.

16. Although not dealing directly with sexuality, Penny Schine Gold (*The Lady and the Virgin*) brings different genres of sources to bear on women in twelfth-century France. My approach comes closest to that of Henry Ansgar Kelly (*Love and Marriage in the Age of Chaucer* [Ithaca, 1975]) who deploys theology, canon law, Ovid, and vernacular literature in fourteenth-century England but with differing results.

17. A recent catalogue of the metaphor is in Jan Ziolkowski, *Alan of Lille's Grammar of Sex: The Meaning of Grammar to a Twelfth-Century Intellectual* (Cambridge, Mass., 1985), 88n.45.

18. For a recent feminist critique of gender categorization see Judith Butler, *Gen-*

der *Trouble: Feminism and the Subversion of Identity* (New York, 1990), esp. ix–xi. Bloch, *Medieval Misogyny*, 5–6, and ch. 3, esp. 89–90.

19. To cite three I found most helpful: *Sexual Meanings: The Cultural Construction of Gender and Sexuality*, ed. Sherry B. Ortner and Harriet Whitehead (Cambridge, 1981); Joan Wallach Scott, *Gender and the Politics of History* (New York, 1988) and Butler, *Gender Trouble*.

20. Linda S. Kauffman, *Discourse of Desire: Gender, Genre, and Epistolary Fictions* (Ithaca, 1986), 60–61.

21. For the theologians see Baldwin, *Masters, Princes, and Merchants*, 1:12–14, 2:241–46, and Beryl Smalley, *The Study of the Bible in the Middle Ages* (Oxford, 1952), 205. For the fabliaux see below pp. 36–42.

22. For two among many recent examples of "cultural constructionism" see Margaret R. Miles, *Carnal Knowing: Female Nakedness and Religious Meaning in the Christian West* (Boston, 1989) and Clarissa W. Atkinson, *The Oldest Vocation: Christian Motherhood in the Middle Ages* (Ithaca, 1991).

23. For recent Freudian interpretations see Henri Rey-Flaud, *La névrose courtoise,* Bibliothèque des analytica (Paris, 1983), esp. ch. 4 for Jean Renart; Jean-Charles Huchet, *L'amour discourtois: La "fin'amors" chez les premiers troubadours,* Bibliothèque historique Privat (Paris, 1987); and Bloch, *The Scandal of the Fabliaux*. Lacanian inspiration may be seen in Leupin, *Barbarolexis*.

24. Rita Lejeune-Dehousse, *L'oeuvre de Jean Renart: Contribution à l'étude du genre romanesque au moyen âge,* Bibliothèque de la Faculté de Philosophie et Lettres de l' Université de Liège, fasc. 61 (Lille, 1935), 332. See also Anthime Fourrier (*Le courant réaliste dans le roman courtois en France au moyen âge 1: Les débuts [XIIe siècle]*) [Paris, 1960], 9) who helped to define the genre. For an earlier statement of what follows see John W. Baldwin, "Jean Renart et le tournois de Saint-Trond: Une conjonction de l'histoire et de la littérature," *Annales: Economies, sociétés, civilisations* 45 (1990), 581–84.

25. Paul Zumthor, *Essai de poétique médiévale* (Paris, 1972), 35. Michel Zink, *Roman rose et rose rouge: Le roman de la rose ou de Guillaume de Dole de Jean Renart* (Paris, 1979), 40, 120–22. See also Michel Zink, *La subjectivité littéraire: Autour du siècle de saint Louis* (Paris, 1985), 42. A comparable stance was taken by Marc-René Jung, "L'empereur Conrad, chanteur de poésie lyrique: Fiction et vérité dans le *Roman de la rose* de Jean Renart," *Romania* 101 (1980), 35–50.

26. Roger Dragonetti, *Le mirage des sources: L'art du faux dans le roman médiévale* (Paris, 1987), 127, 183. In "Double Jeopardy: The Appropriation of Woman in Four Old French Romances of the 'Cycle de la Gageure,'" *Seeking the Woman in Late Medieval and Renaissance Writings: Essays in Feminist Contextual Criticism,* ed. Sheila Fisher and Janet E. Halley (Knoxville, Tenn., 1989), 35–45, Roberta L. Krueger offers a comparable conclusion that Jean Renart has displaced historical women through tricks of language.

27. Bloch, *The Scandal of the Fabliaux*, 90. See also the conclusion of Leupin, *Barbarolexis,* 79–119.

28. Nykrog, *Fabliaux*. Muscatine, *Old French Fabliaux,* 152–69.

29. Augustine, *Confessions* V, 14, and VI, 4, PL, 32:717–18, 721–22; and P. Knöll, Corpus scriptorum ecclesiasticorum latinorum 33, 1, 1 (Vienna, 1969),

111–12, 118–20. Smalley's *Study of the Bible* is fundamental for what follows. On the Church Fathers see 8–24.

30. Paris, Bibliothèque Mazarine, MS 178, which contains the Chanter's commentaries of selected books of the Old Testament, uses these terms in the margins to identify the types of exegesis. The Chanter's commentary on the *Song of Songs* employed only a spiritual interpretation. See below pp. 169–71.

31. Hugues de Saint-Victor, *De scripturis* V, PL, 175:14–15, trans. in Smalley, *Study of the Bible*, 93–94. On Hugues see 83–106.

32. Smalley, *Study of the Bible*, 169. On Andrew see 120–72.

33. Ibid., 214–63. For examples of the Chanter's dependence on André see 180, 199, 203, 232. The Chanter's student Thomas of Chobham (*Summa de arte praedicandi*, 4–6) enumerated the three modes (adding a fourth, *anagoge*), but underlined the importance of *hystoria*.

Chapter One

1. F. S. Gutjahr, *Petrus Cantor Parisiensis: Sein Leben und seine Schriften* (Graz, 1899). Beryl Smalley, *The Study of the Bible in the Middle Ages* (Oxford, 1952), 196–262. Baldwin, *Masters, Princes, and Merchants*, 1:3–16. The Chanter's scriptural commentaries probably date throughout his teaching career; the *questiones* and *Verbum abbreviatum* were begun by 1192/93 and terminated by his death in 1197. The treatment of the Chanter in Müller, *Paradiesesehe* (147–52), is partially based on the version the *Verbum abbreviatum* contained in the manuscripts Munich Clm 17458 and Leipzig, Univ. lat. 432. This version, which I have called "reorganized abridgments," contains materials and opinions not found in the version that circulated in France. (For the other manuscripts see Baldwin, *Masters, Princes, and Merchants*, 2:253–54.) Since it would be hazardous to attribute the reorganized version to the Chanter until it has been compared with the other versions, I have omitted it and that part of Müller's study (150–52) based on it.

2. John W. Baldwin, "Masters at Paris from 1179 to 1215: A Social Perspective," *Renaissance and Renewal in the Twelfth Century*, ed. Robert L. Benson and Giles Constable (Cambridge, Mass., 1982), 149–150.

3. Marcel and Christiane Dickson, "Le cardinal Robert de Courson, sa vie," *Archives d'histoire doctrinale et littéraire du moyen âge* 9 (1934), 53–142. Baldwin, *Masters, Princes, and Merchants*, 1:19–25. The *Summa* can be dated to 1208–1212/13.

4. Chobham, *Summa confessorum*, xxvi–lxxvi. Baldwin, *Masters, Princes and Merchants*, 1:34–36. After completing the *Summa confessorum* Thomas also composed a *Summa de arte praedicandi* which incorporated and summarized sections of the earlier work. For the most recent findings on Thomas's biography see also *Summa de arte praedicandi*, xxxi–vi. Like Chobham's, Pierre de Poitiers's *Summa de confessione* was a product of the Chanter's circle, but his treatment of sexuality is not of sufficient length to treat him separately.

5. Plenius tamen et verius potest solvi sicut asseruit predictus cantor magister noster in extremo anno vite sue cum vivacius de hiis disputatum est quod. . . . Courson, *Summa*, fol. 155rb. See below Appendix 1. Courson's *Summa* transcribes many passages verbatim from the manuscript (W) of the Chanter's *Summa* of Paris,

BN lat. 3477. See Chanter, *Summa* 3(1): 316–17, and Baldwin, *Masters, Princes and Merchants*, 1:24–25, and below p.281n.120.

6. Müller, *Paradiesesehe*, and Zeimentz, *Ehe*, are fundamental studies on the development of the theological schools and their characteristic doctrines on marriage. On Abelard, see Müller, *Paradiesesehe*, 66–69, 276, 280, 293, 298; on Gilbert de la Porrée, see Müller, 60–65; on Hugues de Saint-Victor, see Müller 75–84, 315–16, and Zeimentz, *Ehe*, passim; on the canonists, see Müller, 104–21, and Brundage, *Law, Sex*, chs. 6, 7.

7. Müller, *Paradiesesehe*, 43–56, 96–110. The comprehensive study on the Lombard and his predecessors is Zeimentz, *Ehe*.

8. Müller, *Paradiesesehe*, 19–32. For a recent survey, see Peter Brown, *The Body and Society: Men, Women and Sexual Renunciation in Early Christianity* (New York, 1988), 387–427.

9. Müller, *Paradiesesehe*, 101–3.

10. To *replete terram* (Gen. 1:28): Patet quia dominus coniugium viri et mulieris constituerit in quo confutantur manichei dicentes non posse fieri concubitum sine mortali culpa. Chanter, Paris, Arsenal 44, p.7a; London, Brit. Lib. Roy 2 C 8, fol. 4vb. To *uxorem non dimittat* (1 Cor. 7:11): Hoc heretici dicunt esse rem non bonam, nupcias detestans quas christus aproprians eis interfuit et miraculo confirmavit. Chanter, Paris Mazar. 176, fol. 180va. To *multum est enim* (Ps. 24:11): . . . in quo confutantur cathari qui dicunt non esse remissionem peccatorum post baptismum. Hii heretici dicuntur cathari quia mundos se dicunt, cum potius sint immundi. Hii secundas nuptias dampnant. Paris BN lat. 12011, fol. 42ra. The Chanter also took notice of Pelagian doctrine: to *in quo omnes peccaverunt* (Rom. 5:12): Notandum pelagianos dicere quod nihil est originale peccatum; nec peccatum ade in posterios transiit nisi in illum qui adam imitaretur peccando. Paris, Mazar. 176, fol. 168ra. Chanter, *Summa*, 3(2b):542–43. For Courson see below pp.177–78; 193.

11. The major sources for the condemnations of 1210 and 1215 are *Chartularium universitatis Parisiensis*, ed. Heinrich Denifle and Emile Chatelain (Paris, 1889), 1:70–79; *Chronica anonymi Laudunensis canonici, RHF* 18:714–15; *Oeuvres de Rigord et de Guillaume le Breton*, ed. Henri-François Delaborde (Paris, 1882), 1:231–33; Caesar of Heisterbach, *Dialogus miraculorum* V, 22, ed. Joseph Strange (Cologne, 1851), 1:304–7; trans. H. von E. Scott and C. C. Swinton Bland, *Dialogue on Miracles* (London, 1929), 1:347–51. On David and Amaury before the discovery of the *Quaternuli* see Gabriel Théry, *Autour du décret de 1210: (I) David de Dinant: Etude sur son panthéisme matérialiste;* Germaine Catherine Capelle, *Autour du décret de 1210: (III) Etude sur son panthéisme formel*, Bibliothèque Thomiste 6, 26 (Le Saulchoir, Paris, 1925, 1932). Caesar of Heisterbach identifies the first of the three theologians as *Decanum Salebergiensem*. Since he is not entirely clear on the identities of the three, the name might be an error for Thomas of Chobham who was *subdecanus* of Salisbury. The condemnation falls in one of the periods when Thomas could have been in Paris.

12. *Guillaume le Breton*, 1:232. Caesar of Heisterbach, ed. Strange, 1:304–5; trans. Scott and Bland, 1:348.

13. David de Dinant, *Quaternuli*, passim. Müller, *Paradiesesehe*, 277–78.

14. Brundage, *Law, Sex,* 137, 183, 223.

15. Duby, *Medieval Marriage,* 25–81. Baldwin, *Government of Philip Augustus,* 82–87, 206–7, 210.

16. These are the major themes in Brundage, *Law, Sex.* See the summation on 183.

17. Ibid., 188–89, 235–36, 262–63.

18. Zeimentz, *Ehe,* 104–40, is a thorough discussion of the theologians. For the canonists and papacy see Brundage, *Law, Sex,* 187, 237, 264–68, 331–41.

19. Baldwin. *Masters, Princes, and Merchants,* 1:8, 21.

20. C. 21, in Mansi, 22:1007–10. Baldwin, *Masters, Princes, and Merchants,* 1:49–56. Pierre J. Payer, "Sex and Confession in the Thirteenth Century," in *Sex in the Middle Ages: A Book of Essays,* ed. Joyce E. Salisbury, Garland Medieval Casebooks (New York, 1991), 126–42, is an essay on the implementation of the 1215 decree. For an example of its subsequent influence see the sexual legislation in the synodical statutes of Angers (1217–19) in *Statuts synodaux français,* 1:198–210.

21. Baldwin, *Masters, Princes, and Merchants,* 1:36–38.

22. The details of her life are mainly drawn from Jacques de Vitry, *VMO,* esp. 550, 571–72. Ernest W. McDonnell (*The Beguines and Beghards in Medieval Culture* [New Brunswick, N.J., 1954]), the standard authority on the subject, treats Marie and her influence throughout.

23. Jacques signaled the importance of Pierre the Chanter and his influence on these preachers. *The Historia Occidentalis of Jacques de Vitry,* ed. John Frederick Hinnesbusch, Spicilegium Friburgense 17 (Fribourg, Switzerland, 1972), 94–103.

24. Jacques de Vitry, *VMO,* 564–65.

25. Baldwin, *Masters, Princes and Merchants,* 1:38–39. Jacques de Vitry, *Historia occidentalis,* 5–7.

26. Jacques de Vitry, *VMO,* 547–72. On the date of composition see McDonnell, *Beguines,* 24; and Jacques de Vitry, *Historia occidentalis,* 9. A *Supplementum* to Jacques de Vitry, *VMO* (ed. D. Papebroeck, *AA.SS.* 25 [June 23, V], 572–81), was written by Thomas de Cantimpré shortly after 1227. I have omitted it because of its lateness and secondary nature.

27. Jacques de Vitry, *VMO,* 569–70. McDonnell, *Beguines,* 26, 31.

28. As was the custom in his sermons, Jacques inserted illustrative materials in the *VMO* derived from the Chanter. See, for example, their common views on clothing, pp. 106–8.

29. The comprehensive study is McDonnell, *Beguines.* See pp. 59 and 62 for the houses at Oignes and Nivelles. More recent interpretations of the movement can be found in Brenda M. Bolton, "Mulieres sanctae," in *Women in Medieval Society,* ed. Susan Mosher Stuard (Philadelphia, 1976), 141–58, and Carol Neel, "The Origins of the Beguines," in *Sisters and Workers in the Middle Ages,* ed. Judith Bennett et al. (Chicago, 1989), 240–60. The latter argues that Jacques de Vitry exaggerated the novelty of Marie d'Oignies's contributions.

30. Vincent de Beauvais, *Bibliotheca mundi,* IV: *Speculum historiale* (Douai, 1624), 1240–52. It was inserted between the Albigensian crusade and the Capetians victories at La Roche-aux-Moines and Bouvines.

31. For a convenient summation see John Bugge, *Virginitas: An Essay in the His-*

tory of a Medieval Ideal, International Archives in the History of Ideas, Series Minor 17 (The Hague, 1975).

32. Jacques de Vitry, *VMO,* angels, 548, 550, 554, 555, 558, and further; manual labor, 555; healing, 559; visions, 559, 563, 567, 570; prophecies, 565–67.

33. Unconsecrated host, Jacques de Vitry, *VMO,* 571; *Historia occidentalis,* 206. *VMO,* 549, 552. Caroline Walker Bynum (*Holy Feast and Holy Fast: The Religious Significance of Food to Medieval Women* [Berkeley, 1987], 59, 115–16, 119) has clarified the significance of Marie's alimentary practices.

34. Jean Leclercq, *Monks and Love in Twelfth-Century France: Pyscho-Historical Essays* (Oxford, 1979), 9–12.

35. Six out of twelve surviving manuscripts come from England, two from Paris. On the manuscripts and the masters see Brian Lawn, *The Salernitan Questions: An Introduction to the History of Medieval and Renaissance Literature* (Oxford, 1963), 34–37, and the same author's introduction to the edition, *Prose Salernitan Questions,* ix–xvii. The English masters are named in ibid., 6.

36. Lawn, *Salernitan Questions: An Introduction,* 50–56. Danielle Jacquart, Supplement (Geneva, 1979), to Ernest Wickersheimer, *Dictionnaire biographique des médicins en France au moyen âge* (Paris, 1936), 1:103–5. Guillaume de Conches has been traditionally assigned to the school of Chartres, but the chief source for his intellectual activity is his student John of Salisbury who knew him at Paris. See the revisionist views of Richard W. Southern, "Humanism and the School of Chartres," in *Medieval Humanism and Other Essays* (Oxford, 1970), 71–73.

37. Pope Innocent III recognized the right of the individual faculties to judge the qualifications of their respective members in 1213. *Chartularium universitatis Parisiensis,* 1:75–76. In 1210 the royal historiographer Guillaume le Breton included physicians among those who taught at Paris. *Oeuvres,* 1:230. For the textbooks of Alexander Neckham see below p. 12.

38. On Gilles, see Vieillard, *Gilles de Corbeil,* ch. 1; Karl Sudhoff, "Salerno, Montpellier und Paris um 1200," *Archiv für Geschichte der Medizin* 20 (1928), 51–62; Lawn *Salernitan Questions,* 69–71; Baldwin, *Masters, Princes, and Merchants,* 1:41, 83; and Jacquart, Supplement to Wickersheimer, 90–91. On writing amatory verses, Vieillard, *Gilles de Corbeil,* 65, 195. For the text of the *Diasatyrion,* Vieillard, 346–50, trans. 59–67.

39. For a recent survey of Constantinus Africanus's translations, see Marie-Thérèse d'Alverny, "Translations and Translators," in *Renaissance and Renewal in the Twelfth Century,* ed. Robert L. Benson, and Giles Constable (Cambridge, Mass., 1982), 422–25. Also the introductions to *De coitu, De genecia,* and *Liber minor de coitu.*

40. Corner, *Anatomical Texts,* 30–41. The *Anatomia vivorum* (*Anatomia Richardi Anglici*) is comparatively late (1210–40, probably ca. 1225) and shows the influence of Avicenna and Aristotle. Since it survives in three manuscripts from Paris, it may have been used in the Parisian schools. On the manuscripts and circulation of anatomical works at Paris see Gerhard Baader, "Zur Anatomie in Paris im 13. und 14. Jahrhundert," *Medizinhistorisches Journal* 3 (1968), 45–49.

41. The *Sacerdos ad altare* attributed to Alexander Neckham is edited by Charles

Homer Haskins, "A List of Text-Books from the Close of the Twelfth Century," in *Studies in the History of Medieval Science* (Cambridge, Mass., 1924), 374–75.

42. On the figure of Trotula and the works ascribed to her/him see the recent study of John F. Benton, "Trotula, Women's Problems, and the Professionalization of Medicine in the Middle Ages," *Bulletin of the History of Medicine* 59 (1985), 30–53. The three texts—*Cum auctor, De curis mulierum,* and *De ornatu*—were joined, conflated, and deformed in the *editio princeps* by a certain Kraut, physician at Hagenau in *Trotulae curandarum aegritudinum muliebrium, ante, in et post partum liber unicus, nusquam antea editum,* in *Experimentarius medicinae* (Strasbourg, apud Joannem Schottum, 1544), which was followed by subsequent editions. I shall limit my discussion to the *Cum auctor* which is the only one of the three treatises to receive a critical edition of the twelfth-century text. I am indebted to Monica H. Green for making her edition available to me. The English and French manuscripts consist of Paris BN nouv. acq. lat. 603, fol. 55rb–58ra (1190–1220), and London, British Library, Sloane 1615, fol. 88ra–90vb (ca. 1220–40, France). For a discussion of the gynecology of *Cum auctor* see Monica H. Green, "Transmission," 278–89.

43. *L'art,* 81.

44. Aliud quidam medicus fecit regine Francorum: zinziber, folia lauri terantur simul et pone in olla super carbones uiuos et in sella perforata sedeat ut fumum recipiat. Et redibunt menstrua. Mulier que huiusmodi stupham frequentat, neccesse est uuluam interius inungat unguentis frigidis ne minis calefiat. *Cum auctor* [17].

45. The manuscript is now in New York, Academy of Medicine, MS SAFE. See *Texts and Transmission: A Survey of Latin Classics,* ed. L. D. Reynolds (Oxford, 1983), 32–35; Miriam F. and Israel E. Drabkin in Caelius Aurelianus, v–viii; and E. Seidler, "Die Medizin in der 'Biblionomia' des Richard de Fournival," *Sudhoff's Archiv* 51 (1967), 44–54. Fournival's library passed to master Gérard d'Abbeville and thence to the library of the Sorbonne, but the medical books were sold off according to Gérard's will. For emendations to the text of Caelius see A. Ernout, "Les Gynaecia de Caelius Aurelianus," *Revue de philologie, de littérature et d'histoire ancienne,* 3ème série, 30 (1956), 187–203. According to Richard de Fournival's catalogue, the *Biblionomia,* the library may also have included the *Liber minor de coitu.* Léopold Delisle, *Le cabinet des manuscrits de la Bibliothèque Nationale* (Paris, 1874), 2:535.

46. See above p.5.

47. Nancy G. Siraisi, *Avicenna in Renaissance Italy: The Canon and Medical Teaching in Italian Universities after 1500* (Princeton, 1987), 19–30, 43–44. The possible allusions to Aristotle and Avicenna in the *Prose Salernitan Questions* are of slight consequence. See the few allusions collected on 392–93.

48. *Isagoge Iohannicii,* 1–3. For a fuller interpretation of these fundamental divisions see Nancy G. Siraisi, *Medieval and Early Renaissance Medicine* (Chicago, 1990), 97–109. Lawn, *Salernitan Questions,* 56. *Prose Salernitan Questions,* xvii.

49. See the conclusions of Monica H. Green, "Constantinus Africanus and the Conflict between Religion and Science," in *The Human Embryo: Aristotle and the Arabic and European Traditions,* ed. G. R. Dunstan (Exeter, England, 1990), 47–69.

50. Guillaume de Conches, *De philosophia mundi,* 90; *Dragmaticon,* 244. *Prose Salernitan Questions,* 9–10, 169, 220. See below p.128, 135

51. André, chaplain of the royal hall: Andreas Capellanus, *De amore* I, 6, again II, 6, pp.152, 242; 1174: I, 6, p.156; Gautier: Pref. to III, pp.287, 324. Undoubtedly taking a cue from this reference in the text, three of the major manuscripts call him chaplain of the French king (Vatican, Ottobon. 1463 [13th century]; Paris BN lat. 8756 [14th century]; and Florence, Gadd. 178 [15th century]). The most recent study of authorship is Alfred Karnein, *De Amore,* 21–39.

52. During my research on the court of Philip Augustus in preparation for *The Government of Philip Augustus* I have not found a chaplain called André. Karnein's (*De Amore,* 35–36) attempt to link *Andreas capellanus* with an *Andreas cambellanus* is unconvincing. The confusion of the clerical priestly office of chaplain with the lay domestic office of chamberlain is highly unlikely. That the *Gualterius capellanus noster* in Genoa, 1190 (*Recueil des actes de Philippe Auguste,* ed. H.-F. Delaborde, Chartes de diplômes relatifs à l'histoire de la France [Paris, 1916], 1: no. 365), became Gautier the Young, the chamberlain, thus illustrating a transfer between the two offices, has no corroborating evidence. Henry Ansgar Kelly, *Love and Marriage in the Age of Chaucer* (Ithaca, 1975), 36, simply identifies him as chaplain of the King of Love.

53. He is witness to nine of Marie's charters. John F. Benton, "The Court of Champagne as a Literary Center," *Speculum* 36 (1961), 578–82.

54. Andreas Capellanus, *De amore,* I, 6, p.80. For another reference to Hungary see I, 6, p.100.

55. Karnein, *De Amore,* 37, 110.

56. The citation of the incipit in Pierre d'Etampes's inventory in 1348 leaves no doubt, which Gérard de Montagu's Inventory of 1370 further confirms. *Layettes du Trésor des chartes,* ed. H.-F. Delaborde, Archives nationales, Inventaires et documents (Paris, 1909), 5:xcvi, cxviii. Karnein, *De Amore,* 32–34.

57. Karnein, *De Amore,* 28–32. For Gautier the Young see Baldwin, *Government of Philip Augustus,* 108–9, 408–9. If this Gautier was the dedicatee of André's treatise, the exhortations of the last book were in vain by 1186, the year when Gautier married.

58. The most recent survey of the manuscripts of the *De Amore* has been made by Karnein in *De Amore,* 267–83. Among some forty extant manuscripts only three date from the thirteenth century; of these one is unfortunately inaccessible. The rest are later. The volume in the Trésor des chartes, the French royal archives, has disappeared since the fourteenth-century inventories. Philip Augustus's Register A, which was undoubtedly kept near to Andreas, also left the Trésor des chartes in the sixteenth century but has reappeared in the library of the Cardinal Ottoboni now in Vatican Library as Ottoboni lat. 2796.

The Danish scholar E. Trojel made the only critical edition of the work in 1892 (*Andreae Capellani regii Francorum de Amore libri tres* [Copenhagen]). Although he knew two of the thirteenth-century manuscripts, he based his edition chiefly on two fifteenth-century copies as giving the best text. In his introduction to the manuscripts (xx–liv), however, he reports no serious problems in constructing a critical text. Subsequent editors such as P. G. Walsh (1982) have agreed with this assessment and have reproduced Trojel's text with only minor emendations.

59. Don A. Monson, "Andreas Capellanus' Scholastic Definition of Love" (un-

published paper) demonstrates how André employs the arsenal of available logic from the schools to construct a careful definition of love.

60. Despite these digressions André did not usually forget his original scheme. The clerical classes (clerics and nuns) are briefly treated in I, 7, 8, and the remaining two ways of acquiring love (through riches and granting requests) are summarily treated in I, 9, 10, after the conversations illustrating eloquence are terminated. André omits the dialogue between the man and the woman from the higher nobility, presumably because of the futility of proceeding further after the lack of success with the woman of his own station.

61. This is the distinctive contribution of Rüdiger Schnell, *Andreas Capellanus*.

62. Andreas Capellanus, *De amore*, I, 6, p.178.

63. Don A. Monson, "*Auctoritas* and Intertexuality in Andreas Capellanus's *De amore*," in *Poetics of Love in the Middle Ages*, ed. Moshe Lazar and Norris J. Lacy (Fairfax, Va., 1989), 69–79, esp. 77, argues from André's use of heterogeneous authorities that it was impossible for him to arrive at consistent conclusions. His work resembles more the *sic et non* technique of Abelard.

64. Schnell, *Andreas Capellanus*, 27–33 has analyzed the sophistry of the higher nobleman's argument in the eighth dialogue.

65. The most recent and thorough study of the later readership is Karnein, *De Amore*. For these particular examples see 110–14, 168–75, 179–84, 184–87.

66. Gaston Paris, "Etudes sur les romans de la table ronde: Lancelot du Lac," *Romania* 12 (1883), 459–534.

67. The fullest statement of the position of D. W. Robertson, Jr., is in *A Preface to Chaucer: Studies in Medieval Perspectives* (Princeton, 1962), 391–448. For a recent survey and perceptive critique of the ironist and humorist interpretations see Don A. Monson, "Andreas Capellanus and the Problem of Irony," *Speculum* 63 (1988), 539–72. The most recent of sustained attempts to arrive at an overarching understanding of André are Schnell, *Andreas Capellanus* (1982), and Karnein, *De Amore* (1985). Kelly, *Love and Marriage*, 36–39, is an example of critics who do not take André seriously.

68. This is the conclusion of Schnell, *Andreas Capellanus*, 172, and to a lesser degree Karnein, *De Amore*, 107.

69. The text was edited by A. Morel-Fatio, "*Facetus*," *Romania* 14 (1886), 224–35, and reproduced and trans. Alison Goddard Elliot, "The *Facetus*: or the Art of Courtly Living," *Allegorica* 2 (1977), 27–57. See also the studies of Peter Dronke, "Pseudo-Ovid, Facetus, and the Arts of Love," *Mittellateinisches Jahrbuch* 11 (1976), 126–31, and of C. Stephen Jaeger, *The Origins of Courtliness: Civilizing Trends and the Formation of Courtly Ideals 939–1210* (Philadelphia, 1985), 166–68.

70. The fundamental study of this literature which stresses the interrelations between Latin and vernacular love lyric is Peter Dronke, *Medieval Latin*.

71. For a recent introduction and bibliography on the so-called medieval Latin comedies see Elliot, *Seven Medieval Latin Comedies*, xiii–xlix.

72. Statistics compiled from Birger Munk-Olsen, *L'etude des auteurs classiques latins aux IXe et XIIe siècles* (Paris, 1982–87), 1:88, 2:126–74, 282. See also his "Ovid au moyen âge (du IXe au XIIe siècle)," in *Le strade del testo*, ed. Guglielmo Cavallo (Bari, 1987), 67–97, but I have difficulty in reconciling his figures with data ob-

tained from his *Etude*. E. J. Kenney, "The Manuscript Tradition of Ovid's *Amores, Ars amatoria,* and *Remedia amoris,*" *Classical Quarterly,* 12 (1962), 1–31, is a survey of the most important manuscripts.

73. On the accessus and glosses see *Accessus ad auctores: Bernard d'Utrecht, Conrad d'Hirsau, Dialogus super auctores,* ed. R. B. C. Huygens (Leiden 1970), and Ralph J. Hexter, *Ovid and Medieval Schooling: Studies in Medieval School Commentaries on Ovid's Ars Amatoria, Epistulae ex Ponto and Epistulae Heroidum,* Münchener Beiträge zur Mediäevistik und Renaissance-Forschung 38 (Munich, 1986). For recent work in progress on the Orléans school see Hugues-V. Shooner, "Les *Bursarii Ovidianorum* de Guillaume d'Orléans," *Mediaeval Studies* 43 (1981), 405–24, and Frank T. Coulson, "Hitherto Unedited Medieval and Renaissance Lives of Ovid," *Mediaeval Studies* 49 (1987), 142–57. *Incipiunt glosule Ovidii de arte amandi. . . .* Intentio vero ipsius est iuvenes et puellas in amoris arte instruere et peritos reddere, et hoc est principalis intentio que per totum libri discurrit textum. Paris BN lat. 5137, fol. 102ra; and 8302, fol. 69va.

74. Haskins, *Studies in the History of Medieval Science,* 372.

75. Caesarius of Heisterbach, *Dialogus miraculorum* V, 22, 1:304; trans. Scott and Bland, *Dialogue on Miracles,* 1:348.

76. Two recent introductions to Ovid and his love poetry are Sara Mack, *Ovid* (New Haven, 1988); and Molly Myerowitz, *Ovid's Games of Love* (Detroit, 1985).

77. *Maître Elie's Uberarbeitung der ältesten französischen Ubertragung von Ovid's Ars Amatoria,* ed. H. Kühne et E. Stengel, Ausgaben und Abhandlungen aus dem Gebiete der romanischen Philologie 47 (Marburg, 1886). The author referred to finding women at Saint-German-des-Prés, for example, or at the markets of Champeaux or Place de Grève.

78. For an introduction see *L'art,* 3–59. The translation of Ovid's third book dates from the late thirteenth century.

79. *L'art* 65–67. Scattered in the commentary, the author demonstrates a modicum of medical knowledge normally reserved for clerics. For example, 81 and 158.

80. Ibid., 67–68, 64.

81. Munich Clm 5426, fol. 163 rb. Latin text in John W. Baldwin, "*L'ars amatoria* au XII^c siècle en France: Ovide, Abélard, André le Chapelain, et Pierre le Chantre," *Histoire et société: Mélanges offerts à Georges Duby* (Aix-en-Provence, 1992), 1:26.

82. *Accessus ad auctores,* ed. Huygens, 34. This interpretation was not followed by all the French commentaries. See some differing opinions in Baldwin, "*L'ars amatoria*" at n.14. Aurigen's *Facetus* teaches lovers to love *caute* (for example, *cautius urit amor*), but this is not a warning against love itself, ed. Morel-Fatio, 228; trans. Elliot, 38–41.

83. Andreas Capellanus, *De amore* I, 6, p.184; I, 8, p.212; Pref., p.30; and III, p.286.

84. Andreas Capellanus, *De amore* I, 6, p.180.

85. "Jehan Renart," *Lai de l'ombre,* v.953. The *engin* is found in three passages which call attention to nomenclature (*sornom*) and can be deciphered by reading backward: *Escoufle*—fait par bien povre = povRE bieN pAR faiT (v.9100) and

povRE seurnoN A coRT (vv.9100–9101). *Roman*—qu'il enTRA eN REligion (v.5655). Joseph Bédier made this discovery in his edition to the *Lai de l'ombre:* Société des anciens textes français (Paris, 1913), vii–xx.

86. The *Lai de l'ombre,* vv. 22–23, contains a clear reference to *Escoufle,* as does the *Roman,* v.5417. Similarly, the *Roman* (vv.661–69) takes note of a story of a brave knight from Champagne who loved a women on the march of Perthois, which appears to allude to *Lai de l'ombre.*

Because of the wealth of contemporary personages included by Jean Renart in his two romances, modern scholars have been tempted to date these works within precise limits. This has led to much disagreement in which negative arguments destroying rival positions have predominated over positive alternatives. Perhaps the most secure dates can be provided by the careers of the personages to whom the three works were addressed. Count Baudouin VI of Hainaut (IX of Flanders) to whom Jean Renart most certainly addressed the *Escoufle* as *conte en Hainaut* (vv.9060, 9079–80) acceded to his position in 1195 and left Hainaut in 1202 for the East on crusade never to return. Since *Escoufle* begins with a crusade, Jean most likely wrote it after 1200 when Baudouin took the cross. The *Roman* was addressed to Milon de Nanteuil while he was at Reims (vv.1–7). This period extended at least from 1202 when Milon became a candidate for the archbishop, through his tenure as prévôt of the chapter, and until he was elected bishop of Beauvais in 1217. (He remained in Reims into 1218 as custodian for the absent archbishop.) The *Roman* contains a fictional and friendly tournament at Saint-Trond between French and German parties composed of contemporary figures, some of whom participated in the battle of Bouvines of 1214. Since the Germans win at the fictional Saint-Trond, but the French win at the historical Bouvines, it is most likely that the *Roman* preceded 1214. The *Lai de l'ombre* was dedicated to a certain *Eslit* (bishop-elect) (vv.38–41). Scholars have generally assumed that this was Milon de Nanteuil when he was elect of Beauvais (1217–22). As Rita Lejeune has argued ("Le *Roman de Guillaume de Dole* et la principauté de Liège," *Cahiers de civilisation médiévale* [1974], 1–24, esp. 19), another candidate for the bishop-elect could be Hugues de Pierrepont who was bishop-elect at Liège from 1200 to 1202. In this way the *Lai* could fit chronologically between the two romances as suggested by the mutual references.

87. Lecoy has repertoried these songs in Jean Renart, *Roman,* xxii–xxix. Michel Zink (*Roman rose et rose rouge* [Paris, 1979], 29) argues that the plot was constructed from the songs themselves.

88. For the Provençal version of *Bele m'est la voiz altane,* see *Provenzalische Inedita aus Pariser Handschriften,* ed. Carl Appel (Leipzig, 1892), 87. Its attribution to Daude de Pradas has been disputed by Alexander H. Schutz, *Poésies de Daude de Pradas* (Toulouse, 1937), xxvi.

89. For a recent introduction to this genre see Paden, *Medieval Pastourelle,* 1:ix–xiv. Pastourelles are relevant for our purposes in matters of nonconsensual sex. See below pp.201, 204–5.

90. This stanza, however, is missing in the extant versions. Félix Lecoy, "Sur *Gerbert de Metz: Lieu et date,*" *Romania* 77 (1956), 433.

91. For the full repertory—*Chanson de Roland: Escoufle,* vv.1282–87; *Roman,*

vv.1746–48, 2755, 4509–10; *Guillaume d'Orange: Roman*, v.2304; *Gerbert de Metz: Roman*, vv.1335–67; *Roman de Troie: Escoufle*, vv.7674–75; *Roman*, vv.5324–51; *Roman d'Alexandre: Roman*, vv.2880–81, 5320–21; Perceval, *Roman*, vv.1746–48, 2880–81; Gauvin: *Escoufle*, vv.988–89; *Lai*, v.61; Keu: *Roman*, vv.3159–64; Sagremor: *Roman*, v.365; Arthur: *Escoufle*, vv.786, 988–89; *Roman*, vv.4619, 4681; *Graelent Muer: Roman*, v.2546; *Lai de Lanval: Roman*, vv.5511–12; *Piramus et Tisbé: Escoufle*, vv.6360–87; *Roman de Renart: Roman*, vv.444, 5421.

92. E. Hoepffner ("Les lais de Marie de France dans Galeran de Bretagne et Guillaume de Dole," *Romania* 56 [1930], 226–30) also argues for the influence of Marie's *Lanval* on Jean Renart's depiction of Lïenor's entry into Mainz.

93. From the great body of scholarship on the lais of Marie de France see, most recently, the introduction by Robert Hanning and Joan Ferrante, *The Lais of Marie de France*, 1–27; and Glyn S. Burgess, *Marie de France*. The latter is particularly helpful in establishing Marie's lexicography.

94. Aelis's beauty is compared with Iseut's (*Escoufle*, vv.3450–55, 8846–49); Count Richard's marriage to the lady of Genoa to King Marc with Iseut (*Escoufle*, vv.1715–17); Conrad's hunt to Marc's (*Roman*, v.170); Guillaume's and Aelis's triumphal entry into Rome to Tristan's and Iseut's joy (*Escoufle*, vv.8774–75).

95. The scenes are divided into four groups—(1) interior: early episodes, (2) on the stem: a hunting scene in the forest, (3) on the cover: Marc spying on the nude lovers lying together but separated by a sword, and (4) on the handle: incident of the dwarf. See the discussions of Léopold Sudre, "Les allusions à la légende de Tristan dans la littérature du moyen âge," *Romania* 15 (1886), 536–42; Rita Lejeune, "La coupe de la légende de Tristan dans l'*Escoufle* de Jean Renart," in *The Medieval Alexander Legend and Romance Epic: Essays in Honor of David J. A. Ross*, ed. Peter Noble, Lucie Polak, and Claire Isoz (Millwood, N.Y., 1982), 119–24; and Linda Cooper, "L'ironie iconographique de la coupe de Tristan dans l'*Escoufle*," *Romania* 104 (1983), 157–76, who discusses the incongruity of the gift in terms of irony.

96. A recent and helpful introduction to the legend is Emmanuèle Baumgartner, *Tristan et Iseut: De la légende aux récits en vers* (Paris, 1987).

97. For his derision about the Flemish-Germanic language see *Roman*, vv.2406–9. The linguistic confrontation at Saint-Trond was noted as early as the beginning of the twelfth century by the local chronicler. *Chronique de l'abbaye de Saint-Trond*, ed. C. de Borman (Liège, 1877), 1:5–6, 70, 122. See the discussion of Albert Henry, *Esquisse d'une histoire des mots wallon et wallonie*, 3d ed (Mont-sur Marchienne, 1990), 18–19. I am grateful to Paul Meyvaert for these references.

98. He also refuses to follow the mere belief or suspicion that brought about Piramas's and Tisbé's death. *Escoufle*, vv.6360–79.

99. Jean Frappier, *Chrétien de Troyes*, new ed. (Paris, 1968); English trans. by Raymond J. Cormier (Athens, Ohio, 1982) remains a standard introduction.

100. Rita Lejeune, "Le *Roman de Guillaume de Dole* et la principauté de Liège," 1–16.

101. Bradford B. Broughton, *The Legends of King Richard I, Coeur de Lion* (Hague, 1966), 116–17. Anthime Fourrier, "Les armoiries de l'empereur dans *Guillaume de Dole*," in *Mélanges offerts à Rita Lejeune* (Gembloux, 1969), 2:1211–26.

102. See the discussion of Charles Muscatine, "Courtly Literature and Vulgar

Language," in *Court and Poet: Selected Proceedings of the Third Congress of the International Courtly Literature Society* (Liverpool, 1981), 1–19, resumed in *Old French Fabliaux,* 133–42, 151.

103. Joseph Bédier, *Les fabliaux: Etudes de littérature populaire et d'histoire littéraire du moyen âge,* 4th ed. (Paris, 1925), was the first modern critical and comprehensive treatment. Per Nykrog's *Fabliaux* remains the standard study of the genre. Charles Muscatine's *Old French Fabliaux* is the most recent in English of a plethora of surveys on the subject. *The Humor of the Fabliaux: A Collection of Critical Essays,* ed. Thomas D. Cooke and Benjamin L. Honeycutt (Columbia, Mo., 1974), contains an important collection of studies.

104. On *Richeut* see Vernay's introduction to the poem and Donald Eugene Ker, "The Twelfth-Century French Poem of *Richeut:* A Study of History, Form, and Content" (Ph.D. diss., Ohio State University, 1976). Bédier and Muscatine have accepted *Richeut* into the fabliaux corpus; Nykrog, 255, excluded it on formal grounds but nonetheless admitted its unavoidable relevance.

105. The comprehensive study is Charles Foulon, *L'oeuvre de Jehan Bodel,* Travaux de la Faculté des lettres et sciences humaines de Rennes, 1st sér., 2 (Paris, 1958). On a hypothetical chronology of his career and works, 9–18; on the *Congés,* 707–15; on Jean de Boves, 68. The catalogue of his fabliaux and the allusion to Jean de Boves appears in *Des deux chevaus,* vv.1–24, ed. Nardin 149–50. His name "Bodel" was added to the necrology between 2 February and 6 June 1210. Roger Berger, *Le nécrologie de la confrérie des jongleurs et des bourgeois d'Arras (1194–1361),* Mémoires de la Commission départementale des Monuments Historiques du Pas-de-Calais 11 (2), (Arras, 1963), 110.

106. Lists of extant fabliaux have been compiled by Bédier (*Fabliaux,* 436–40), Nykrog (*Fabliaux,* 310–25), and Muscatine (*Old French Fabliaux,* 201–14). For my sample of fifty see "Short Titles" (designated by "F").

107. For example, Jean Bodel, *Vilain,* vv.1, 114; *Gombert,* vv.1, 192. Muscatine, *Old French Fabliaux,* 22–23. One version of the *Roman de Renart* from 1175 to 1176 appears to use the term, but the manuscript tradition is not entirely clear. See the discussion by Knud Togeby, "The Nature of the Fabliaux," in *The Humor of the Fabliaux,* 11.

108. *Dame escolliee,* 95, is another rare example of the mention of writing. Jean Rychner, *Contributions à l'étude des fabliaux: Variantes, remaniements, dégradations,* Université de Neuchatel, Recueil de travaux publiés par la Faculté des Lettres 28 (Neuchatel, 1960), 2 vols., is the fundamental study of these variants, which in turn led to the publication of the NRCF which takes into account the manuscript differences and traditions. See 132–33 for his conclusions on oral transmission. A convenient list of the major manuscripts is given on 9–10. Except for one (Paris BN fr. 2173) dated early (?) in the thirteenth century, all, including the most important, are from the late thirteenth or fourteenth centuries.

109. Over half of the fabliaux in our sample offer an explicit moral at the end. For other citations of the word *example/essample* see *Prestre crucefie* (v.93), *Dame escolliee* (95), and *Chevaliers, de deus clercs* (v.34).

110. This holds true for the fabliaux in general: Bedier, *Les fabliaux,* 43; Muscatine, *Old French Fabliaux,* 24–25; Foulon, *L'oeuvre de Jehan Bodel,* 121–22.

111. On the social world of the fabliaux see below pp.53–56, 60–61.

112. Nykrog (*Fabliaux,* 55) estimated that of 147 themes found in the fabliaux, 106 were erotic in various permutations and only 41 nonerotic.

113. *Enfant qui fu remis,* for example, has a direct counterpart in Latin. Edmond Faral, ("Le fabliaux latin au moyen âge," *Romania* 50 [1924], 321–85) argued for close affinities. See also Muscatine, *Old French Fabliaux,* 14–15. In the *Humor of the Fabliaux* this position has found support in Wailes (56) but rejection in Beyer (24).

114. Nykrog, *Fabliaux,* 83; in *Humor of the Fabliaux,* 65, 72–73. Huguette Legros, "Un auteur en quête de son public: Les fabliaux de Jean Bodel," *Romania* 104 (1987), 107–108.

115. *Les deus chevaus,* v.8, ed. Nardine, 149.

116. The phrase is Muscatine's (*Old French Fabliaux,* 133). See also Sarah Melhado White, "Sexual Language and Human Conflict in Old French Fabliaux," *Comparative Studies in Society and History* 24 (1984), 185–210.

117. Subculture is the hypothesis of Muscatine (*Old French Fabliaux,* 109, 151, 155). Naughty children is the image of Nykrog (*Fabliaux,* 216.) R. Howard Bloch's scandal (*The Scandal of the Fabliaux* [Chicago, 1986], 90) is, to be sure, linguistic or rhetorical but not sexual.

118. Nykrog, *Fabliaux,* 21–22. In *Barat* Jean Bodel addresses *baron* (v.1), but it may depend on the rhyme with *larron* in the next line. He also may be heard to dialogue with a peasant audience. See Foulon, *L'oeuvre de Jehan Bodel,* 85–86.

119. Bédier, *Fabliaux,* 371. In the case of Jean Bodel, Huguette Legros (*Romania* 104 [1983], 111–12) notes that the population at Arras included both nobility and bourgeoisie but concludes that Jean essentially intended the latter. Nykrog, *Fabliaux,* 227, 241. Muscatine, *Old French Fabliaux* 45. Rychner, *Contributions,* 1:145; on *La damoisele qui ne pooit oïr,* 1:84–91. On the variety in the manuscripts see Nykrog, *Fabliaux,* 25–26, 228.

120. Item quidam adulter consuevit habere accessum ad quandam adulteram, et cum una vice supervenisset proprius adultere maritus, adultera clausit suum adulterium in archa quadam. Quod comperiens ille maritus, aperuit archam. Et adulter percussit illico eum cultro, et effudit viscera eius. . . . Chanter, *Summa* BN lat. 3477, fol. 140ra–rb; and Courson, *Summa* XXVI, 20, fol. 94rb. The texts are nearly identical. The Chanter also raised the case of a chamberlain who slept with the wife of his lord. *Summa,* 2:319–20.

121. Lambert d'Ardres, *Historia comitum Ghisnensium,* ed. Joh. Heller, MGH SS 24:598.

122. See below p.114.

Chapter Two

1. Lev. 18:22; 20:13. 1 Cor. 6:7; 1 Tim. 1:9–10; Rom. 1:26–27.

2. For a summary of the penitentials see Pierre J. Payer, *Sex and the Penitentials: The Development of a Sexual Code, 550–1150* (Toronto, 1984), 135–39. Gratian, *Decretum,* C.32, q.7, c.11 *Adulterii.* Lombard, *Sententiarum,* 4.38.2 (PL, 192:933, Q 2:481–82). John Boswell, *Christianity, Social Tolerance,* 226–28, explains this absence as the result of unprecedented permissiveness of homosexual expression in the early twelfth century.

3. C.11, Mansi, 22:224–25.

4. Chanter, *Verbum abbreviatum*, PL, 205:333–35 (short version) and Appendix 2 (long version). For the Chanter's importance and a translation of the short version see Boswell, *Christianity, Social Tolerance*, 277–78 and 375–78.

5. To *masculorum concubitoribus* (1 Tim. 1:10): Et nota quod cantor Parisiensis dicebat se legisse in scripturis Hieronymi, quod ea nocte qua natus est salvator, mortui sunt omnes sodomitae ubicumque erant, cujus talem assignabat rationem beatus Hieronymus. Iustum erat, ut auctore naturae nascente morerentur hostes naturae, non valentes sustinere adventum et splendorem ipsius. *Hugonis Sancto Charo . . . in epistolis Pauli* (Venice, 1703), 7, fol. 209rb. I wish to thank Wayne Dynes and Philippe Buc for calling my attention to this text. I have not been able to locate it either in Jerome or Pierre the Chanter.

6. See a preliminary discussion of hermaphrodites in the Chanter's commentary to Gen. 1:27: Sic construe ut locum habeat ratio quod deus creavit hominem non solum unum hominem sed duos, nec in uno tantum sexu sed in utroque *quia masculum et feminam creavit eos* non androgeos, id est, non ermafroditos qui viri et mulieris simul habent instrumentum. Ergo plura dicit ne putaret homo sodomita posse abuti homine loco mulieris quod homo utrumque haberet etiam instrumentum contra tales. Paris, Arsenal 44, p.7a, and London, British Library, Roy 2 C 8, fol. 4va. Courson continued the discussion in his *Summa* XLII, 18. See his conclusion: Solutio ut tradunt phisici non potest contingere quod duo sexus in ermafrodito equaliter vigeant. Immo oportet quod semper unus obtineat privilegium et si secundum sexum illum possit reddere debitum secundum illum poterit contrahere quia ut dicit lex humana semper sexus incalescentis etatis preiudicat in talibus. Si autem secundum neutrum sexum possit talis reddere debitum, persona est illegitima ad contrahendum. Paris, BN lat, 14524, fol. 144va.

7. Aliquis habet uxorem nullo modo vult cognoscere eam in vase nature sed extraordinarie polluit eam more sodomorum. Si autem uxor hoc nolit pati et separet se ab eo, ipse forte abutetur masculis sicut prius consuevit et violentia est ad hoc presumptio. Quid faciet uxor? Contrarium quod nullo modo debet exhibere corpus suum instrumentum mortalis peccati immo potius esset ei moriendum. Credimus quod per sagaces amiculas videri debet si uxor illa dicit se esse virginem, utrum porta illa sit clausa nature et cogendus est vir per ecclesiam. Sed quid si illa prius fuerit vidua et nullo modo possit probare quod ita ut eam extraordinarie polluat? Consilium nostrum est quod cum vir exigit ab uxore ut ita turpiter coeat, ipsa debet se supponere ordine naturali et manibus, etiam per violentiam, si potest immittere virgam in vas naturale, et ita forte poterint eum revocare. Chanter, *Summa* Paris BN lat. 3477, fol. 49rb. For Augustine's passage in the Lombard and Gratian see below p.213.

8. Chobham, *Summa confessorum*, 398–403. See also Pierre de Poitiers, *Summa de confessione*, 16–17.

9. Gilles de Corbeil, *Hierapigra*, edited in Vieillard, *Gilles de Corbeil*, 351–52 (trans. 217), and 362 (trans. 261). Compare the parallel passages in Alain de Lille, *De planctu naturae*, ed. Nikolaus M. Häring, *Studi medievali* 19 (1978), 806, vv.15–22, and 846, vv.50–57. For a recent and full discussion see Jan Ziolkowski, *Alan of Lille's Grammar of Sex: The Meaning of Grammar to a Twelfth-Century Intellectual*

(Cambridge, Mass., 1985), on Alain (15, 35–38), on the vernacular writer Gautier de Coincy (35), on Gilles de Corbeil (68), and on other contemporary writers (ch. 2).

10. For the thirteenth-century discussion see Boswell, *Christianity, Social Tolerance*, 310–32.

11. Ovid, *Ars amatoria* II, vv.682–84. *L'art* 68. Andreas Capellanus, *De amore* I, 2, p.34. *Eneas*, ed. J.-J. Salverda de Frave (Paris, 1929), vv.8565–95. See also Raphael Levy, "L'allusion à la sodomie dans *Eneas*," *Philological Quarterly* 27 (1948), 372–76. Marie de France, *Lanval*, vv.278–82. A similar attitude was expressed in Occitan. Alfred Pillet and Henry Carstens, *Bibliographie der Troubadours* (Halle, 1933), 461, 127. See Angelica Rieger, "Was Dieris de Romans Lesbian?" *The Voice of the Trobaritz*, ed. William D. Padden (Philadelphia, 1989), 77.

12. Nykrog, *Fabliaux*, 180. Muscatine, *Old French Fabliaux*, 124–25.

13. *Prestre et le chevalier*, 81–82, 84, 88. Pierre de Poitiers, *Summa de confessione*, 17. The chief exception to silence over lesbians from an earlier generation (1174–78) is Etienne de Fougères, *Le livre de manières*, ed. R. Anthony Lodge (Geneva, 1979), vv.1097–1124.

14. Guillaume de Conches, *De philosophia mundi*, PL, 172:88; *Dramaticon*, 240. *Salernitan Questions*, 6. Similarly, following Soranus's doctrine (pp.31, 32), Caelius Aurelianus, 13, asserted that women are most apt to conceive between 14 and 40.

15. Brundage, *Law, Sex*, 357. W. Onclin, "L'age requis pour le mariage dans la doctrine canonique médiévale, "*Proceedings of the Second International Congress of Medieval Canon Law (1963), Monumenta iuris canonici*, ser. C: Subsidia (Vatican, 1965), 1:239–43. Chobham, *Summa confessorum*, 157, 158 and 153 (on free consent).

16. Andreas Capellanus, *De amore* I, 5, pp.38, 40.

17. Ovid, *Ars amatoria* III, vv.61–62. In the Latin comedies the male lovers divide about equally between young and mature men.

18. *Jouglet* retails the preparation of the inexperienced Robinet for his marriage by the jongleur Jouglet, and *Damoiselle qui ne pooit oïr* recounts the sexual initiation of a prudish girl. In the *Guillaume au faucon* a damoiseau is introduced to courtly love, but he is not a child having served the châtelain for seven years.

19. Gottfried von Strassburg, *Tristan*, v.2131. Chrétien, *Cligès*, vv.2724–25.

20. When Guillaume recapitulates at the end of the romance, he admits that the youthful pair lived together in the nursery as married, although they were not yet of age. *Escoufle*, vv.7498–7509.

21. Guillaume de Conches, *De philosophia mundi*, PL, 172:88. *Salernitan Questions*, 22.

22. Andreas Capellanus, *De amore* II, 5, 7, pp.38, 268. See the discussion of Schnell, *Andreas Capellanus*, 92, on possible Roman law precedents.

23. Ovid, *Amores*, I, 9, vv.3–4.

24. See Brundage, *Law, Sex*, 290–92, 376–78, for the contemporary canonist discussion. Courson offered an extensive discussion, *Summa* XLII, 17, fol. 142rb–44va summarized in Chobham, *Summa confessorum*, 183–87. In his manual Flamborough, *Liber poenitentialis*, 86, mentioned the physiological impediments only in passing. For further discussion see p.96 Andreas Capellanus, *De amore* II, 5, p.40. On their relevance to his theories of sexuality see p.140. In a love-judgment André (II, 7, pp.262–64) also considered whether a lady can reject a lover who has subse-

quently lost an eye or otherwise been physically maimed in battle. Ermengard of Narbonne decided that since it was the knight's original bravery that won the lady's love, she should not refuse him for the consequences of that bravery.

25. See the summations in Chobham, *Summa confessorum,* 176–78, and Flameborough, *Liber poenitentialis,* 78.

26. Ovid, *Ars amatoria* II, vv.478–80 (on the beginnings of the world); *Amores* III, 11, v.10, and I, 3, vv.6–7 (on his personal status).

27. Ovid, *Ars amatoria* I, v.36. Moreover, the notion of *servitium amoris,* which connoted the abject servility of the lover to his condition in Propertius and Tibullus, when transmitted by Ovid could also suggest the service of knights to a medieval audience. On the background of the Latin elegists see R. O. A. M. Lyne, *The Latin Love Poets: From Catullus to Horace* (Oxford, 1980), 71, 72.

28. In addition to Guillaume de Blois's *Alda* and Arnoul d'Orléan's *Lidia,* these include the *Miles gloriosus,* ed. Robert Baschet in Cohen, *La "Comédie" latine* 1:196–210; Mathieu de Vendôme, *Milo,* ed. Marcel Abraham, in Cohen, 1:168–77, and *Babio,* ed. Henri Laye, in Cohen, 2:30–56.

29. For an extensive analysis see Glyn S. Burgess, "Social Status in the *Lais* of Marie de France," in *Spirit of the Court: Selected Proceedings of the Fourth Congress of International Courtly Literature Society,* ed. Glyn S. Burgess and R. W. Taylor, (Cambridge, 1985), 69–78, summarized in Burgess, *Marie de France,* 71–76, 102–4, 128–29.

30. For some examples among many in Andreas Capellanus, *De amore: ordo* I, 6, p.46; *genus* I, 6, p.44; *gradus* I, 7, p.208; *ordo* and *genus* undifferentiated I, 6, p.62; *genus* as family or lineage I, 6, p.48.

31. A clear statement of the trifunctional scheme is found only in the eccentric version of the Chanter's *Verbum abbreviatum* that circulated in southeastern Germany and Italy. Richard C. Trexler, *The Christian at Prayer: An Illustrated Prayer Manual Attributed to Peter the Chanter (d. 1197)* (Binghamton, N.Y., 1987), 224–26. The treatises of the Chanter and his circle produced at Paris appear to ignore the traditional scheme, preferring more nuanced divisions based on professions. Baldwin, *Masters, Princes, and Merchants,* 1:56–58; and Georges Duby, *Les trois ordres ou l'imaginaire du féodalisme* (Paris, 1978), 373–77, which is the classic study on the trifunctional scheme.

32. *L'art,* 209.

33. Andreas Capellanus, *De amore* I, 11, p.222; *L'art,* 209. On rape see p.204.

34. Andreas Capellanus, *De amore* I, 6, pp.44, 62, 66.

35. Ibid. I, 6, pp.44, 46, 74, 120, 122; II, 7, pp.250–70. *Les registres de Philippe Auguste,* ed. John W. Baldwin et al., Recueil des historiens de la France, Documents financiers et administratifs 7 (Paris, 1993), 333–35. On vavasseurs in romance see Brian Woledge, "Bon vavasseurs et mauvais sénéchaux," in *Mélanges offerts à Rita Lejeune* (Gembloux, 1969), 2:1263–77.

36. Andreas Capellanus, *De amore* I, 6, pp.46–208: the response of the plebian woman to the plebian man, p.58; the arbitration of the countess, p.154–56.

37. Fabliaux containing sexually active characters classified by social group [table 1]. Nykrog, *Fabliaux,* ch. 4 analyzes the social world from a larger sample.

38. Doubtful cases include Boivin, who travels to Provins with his purse

(*Boivin*), the knight who is the son of a *vilain* but a very rich usurer (*Berengier*) and the *vilain* in town who offered hospitality to the poor cleric (*Povre clerc*).

39. For example, *Cuvier, Enfant fu remis, Prestre et la dame, Segretain moine*, and perhaps *Estormie*.

40. Money changers, *Deus changeors;* fishermen, *Pescheor;* butchers, *Bouchier;* millers, *Meunier;* blacksmiths, *Fevre;* cobblers, *Prestre qui fu mis;* and crucifix makers, *Prestre crucefié*.

41. Bourgeois—*Borgoise, Saineresse,* and *Auberee. Prodon*—Jean Bodel, *Sohaiz;* Jehan who pretends to leave town is also called *preudomme. Estormi*.

42. Multiple categories exist in individual fabliaux but moving from the more general to the specific: knights—*Chevalier qui fist sa fame, Chevalier qui recovra, Chevalier qui fist parler, Tresces;* vavassors—*Jouglet, Chevalier a la robe,* and *Aloul; châtelain*—*Berengier (I, II),* and *Guillaume au faucon*.

43. Andreas Capellanus, *De amore* I, 6, pp.62, 70, 72.

44. Ibid. I, 6, pp.50, 76.

45. Ibid. I, 6, pp.48, 66, 78.

46. *Damoisele qui ne pooit oïr (I)* also suggests downward *mésalliance* for the woman.

47. In *Jugemenz des cons* the three daughters, although richer than Robinet, apparently hope to marry upward because the young man's lineage will honor their family. These examples of men marrying downward should nuance the conclusions of Marie-Thérèse Lorcin that the wife always marries down and that money, not love, is the sole reason for *mésalliance* in the fabliaux: "Quand les princes n'épousaient pas les bergères, ou mésalliance et classes d'âge dans les fabliaux," *Mediaevo romanzo* 3 (1976), 197–208.

48. Louis had five marriageable daughters. See his complaint at the time of Philip Augustus's birth. Alexander Cartellieri, *Philip II. August, König von Frankreich* (Leipzig, 1899), 1: Beilagen 49. Elsewhere daughters from the royal houses of Scotland, Iceland (Ireland?), and England are offered as alternatives (Jean Renart, *Roman*, vv.3530–31, 3575).

49. Simile de facto acidit de principe huius regni qui consensit matrimonialiter in filiam imperatoris pro qua ancilla eius fuit ei supposita et illam ancillam duxit in uxorem ex qua spurios suscepit filios qui postmodum subverterunt regnum. Rex non cognoscens hanc ancillam; eam maritali cognoscit affectu. Ergo eam sic cognoscendo non peccat sicut vir non peccat cognoscendo aliquam putando uxorem eam suam esse cum tamen non sit sed contra iste modo consentit istam carnaliter et illa in istum et solus mutuus consensus facit matrimonium. Ergo hic non est fornicatio vel adulterium. . . . Courson, *Summa* XLII, 12, fol. 137va.

50. For a summary of the ecclesiastical movement to promote clerical celibacy see Brundage, *Law, Sex*, 183, 214–23, 251–53, 342–43. See below on the definition of the lower limits of holy orders pp.61–63.

51. Abelard, *Historia calamitatum*, in *Letters*, 12:175.

52. On the first expressions of this debate literature found in the *Altercatio Phyllides et Floriae* and the *Concilium Romarici Montis*, see F. J. E. Raby, *A History of Secular Latin Poetry in the Middle Ages* (Oxford, 1957), 2:290–97.

53. Andreas Capellanus, *De amore* I, 8, pp.210–12. The corruption of nuns was

forbidden in Roman law (*Codex* 1, 3, 5; ed. P. Krueger, *Corpus iuris civilis* [Berlin, 1914], 2) and repeated by Gratian (*De poen*, D.1, c.6 and C.36, q.2, c.3). Schnell, *Andreas Capellanus*, 114. See also the views of the penitentialists Chobham, *Summa confessorum*, 390–93; and Pierre de Poitiers, *Summa de confessione*, 15–16. In the Synod of Angers (1217–19) penance for the seduction of nuns could be administered only by bishops. *Statuts synodaux français*, 1:202.

54. Andreas Capellanus, *De amore* I, 7, pp.208–10.

55. Ibid. I, 6, pp.182–88.

56. The clerics are associated with schools in *Borgoise, Cuvier,* and *Povre clerc* (at Paris). See the comments of Marie-Thérèse Lorcin ("Quand les princes. . . ." 213–14, 218–19) on the age of clerics.

57. The topos of lovers dissuading the husband of what he sees finds precedent in Latin comedy in Arnould d'Orléans, *Lidia*, 226–46.

58. Table: *Boucher, Borgeoise, Perdriz, Prestre crucefié, Povre clerc, Prestre et la dame,* and *Prestre qui fu mis.* Bath: *Cuvier, Prestre et la dame,* and *Prestre qui fu mis.* In all these cases if the couple does not retire to bed the intent is nonetheless obvious. Sexual relations between women and their priests were of such enormity that the Synod of Angers (1217–19) required that they be referred to the bishop for adjudication. *Statuts synodaux français*, 1:202.

59. *Cuvier* (involving a cleric); *Povre cleric.* The *Borgoise* involves a cleric and punishes the husband. For the castration stories see below pp.69, 109–10.

60. In *Bouchier* a clever butcher takes similar revenge on an avaricious and inhospitable priest.

61. *Salernitan Questions*, 6. Brian Lawn, *Salernitan Questions*, (Oxford, 1963), 35.

62. Mansi, 20:437. Comestor reported by Gerald of Wales, *Gemma ecclesiastica* II, 6, in *Opera*, ed. J. S. Brewer (London, 1862), 2:187–88. For a fuller discussion see John W. Baldwin, "A Campaign to Reduce Clerical Celibacy at the Turn of the Twelfth and Thirteenth Centurie," *Etudes d'histoire du droit canonique dédiées à Gabriel Lebras* (Paris, 1965), 2:1041–53; and Baldwin, *Masters, Princes, and Merchants,* 1:337–41.

63. Chobham, *Summa confessorum*, 376–78; Courson, *Summa* XXIII, 3, 6 (texts edited in Baldwin, *Masters, Princes, and Merchants,* 2:231–32nn.218–19); Gerald of Wales, *Gemma ecclesiastica* II, 5, 6, in *Opera*, 2:186–87.

64. Raoul Ardent, *Speculum universale* X, 36 (text edited in Baldwin, *Masters, Princes, and Merchants,* 2:229n.212).

65. C.1, (1208) Mansi, 22:763. Gilles de Corbeil, *Hierapigra* I, vv.613–43, in Vieillard, *Gilles de Corbeil,* 364–65. (1207) *Compilatio* 3:1.9.6, in *Quinque compilationes antiquae*, ed. A. Friedberg (Leipzig, 1882), and *Decretales Gregorii IX*:1.14.9, *A multis*, ed. A. Friedberg, *Corpus iuris canonici* (Leipzig, 1881), 2; c.14, (1215) Mansi, 22:1003.

66. Lombard, *Sententiarum*, 4.2.1; 4.26.6; (PL, 192:841–42, 909–10; Q. 2:139–40, 419–20). Constat quod matrimonium est sacramentum quod est sacre rei signum et hec dupliciter. Est enim signum illius sacro[san]ctissime et ineffablilis copulationis divinitatis scilicet et humanitatis facte in utero virginali, sicut enim per matrimonium vir et uxor contrahendo in ecclesia fuerit una caro ita in divinitate assumente et in humanitate assumpta verbum factum est una caro scilicet Christus

Jesus unus deus et unus homo. . . . Est autem matrimonium copulationis divinitatis et humanitatis et copulationis Christi et ecclesie significativum. Ideo dicitur sacramentum quia est utriusque tam sacre rei signaculum. Courson, *Summa* XLII, 2, fol. 129vb, 130ra. In general see Jean Gaudemet, *Le mariage en Occident* (Paris, 1987), 188–91.

67. A negative definition of marriage in the synod of Angers (1217–19) underscored its unequivocal character: "quod omnis voluntaria seminis effusio est mortale peccatum tam in mare quam in femina, nisi per legitimum conjugium excusetur. *Statuts synodaux français*, 1:232–34.

68. Chanter, *Verbum abbreviatum*, 332. Chobham, *Summa confessorum*, 341–44. For contemporary canonist discussion of fornication and adultery see Brundage, *Law, Sex*, 247–48, 380–89. For penance enjoined on fornicators and adulterers see the synod of Angers (1217–19), *Statuts synodaux français*, 1:232–34.

69. Chanter, *Verbum abbreviatum*, 333. Cf. the long version, Vatican Reg. Lat. 106, fol. 152vb, and Paris Mazar, 772, fol. 43rb–va: Adulterium quoddam est simplex, quoddam vero dupplex. Simplex vero adulterium est soluti cum coniugata vel econverso. Dupplex est autem et maius coniugati scilicet cum coniugata. Adulterium homicidio videtur esse par crimen, unde dominus adulteros in lege sine remedio precipit lapidari. Maioritas autem criminum patet per maioritatem penarum. Nam iuxta quantitatem criminum statuit lex quantitatem penarum. Unde maxime timendum quod ecclesia erret cum hec instituta a domino non observet. Nam maiora crimina non punit ut crimen adulterum et incestus et vitium contra naturam. Furta vero et huiusmodi minora morte punit quod contrarium est legi. See a similar passage in Courson, *Summa* XXX, 7, fol. 106rb, vb, text in Baldwin, *Masters, Princes, and Merchants*, 2:214–15n.34. The Chanter offered another summary of his views in the *Summa Abel* v°: fornicatio, Paris BN lat. 455, fol. 68va. Chobham, *Summa confessorum*, 192, 362. On contemporary canonist opinion concerning killing those caught in adultery see Brundage, *Law, Sex*, 208, 307, 388.

70. Ovid, *Amores* I, 4; II, 12, vv.1–4; *Ars amatoria* I, v.579; II, vv.369–70, 544–46. Among the Latin comedies *Milo, Miles gloriosus, Lidia,* and *Babio* treat adulterous themes.

71. Mathieu de Vendôme, letter in F. J. E. Raby, *Secular Latin Poetry in the Middle Ages* (Oxford, 1957), 2:33,34; Abelard, *Historia calamitatum* in *Letters*, 12:185–89; *Epistola I*, in *Letters*, 15:70–71.

72. Andreas Capellanus, *De amore* III, pp.286–88.

73. Ibid. I, 6, p.178. On the identification of the celebrated maidens in literature p.18.

74. Andreas Capellanus, *De amore* I, 6, pp.146–48, 150–52, 156. To counter the woman's distinction between *maritus* and *amans,* the man makes a further division between *amantes* and *amicus/amica* as mere friends, p.150. For marital affection see below p.138, and for the marital debt see pp.192–94. On the incongruity of citing the *vehemens amator* opinion see below p.138.

75. Ibid. III, p.290; I, 6, pp.170–72; II, 4, p.232; II, 8, p.282; and for the judgments II, 7, pp.256, 266, 258.

76. *L'art*, 210, to *Ars amatoria* II, vv.545–46; and 213 to *Ars* II, v.600.

77. [Table 2.] See the conclusions of Nykrog, *Fabliaux*, 55, based on a larger corpus.

78. *Crote* also expresses, albeit crudely, the connubial contentment of a married peasant couple. In *Dame qui aveine demandoit* the wife's marital expectations exceed the capabilities of her husband.

79. Connubial happiness is likewise impossible with the knight and the shrewish wife in the *Dame escolliee*.

80. Other peasant examples include *Aloul* and *Perdriz*.

81. Traveling husband: *Enfant qui fut remis, Cuvier, Prestre et la dame,* and *Segretain moine.* Other bourgois situations: *Deus changeors, Prestre crucefié, Saineresse,* and *Prestre qui fu mis.*

82. For other adulterous clerics: *Borgoise, Cuvier,* and *Meunier.*

83. For other adulterous priests: *Vilain, Estormi, Aloul, Perdriz, Prestre crucefié, Pescheor, Povre clerc, Prestre et de la dame,* and *Prestre ki abevette.*

84. For other aristocratic adultery: *Chevalier qui fist sa fame, Berengier (I),* and *Chevalier qui recovra.*

85. *Deus changeors, Saineresse, Fevre,* and *Auberee.*

86. For other examples of near castration: *Aloul,* and *Perdriz.*

87. Roger Dubuis, "*Dru* et *drüerie* dans le *Tristan* de Béroul," *Mélanges de langue et littérature françaises du moyen âge offerts à Pierre Jonin, Sénéfiance* 7 (1979), 221–31, provides a comprehensive analysis of the terms.

88. See the conclusions in Burgess, *Marie de France,* 125–26, 139, 169.

89. Others include *Bisclavret, Yonec, Laustic* (sublimated), and *Eliduc* (technically not consummated).

90. There is also awareness of potential and unlawful bigamy (vv.601, 1127).

91. Burgess (*Marie de France,* 217n.18) notes that the term was used fourteen times by Marie and catalogues the scope of its usage.

92. *Les registres de Philippe Auguste,* ed. Baldwin, 465–66. The Capetian chancery copied the charter into a register, but the original, to which the ribbon and seal were attached, survived in Normandy.

93. The adulterous relation between the count of Saint-Gilles and the lady of Montpelliers is underscored by his jealousy over the *gage d'amour. Escoufle,* vv.5846–53.

94. The exception is Count Richard's presentation of a gold chalice to the church of the Holy Sepulchre in Jerusalem on which the adultery scenes of Tristan and Iseut are explicitly depicted. *Escoufle,* vv.579–616. See above p.30.

95. In similar fashion, the imperial coronation at Rome in *Escoufle* (vv.9008–24) offers an occasion for knights and maidens to form new loves.

96. *La chronique de Gislebert de Mons,* ed. Léon Vanderkindere, Recueil de textes pour servir à l'étude de l'histoire de Belgique (Brussels, 1904), 191–92. This Marie was the daughter of Henri I, count of Champagne, and Marie, daughter of Louis VII and Eleanor of Aquitaine.

97. Flameborough, *Liber poenitentialis,* 66–98. Chobham, *Summa confessorum,* 154–93.

98. For a summation of these definitions see Brundage, *Law, Sex,* 87–88, 182–203, 242–45, 288–89, 331–37. Gaudemet, *Mariage,* 197–219, 239–62. Duby, *Medi-*

eval Marriage, 15–22. In the twelfth century the method of computation was "medieval-Germanic" (counting from each spouse to the common ancester) and not Roman (counting from one spouse to the common ancestor and then down to the other spouse).

99. Duby, *Medieval Marriage,* 3–15, 25–81. Duby argues for endogamy primarily on the basis of royal evidence. Constance B. Bouchard ("Consanguinity and Noble Marriages in the Tenth and Eleventh Centuries," *Speculum* 56 [1981], 268–87) maintains that the nobility of the earlier period attempted to respect the limits of consanguinity, although she concedes that in the twelfth century they were frequently willing to transgress the ecclesiastical boundaries. The twelfth-century nobility deserve a study comparable to hers on the preceding period. On Philip and Ingeborg see Baldwin, *Government of Philip Augustus,* 83. The falsity of the alleged relationship was recognized even in the genealogy of Ingeborg compiled in the royal registers. *Les registres de Philippe Auguste,* ed. Baldwin, 549–53.

100. Jean-Baptiste Molin and Protais Mutembe, *Le rituel du mariage en France du XIIᵉ au XVIᵉ siècle* (Paris, 1973), include in their study an examination of seven marriage *ordines* prior to the thirteenth century and three from the thirteenth century (283). In this pargraph I have sketched the salient steps of the marriage ritual from these *ordines:* 49–50, 64–66, 79–82, 89, 136–37, 160, 180, 231. In the twelfth century one *ordo* in southern France was unusual when it instructs the priest to ask the couple whether they love each other (*Si est amor inter illos*) (65). No ritual appears for engagement until the thirteenth century (50). Nor does the priest usurp the father's role as *coniunctor* of the couple until the thirteenth century (92–93).

101. In *Dame escolliee* (105) the count states that he has put a ring on his bride's finger.

102. After Erec and Enide's wedding the archbishops and bishops accompany the couple to the nuptial chamber (v.2020).

103. Otto of Brunswick, who may be the contemporary prototype for Conrad, was married to his second wife in 1214 neither by a bishop or priest but by William, count of Holland. Molin and Mutembe, *Rituel de mariage,* 92.

104. Eilhart von Ohberg, *Tristan,* trans. J. W. Thomas (Lincoln, Nebr., 1978), 74.

105. That this marriage was fully arranged was emphasized later when Guillaume explained that his father Richard had warred against the Pisans and Genoese and taken his mother captive before the emperor gave her to him to marry. *Escoufle,* vv.7477–89.

106. In the *Vallet aus douze fames* a young man aspires to hyperpolygamy but does not succeed.

107. On the papal policy and the Chanter's reform see Baldwin, *Masters, Princes, and Merchants,* 1:332–37.

108. Chanter, *Verbum abbreviatum* (long version), in Baldwin, *Masters, Princes, and Merchants,* 2:224n.170.

109. Chanter, *Verbum abbreviatum* (long version), in Baldwin, *Masters, Princes, and Merchants,* 2:225n.179.

110. Innocent III, *Regesta,* PL, 214:1015. A. Potthast, *Regesta pontificum Romanorum* (Berlin, 1874), 1:no. 1713.

111. Chanter, *Verbum abbreviatum*, PL, 205:164, and Baldwin, *Masters, Princes, and Merchants*, 2:226n.186.

112. C.50, Mansi, 22:1035–38.

113. Andreas Capellanus, *De amore* I, 6, pp.102–16.

114. See the overview of Leah L. Otis, *Prostitution in Medieval Society: The History of an Urban Institution in Languedoc* (Chicago, 1985), 9–39.

115. Ovid, *Amores* I, 10, vv.11–34. For example, avoid her birthday because of the expense of gifts. *Ars amatoria* I, vv.417–20.

116. Andreas Capellanus, *De amore* I, 6, 9, 12, pp.192, 212, 222. On the absence in romance see the comprehensive index on women in Marie-Luce Chênerie, *Le chevalier errant dans les romans arthuriens en vers des XIIe et XIIIe siècles*, Publications Romanes et Françaises 172 (Geneva, 1986), 728–30. See also feminine hospitality, 559–76. None of the examples cited in Marie-Luce Chênerie, " 'Ces curieux chevaliers tournoyeurs . . . ' Des fabliaux aux romans," *Romania* 97 (1976), 347–50, produce clear cases of women who charge money in the romances.

117. Baldwin, *Masters, Princes, and Merchants*, 1:133–37. For penance enjoined on clients of prostitutes see the synod of Angers (1217–19), *Statuts synodaux français*, 1:198–200.

118. Ulpian in *Digesta*, 33.2.43. Gratian, *Decretum* D.34, c.16. Adolf Berger, *Encyclopedic Dictionary of Roman Law, Transactions of the American Philosophical Society*, n.s. 43, no. 2 (1953), v°. *meretrix*. Brundage, *Law, Sex*, 44, 248.

119. Chobham, *Summa confessorum*, 346, 348. Chanter, *Summa*, 3 (2a):173–74.

120. Gratian, *Decretum*, C.32, q.4, c.11. Chobham, *Summa confessorum*, 347, 296. See also Chanter, *Summa* 3(2a):172.

121. *Digesta*, 12.5.1 and 3. *Digesta*, 12.5.4, par.3. Chanter, *Summa* 3(2a):171–73. Courson in Baldwin, *Masters, Princes, and Merchants* 2:92n.128. Chobham, *Summa confessorum*, 296, 351–52.

122. Chanter, *Summa* 3(2a):171, 173, 175. Courson, *Summa* in Baldwin, *Masters, Princes, and Merchants*, 2:92–93n.128, 94–95n.141. Chobham, *Summa confessorum*, 297, 348–49, 352. On contemporary canonists see Brundage, *Law, Sex*, 393–94.

123. Ulpian in *Digesta*, 33.2.43. Chobham, *Summa confessorum*, 347.

124. See the comment of Marie-Thérèse Lorcin, "La prostituée des fabliaux: Est-elle integrée ou exclue?" *Senefiance* 5 (1978), 111.

125. Chobham, *Summa confessorum*, 404. It was apparently on his mind, because he cites the example also on 339 and 367. The penance enjoined on pimps was no more severe than on prostitutes in the synod of Angers (1217–19), *Statuts synodaux français*, 1:210.

126. Chanter, *Summa* 3(2a):172–73. Chobham, *Summa confessorum*, 352–53. Courson, *Summa*, in Baldwin, *Masters, Princes, and Merchants*, 2:92–93n.128.

127. See the observation of Lorcin, "La prostituée . . . ," 111–14.

128. Chanter, *Summa*, 2:351–52; 3(2a):239, 242. Chobham, *Summa confessorum*, 349.

129. Otis, *Prostitution*, 25–26.

130. Chobham, *Summa confessorum*, 403–4. See the legislation against procurers in the south of France, Otis, *Prostitution*, 89.

131. On Foulque's campaign, see Baldwin, *Masters, Princes, and Merchants*,

1:136–37. Otto of Saint-Blaise, *Chronicon* (1198), in *MGH, SS,* 20:330. For the canonist discussion, Brundage, *Law, Sex,* 309–10. Innocent III, *Regesta,* PL, 214:102 (20 April 1198). Potthast 1:no. 114.

132. Courson, *Summa,* in Baldwin, *Masters,* 2:94–95nn.141, 145. Mansi, 22:854. Otis, *Prostitution,* 17, 22–23.

133. In opposition to the conclusions of Lorcin, "La Prostituée . . . " 110.

134. Chobham, *Summa confessorum,* 347–48. Augustine, *De ordine* II, 4, 12, ed. PL, 32:1000, and W. M. Green, Corpus christianorum 29 (Turnholt, 1970), 114. Chanter, *Summa* 3(2a):172, 174.

135. Otis, *Prostitution,* 103–4. The conditions surrounding prostitution of the later Middle Ages, studied in Jacques Rossiaud, *La prostitution médiévale* (Paris, 1988), and Ruth Mazo Karras, "The Regulation of Brothels in Later Medieval England," *Signs* 14 (1989), 399–433, differ significantly from those of the turn of the twelfth and thirteenth centuries.

136. On the trisexual system see Matthäus Bernards, *Speculum virginum: Geistigkeit und Seelenleben der Frau im Hochmittelalter,* Beihefte zum Archiv für Kulturgeschichte 16 (Cologne, 1955), 40–44. A treatise from Pierre the Chanter's circle included the ancient schema. *The Christian at Prayer,* ed. Trexler, 253.

137. *The Historia Occidentalis of Jacques de Vitry: A Critical Edition,* ed. John F. Hinnebusch, Spicilegium Friburgense 17 (Fribourg, Switzerland, 1972), 165–66.

138. Jacques de Vitry, *VMO* 547–48.

139. Ibid., 550.

Chapter Three

1. Et haec fuit prima humani corporis immortalis, scilicet, posse non mori. Lombard, *Sententiarum,* 2.19.1, (PL, 192:690, Q.1:422); . . . in paradiso carnali copula convenisset, et esset ibi thorus immaculatus, et commixtio sine concupiscentia; atque genitalibus membris sicut ceteris imperarent, ut ibi nullum motum illicitum sentirent. Et sicut alia membra corporis aliis admovemus, ut manum ori, sine ardore libidinis, ita genitalibus uterentur membris sine aliquo pruritu carnis. . . . Incredibile enim non est Deum talia fecisse illa corpora . . . illis membris sicut pedibus imperarent. Ibid., 2.20, 1 (PL, 192:692, Q.1:427–28); Firmissime tene, et nullatenus dubites, omnem hominem . . . cum originali peccato nasci, impietati subditum, mortique subjectum. . . . fomes peccati, scilicet concupiscentia vel concupiscibilitas, quae dicitur lex membrorum, sive languor naturae, sive tyrannus qui est in membris nostris, sive lex carnis. . . . Ibid., 2.30.7,8 (PL, 192:722, Q.1:499–500).

2. Augustine, *De Genesi ad litteram* XI, 1, 32. *De civitate dei* XIV, 17, 18.

3. Chanter to: *erat uterque nudus et non erubescebant* (Gen. 2:25) *Nil putabant velandum quia nil senserant refrendandum* (*Glossa ordinaria*) sicut non erubescimus si quis viderit manus. Inordinatus enim motus facit pudenda ut vides in puero qui non erubescit videri pudenda sua, qui motum erubescibilem beneficio etatis non sentit. Quique est inordinatus ideo est pudendus quia sine peccato non fit. . . . To: *aperti sunt oculi amborum* (Gen. 3:7) id est, tale quid visu perceperunt quod non ante; id est, disconvenientiam nuditatis. . . . Quare manifestum est quod ante peccatum nuditatem suam non cognoscebant. Ergo hic dicimus oculos concupiscentiam et

eius cognicionem. Erant enim in eis naturales motus concupiscentie, sed repressi et clausi quantum ad visum, ut in pueris usque ad pubertatem. Sed tunc tanquam rivuli aperti sunt et ceperunt diffundi et moveri quos cum prius non sensisset in se esse. . . . Sed forte propter peccatum infusus est eis . . . ut sentirent pruritum ut bruta quibus infusus est in ipsa eorum formatione quam a sui persona formatione sentiebant ut nunc sentiunt post peccatum. Ergo membra ceperunt moveri contra suuum superiorem, id est, rationem, sicut parentes fuerint superiori inobedientes. Paris Arsenal 44, pp.10b, 11b; London, Brit. Lib. Roy. 2 C 8, fol. 6vb, 7ra, rb.

4. *Prose Salernitan Questions*, 1–2.

5. *Anatomia Ricardi Salernitani*, 79. *Anatomia magistri Nicolai* 30. Chanter, *Verbum abbreviatum*, 337,338. On anatomy in general see Jacquart et Thomasset, *Sexuality and Medicine*, 22–41.

6. *Anatomia Ricardi Salernitani*, 80.81. *Anatomia magistri Nicolai*, 33, 35, 36. For the widespread acceptance of the division of brain, heart, and liver in French circles see Bernardus Silvestris, *Cosmographia*, XIII, 19, XIV, vv.153–70, ed. Peter Dronke, Textus minores 53 (Leiden, 1978), 148, 154, trans. Winthrop Wetherbee (New York, 1973), 121, 126, and Alain de Lille, *De planctu naturae*, ed. N. M. Häring, *Studi medievali*, 3d ser. 19 (1978), 828; trans. James J. Sheridan, *The Plaint of Nature*, Pontifical Institute of Medieval Studies, Medieval Sources in Translation 26 (Toronto, 1980), 121–22.

7. Galen, *On the Useful Parts of the Body*, trans. Margaret Tallmadge May (Ithaca, 1968), 2:628–31. Thomas Laqueur, *Making Sex: Body and Gender from the Greeks to Freud* (Cambridge, Mass., 1990), 25–34, has summarized the basic Galenic and Aristotelian positions, which he terms the "one-sex" model. For a more nuanced treatment of Aristotle and Galen, see Green, "Transmission," 40–42.

8. Nemesius of Emesia, *De natura hominis*, trans. by Nicolas Alfanus, ed. Karl Burkhard (Leipzig, 1917), 142. It was also translated by Burgundio of Pisa, ed. G. Berbeke and J. R. Moncho. Corpus Latinum commentariorum in Aristotelem Graecorum, Suppl. 1 (Leipzig, 1975), 109. Constantinus, *De genecia*, 313. See also Rouselle, *Porneia*, 26–27.

9. David de Dinant, *Quaternuli*, 31–32. Avicenna, *Liber canonis*, 3.21.1.1, fol. 285v.

10. *Anatomia vivorum*, 21–22.

11. *Anatomia Richardi Salernitani*, 90. *Anatomia magistri Nicholai*, 56. Caelius Aurelianus, 5. Muscio, 10. Constantinus, *De genecia* 314. *Prose Salernitan Questions*, 103. Caelius thought that they were softer than the males; Constantinus, harder.

12. *Anatomia Richardi Salernitani*, 90. *Anatomia magistri Nicolai*, 36, 56.

13. *Anatomia Richardi Salernitani*, 90–91. *Anatomia magistri Nicolai*, 36, 57.

14. Constantinus, *De genecia*, 322–23.

15. *Anatomia Richardi Salernitani*, 84, 92. *Anatomia magistri Nicolai* 43.

16. Constantinus, *De Genecia* 323. The *Anatomia vivorum*, 24, further expanded on Constantinus's account. The penis, erect with spirit or air, extends six inches so that it can reach the destined place for projecting the seed. It has two ducts, one for the sperm from the testicles and the other for the urine from the bladder which join at the neck of the penis. It also has two pairs of muscles, one which governs the

length and extension of the erection and the other which keeps it straight. After injection of the sperm, it returns to its former size.

17. Guillaume de Conches, *Dragmaticon*, 240–41. *Prose Salernitan Questions*, 8.

18. *Anatomia magistri Nicolai*, 57–58. Guillaume de Conches, *De philosophia mundi*, 88–89; *Dragmaticon*, 241. *Prose Salernitan Questions*, 8. *Anatomia Richardi Salernitani*, 91. Robert Reisart, *Der siebenkammerige Uterus: Studien zur mittelalterlichen Wirkungsgeschichte und Entfaltung eines embryologischen Gebärmuttermodells*, Würzburger medizinhistorische Forschungen 39 (Hannover, 1986), 46–51, 65–69. See below, pp.207–8. The tradition of Soranus (*Gynecology*, 8–14) which described the shape of the uterus as consisting of orifice (*orificium*), neck (*collum*), isthmus (*cervix*), shoulders (*umeri*), sides (*latera*), and base (*fundus*) (Caelius Aurelianus, 3–6, and Muscio, 6–10) was not followed by the Salernitans.

19. *Anatomia Richardi Salernitani*, 91. *Anatomia magistri Nicolai*, 51.

20. *Anatomia Ricardi Salernitani*, 84. *Anatomia magistri Nicolai*, 43.

21. Caelius Aurelianus, 1, 4, 6–7. Muscio, 8–9. Compare Soranus, *Gynecology*, 14. The clitoris was further treated in Caelius Aurelianus, 113, and Muscio, 106. See below p.130. The inability to describe the external female organs was shared with ancient medicine. Rousselle, *Porneia*, 27. Constantinus, *De genecia*, 313–14.

22. *Anatomia Ricardi Salernitani*, 90. *Anatomia magistri Nicolai*, 56. See Green, "Transmission," 44–45. Caelius Aurelianus, 6. Soranus, *Gynecology*, 14.

23. Isidore of Seville, *Etymologia sive originum* XI, 1, 75–77, ed. W. M. Lindsay (Oxford, 1911), 2: trans. William D. Sharpe, *Isidore of Seville: The Medical Writings*, Transactions of the American Philosophical Society, n.s., 54(2) (1964), 43. Constantinus, *De genecia*, 321–22. *Prose Salernitan Questions*, 195–96. See the discussion of Jacquart and Thomasset, *Sexuality and Medicine*, 11–12, 34.

24. Chobham, *Summa confessorum*, 465.

25. *Anatomia Richardi Salernitani*, 90. *Anatomia magistri Nicolai*, 56.

26. Allen, *The Concept of Woman*, 47–52, 187–89. Michael Boylan, "The Galenic and Hippocratic Challenges to Aristotle's Conception Theory," *Journal of the History of Biology* 16 (1983), 87–92, 100–105. Galen, *On the Useful Parts of the Body*, 2:631–34. Guillaume de Conches, *De philosophia mundi*, 89. *Dragmaticon*, 237, 239, 240, 242. *Prose Salernitan Questions*, 3, 4, 6–7, 9, 21. See below pp.134–35.

27. *Anatomia magistri Nicolai*, 57. Guillaume de Conches, *De philosophia mundi*, 88; *Dragmaticon*, 236. *Prose Salernitan Questions*, 3, 11, 220. (The Latin translations of Nemesius of Emesia [*De natura hominis*, ed. Burckhard, 141; ed. Verbeke and Moncho, 108–9] present a different scheme.) Constantinus, *De coitu*, 86. See also Jacquart and Thomasset, *Sexuality and Medicine*, 50–55.

28. David de Dinant, *Quaternuli*, 12, 23. On the complexities of the Galenic and Aristotelian schemes, see Michael Boylan, "The Galenic and Hippocratic Challenges," 83–112. On the conflict between Aristotle and Galen, and its repercussions in Avicenna, see B. F. Musallam, *Sex and Society in Islam: Birth Control before the Nineteenth Century*, Cambridge Studies in Islamic Civilization (Cambridge, 1983), 43–49.

29. Gerda Lerner, *The Creation of Patriarchy* (New York, 1986), 192.

30. On Augustine's reticence and a possible acceptance of the two seed theory:

Utrum autem utriusque sexus semina in muliebri utero cum voluptate misceantur, viderint feminae quid in secretis visceribus sentiant; nos non decet inaniter usque ad ista esse curiosos. *De nuptiis et concupiscentia* II, 13, 26. On the predominance of the agricultural metaphor for conception: *De nuptiis et concupiscentia* II, 14, 15, *De civitate dei* XIV, 23, 24, 26. See the conclusions of Elizabeth A. Clark, "Vitiated Seeds and Holy Vessels: Augustine's Manichean Past," in *Ascetic Piety and Woman's Faith: Essays on Late Ancient Christianity* (Lewiston, Queenston, 1986), 310–12.

31. *Anatomia vivorum*, 23.

32. quod *enim in iniquitatibus conceptus sum* (Ps. 50:7) . . . unde notandum quod duplex est conceptio. Prima fit quando semina duorum, scilicet, viri et femine, in matrice concipiuntur, et est conceptio carnis, et in ista fit causa originalis. Secunda fit quando anima infunditur corpori, et ista fit effectus originalis. Chanter, Paris BN lat. 12011, fol. 94vb. *Statuts synodaux français*, 1:232–34.

33. David de Dinant, *Quaternuli*, 23, 24, 31. See also Nemesius of Emesia, *De natura hominis*, ed. Burkhard 142; ed. Verbeke and Moncho, 109. Rousselle, *Porneia*, 30–31. Jacquart and Thomasset, *Sexuality and Medicine*, 50, 54.

34. Chobham, *Summa confessorum*, 183–87. Sequitur de alio impedimento matrimonii quod est impossiblitas coeundi que provenit multiplici de causa quia quandoque provenit ex frig[id]itate, quandoque ex malefico, quandoque ex defectu vel ex vicio membrorum, quandoque ex infectione abusionis. . . . Ad sequens dicimus quod in omnibus probationibus attendere debemus . . . et hoc pro generali regula habere debemus quod semper standum est veris rationibus potius quam verisimilibus. . . . cum ille de quo dubitatur an sit naturaliter frigidus vocatur inter pulcherrimas mulieres et contrectatur ab illis et cum tandem frigidus invenitur ab omnibus tunc primo constare debet per huiusmodi veras probatones quod frigidus est. Simili modo dicimus de artis mulieribus de quibus probandis. . . . de illis probandis an sint arte est cum a discretis mulieribus oculata fide ostenduntur et per contrectationem et inspectionem deprehenduntur esse arte et omnino impotentes ad reddendum debitum. . . . Courson, *Summa* XLII, 16, fol. 142rb, 143rb, va. Chobham also recommended midwives (*sagaces matrone*) for examining men (184). For examples of this procedure in fifteenth-century England see Richard H. Helmholz, *Marriage Litigation in Medieval England*, Cambridge Studies in English Legal History (Cambridge, 1974), 87–90.

35. Ovid, *Amores*, II, 7; II, 15.

36. Ibid., I, 5.

37. *Ars amatoria*, II, vv.609–18; III, vv.669–82, 807–8. *Remedia*, vv.411–12.

38. See below pp.108,110.

39. Guillaume de Blois, *Alda*, vv.125–36. Arnoul d'Orléans, *Lidia*, vv.443–50; *De nuncio sagaci*, vv.36–47; *De tribus puellis*, vv.31–56. See also *Facetus*, vv.215–34, ed. Morel-Fatio, 229, trans. Elliot, 41–43. (See above pp.20–21.)

40. Mathieu de Vendôme, *Ars versificatoria* I, 56, 57. Geoffroi de Vinsauf, *Poetria nova*, vv.563–97, 773–75; *Documentum* II, 2, 3. The clerical verse is in Dronke, *Medieval Latin*, 2:450–52. The wide-reaching influence of this model is also seen in the description of Prudence in Alain de Lille's *Anticlaudianus* (I, vv.270–303, ed. Robert Bossuat, Textes Philosophiques du Moyen Âge 1 [Paris, 1955], 65–66; trans. James J. Sheridan [Toronto, 1973], 56–57) and of Nature in his *De planctu naturae*

(ed. Häring 809, trans. Sheridan, 73–75). For a general treatment of canonical beauty in the Latin rhetoricians see Alice M. Colby, *The Portrait in Twelfth-Century French Literature* (Geneva, 1965), 89–96.

41. *De tribus puellis*, vv.45–50. Ovid, *Ars amatoria* III, v.274; *Remedia*, vv.327, 337–38.

42. Mathieu de Vendôme, *Ars versificatoria* I, 67. Ovid, *Ars amatoria* I, v.509.

43. Andreas Capellanus, *De amore* I, 1, 6, pp.34, 42, 198–200.

44. Andreas Capellanus, *De amore* I, 6, pp.96–118. Betsy Bowden has interpreted this allegorical passage as a series of sexual puns ("The Art of Courtly Copulation," *Medievalia et humanistica* n.s. 9 [1979], 67–85). Although the imagery of the metaphors seems plausible, her use of *poenis* =penis and *probitas*=uprightness= erection is less convincing. *Penis* fell out of use in Late Latin (J. N. Adams, *The Latin Sexual Vocabulary* [Baltimore, 1982], 35–36), and I have found it rarely attested in the contemporary Latin poets and prose authors, in contrast to the frequency of *virga*. For a summary of the question and other hesitations see Don A. Monson, "Andreas Capellanus and the Problem of Irony," *Speculum* 63 (1988), 556–66.

45. Colby (*The Portrait*, 5, 102–3, 178) modifies the conclusions of Edmond Faral (*Recherches sur les sources latines des contes et romans courtois du moyen âge* [Paris, 1913]) that the Latin rhetoricians' models were determinant in shaping romance description. Although Colby demonstrates how the romance poets could work independently of the prescriptions of the rhetorical models, she nonetheless concedes that they worked within the Latin framework.

46. In addition to the general studies of Camille Enlart, *Le costume* in the *Manuel d'archéologie française depuis les temps Mérovingiens jusqu'à la Renaissance* (Paris, 1916), 3:23–69, and François Boucher, *20,000 Years of Fashion: The History of Costume and Personal Adornment* (New York, 1967), 164–89, the study of Eunice Rathbone Goddard, *Women's Costume in French Texts of the Eleventh and Twelfth Centuries*, The Johns Hopkins Studies in Romance Literatures and Languages 7 (Baltimore and Paris, 1927) is of particular value. See also Michel Pastoureau, *La vie quotidienne en France et en Angleterre au temps des chevaliers de la table ronde* (Paris, 1976), 89–100.

47. On the *pliçon* and the *emigaut* (opening) see Goddard, *Women's Costume*, 187–93 and 111–12.

48. For an interpretation of this passage from the standpoint of couture see Goddard, *Women's Costume*, 158–59.

49. Colby, *The Portrait*, 112–21.

50. Equally conventional is the description of the seneschal's wife's beauty in *Equitan*, vv.31–37.

51. See the discussion of Colby, *The Portrait*, 144–58, and her conclusion on Chrétien's originality (180).

52. See the well-known statement in *Galeran de Bretagne*, ed. Lucien Foulet, Classiques français du moyen âge (Paris, 1975), vv.1306–8: Soubz la pelice ou la chemise, / Que courtoisie me deffent / Que je ne nomme appertement. In Colby's exhaustive survey of twelfth-century romance, she has found only one mention of the pudenda (*cunet* in Hue de Roteland). *The Portrait*, 62.

53. Gottfried phrases the crucial formula: "Lay in my arms or beside me" (vv.15, 710–11).

54. For the wearing of the *ceinture* see Enlart, *Le costume*, 36, Boucher, *20,000 Years*, 171, and Goddard, *Women's Costume* 65.

55. On the breasts in romance see Colby, *The Portrait*, 59–60, 156–57. For the necklace see Arnoul d' Orléans, *Lidia*, vv.449–50. This necklace was incorporated into Geoffroi de Vinsauf's canon on dress. *Poetria nova*, v.604.

56. As Marc spies on the sleeping lovers in the cave, his attention is drawn to her throat, breasts, arms, and hands. Gottfried (vv.17, 600–603).

57. Enlart, *Le costume*, 32–36. Boucher, *20,000 Years*, 171, 179.

58. On Lïenor's *cote* see Goddard, *Women's Costume*, 105.

59. The term "male gaze" appears to have surfaced first in film criticism. See Laura Mulvey, "Visual Pleasure and Narrative Cinema," *Screen* (1975), reprinted in Laura Mulvey, *Visual and Other Pleasures* (Bloomington, 1989), 14–26.

60. *Remedia*, vv.343–44. For an example of this quotation in another context, see Chanter, *Verbum abbreviatum*, 26.

61. Geoffroi de Vinsauf, *Poetria nova*, vv.600–621.

62. Erec's coronation *mantel* is adorned with gems and gold and embroidered by four fairies with designs of the seven liberal arts from Macrobius (*Erec*, vv.6671–6747). Lïenor's coronation gown was lined with silks and furs. Similar to Erec's mantel, it was embroidered with the story of the burning of Troy and took seven to eight years to complete (*Roman*, vv.5324–61).

63. Exceditur hodie in vestis materia, in tinctura, in forma, in composicione, in diversificacione, in materie mutacione. Quia hodie erubesceret etiam servus tegere nuditatem suam illa veste quam primis omnium inventium parentibus in paradiso preparavit et post lapsum eis compatiens dedit. Nempe illis ad tegendam erubescibilem nuditatem et turpitudinem suam dominus tunicas fecit pelliceas unde in Genesi [3:21]. . . . Si fuerint consuti vel forsipe cese vel arte pelliparii parate non querens a me quia nescio. Credo tamen eas rudes fuisse. Ecce rudis et simplex materia vestis a qua per humanum vel potius vanum curiositatem ventum est non solum ad corium animalium vel animantium, ad lanum ovium, ad linum vel canabrum agrorum. Que quidam tolerabilia essent si in naturali colore [*ms:* calore] subsisterent quia omnia illa profert nobis tellus et naturalia sunt, sed nec hic subsistere volumus imo processum est usque ad plumas avium ut moveat cornicula risum, ad stercora vermium quorum delicias pannus bobianus urit usque etiam ad aurifrigium nendo filum ex auro. Nec ultra possunt nisi ad telas aranearum procedere velit hominis inconstantia. Attende etiam quantus excelsus sit in colorum varietate. Naturalem enim colorem corrumpit vanitas hominum nunc pervertendo in rubeum, nunc in subrubeum, nunc in viridem, nunc in croceum, nunc in violaceum, nunc in quemlibet alium mixtum et confusum ut tria solo colore vestium perstringentur oculi intuentium et in admirationem rapiantur cum natura singulis rebus et maxime floribus innatum adeoque pulcrum colorem dederit quali non poterat operari Salomon in omni gloria sua (Mat. 6:29) . . . Chanter, *Verbum abbreviatum*, fol. 111ra–rb. See also the short version in PL, 205:251.

64. *Contra formam vestium*. Suggillavimus superfluitatem et luxum vestium, quo ad materiam et colorem. Suggillandus est luxus earum, quo ad formam. Formam

attendimus in duobus: in colorum diversificacione et in modo composicionis. In colorum diversificacione ut in veste bipertita, tripertita, quadripertita, vel multipertita; bicolore vel multicolore quod ad diversorum variata pictacia. In modo composicionis, ut in modo cedendi, scindendi, consuendi, eligandi, fraccillandi, caudandi. Cuius in composicio in composicionem mentalem innuit. Cum enim natura hominem a bruto insigni et honesto caractere distinxerit, quod natura homini negavit, scilicet caudam, ipse per artificium illud in veste caudata. . . . Unde Tornacensis episcopus in sermone suo: non decet, inquit, matronas christianas vestes habere subtalares et post se trahentes quibus verrant sordes pavimenti et viarum. Chanter, *Verbum abbreviatum* Ste.-Gen. 137rb, va. Vat. fols. 111vb–112ra. Short version, PL, 205:252. See also *Summa*, 2:239–43.

65. Ovid, *Amores* III, 2, vv.25–28, repeated in *Ars amatoria* I, vv.153–56, and by the vernacular *L'art*, 88.

66. In the eleventh century the criticism was directed against male fashion. H. Platelle, "Le problème du scandale: Les nouvelles modes masculines aux XIᵉ et XIIᵉ siècles," *Revue belge de philologie et d'histoire* 53 (1975), 1071–78. Goddard, *Women's Costume*, 98–99, 215. Boucher, *20,000 Years*, 171.

67. *De ornatu mulierum*. . . . forte possimus dicere quod sufficit uxori facere tantum ne displiceat et aliquid medium inter placere et displacere, sed difficile est illud observare. . . . Chanter, *Summa de sacramentis*, Paris BN lat. 3477, fol. 48vb.

68. Jacques de Vitry, *VMO*, 550, 555. *Estamine* in Old French could mean either a light wool cloth or a sieve.

69. Guillaume de Blois, *Alda*, vv.467–514.

70. In *Barat* (vv.84–87) the peasant Haimet, who was up a tree without his shorts, exposes his balls and prick.

71. The exaggeration of the penis became a topos. In *Prestre et le chevalier* (p.82) it is longer than a knife. On human genitals see the summaries of Nykrog, *Fabliaux*, 211–12, Muscatine, *Old French Fabliaux*, 112–15, and the study of Sarah Melhado White, "Sexual Language and Human Conflict in Old French Fabliaux," *Comparative Studies in Society and History* 24 (1984), 185–210. She calculates that 13% of the fabliaux evoke the genitals in a literal way (191).

72. Andreas Capellanus, *De amore* I, 6, p.200.

73. See the observation of White, "Sexual Language," 194, 204.

74. *Damoiselle qui ne pooit oïr (I)*, vv.49–96, *(II)* vv.128–87, *(III)* vv.143–94.

75. Cf. the Latin version: vulva trahit corda plus quam fortissima chorda. *Proverbia sententiaeque latinitatis medii aevi*, ed. Hans Walter, Carmina medii aevi posterioris latina 2 (Göttingen, 1967), 5:no.34265. For the French version: *Proverbes français antérieurs au XVᵉ siècle*, ed. Joseph Morawski, Classiques français du moyen âge (Paris, 1924), no. 1654. That *cul* could be interchangeable with *con* in Latin, see J. F. Adams, *The Latin Sexual Vocabulary* (Baltimore, 1982), 96, 116–17.

76. *Lai du lecheor*, ed. Gaston Paris, *Romania* 8 (1879), 65–66; trans. Paul Brians, *Bawdy Tales from the Courts of Medieval France* (New York, 1972), 124–26.

Chapter Four

1. Aristotle, for example, asserted that desire is always an appetite for an agreeable thing, thus creating a necessary circularity. See Michel Foucault, *History of*

Sexuality 2: The Use of Pleasure (New York, 1985), 42–43. A preparatory sketch for this chapter may be found in John W. Baldwin, "Five Discourses on Desire: Sexuality and Gender In Northern France around 1200," *Speculum* 66 (1991), 797–819.

2. See above pp.3–4.

3. Zeimentz, *Ehe,* is the fullest treatment of the twelfth-century theologians through Pierre the Lombard.

4. Lombard, *Sententiarum,* 2.20.1, (PL, 192:692; Q. I, 427–28). For fuller discussion see above p.88 and below p.174.

5. Lombard, *Sententiarum,* 2.22; 2.30.2, 5, 8 (PL, 192:697, 720–22; Q. I, 439–40, 496–500).

6. Augustine, *De Genesi ad litteram* XI, 31–32; *De nuptiis et concupiscientia* I, 6; II, 3, 5, 7, 30–31. Haec autem sibi non solum totum corpus nec solum extrinsecus, verum etiam intrinsecus vindicat totumque commovet hominem, animi simul affectu cum carnis appetitu coniuncto atque permixto, ut ea voluptas sequatur, qua maior in corporis voluptatibus nulla est; ita ut momento ipso temporis, quo ad eius pervenitur extremum, paene omnis acies et quasi vigilia cogitationis obruatur. . . . sed aliquando inportunus est ille motus poscente nullo, aliquando autem destituit inhiantem, et cum in animo concupiscentia ferveat, friget in corpore; atque ita mirum in modum non solum generandi voluntati, verum etiam lasciviendi libidini libido non seruit, et cum tota plerumque menti cohibenti adversetur nonnumquam et adversus se ipsa dividitur commotoque animo in commovendo corpore se ipsa non sequitur. *De civitate dei* XIV, 16.

7. Augustine, *De Genesi ad litteram* XI, 32; *De nuptiis et concupiscentia* I, 22; II, 5, 30; *De civitate dei* XIV, 17, 18; on modest speech: XIV, 23, 26. On the Chanter's recapitulation see above p.88.

8. Chanter to: *aperti sunt oculi amborum* (Gen. 3:7). For the text, see p.291–92n.3.To: *omnis qui viderit* (Matt. 5:27) *non ait qui concupierit (Glossa ordin.)* primo motu qui non est in nostra postestate *sed qui viderit ad concupiscendum eam,* id est, hoc fine et animi proposito *attenderit,* id est, eo intuitu in causa visum direxerit ut eam concupiscat *quod iam non est titillari* moveri, scilicet, primo motu, *sed plene consentire libidini ut si facultas sit (Glossa ordin.)* et loci et temporis oportunitas perficiatur quod intendebat. Titillacio enim anime pro passio dicitur que et si culpam habent, non tantum crimen quia pro isto primo motu non dampnatur. Ex hac glosa manifestum huius argumenti quia primus motus culpa est sed venialis, et est pro passio subitus motus sine deliberatione boni vel mali operis. . . . Paris BN lat. 15585, fol. 48vb.

9. For the less frequent terms: . . . *desideria, quae sunt actuales* Lombard, *Sententiarum,* 2.30.8, (PL, 192:722; Q.1:500); *titillatio* 2.21.6 (PL, 192:696; Q.1:437); *voluptas,* 4.31.5 (PL, 192:920; Q.2:447); *delectatione carnali,* 4.33.1 (PL, 192:925; Q.2:459). For the vocabulary of the preceding theologians of the twelfth century see Zeimentz, *Ehe,* 71.

10. Lombard, *Sententiarum,* 2.30, 31 (PL, 192:720–26; Q.2:442); 4.1.9 (PL, 192:841, Q.2:238). For a full discussion of the early theologians see Odon Lottin, *Pyschologie et morale aux XIIe et XIIIe siècles* (Louvain, 1954), 4(1):11–76.

11. For the theologians of the second half of the century see Lottin, *Pyschologie et*

morale 4(1):88–106. Lottin remarks that he has found no discussions from the Chanter or Courson, 4:89n.1.

12. Augustine, *De bono conjugali,* 24(29). Lombard, *Sententiarum,* 4.31.1 (PL, 192:918; Q.2:442) on the goods of marriage; 4.2.1 (PL 192:842, Q.2:240).

13. Lombard, *Sententiarum,* 4.30.3 (PL, 192:918, Q.2:441); 4.31.5 (PL, 192:920, Q.2:446); 4.32.1 (PL, 192:922, Q.2:452).

14. Lombard, *Sententiarum,* 4.31.5, (PL, 192:920, Q.2:447). Jerome, *Adversus Jovianum* II, 49, PL, 23:281; *In Eph. 5:25,* PL, 26:532. *The Sentences of Sextus: A Contribution to the History of Early Christian Ethics,* ed. H. Chadwick (Cambridge, 1959), 39; trans. Richard A. Edwards and Robert A. Wild, Texts and Translations 22, Early Christian Literature Series 5 (Chico, Calif., 1981), no. 231. See Zeimentz, *Ehe,* 230. The Sextus dictum was also known to Gratian, *Decretum* C.32, 4, 5.

15. Lombard, *Sententiarum,* 4.31.8 (PL, 192:921, Q.2:450). For the theological preparation for this discussion, see Zeimentz, *Ehe,* 83–85.

16. Augustine, *De bono conjugali,* 16. Lombard, *Sententiarum,* 4.32.2 (PL, 192:925, Q.2:459).

17. The fullest collection and discussion of Huguccio's many and complex texts remains Müller, *Paradiesesehe,* 110–17, summarized by Brundage, *Law, Sex,* 281–82. See also Henry Ansgar Kelly, *Love and Marriage in the Age of Chaucer* (Ithaca, 1975), 248–54. The complexity of the canonist's position deserves further treatment. Typical of many passages defining desire is: to *voluptas:* D.5, c.2: id est, delectatio que habitur in coitu *est in culpa,* id est, culpa et peccatum. Numquam coitus coniugalis potest exerceri sine peccato saltem cum veniali quia ad minus est ibi fervor quidam, purritus quidam, voluptas in ipso opere que est peccatum veniale ut C.33, q.4, c.7. Huguccio *Summa decretorum,* Paris BN lat. 15936, fol. 6va.

In addition to the excerpts transcribed in Müller the two following glosses best encapsulate the range of his argumentation: to *voluptas:* C.33, q.4, c.7: que est in coitu *nullatenus potest esse sine culpa,* id est, non potest esse quin ipsa fit culpa et peccatum et hinc expresse colligitur quod opus coniugale non potest exerceri sine peccato licet ipsum quandoque non sit peccatum quia semper est vel quidam pruritus carnis et quedam voluptas in emissione spermatis que semper est peccatum, licet venialissimum, ut hic dicitur et D.5, c.1, et ideo est quod christus noluit nasci de coitu quia sine peccato exerceri non potest etiam si sanctus sit qui coeat ut C.27, q.2, c.10, et C.32, q.2, c.4, sed secundum hoc videtur quod quis ex necessitate teneatur peccare cum ex necessitate teneatur debitum reddere, sed dico quod non tenetur ad peccandum licet teneatur ad id expleri non potest sine peccato, sicut iste tenetur ire ad sanctum iacobum non tamen potest hoc explere quin peccet quandoque. Similiter iste tenetur diligere deum ex caritate, nec hoc potest facere sine caritate et modo non tenetur operari caritatem vel etiam habere secundum quos-dam. Item iste tenetur cantare missam; [presbyter plebanus] hoc non potest facere sine lingua; non tamen tenetur habere linguam sed quid hoc ex necessitate videtur homo peccare in primis motibus quia non sunt in nostra potestate et sepe oriuntur in nobis nolentibus, unde apostolus: ago quod nolo et tamen imputantur quia peccata sunt. Huguccio, *Summa decretorum,* Paris BN lat. 15397, fol. 195vb (cf. Rom.

7:15–24). See the summary in Johannes Teutonicus, *Glossa ordinaria,* to C.33, q.4, c.7, Gratian, *Decretum* (Venice, 1572), 1199b–1200a.

To *sed alia plura sunt* . . . C.32, q.2, c.4: . . . [after discussing the divine commandment to increase and multiply] Hec solutio plane potest dici quod deus multa precipit et facit que non sunt nec esse possunt sine peccato; nonne facit animas que numquam possunt esse sine peccato in hac vita ut de cons. D.4, c.9. Precipit etiam filios et uxores diligamus et ut curam eorum agamus, et unde vix sine peccato hoc fiunt ut D.25, c.4, et de poen D.5, c.6, et [de poen] D.7, c.6. Item hoc capitulum et multa alia expresse contradicunt manducatori et petro lombardo qui dicunt quod coitus causa prolis vel causa reddendi debitum potest expleri sine peccato et dicunt quod heretici hoc dicebant scilicet quod concubitus non potest fieri sine peccato quod tamen ego credo esse catholicum sed credo quod heretici intelligebant sine peccato mortali. Huguccio, *Summa decretorum,* Paris BN lat. 15397, fol. 84rb. Johannes Teutonicus *Glossa ordinaria* to *presentia:* C.32, q.2, c.4, sided with Pierre Manducator against Huguccio.

For other texts see below pp.300–301n.23, 315n.50.

18. See its formulation in Lombard, *Sententiarum,* 4.31.8, (PL, 192:922, Q.2:450). On its popularity see Zeimentz, *Ehe,* 76–77.

19. For the text see Appendix 1. See also the discussion of Müller, *Paradiesesehe,* 152–58. For fragments of the Chanter's contribution to Courson's *questio,* see *Summa,* 2:385, 3(2b):542–43.

20. Attending church for amorous assignations was a contemporary topos. See *L'art,* 76.

21. Müller, *Paradiesesehe,* 153–54. Chobham, *Summa confessorum,* 334. The canonists Laurentius Hispanus and Johannes Teutonicus took a position comparable to the Chanter's school. Kelly, *Love and Marriage,* 248–54.

22. [Concubitus est:] Item. carnalis, quando vir abstinere non potest, quod esset mortale peccatum, nisi per bona coniugii excusaretur, sed est veniale. Item concubitus duplex est impetuosus, cum fit in loco sacro vel cum menstrua patitur mulier et tunc est mortale [peccatum]. Item. conjugalis, cum fit tantum causa procreande sobilis, et tunc est meritorius, et iste semper bonus, alii semper mali, unde omnis concubitus preter legitimum cohoperatur gehennam, unde apostolus: fornicatores et adulteros iudicabit deus (Heb. 13:4). Chanter, *Summa Abel,* Paris BN lat. 455, fol. 63va.

To 1 Cor. 7:4: Cohitus maritalis fit quandoque sine peccato cum exigitur debitum ab eo a quo exigitur vel cum causa procreande prolis ad cultum dei, forte tamen adheret hic macula venialis quamvis totalis cohitus non sit peccatum, quoddam tamen peccatum veniale; quandoque [est veniale, quando] fit causa vitande fornicationis; quandoque est criminale quando fit causa explende voluptatis inmoderate, unde vehemens amator proprie uxoris adulter est. Chanter, Paris Mazar. 176, fol. 180rb. Müller, *Paradiesesehe,* 148–49nn.68, 69. In a fragmentary sketch the Chanter had considered Huguccio's proposition that returning the marital debt was venial sin. *Summa,* 2:156.

23. For Courson, see Appendix 1. To *quod enim,* C.32, q.2, d.p.c.2: . . . Notandum quod vir commiscetur uxori iiii de causis scilicet causa prolis, causa reddendi debitum, causa incontinencie, causa exsaturande libidinis vel explende voluptatis.

Cum causa prolis tunc ipse coitus nullum peccatum est veniale vel mortale, immo si ficiat ex caritate meritorius est vite eterne ut D.13, c.2, et D.25, d.p.c.3. Idem ex toto cum causa reddendi debitum ei commiscetur ut C.33, q.5, c.1. Item causa incontinentie tunc ipse coitus veniale peccatum est et venialiter vir peccat ut hic et in proximo sequenti capitulo et C.27, q.2, c.10, et C.33, q.4, c.7. Causa explende libidinis sive voluptatis tunc ipse coitus mortale peccatum est et mortaliter vir peccat ut C.32, q.4, c.5, licet minus propter bonum coniugii punitur scilicet ad modum veniale ut C.32, q.7, c.11. Huguccio, *Summa decretorum,* Paris BN lat. 15397, fol. 84ra.

24. Chobham, *Summa confessorum,* 333–39.

25. Huguccio agreed that it belonged to the category of mortal sin. Because of the *bonum* of marriage, however, its punishment should be reduced to the level of venial sin.

26. To *Qui autem fornicatur peccat in corpus suum* (1 Cor. 6:18): id est, isto libidinis ardore, quo nullus maior est, sic homo totus absorbetur, ut nihil aliud possit agere nec animus aliud cogitare, sed totus homo caro fit, ut secundum hoc animus et caro possint dici duo in carne una, quia voluptas corporis animum tenet servum et efficit captivum et quasi transire cogat in corpus. Chanter, Paris, Mazar. 176, fol. 180ra. See the discussion of Müller, *Paradiesesehe,* 147–52.

27. Chobham, *Summa confessorum,* 335–36. See also *Summa de arte praedicandi,* 255, and the *Summa de commendatione virtutum* in ibid., xix.

28. See the appraisal of Müller, *Paradiesesehe,* 158–59.

29. To 1 Cor. 7:5: In naturalem usum ubi vel nulla est culpa vel venialis, nisi immoderata intervenerit libidinis voluptas. Chanter, Paris, Mazar. 176, fol. 180rb. For canonist discussion of the four causes, see Kelly, *Love and Marriage,* 254–60. The canonists Laurentius Hispanus and Johannes Teutonicus approximated the interpretation of *vehemens amator* in the Chanter's circle.

30. *Prose Salernitan Questions,* 9. Caelius Aurelianus, 15. Constantinus, *De coitu,* 80. Despite the English title of her book *Porneia: On Desire and the Body in Antiquity,* Aline Rousselle in fact demonstrates that ancient physicians took little interest in *porneia* (the desire of another's body), 15. At most it was a pathology (63–77) and of greater interest to Christian ascetical writers (141–59).

31. *Prose Salernitan Questions,* 10.

32. Ibid., 169, 220.

33. See below pp.175–76.

34. *Prose Salernitan Questions,* 10–11, 160, 169, 21. Master Johannes Ieiunus has not been identified. See also Galen's physiological explanations of delight, *On the Usefulness of the Parts of the Body,* trans. Margaret Tallmadge May (Ithaca, 1968), 2:640–41.

35. *Prose Salernitan Questions,* 10–11, 161. On the ancient Greeks see Foucault, *The History of Sexuality: 2* 40–4. Jacquart and Thomasset (*Sexuality and Medicine,* 82–85) stress the novelty of the psychological dimension in the medieval analysis.

36. *Prose Salernitan Questions,* 11, 20–21, 12.

37. Muscio, 57, and Caelius Aurelianus, 75, based on Soranus, *Gynecology,* 148. Muscio, 109, which is missing in Soranus and Caelius. The gynecological treatise *Cum auctor* merely prescribed herbal remedies without inquiring into the causes:

[De pruritu uulue] Quandoque sentitur pruritus in uulua. Tunc accipe crocum, camphoram, litargium, baccas lauri, et albumen oui, et fiat clistere uel pessarum. Diascorides dicit quod puluis fenugrecum per se cum sanguine anseris iniecus ualet contra duriciem matricis [41].

38. *Prose Salernitan Questions,* 275–76. The most recent and authoritative discussion of *amor heroicus* is Wack, *Lovesickness,* which includes new editions and translations of the texts of Constantinus Africanus (188–93) and Gérard de Bourges (199–205). See also her extensive discussion of the two physicians (31–73). Wack dates Gérard's commentary to 1180–1200 on inferential grounds. It was certainly completed by 1236 when it was known to Hugues de Saint-Cher (52–53). The use of Avicenna's *Canon,* however, may suggest the third decade of the thirteenth century, when the latter work entered the Parisian scene. See pp.13–14. If Gérard's work is earlier, it then represents a precocious use of Avicenna's medical treatise (54).

Another enigmatic figure, Giles of Portugal, perhaps identified with Giles of Santarem, a physician and Dominican friar, who taught in Paris in the first two decades of the thirteenth century, devoted a *questio* to specific aspects, namely, to situating the malady in the brain (1–16) and to evaluating the effects of wine (17–38). See Wack, 206–11 (text and translation) and 76–82 (discussion).

39. Avicenna, *Liber de anima seu sextus de naturalibus I–III,* I, 5, ed. S. Van Riet, Avicenna Latinus (Louvain, 1972), 1:87–101. On the medical tradition of the psychological faculties as found in Avicenna see Murray Wright Bundy, *The Theory of Imagination in Classical and Mediaeval Thought* in *University of Illinois Studies in Language and Literature* 12 (2–3) (Urbana, 1927), 182–85; E. Ruth Harvey, *The Inward Wits: Psychological Theory in the Middle Ages and the Renaissance,* Warburg Institute Surveys 6 (London, 1975), 35–47; Anne-Marie Bautier, "*Phantasia-Imaginatio:* De l'image à l'imaginaire dans les textes du haut moyen âge," in *Phantasia-Imaginatio* (Rome, 1986), 81–104.

40. *Prose Salernitan Questions,* 275–76.

41. On Alain and Gérard see Wack, *Lovesickness,* 56–59.

42. Ibid., 66.

43. Chobham, *Summa confessorum,* 389–90. See also the version in *Summa de arte praedicandi* (304) and another case of a cleric afflicted by *insano amore* (52). In diagnosing nocturnal illusions (wet dreams) Chobham (330) also applied medical theory. They can be caused by a superfluity of humors the body seeks to discharge. Physicians claim that this kind is caused more by sickness than by lust. For penance enjoined for nocturnal emissions see the Synod of Angers (1217–19), *Statuts synodaux français,* 1:208.

44. Guillaume de Conches, *Dragmaticon,* 238–39. Guillaume's most extensive discussion occurs in his *Glossae super Macrobium,* Copenhagen Kgl Bibl. MS G.Kgl.S. 1910, fol. 40r-v, edited in Helen Rodnite Lemay, "William of Saliceto on Human Sexuality," *Viator* 12 (1981), 172n.46. (Guillaume refers to Ovid's story of Tiresias. See p.143. *Prose Salernitan Questions,* 4. *Anatomia magistri Nicolai,* 59. Jacquart and Thomasset, *Sexuality and Medicine,* 81.

45. Viellard, *Gilles de Corbeil,* 346–47, trans. 59–60.

46. Guillaume de Conches, *Dragmaticon*, 240. *Prose Salernitan Questions*, 6. See above, p.79 and pp.216–17 for the infertility of the prostitute's womb.

47. Guillaume de Conches, *De philosophia mundi*, 89; *Dragmaticon*, 241–42. *Prose Salernitan Questions*, 6–7.

48. *Prose Salernitan Questions*, 186–87.

49. Ibid., 22. *Anatomia magistri Nicolai*, 59. Constantinus, *De genecia*, 315.

50. Guillaume de Conches, *Dragmaticon*, 245. *Prose Salernitan Questions*, 13–14, 186, 220. *L'art* 117.

51. David de Dinant, *Quaternuli*, 23, 31. Aristotle's original treatment of male and female desire is not as categorical as this version. Thomas Laqueur, *Making Sex: Body and Gender from the Greeks to Freud* (Cambridge, Mass., 1990), 47–49.

52. On the lack of female desire: Nam si ad inpedimentum serendae prolis esset libido detrahenda, viris esset detrahenda, non feminis. Femina enim posset voluntate concumbere etiam desistente libidine qua stimularetur, si viro non deesset qua excitaretur. Augustine, *De nuptiis et concupiscentia* II, 15.

53. . . . nec Veneris gaudia nosse potes. Ovid, *Amores* II, 3, v.2; . . . quo nunc mea gaudia defers? *Amores* II, 5, v.29; . . . quid mutua differs / gaudia *Amores* III, 6, vv.87–88; at quae non tacita formaui gaudia mente *Amores* III, 7, v.63; . . . et quaedam gaudia noctis habe *Ars amatoria* II, v.308; . . . Veneris da gaudia flenti *Ars* II, v.459; arte Venus nulla dulce peregrit opus. / ales habet, quod amet; cum quo sua gaudia iungat, *Ars* II, vv.480–481; gaudia post Veneris quae poscet munus amantem, *Ars* III, v.805; Even when the woman is incapable of pleasure, she should dissemble her joy: tu quoque, cui Veneris sensum natura negauit, / dulcia mendaci gaudia finge sono. *Ars* III, vv.797–98.

54. . . . in corde sagittae, / et possessa ferus pectora uersat Amor. . . . accendimus ignem? . . . crescere flammas. Ovid, *Amores* I, 2, vv.7–11.

55. quod licet, ingratum est; quod non licet, acrius urit: Ovid, *Amores* II, 19, v.3; uror, et in uacuo pectore regnat Amor. I, 1, v.26.

56. Ovid, *Ars amatoria* I, vv.9–10; . . . ualidoque perurimur aestu, III, v.543; I, vv.734–36, 729.

57. Andreas Capellanus, *De amore* I, 6, pp.148–50.

58. Ibid., I, 6, p.146. Among the judgments of love, the countess Ermengard also excluded martial affection from the definition of love. II, 7, p.258. [matrimonium] non enim coitus facit, sed maritalis affectio. *Digesta*, 24.1.32.13. For contemporary canonists see John T. Noonan, "Marital Affection in the Canonists" (Collectanea Stephan Kuttner) *Studia Gratiana* 12 (1967), 2:477–509. Apparently the problem of proving marital affection in law restrained canonists from using this concept as a necessary requirement for establishing marriage. Michael M. Sheehan suggests ("*Maritalis Affectio* Revisited," in *The Olde Daunce: Love, Friendship, Sex and Marriage in the Medieval World*, ed. Robert R. Edwards and Stephen Spector [Albany, N.Y., 1991], 32–43) that the concept deserves further study.

59. Andreas Capellanus, *De amore* I, 1, 6, pp.34, 146, 182.

60. Ibid., III, pp.286, 294–98.

61. His definition of sleep, for example, in ibid., III, p.305, can be found in Guillaume de Conches, *Dragmaticon*, 264, and *Salernitan Questions*, 186. André at-

tributed it to a certain Johannitius. See Mary C. Wack, "Imagination, Medicine and Rhetoric in Andreas Capellanus' 'De Amore,'" in *Magister Regis: Studies in honor of Robert Earl Kaske,* ed. Arthur Groos (New York, 1986), 104–5.

62. Andreas Capellanus, *De amore* I, 6, 5, pp.64, 40. See also I, 6, 10, pp.108, 220.

63. Ibid., I, 6; III, pp.180, 202, 322. This term was also appropriate for love of the lower parts. I, 6, p.203. For samples of other uses of *delectatio* and *voluptas,* see I, 6, pp.148, 182; I, 7, p.210; I, 10, p.220; II, 8, p.284; III, pp.294, 302.

64. Ibid., I, 10; II, 8, pp.220, 284. It may also have been implied in the fleshly temptation to sin among clerics (ut carnis ab eis stimulum et peccati fomitem removeret . . .). Ibid., I, 6, p.182.

65. . . . si quis in igne positus non uratur. Ibid., I, 6, p.180. . . . qui in igne positus nescit ardere. Lombard, *Sententiarum,* 4.31.8, PL, 192:922, Q.2:451). A similar phrase is in *De amore* III, p.302. For the ubiquitous metaphor of fire and its linkage with the eyes see the examples in Latin comedy: . . . Nam quociens oculos domine vultusque videbam / Igne calescebam corpora nostra grato / . . . . Neque spectare diucius illam / Nec tamen aspicere candida membra nimis. / Quanto magis specto, tanto magis igne calesco, / Res eadem nobis et nocet atque iuuat. *De tribus puellis,* vv.195–96, 265–68.

66. Andreas Capellanus, *De amore* I, 6; III, pp.172, 286.

67. Ovid, *Ars amatoria* II, vv.519–20.

68. Andreas Capellanus, *De amore* I, 1, 3, 1, pp.32, 36, 34. These elements reappear in I, 5, 6; II, 2, pp.40, 206, 228.

69. Ibid., I, 5; II, 2, pp.40, 228.

70. Ibid., I, 6, pp.96–98, 60. See the discussion of Wack, "Imagination," 111–12.

71. *L'art* 91, 224. Cf. Chrétien *Cligès,* vv.725–28 and below p.148. For orgasm see below p.196.

72. Andreas Capellanus, *De amore* I, 1, p.34. See also a parallel example provided by the medical authority Urso of Calabria in Wack, "Imagination," 106n.22.

73. Andreas Capellanus, *De amore* I, 6, pp.180, 204.

74. Ibid., II, 8, pp.282–84.

75. *Prose Salernitan Questions,* 220. See above pp.131–3.

76. For examples of *imaginatio* linked with *cogitatio* see Andreas Capellanus, *De amore* I, 1, 6; II, 8, pp.34, 206, 284. For discussions of André and medical theory see Wack, "Imagination," 101–15. Karnein, *De Amore,* 63–68. Schnell, *Andreas Capellanus,* 159–64.

77. Andreas Capellanus, *De amore* I, 1, 5, 6, pp.32, 34, 40, 206.

78. Ibid., I, 6, pp.146, 148. See also II, 7, p.250.

79. Ibid., I, 6, pp.148, 150.

80. Ibid., III, pp.304–6. For the theological discussion see above pp.120, 125–27.

81. *Prose Salernitan Questions,* 11. See above pp.128–29.

82. Constantinus, *Viaticum,* 2–3 in Wack, *Lovesickness,* 188. *Prose Salernitan Questions,* 276.

83. Andreas Capellanus, *De amore* III; I, 6, pp.298, 133–209. Gérard de Bourges, *Glosses,* 31–34, 57–59, in Wack, *Lovesickness,* 200, 202. See Wack, "Imagination," 114.

84. Ovid, *Ars amatoria* I, v.735. Andreas Capellanus, *De amore* III, p.304. Con-

stantinus, *Viaticum*, 1, 22, in Wack, *Lovesickness*, 188. Gérard de Bourges, *Glosses*, 1, in Wack, *Lovesickness*, 198.

85. Andreas Capellanus, *De amore* I, 6, 4, pp.52, 38.

86. Ovid, *Ars amatoria* I, v.729. Andreas Capellanus, *De amore* I, 1; II, 5, pp.32, 236.

87. Andreas Capellanus, *De amore* III, pp.286–306.

88. Ibid., III, p.318.

89. *L'art*, 81, 149, 104–6.

90. Ovid, *Metamorphoses* III, vv.316–38, ed. F. J. Miller, Loeb Classical Library (Cambridge, Mass., 1984), 1:146–48. *L'art* 102–3. Laqueur, *Making Sex*, 102–3. Isidore of Seville had observed that the word *femina* was derived from "force of fire" in Greek etymology because women are more libidinous than men. *Etymologiarum sive originum* XI, ii, 24, ed. L. M. Lindsay (Oxford, 1911), 2: trans. William D. Sharpe, *Isidore of Seville: The Medical Writings*, Transactions of the American Philosophical Society, n.s. 54(2), (1964), 50.

91. Glynnis M. Cropp, *Vocabulaire courtois des troubadours de l'époque classique*, Publications romanes et français 135 (Geneva, 1975), 317–53, 280–93, 265–74. The massive and exhaustive treatment of the full linguistic spectrum of *joie-dolor* in the troubadour and trouvère lyrics is Georges Lavis, *L'expression de l'affectivité dans la poésie lyrique française du moyen âge (XIIe–XIIIe siècle): Etude sémantique et stylistique du réseau lexical joie-dolor*, Bibliothèque de la Faculté de Philosophie et Lettres de l'Université de Liège, 200 (Paris, 1972), 155–333. Lavis, however, does not treat the larger corpus of northern French romances. On desire see 62–89.

92. *aveir cure* is synonymous for *talent* (*Guigemar*, v.58, *Lanval*, v.270) as is *desir* (*Lanval*, v.130) and *voleir* (Lanval, v.266). For other examples of *talent*, see *Lanval*, vv.137, 168. See also Burgess, *Marie de France*, 145–46.

93. See the extensive analysis in Burgess, *Marie de France*, 170–78, and the inventory of vocabulary, 219n.25.

94. Cropp, *Vocabulaire courtois des troubadours*, 254–64. Philippe Ménard, "Le coeur dans les poésies de Bernard de Ventadour," in *Présence des troubadours*, ed. Pierre Bec, Annales de l'Institut d'études occitanes, 4th ser., V (Toulouse, 1970), 119–30.

95.
> Onques del bevraje ne bui,
> don Tristans fu anpoisonez,
> mes plus me fet amer que lui
> fins cuers et bone volantez.
> bien an doit estre miens li grez,
> qu'ains de rien esforciez n'an fui,
> fors de tant, que mes iauz an crui, . . .

Chrétien de Troyes, *D'amours qui m'a tolu a moi*, ed. Wendelin Foerster, *Kristian von Troyes, Wörterbuch zu seinen sämtlichen Werken*, Romanische Bibliothek 21 (Halle, 1914), 208*, vv.28–34. The lyrics cannot be dated but are usually assumed to be early works.

96. For a sustained analysis see Ruth H. Cline, "Heart and Eyes," *Romance Philology* 25 (1971), 263–67.

97. Throughout the entire courtship the only *delite*, *anvoise*, and *solace* enjoyed by

the lovers was that of Alexandre when he passed a night with a shirt into which Soredamor had woven her golden hair (vv. 1616–18).

98. *Deduit* is a conjecture for a missing line that follows *nuit* of the preceding line (v. 1749).

99. Ovid, *Metamorphoses* IV, vv. 55–166. *Piramus et Tisbé,* ed. C. de Boer (Paris, 1921), Classiques français du moyen âge.

100. The contributions of the *chansons* to the narrative have been examined by Marc René Jung, "L'empereur Conrad chanteur de poésie lyrique," *Romania* 101 (1980), 35–50; Emmanuèle Baumgartner, "Les citations lyriques dans le *Roman de la Rose* de Jean Renart," *Romance Philology* 35 (1981), 260–66; and Sylvia Huot, *From Song to Book: The Poetics of Writing in Old French Lyric and Lyrical Narrative Poetry* (Ithaca, 1987), 108–16.

101. Michel Zink, *Roman rose et rose rouge* (Paris, 1979), 100–109, noted the significance of Conrad's not seeing Lïenor and of her name. In Marie de France's *Lanval,* vv. 118–19, to which Jean Renart later alludes, the image of the spark is also love's occasion. Equitan, Gurun, and Milun all fall in love from hearsay. Burgess, *Marie de France,* 165.

102. Jean Renart's French version is closest to the Provençal versions in MSS. W and X, ed. Rupert T. Pickens, *The Songs of Jaufré Rudel* (Toronto, 1978), 206–13. For the interpretation of the *vida* and the MSS. A and B see Don A. Monson, "Jaufré Rudel et l'amour lointain: Les origines d'une légende," *Romania* 106 (1985), 36–44. For examples of different readings of the poem see the celebrated dispute between Grace Frank and Leo Spitzer: Grace Frank, "The Distant Love of Jaufré Rudel, *MLN* 57 (1942), 528–34; Leo Spitzer, "*L'amour lo[i]ntain de Jaufré Rudel et le sens de la poésie des troubadours,*" North Carolina University, Studies in the Romance Languages and Literatures 5 (Chapel Hill, 1944); and Grace Frank, "Jaufré Rudel, Casella and Spitzer," *MLN* 59 (1944), 526–31. See also the social interpretation by Erich Köhler, "*Amor de lonh,* oder: Der 'Prinz' ohne Burg," *Orbis mediaevalis: Mélanges de langue et de littérature médiévale offerts à Reto Radulfo Bezzola* (Bern, 1978), 219–34; and Pierre Bec, "Amour de lon' et 'dame jamais vue.' Pour une lecture plurielle de la chanson VI de Jaufré Rudel," in *Miscellanea di studi in onore di Aurelio Roncaglia: A cinquantanni della sua laurea* (Modena, 1989), 101–18.

103. Cf. *Chansons attribuées au Chastelain de Couci,* ed. Alain Lerond (Paris, 1964), 76. (Had the audience been familiar with the remaining stanzas of the poem, not reproduced by Jean Renart, they would have been averted to impending trouble.) Sylvia Huot, *From Song to Book,* 111–12.

104. Baumgartner ("Les Citations lyriques . . . , 263–65) suggests the hypothesis that Jean Renart intended the dance songs to represent Lïenor in contrast to the *grand chant cortois* for Conrad, but little support is offered from the text.

105. Compare Lerond, p. 148.

106. In the very first example, a woman sings:

> E non Deu, sire, se ne l'ai,
> l'amor de lui, mar l'acointai. (Vv. 291–92)

In God's name, lord, if I have not his love, I have met him unhappily.

Another complains:

> Vos ne sentez mie les maus d'amer
> si com ge faz! (Vv.518–19)

You do not feel the ills of love as I do.

107. Cf. the Provençal text in Carl Appel, ed., *Provenzalische Inedita aus Pariser Handschriften* (Leipzig, 1892), 87.

108. Huot, *From Song to Book,* 113–14. The *chansons de toile* have been reedited by Michel Zink, *Les chansons de toile* (Paris, 1977), 158–64. See also Zink's comments 4–12.

109. Cf. the text in Bernard de Ventadour, *Chansons d'amour,* ed. Moshé Lazar, Bibliothèque française et romane, Série B: Editions critiques de textes 4 (Paris, 1966), 180, and Carl Appel, ed., *Bernart von Ventadorn: Seine Lieder mit Einleitung und Glossar* (Halle, 1915), 249–55. Bernart de Ventadour's *chanson* is followed directly by one from Gautier de Soignes (*Lors que florist la bruiere,* vv.5232–52) which gives perhaps the strongest expression of the pains of love in Jean Renart's repertory.

110. See above pp.144ff.

111. Other comparable terms are *covoitise* and *desir. Dame qui aveine demandoit,* pp.319, 320.

112. Jean Bodel, *Sohaiz,* vv.62–70.

113. Item sicut in ecclesiastica le[genda] quendam adholescentem quem non movere tormenta moverint libidinis blandimenta. Cum enim non posset ad idolatriam inpertrahi, ligatis manibus cathenula aurea eoque posito in loco ameno floribus pleno missa est ad eum mulier pulcra facie ut per lubricum carnis caderet a religione et proposito suo. Quem ipsam agrediens et deosculans et palpans cum iam titillaret caro eius ipse sibi dentibus partem lingue propie abscidit et sanguinem in os meretricis expuit, sicque liberatus eam a se fugavit dolerem dolore retundens. . . . Chanter, *Unum ex quatuor,* Paris BN lat. 15585, fol. 49rb–va. Jerome, *Vita Pauli eremte,* PL 23:17–30. Chobham, *Summa,* 335.

114. Constantinus, *De coitu,* 160.

115. For numerous other examples: *Meunier,* p.91; *Borgoise,* v.111; *Vallet aux douze fames,* vv.54–56; *Segretain moine,* p.219; *Jouglet* v.136; *Saineresse,* vv.44–46. As in the romances, in those fabliaux that deal chiefly with the aristocracy, the only lovemaking to be mentioned is embraces and kisses: *Guillaume au faucon,* p.104; *Berengier,* v.266.

116. When the wife receives both husband and lover in bed simultaneously, foreplay is also omitted: *Prestre et la dame,* p.239; *Aloul,* vv.249–59.

117. Ovid, *Amores* I, 5.

118. Ibid., I, 4; II, 15; III, 7, 22.

119. Ibid., (thousand ways) III, 14, v.24; (embraces) III, 7, v.8; (thighs and feet) I, 4, vv.43–44, II, 7, v.10; (breasts) I, 4, vv.6, 37; II, 15, vv.11–12; (words) III, 7, vv.11–12; III, 14, v.25; (tongue) III, 7, v.9; II, 5, vv.23–24, 57; II, 14, v.23.

120. Ovid, *Ars amatoria* III, v.787.

121. Ibid., II, vv.703–20; III, vv.771–800.

122. Abelard, *Historia calamitatum* in *Letters,* 12:183–84.

123. The basic studies on the topos remain: Karl Helm, "Quinque lineae amoris," *Germanisch-Romanische Monatsschrift* 19 (1941), 236–47, and Lionel J. Friedman, "Gradus Amoris," *Romance Philology* 19 (1965), 167–77. Porphyrio, *Commentum in Horatium Flacum,* ed. Alfred Holder (Otting, 1894), 21. Donatus, in *Scholia Terentiana,* ed. Friedrich Schlee (Leipzig, 1893), 106. Latin school poetry, Dronke, *Medieval Latin,* 2:488. Mathieu de Vendôme, *Ars versificatoria* II, 13. Honorius Augustodunensis, *Expositio in Cantica canticorum,* PL, 172:351. Alain de Lille, *Summa de arte praedicatoris* 5, PL, 210:122. William de Montibus, *Distinctiones theologice,* in *William de Montibus (c. 1140–1213): The Schools and Literature of Pastoral Care,* ed. Joseph Goering, Pontifical Institute of Medieval Studies, Studies and Texts 108 (Toronto, 1992), 270. Robert of Flameborough (*Liber poenitentialis* 199) also reflects the formula in questions to be posed to men and women interogated about *luxuria:* Multos personas, et masculos et feminas, male aspexisti, concupisvisti, sollcitasti, tractasti, osculatus es. The Synod of Angers (1217–19) enumerated sight, touching, kissing with the tongue, and touching the breasts and vagina, *Statuts synodaux français,* 1:210.

124. Andreas Capellanus, *De amore* I, 6, p.56.

125. Ibid., I, 6, p.170, repeated in II, 6, p.244.

126. Ibid., I, 6, p.180. Don A. Monson ("*L'amour pur* d'André le Chapelain et la poésie des troubadours," in *Chrétien de Troyes and the Troubadours: Essays in Memory of the Late Leslie Topsfield,* ed. Peter S. Noble and Linda M. Paterson [Cambridge, 1984], 78–89) argues that André's *amor purus* is merely an elaborate "stratégie galante"—a sophistic ploy—for seducing the woman of the higher nobility. Since it is only a rhetorical device, it cannot be considered a current theory of erotic deportment. Monson nonetheless contends that André's *amor purus* arises from bases common to contemporary troubadour love. If we consider the *De amore* to be a loose compendium of erotic lore, the rhetorical designs would not necessarily negate the possibility of *amor purus* to be a viable amorous practice in the twelfth century.

127. Andreas Capellanus, *De amore* I, 6, p.202. On higher and lower love see pp.199–204.

128. Ibid., II, 6, p.240.

129. René Nelli, *L'érotique des troubadours* (Paris, 1974), 1:381–82 has devised an influential schema of four stages of progression of troubadour love: (1) aspirant (*fenhedor*), (2) suppliant (*precador*), (3) recognized suitor (*entendedor*), and (4) accepted lover (*drut*). See L. T. Topsfield, *Troubadours and Love* (Cambridge, 1975), 113. F. R. P. Akehurst, "Les étapes de l'amour chez Bernard de Ventadour," *Cahiers de civilisation médiévale* 16 (1973), 133–47, has attempted to apply this schema to Bernart. Although the four stages imply a progression like the *Quinque lineae,* their contents are not identical, as Nelli (1:389) has pointed out.

130. Bernart de Ventadorn, *Songs,* ed. and trans. Stephen G. Nichols, Jr., et al., University of North Carolina Studies in the Romance Languages and Literatures 39 (Chapel Hill, 1962).

131. Moshé Lazar, *Amour courtois et "fin'amors" dans la littérature du XIIᵉ siècle,* Bibliothèque française et romane, Série C: Etudes littéraires 8 (Paris, 1964),

118–34, has argued for the sensuality of the troubadours. See the reservations summarized in Cropp, *Vocabulaire courtois des troubadours,* 357–78. William D. Paden, Jr., "*Utrum copularentur:* of *Cors,*" *L'ésprit créateur* 19 (1979), 70–82, emphasizes the ambiguity and self-consciousness of troubadour language. At times, troubadours could be explicitly obscene. See Pierre Bec, *Burlesque et obscénité chez les troubadours: Le contre-texte au moyen âge* (Paris, 1984).

132. This literature has received two recent studies: E. Ann Matter, *The Voice of My Beloved: The Song of Songs in Western Medieval Christianity* (Philadelphia, 1990), and Ann W. Astell, *The Song of Songs in the Middle Ages* (Ithaca, 1990).

133. The commentary is unedited but may be found in the MSS: Paris BN lat. 15565, fol. 52rb–66vb, and Mazar. 178, fol. 41ra–50vb. A good text for the *Glossa ordinaria* is *Biblia latina cum glossa* (Strassburg, 1480), 2: fol. 127va–135va. The text of the preface furnished in PL, 113:1125–28, follows that of the 1480 edition closely.

134. Salomon iuxta numerum vocabulorum tres libros fecit. . . . Iuxta hoc vocabulum composuit parabolas scilicet libros proverbiorum in quo docet incipientes et parvulos. . . . vocatus est et ecclesiastes, id est concionator quo nomine censetur et secundum opus eius in quo construit graniunculos et proficientes. . . . Iuxta hoc nomen composuit cantica canticorum in quo libro docet maturos perfectos et pervenientes de solo amore et pace dei. . . . In proverbiis Sal[omon] fuit ethicus tractans de moribus; in ecclesiaste phisicus naturas rerum docens; in canticis canticorum theologus sermocinans de divinis figurabatur. . . . Chanter, BN 52rb–va, Mazar. fol. 41ra–rb. *Glossa ordinaria,* PL, 113:1125–27.

135. . . . scilicet apud hebreos hanc observantiam esse ne cuiquam hunc librum permitterent legere nisi viro perfecte scientie et fidei roborate ne forte per imbecillitatem infantie et fidei impericiam; non tamen erudiret cognitio lubricas mentes quam textus converteret ad concupiscentias carnales. Chanter, BN fol. 66vb, Mazar. 50vb. *Glossa ordinaria,* PL, 113:1127. Chanter, *Verbum abbreviatum,* PL, 205:32, 188. Baldwin, *Masters, Princes, and Merchants,* 1:94, 2:65n.37.

136. Tu igitur ut spiritualis audi spiritualiter verba amatoria cantari et disce motum anime tue et naturalis amoris incendium ad meliora transferre. Chanter, BN fol. 52vb, Mazar. 41rb. *Glossa ordinaria,* PL, 113:1128.

137. Ad hoc dicendum quod quadruplex est amor. Est enim amor divinus vel ethereus de dilectione dei et proximi, et hic in precepto consistens meritorius est. Est et alius diabolicus venereus libidinosus et huiusmodi et hic dampnabilis est. Est et alius carnalis quo quis carnem propriam vel parentes diligit qui si moderatus est et sub deo tolerabilis est. Si inmoderatus, execrebilis est. Qui amat parentes etc. (Matt. 10:37). Et alius mundialis qui moderatus licitus est; si inmoderatus et contra deum, et detestabilis et pernitiosus quia amicus mundi inimicus dei etc. (James 4:4). Chanter, BN 52vb, Mazar. 41va.

138. Materia sunt sponsus et sponsa, caput et membra, christus et ecclesia. Chanter, BN 52va, Mazar. 41rb. *Glossa ordinaria,* PL, 113:1127. Contrast Chanter (see above n.134) with *Glossa ordinaria,* PL, 113:1127. On the influence of Robert of Tombelaine on the *Glossa ordinaria* see Matter, *Voice of My Beloved,* 47nn.62, 107, 121n.79.

139. Chanter, to *osculetur* (1:1): Item nota quod os patris dicitur. . . . etiam

dicitur sacra scriptura. . . . Item os etiam dicitur predicator . . . BN 53ra, Mazar. 41vb. To *sicut labia* (4:3): predicatores qui quandoque dentes quandoque labia dicuntur. Dentes eo quod terant, id est, quod exponant scripturam sacram, labia eo quo attricta aliis aperiant et predicent. Dentes ergo proprie dicuntur exponitores, labia predicatores. BN 59rb, Mazar. 46va. To *collum* (4:4): predicatores. To *duo ubera* (4:5): predicatores lac parvuli in christo propinantes. BN fol. 59vb, Mazar. 46va–vb. To *sexaginta sunt regine* (6:7): predicatores, scilicet, qui se regunt et generant prolem et filios sponso ex amore eius. BN fol. 63rb, Mazar. 49ra. To *iunctura* (7:1): ita iunctura illa, id est, predicatores coniugentes per spiritualem intelligentiam ornant et munitant fideles. BN fol. 64rb, Mazar. 49va. To *duo ubera* (7:3): doctores rudium qui non sua predicant sed ex eloquiis utriusque testamenti summunt. BN fol. 64ra, Mazar. 49va. To *sugentem ubera matris mea* (8:1): interrogantem precipuos doctores qui erant ubera matri mee, id est, legis vel sinagoge illius carnali intelligentia nutritus fui. BN fol. 65va, Mazar. fol. 50ra.

140. In primo cantico incepit diligi tanquam pater instruans. In secundo desiderari per operum illius cognitionem. In tertio amplius et quasi possideri. Chanter, BN fol. 52va, Mazar. 41rb.

141. . . . requiescant inter brachia et amplexus sponsi unde canticum canticorum dicitur sua dignitate omnia alia excedens. Chanter, BN fol. 52rb, Mazar. fol. 41ra.

142. Modus agendi est ostendere quali desiderio membra capiti cohereant et ei placere contendant et . . . quali affectione sponsus ecclesiam diligat eam laudans . . . ammonens, et confortans . . . Chanter, BN 52va, Mazar. 41rb.

143. For summaries of Bernard of Clairvaux's exposition of the kiss, see Matter, *Voice of My Beloved,* 123–33, and Astell, *Song of Songs,* 89–96. For the Chanter's categories to *osculetur* (1:1): Nota quia est osculum lascive ut meretricis. . . . osculum perfidie. . . . osculum casti amoris. . . . osculum pacis et reconciliationis. . . . osculum astucie. . . . osculum reverentie. . . . BN. fol. 53ra, Mazar. fol. 41vb. This analysis does not entirely overlap with that in the *Summa Abel* vº *osculum,* Paris BN 455, fol. 79va–vb.

144. To vel *amore languo* (2:5): spiritualiter, id est, pro delectione sponsi et ecclesie penas carius sustineo quia palleat omnis amans. Hic est color aptus amantis. Chanter, BN fol. 56ra, Mazar. 44rb. Ovid, *Ars amatoria* I, v.729.

145. Jacques de Vitry, *VMO,* 547, 549, 554.

146. Ibid., 568–69, 571.

147. Ibid., 572.

Chapter Five

1. Coitus est viri ac mulieris commixtio ex utriusque naturali ac voluntaria coniunctionis actione cum spermatis emissione, fetus procreatio, operis multa comitante delectatione. *Salernitan Questions,* 9.

2. Ovid, *Ars amatoria* II, vv.467–88. Ovid introduced this myth to justify a lover's assuaging his mistress's jealousy by forceful lovemaking. *L'art,* 204–5.

3. See above p.88. Augustine, *De Genesi ad litteram* IX, 10; *De civitate dei* XIV,

16, 23, 24; Lombard, *Sententiarum*, 2.19.1, 2.20.1, and 2 (PL, 192:690, 692; Q.1:421, 427–28).

4. Chanter to: *replete terram* (Gen. 1:28) prolis posteritate quia qui sine coniunctione eorum fieri non potuit. Patet quia deus coniugium viri et mulieris constituerit in quo confutantur manichei dicentes non posse fieri concubitum sine mortali culpa. Si non peccas, sed homo sicut digitus digitum tangit sine voluptate. Sic homo uxorem cognosceret ad prolis procreationem, et cum deus vellet, homines in empireum sine morte transferet. Paris Arsenal 44, p.7a, London, Brit. Lib. Royal 2 C 8, fol. 4vb. Incorporated by Courson: Magister noster cantor dicit . . . quod per primum hominem qui si cognoscere vellet uxorem suam in primo statu non plus pruriret caro quam si digitus digitum tangeret. *Summa* XLII, 31, fol. 154vb. Chobham, *Summa confessorum*, 343. The phrase also appears in the *Glossa ordinaria* to *sine ardore:* Gratian, *Decretum*, C.32, c.2, *post* c.2.

5. On the origins of concupiscence, see pp.117–18. Chanter to *aperti sunt oculi amborum* (Gen. 3:7). (For the first part of the commentary see above p.291n.3.). . . . Primum autem motum concupiscentie contrarium rationi senserunt in gentitalibus et contra se videntes ea moveri erubuerint. Unde et illa dicta sunt pudenda. Econtraria hominis membra ad nutum hominis stant et moventur, nec dicuntur pudenda et hec inobedientia pudendorum que suo non obediunt superiori et sunt quasi porta generis humani. Signum est inobedientie parentum qui inobedientes fuerint suo creatori. Paris Arsenal 44, p.11b, London Brit. Lib. Royal 2 C 8, fol. 7ra.

6. Duplex autem fuit causa matrimonii institutionis: una ante peccatum facta in paradiso ad officium ubi esset coitus immaculatus et conceptio sine ardore et partus sine dolore; altera post peccatum ad remedium facta extra paradisum propter licitum motum refrenandum. Prima facta est ut natura multiplicaretur; secunda ut vitium cohiberetur. . . . Est enim matrimonium de iure naturali et naturalia iura cum creaturis sunt prodita sicut dicitur d. vi. in fine. . . . Courson, *Summa* XLII, 4, fol. 131rb, va. See the passage of Isidore in Gratian, *Decretum*, D.1, c.7.

7. Constantinus, *De coitu*, 80, 82–84. Guillaume de Conches, *Dragmaticon*, 239. *Prose Salernitan Questions*, 3–4, 10–11.

8. For the four complexions see above p.15. Guillaume de Conches, *Dragmaticon*, 238. *Prose Salernitan Questions*, 4. See the parallel discussion in Constantinus, *De coitu*, 96–100.

9. Guillaume de Conches, *Dragmaticon*, 240, merely raises the question, to which the *Prose Salernitan Questions*, 7–8, provides extended discussion.

10. Guillaume de Conches, *Dragmaticon*, 239. *Prose Salernitan Questions*, 5. André the Chaplain (*De Amore* I, 6, p.174) was also aware of the effects of heat and cold on sexuality. See above on the gender distinction of desire p.134.

Absent from the discussions in the *Prose Salernitan Questions* was any consideration of venereal disease. The only mention of a venereally transmitted disease that I have been able to discover in the five discourses is leprosy. In Béroul (vv.3760–73) Tristan, who was disguised as a leper, asserts that he contracted the disease from an *amie* who was married to a leper.

11. Jean-Louis Flandrin's *Un temps* is the exhaustive study of the penitentials. See esp. 20–33. See also the contributions of Pierre J. Payer, "Early Medieval Regula-

tions concerning Marital Sexual Relations," *Journal of Medieval History* 6 (1980), 365–67, 372, and *Sex and the Penitentials: The Development of a Sexual Code* (Toronto, 1984), 23–28 and 127–28 as well as the general summary in Brundage, *Law, Sex,* 157–61.

12. Flandrin, *Un temps,* 42.

13. Flandrin (see *Un temps,* 6) has promised a second volume devoted to the modification of the calendar of the penitentials. See his suggestions in ibid., 29, 37, 70, 136–38. Gratian, *Decretum,* C.33, q.4, c.2, c.4, c.5. Lombard, *Sententiarum,* 4.32.3 (PL, 192:923, Q.1:455. Brundage, *Sex, Law,* 242, 604.

14. Chobham, *Summa confessorum,* 336–37. By quoting the canonical materials he also included Rogation days (366).

15. Ibid., 188. More specifically, from Advent (four Sundays before Christmas) through the week of Epiphany (6 January) and from Septuagesima (third Sunday before Ash Wednesday) through the Easter week. This was based on the canons in Gratian, *Decretum,* C.33, q.4, c.8–11. See also the Lombard, *Sententiarum,* 4.32.4, PL, 192:924, Q.2:456.

16. Robert of Courson, *Summa* XLII, 31, 32, fol. 155vb, 156ra. Text in Appendix 1.

17. Léopold Delisle, *Catalogue des actes de Philippe Auguste* (Paris, 1856), lxviii.

18. Jean Renart sews chronological clues in abundance: the tournament at Saint-Trond was held on the feast of Saint George (23 April). *Roman,* vv.2320–21. The emperor orders his assembly to open at Mainz on 1 May (vv.3079, 3484, 4252) Lïenor will vindicate herself before the end of April (v.4026). Jean's statement that a fortnight (*quinzaine deerraine*) passes before the barons will arrive at Mainz (v.4144) is an uncharacteristic slip. On the seasonal framework for the romances in general see Marie-Luce Chênerie, *Chevalier errant dans le romans arthuriens en vers des XIIᵉ et XIIIᵉ siècles,* Publications romanes et françaises 172 (Geneva, 1986), 242–46. The gallant hunting scene is situated in *esté* (v.140), but the term could include springtime as well (Chênerie, *Chevalier,* 243) as is required by the romance narrative.

19. This is a leitmotif in Michel Foucault's *History of Sexuality: 2: The Use of Pleasure* and *3: The Care of Self* (New York, 1985–86).

20. Constantinus, *De coitu,* 142–56, 96.

21. Ibid., 142–84. *Liber minor de coitu,* 86–100. Vieillard, *Gilles de Corbeil,* 346–50, trans. 59–63.

22. Constantinus, *De coitu,* 114–18. Guillaume de Conches, *Dragmaticon,* 238–39. *Prose Salernitan Questions,* 5.

23. Ovid, *Amores* I, 4; *Ars amatoria* I, vv.229–44, reexpressed in III, vv.761–62; *Remedia,* vv.805–6. *L'art,* 98–99.

24. Andreas Capellanus, *De amore* III, p.304.

25. To Gen. 3:5: Super hunc locum dicit Gregorius *primum parentem* [*dyabolus tribus modis*] temptavit: gula, vana gloria, et avaritia. Gula cum *cibum vetitum suasit* [*ad*] *comedendum (Glossa ordinaria).* . . . Gula est immoderata cibi aviditas, id est, vicium quo immoderate dicitur appetere gula. Paris Arsenal 44, p.11a. See also Chobham, *Summa de arte praedicandi,* 251.

26. Et dictum est per sepe sanguissuge due sunt filie dicentes: affer, affer (Prov. 30:15), scilicet ventris ingluvies et libido inexpleta. Gula esuriens clamat ad

manum, affer, affer; stomachus nimis distentus clamat ad pudendorum clep-
sedram, affer, affer. Evacua quia rumpor . . . Sunt autem plures libidinis species
illicite que ex gulositate nascuntur, fornicatio simplex, adulterium, incestus, et ig-
nominiosa turpitudo vicii sodomorum. Chanter, *Verbum,* Vat. Reg. lat. 106, fol.
152va, and Paris Mazar. 772, fol. 43ra. PL, 205:329A, 330A, 331B,D, 332D. For
the verses of Ovid, see above p.181. On Terence *Eunuchus,* 4.5.732, see Baldwin,
Masters, Princes, and Merchants, 2:91n.116. Chobham, *Summa confessorum,* 409–12,
repeats the Chanter's arguments on drunkenness and sexuality; *Summa de arte
praedicandi,* 247–48, repeats the relationship between gluttony and lust. Pierre de
Poitiers, *Summa de confessione,* 11, also links gluttony and lust and quotes Proverbs
30:15. For penance enjoined on gluttons see the Synod of Angers (1217–19), *Statuts
synodaux français,* 1:196–98.

27. *Tresces,* vv.64–66, gives a rare example of a knight and his wife eating, but
the purpose is to put the knight to sleep so that the wife's lover can join the two in
bed.

28. From our sample of fabliaux nearly all the adulterous situations between a
wife and a priest situate the couple at table: *Prestre et Alison, Povre clerc, Prestre qui fu
mis, Prestre crucifié, Perdriz,* and *Prestre et la dame.*

29. Andreas Capellanus, *De amore* III, p.311.

30. Constantinus, *De coitu,* 112, 120–28, 132–34. In the Galenic tradition *Cum
auctor* recommended therapeutic intercourse for amenorrhea. Among the cures: . . .
Valet et coitus . . . [18].

31. The comprehensive study of the role of intercourse and virginity for women
in ancient and medieval medicine is Green, "Transmission," 19–22, 25–36, 46–52,
135–37, 267–68, 276–77, 294.

32. Muscio, 10. Caelius Aurelianus, 12–13.

33. Green, "Transmission," 276–77. Contingit autem hoc quia uiris non utuntur, et maxime uiduis que uti consueuerunt carnali comercio uirorum. Virginibus
solet euenire cum ad annos nubilos uenerint nec possunt uti ueneriis quia tunc in eis
sperma habundat quod natura uellet expellere. *Cum auctor* [26].

34. Andreas Capellanus, *De amore* III, p.304. Guillaume de Conches, *Dragmaticon,* 214. *Prose Salernitan Questions,* 182. The quotation attributed to Johannicius
was identified by Mary F. Wack, "Imagination, Medicine, and Rhetoric in Andreas
Capellanus' 'De Amore,'" *Magister Regis: Studies in Honor of Robert Earl Kaske,* ed.
Arthur Groos (New York, 1986). Elsewhere (II, 7, p.268), André urged consulta-
tion of medical opinion to explain the sexual preferences of the young and old.

35. The commentary to the *Song of Songs* would have been the appropriate place
to discuss virginity, but the Chanter was so engrossed in the ecclesiological tradition of exegesis that he neglected to consider the Marian interpretation most suited
for treatment of virginity. See above pp.169–71.

36. Virginitas que est castitas . . . de hac dicitur virginitas replet celum sicut terram coniugium. Virginitas castica est que pro eternis tantum servatur et maior
virtus est. Talis virginitas quam martirium, nam uno momento fit martirum sed
virginitas cum lucta et pugna longa. . . . Nichil prodest virginitas corporis ubi
operatur corruptio mentis. . . . Item virginitas in corpore nil proderit si caritas aut
humilitas a corde discessit. Melior est humilis coniugalitas quam superba virgini-

tas. Chanter, *Summa Abel,* Paris BN lat. 455, fol. 92va. On the Chanter's acknowledgment of Bernard de Clairvaux see Baldwin, *Masters, Princes, and Merchants,* 1:49, 66, 67, 70, 99, 107, 186, 256.

37. Chobham, *Summa confessorum,* 392–93; see also *Summa de arte praedicandi,* 254. Vieillard, *Gilles de Corbeil,* 370–71, trans. 282–84. Vieillard, *Gilles de Corbeil,* 370–71, trans. 282–84.

38. Jacques de Vitry, *VMO,* 550.

39. Guillaume de Conches, *Dramaticon,* 244. *Prose Salernitan Questions,* 9–10.

40. For representative examples from the *Prose Salernitan Questions* (abbreviated *PSQ*), Courson (*Summa*), and Chobham (*Summa confessorum*): *Coitus: PSQ,* 3, 160; Courson, fol. 131rb, 132va, and 155vb; Chobham, 333. *Coniunctio: PSQ,* 9; Courson, fol. 155vb; Chobham 145. *Commixtio: PSQ,* 9, Courson, 131va, 155vb. *Concubitus: PSQ,* 186, Chobham, 339. *Opus veneris: PSQ,* 11. *Actio veneris: PSQ,* 7, 103. *Copulatio:* Courson, fol. 129vb, 155vb; Chobham, 149. *Cognoscere:* Courson, 154vb. *Debitum: PSQ,* 7, 11; Courson, fol. 155ra; Chobham, 334. *Carnale commercium:* Courson, 154ra. For the semantic context see J. N. Adams, *The Latin Sexual Vocabulary* (Baltimore, 1982), 177–80, 188–90.

41. Ovid, *Amores* I, 5, vv.23–25; *Ars amatoria* II, vv.703–8.

42. Use of *Veneris* . . . : Ovid, *Amores* I, 4, v.21; II, 3, v.2; II, 7, v.21; II, 8, v.8; *Ars amatoria* III, vv.787, 797, 805. Beasts: *Ars* II, v.615. *Remedia amoris,* vv.399, 725–26. See the conclusion of Adams, *Latin Sexual Vocabulary,* 224–25, on Ovid's euphemisms.

43. In Ovid *solacium* occurs only three times in the *Remedia amoris,* vv.241, 449, 483, the last two with sexual connotations. *Solacium/solatium* is not attested with sexual connotations in C. Du Cange, *Glossarium mediae et infimiae latinitatis,* ed. L. Favre (Paris, 1883–87); J. F. Niermeyer, *Mediae Latinitatis Lexicon* (Leiden, 1984); and R. E. Latham, *Revised Medieval Latin Word List* (London, 1965). *L'art* 221, 223, 225.

44. Glynnis M. Cropp, *Vocabulaire courtois des troubadours de l'époque classique,* Publications romanes et françaises 135 (Geneva, 1975), 327–31, 334–40.

45. The line after *Escoufle,* v.1749 (*Les gens cele premiere nuit*), is missing. The scribe may have omitted it out of modesty, but most likely the last word was *deduit* as in *Roman,* v.5503, to rhyme with *nuit.*

46. *Ars amatoria* I, vv.669–70.

47. To *vir reddat debitum uxori et uxor viro* (1 Cor. 7:3) et hoc est in precepto et hoc debet *quia vir non habet postestatem corporis sui* ad aliam *nec mulier habet potestatem sui corporis* quia non potest continere si mulier exigit ab eo debitum. Similiter *nec mulier.* In hoc enim pares sunt vir et mulier, nec in hoc tollitur viro dominium in muliere sed vicium. Cohitus maritalis fit quandoque sine peccato cum exigitur debitum ab eo a quo exigitur. . . . Paris Mazar. 176, fol. 180rb. Cf. Lombard, *Sententiarum,* 4.32.1, PL, 192:922, Q.2:451. The phrase *sed vicium* originates from Augustine's Sermon 332, PL, 38:1463, transmitted by Lombard, *Sententiarum,* 4.32.1, PL, 192:922, Q.2:452. It appears to mean that returning the marital debt removes sin but not the dominium due to the husband. See the rendition in the Dominican compilation attributed Hugues de Saint-Cher: to 1 Cor. 7: Carnis concupiscentiae non servit (*Rom. 8b*) non nisi ad propagandam prolem, intellige precipue: in lege

naturae, id est, in opere naturali et reddendo debito. In hoc pares, quia neque etc. post consummationem matrimonii.

Sed vicium, id est, occasio peccati. . . . *Opera omnia* (Venice, 1703–54), 7:88.

48. Gratian, *Decretum*, C.33, q.4, d.p.c.11. See also the comment of Rufinus, *Summa decretorum*, to C.33, q.4, pr., ed. H. Singer, (Paderborn, 1902), 503.

49. Rufinus, *Summa decretorum*, to C.32, q.2, c.1, pp.479–80.

50. To *Item adversus*, D.13, pr.: . . . Item ego habeo uxorem instanter petit debitum. Si pecco mortaliter quia facio contra preceptum ut C.33 q.5 c.1. Si reddo, pecco saltem venialiter quia in quolibet coitu subest quidam pruritus, quedam delectatio que non potest non esse peccatum ut C.33, q.4, c.7, et sic videor esse perplexus. . . . In quarto exemplo scilicet de uxore petenti debitum dico quod non sum perplexus quia possum eam eludere multipliciter scilicet ratione temporis, ratione loci, vel promittendo me postea facturum donec illa efferbeat et petere desinat. Si nec sic illa desistit, possum ei reddere debitum sine omni peccato coniugem reddere debitum coniugi. Huguccio, Paris BN lat. 15396, fol. 13ra, rb. See the summary of Huguccio in the *Glossa ordinaria* to the same passage.

51. *Glossa ordinaria* to *debeamus*: C.33, q.4, c.1. See the discussion of James A. Brundage, "Sexual Equality in Medieval Canon Law," *Medieval Women and the Sources of Medieval History*, ed. Joel T. Rosenthal (Athens, Ga., 1990), 66–79, and Elizabeth M. Makowski, "The Conjugal Debt and Medieval Canon Law," *Journal of Medieval History* 3 (1977), 99–114. The casuistry of the problem deserves further study in canon law.

52. See above pp.177–78 and 244–45.

53. See above p.300n.22 for the text.

54. *Liber minor de coitu*, 98.

55. *Prose Salernitan Questions*, 7.

56. Ovid, *Amores* III, 14, vv.21–28.

57. Ibid., III, 7, vv.63–64, 23–26. For bodily images see above p.97.

58. Ovid *Ars amatoria* II, vv.704–28.

59. *L'art*, 222–25.

60. Marie de France also alludes to Ovid's magisterial reputation in *Guigemar* when she depicts a mural in a chapel where Venus consigns to the flames Ovid's book, the one in which he teaches how to control love (vv.239–40).

61. Andreas Capellanus, *De Amore* I, 6, pp.180, 198–202; II, 6, p.244.

62. *Babio*, vv.272, 278, ed. and trans. Henri Laye, in Cohen, *La "Comédie" latine* 2:44. See Adams, *Latin Sexual Vocabulary*, 151–52.

63. For other examples: *deduit*, *Guillaume au faucon*, p.112; *solas*: *Auberee*, v.423; *Segretain Moine*, p.227 puts it more directly: Amiez vos donc son solaz / En mi voz janbes à sentir? *Meunier*, p.91, which imitates Jean Bodel, uses *deduit*. For discussions of sexual obscenity in the fabliaux see Nykrog, *Fabliaux*, 209–23, and Muscatine, *Old French Fabliaux*, 105–51.

64. *culeter*: *Damoisele qui ne pooit oïr (I)*, v.8. *vertoillie*: *Fevre*, v.135. *arecier*: *Boivins*, v.275. *locier*: Jean Bodel, *Villain*, v.92. *feru et heurté*: *Prestre ki abevete*, p.56. On the use of *foutre* see Nykrog, *Fabliaux*, 210–11, and Muscatine, *Old French Fabliaux*, 110.

65. *Estormi*, v.67; *Prestre ki abevete*, p.56; *Prestre et le chevalier*, pp.81, 88. For the

horse metaphor, *Aloul*, vv.63, 261–62. See Brundage, *Law, Sex*, 286, for the canonists. *Prestre et de la dame*, p.239: Après si l'a envers mise; / Entre les cuisses si i entre, is ambiguous as to position.

66. Pierre de Poitiers, *Summa de confessione*, 16. Chobham, *Summa confessorum*, 336, 298. See above p.45. Pierre de Poitiers, 19, condemned masturbation as monstrous because it combines the male-active and female-passive roles in one person as if a hermaphrodite. See the severe penance enjoined in the Synod of Angers (1217–19), *Statuts synodaux français*, 1:208.

67. See above pp.55–56.

68. *Prose Salernitan Questions*, 20.

69. Chobham, *Summa confessorum*, 333, 335.

70. *Prose Salernitan Questions*, 9.

71. Andreas Capellanus, *De amore* I, 6, p.156. Burgess, *Marie de France*, 137–38.

72. Baldwin, *Masters, Princes, and Merchants*, 1:34, 2:92–93n.128.

73. *Damoisele qui ne pooit oïr (I–III)*.

74. On the *pastourelle* see above p.28.

75. Paden, *Medieval Pastourelle*, 1:68–71, 2:547. This *pastourelle* is attributed to Jean Bodel in Paris BN franc. 844, fol. 99. On the historical context see Charles Foulon, *L'oeuvre de Jehan Bodel*, Travaux de la Faculté des Lettres et Sciences humaines de Rennes, Série 1, 2 (Paris, 1958), 188–205.

76. Philippe de Beaumanoir, *Coutumes de Beauvaisis*, 829–30, ed. A. Salmon, Collection de textes pour servir à l'étude et l'enseignement de l'histoire (Paris, 1899), 24:430. On *raptus* see Brundage, *Law, Sex*, 47–48. The most recent and comprehensive study on rape in medieval literature is Kathryn Gravdal, *Ravishing Maidens*. For a study of rape in France based on the *coutumiers* and decisions of courts in the thirteenth and fourteenth centuries see A. Porteau-Bitker, "La justice laïque et le viol au moyen âge," *Revue historique de droit français et étranger* 66 (1988), 491–521.

77. Chobham, *Summa confessorum*, 353. The major tenants of the canon law on rape are discussed by Brundage, *Law, Sex*, 209–10, 249–50, 311–13, 396–98.

78. See above pp.161–62 and 307n.113.

79. Jacques de Vitry, *VMO*, 548, 560. The rape involved in the sack of Liège in 1212 elicited comment from numerous contemporary chroniclers. See *Reineri Annales*, ed. G. H. Pertz, *MGH SS* 16:664, and the further discussion in Ernest W, McDonnell, *The Beguines and Beghards in Medieval Culture* (New Brunswick, N.J., 1954), 130n.53.

80. Guillaume de Conches, *De philosophia mundi*, 89; *Dragmaticon*, 241. *Prose Salernitan Questions*, 6–7. See above p.135.

81. For an examination of rape in Chrétien see Gravdal, *Ravishing Maidens*, 43–68.

82. See the single example uncovered by Nykrog, *Fabliaux*, 89–91.

83. See Gravdal, *Ravishing Maidens*, 60–61.

84. Andreas Capellanus, *De amore* I, 11, p.222.

85. Paden, *Medieval Pastourelle*, 1:70–73, 2:548. Paris BN franc 844, fol. 98, attributes the piece to Jean Bodel.

86. For an extensive discussion of rape in the *pastourelles* see Kathryn Gravdal,

"Camouflaging Rape: The Rhetoric of Sexual Violence in the Medieval Pastourelle," *Romanic Review* 76 (1985), 361–73; William D. Paden, "Rape in the Pastourelle," *Romanic Review* 80 (1989), 331–49; and Gravdal, *Ravishing Maidens,* 104–21.

Chapter Six

1. Constantinus, *De coitu* 76. *Prose Salernitan Questions* 9.

2. See above p.94 for the competing theories. Guillaume de Conches, *Dragmaticon,* 242, 236. *Prose Salernitan Questions* 7, 3, 92–93. Children of adulterine unions, however, resemble their fathers more than their mothers. One explanation is that unlike marriage governed by mutual consent, in adultery the wills of the two parties are dissimilar, producing conflict. The sperm of the male superimposes itself upon the female, and the child receives the father's form. Another explanation focuses on infection caused by shame. *Prose Salernitan Questions,* 22–23.

3. Guillaume de Conches, *De philosophia,* 90; *Dragmaticon,* 241. *Prose Salernitan Questions,* 6, 8, 103, 14. *Anatomia Ricardi Salernitani,* 92. The *Anatomia magistri Nicolai* (43, 58) added further variations: males and females can be generated on either side, but males generated on the left are effeminate and females on the right viragos. Others say that the sex is determined by the proportion of male and female sperm, just as a high proportion of wine makes water taste like wine and vice versa. The elements of right/left and hot/cold were treated extensively in Constantinus Africanus, *De coitu,* 106–10.

4. [De signis inpregnationis] Ad cognoscendum utrum mulier gestet masculum, accipe aquam de fonte et extrahat mulier gutam sanguinis dextro latere, et in aqua infundat. Et si fundum petat, masculum gestat; non, feminam. Vnde Ypocras dixit: mulier que masculum concepit bene colorata est et dextram mamillam habet grossiorem. Si uero feminam, pallida est, et habet mamillam sinistram grossiorem. *Cum auctor* [57].

5. Fridolf Kudlien, "The Seven Cells of the Uterus: The Doctrine and Its Roots," *Bulletin of the History of Medicine* 39 (1969), 415–23. For the fullest and most recent discussion see Robert Reisert, *Der siebenkammerige Uterus: Studien zur mittelalterlichen Wirkungsgeschichte und Entfaltung eines embryologischen Gebärmuttermodells,* Würzburger medizinhistorische Forschungen 39 (Hannover, 1986), 7–20, 37–53, 65–69. Constantinus, *De genecia,* 320.

6. Guillaume de Conches, *De philosophia,* 90; *Dragmaticon,* 246–48. *Prose Salernitan Questions,* 14–16. See C. S. F. Burnett ("The Planets and the Development of the Embryo," *The Human Embryo: Aristotle and the Arabic and European Traditions,* ed. G. R. Dunstan, [Exeter, 1990], 95–112) who traces this theory back to the *De humane natura* attributed to Constantinus Africanus. Concurrent to the *Prose Salernitan Questions* it was also found in Helinand de Froidment's *Chronica.*

7. Guillaume de Conches, *De philosopia,* 91; *Dragmaticon,* 248–49. *Prose Salernitan Questions,* 103–5.

8. Guillaume de Conches, *De philosophia,* 89; *Dragmaticon,* 244–45, 247. *Prose Salernitan Questions,* 12, 13, 15, 221. *Cum auctor* employed the arboreal imagery of the Salernitan school to discuss morbidities found in females. Menstruation was likened to the flowers of trees that preceded the fruit and served to purge the body

of superfluous humors. Propter hoc inquam ad caloris recompensationem quandam eis purgatione precipuam nature assignari per menstrua, scilicet que apud eas uulgo flores appellantur, quia sicut arbores sine floribus fructum non afferunt, similiter mulieres sine floribus conceptionis officio fraudarentur. . . . *Cum auctor* [3].

Much of the treatise was devoted to menstrual disorders. The fetus is attached to the womb like a fruit of a tree, an observation that opened the discussion of miscarriages. Refert Galienus, ita ligatus fetus in matrice sicut fructus in arbore, qui cum precedat a flore tenerrimus est, et ex qualibet occasione corruit. *Cum auctor* [48].

9. For the commentary to the Psalms see above p.95. To *coagulatus in sanguine matris ex semine hominis* (Wisdom 7:2): hic ostendit differentiam sexus utriusque ut enim aiunt phisici. Semen viri candidum est, mulieris sanguinolentum quorum commixtione certis spatiis corpus formetur donec animatum perveniat ad partum, et alii vii, et alii viii, alii ix mense nascuntur et si qui in decimo perfectores et vitales et sannativi dicuntur esse. Chanter, Paris BN lat. 15565, fol. 129rb.

10. *Le fresne,* vv.9, 69–70; *Bisclavret,* v.309; *Yonec,* v.457; *Milun,* vv.88–89.

11. Augustine, *De Genesi ad litteram* IX, 7; see also *De bono conjugali* 24(29). On the influence of the biblical command in Genesis 1:28 see the full treatment of Jeremy Cohen, *"Be Fertil and Increase, Fill the Earth and Master It:" The Ancient and Medieval Career of a Biblical Text* (Ithaca, 1989), esp. 14, 224, 231, 237, 260.

12. Gratian, *Decretum,* C.27, q.2, c.10. Lombard, *Sententiarum,* 2.31.1, PL, 192:918, Q.2:442.

13. Chanter, London Brit, Lib. Royal 2 C 8, fol. 4vb, Paris Arsenal 44, p.7a. See p.271n.10 for the text. Sequitur de bonis matrimonii. Sunt autem tria bona matrimonii ut dicit Augustinus in libro de bono coniugali sicut habetur, C.27, q.2, c.10 ubi dicitur quod ista tria proles, fides, et sacramentum sunt bona coniugii, et ideo dicuntur bona coniugii quia excusant coitum a mortali peccato. . . . proles . . . quo quis educate prolem ad cultum dei. Courson, *Summa,* XLII, 6, fol. 132vb. Chobham, *Summa confessorum,* 333, repeated the same schema. For the fourfold schema see above pp.124–25.

14. See the discussion of Jean-Baptiste Molin and Protais Mutembe, *Le rituel du mariage en France du XIIe au XVI siècle,* Théologie historique 26 (Paris, 1974), 255–59, 287, 326–27.

15. Chanter, *Summa,* 3(2a): 329.

16. Gratian, *Decretum,* C.32, q.2, c.7, *Aliquando.* Lombard, *Sententiarum libri quatuor,* 4.31.3, PL, 192:920, Q.2:445. The most comprehensive discussion of contraception and abortion is John T. Noonan, Jr., *Contraception,* 214–19. Most recently, John M. Riddle (*Contraception and Abortion from the Ancient World to the Renaissance* [Cambridge, Mass., 1992]) has collected evidence on contraceptive and abortion practices. This study appeared too late for me to take advantage of its findings.

17. Item Augustinus ad idem ait in libro de bono coniugii sicut habetur C.32, q.2, c.6. Ibi invenio quem ad modum has nuptias possumus appellare, videlicet, ubi conditio talis apponitur. Ego contraho tecum si procures nobis non nasci filios per venena sterilitatis vel alio modo. Sic ergo auctoritate Augustini et Urbani pape habetur quod conditio adiecta impedit matrimonii contractum. . . . Courson, *Summa* XLII, 15, fol. 140vb.

Aliqua mulier ex frequenti partu rupta est interius, ita quod constat ei assertione fisicorum quod si, iterum conceperit, morietur. Vir nilominus petit debitum. Queritur an ipsa teneatur reddere.

Dicit magister quod sicut habens panem in extrema necessitate famis et panem unum debeat, non tenetur in tali articulo reddere ei quem debet panem, licet repetat; ita mulier ista, cum certa sit de morte si reddat viro debitum, licet corpus suum viro debeat, non tenetur ei reddere in tali articulo. Et cogendus est vir ille per ecclesiam ab exactione debiti ut expectet, quousque ipsa per senectutem fiat impotens, concipere.

Nec approbat magister opinionem quorundam dicentium ipsam posse procurare venenum sterilitatis, et ita reddere debitum cum secura sit quod non possit concipere. Sic enim occasionaliter esset ipsa homicida proprie prolis. Chanter, *Summa*, Munich Clm 5426, fol. 118ra–rb. This rough version was given a more succinct form in *Summa*, 3(2b):463–64. Galienus dicit mulieres que habent uuluas angustas et matrices strictas non debent uiris uti, ne concipiat et moriantur. Sed omnes tales non possunt abstinere, et ideo nostro indigent auxilio. *Cum auctor* [45].

18. Chobham, *Summa confessorum*, 463–64. The three remaining practices are those of infanticide: (3) refusing the breast, (4) exposure, and (5) overlay.

19. Gratian, *Decretum*, C.32, q.7, c.11 in a section concerning the degrees of fornication. Lombard, *Sententiarum*, 4.38.2, (PL, 192:933; Q.2:481–82) in a section on vows. Duo genera principum non recte operantium in plebe. Unum quod obest alterum quod non prodest; significantur in filiis inde quorum unus malignus ante dominum. Alter fundabat semen in terra ne fecundaret Thamar. Nec sunt amplius quam duo genere hominum inutilia. Nocentes scilicet et prodesse nolentes, et si quid boni habent in hac vita produnt tanquam in terra fundentes et quia in malo peior est qui nocet quam qui non prodest. Ideo maior dicitur malignus non minor qui semen fundebat. *Glossa ordinaria* to Gen. 38:7. For the Chanter's views see above p.45. Noonan, *Contraception*, 219, 275, 287.

20. Flandrin, *Un temps*, 12–20 and 46–70 for the demographic effects. See also Pierre J. Payer, *Sex and the Penitentials: The Development of a Sexual Code, 550–1150* (Toronto, 1984), 23–28.

21. Chobham, *Summa confessorum*, 338, 365–66. See also Pierre de Poitiers, *Summa de confessione*, 16–17.

22. Noonan, *Contraception*, 357–58, for Huguccio. See above p.121. Item. Si quis lubricus est et posset per herbam vel potionem aliquam infrigidare partes genitales ita quod ex toto amitteret potenciam generandi, non peccaret, sed non deberet sibi ferrum inicere nec aliquo modo mutilare fabricam corporis sui a Deo factam, quia nil Deus in homine superfluum creavit. Quidam dicunt quod sicut peccatum est membrum naturale mutilare, ita peccatum est potentiam naturalem quamcumque penitus extinguere. Chanter, *Summa*, Munich Clm. 5426, fol. 101va.

23. Constantinus, *Pantegni (Practica)*, VIII, 3 in *Opera omnia* (Lyon, 1515), pars II, fol. 115rb. His treatment in *De coitu*, 142–84, from the *Viaticum* is limited chiefly to aphrodisiacs and anaphrodisiacs that affect male coitus. See Monica H. Green, "Constantinus Africanus and the Conflict between Religion and Science," *The Human Embryo: Aristotle and the Arabic and European Traditions*, ed. G. R. Dunstan (Ex-

eter, England, 1990), 50–52, 54–56, 59. Noonan, *Contraception*, 246–49, has conveniently summarized Avicenna's material.

24. Muscio, 20. Caelius Aurelianus, 28–31, which resumes Soranus, *Gynecology*, 62–68. Chobham, *Summa confessorum*, 464. Mulier si non uult concipere, carne sua nuda ferat secum matricem capre que numquam habuit fetum. Inuenitur autem quidam lapis gagates qui gestatur a muliere prohibet conceptionem uel etiam gustatus. Aliter, recipe mustelam masculum et auferantur ei testiculi et relinquatur uiuus. Hos testiculos ferat secum in sinu suo et liget eos in pelle anserina uel in alia, et non concipiet. *Cum auctor* [46]. As for abortions, *Cum auctor* merely noted that they were easier early in pregnancy. Sic cum primo educitur infans ex semine concepto, nam tenera et non firma sunt eius ligamenta, quibus ligatur matrici et de leui emittitur per aborsum [48].

25. Guillaume de Conches, *De philosophia*, 89; *Dragmaticon*, 242–43. *Prose Salernitan Questions*, 8–9. Sicut testatur Ypocras, mulieres inutiles sunt ad conceptionem aut nimis macie uel tenues, uel quia pinguedo circumuoluta orificio matricis ipsam constringit et non permittit eam semen recipi in matricem. Quedam habent matrices sic lubricas ut semen intus retineri non possit. Contingit quandoque uicio uiri quia semen nimis tenue et infusum matrici sua liquiditate elabitur. Quidam habent etiam testiculos frigidos et siccos, et isti aut numquam aut raro generare possunt, quia semen eorum est generationem inutile. *Cum auctor* [42]. On the sterility test: Si maneat sterilis mulier, hoc modo scies utrum uicio uiri uel eius contingat. Accipe duas ollas et in unaquaque pone cantabrum, et de urina uiri in una, et in altera de urina mulieris, et sic per .ix. dies dimitantur uel etiam amplius. Et si contigat uicio mulieris, inuenies in olla uermes quosdam et cantabrum eius fetidum. Si ex uicio uiri similia inuenies. Si in neutra inueneris, in neutro est causa, et beneficio medicine poteris iuuare, ut concipiat. *Cum auctor* [43].

26. Guillaume de Conches, *De philosophia*, 89; *Dragmaticon*, 240–41. *Prose Salernitan Questions*, 6, 8.

27. Augustine, *De bono conjugali*, 11. The following section that pronounced extravaginal sex with a wife to be more damnable than with a prostitute was better circulated in the twelfth century. The version for *De adulterinis conjugiis* was repeated in Gratian, *Decretum*, C.32, q.7, c.11, and Lombard, *Sententiarum*, 4.38.2, PL, 192:933, Q.2:482. Augustine, *De nuptiis et concupiscentia* I, 9.

28. Chobham, *Summa confessorum*, 338. See above pp.135–36.

29. Ovid, *Amores* II, 13, and 14, particularly vv.9–10, 19–20. *Ars amatoria* II, vv.467–88; III, vv.81–82. The *Amores* III, 14, v.7, also acknowledges a cosmetic application for abortions—to prevent stomach wrinkles. Twelfth-century Latin poets like Bernardus Silvestris (*Cosmographia* XIV, vv.153–70, ed. Peter Dronke, Textus minores 53 [Leiden, 1978], trans. Winthrop Wetherbee [New York, 1973], 126) and Alain de Lille (*De planctu nature* I, ed. N. M. Häring, *Studi medievali*, 3d. ser., 19 [1978], 806–8, trans. James J. Sheridan, Medieval Sources in Translation 26 [Toronto, 1980], 67–72) did not neglect, however, the importance of generation in the natural cosmos.

30. Andreas Capellanus, *De amore* I, 6, p.150. In III, for example, see pp.288, 300.

31. Ibid., I, 6, pp.180, 198–200.

32. Ibid., III, p.288.

33. Employing indirect evidence, P. P. A. Biller argues for greater use of contraception in the high Middle Ages than formerly assumed. "Birth-Control in the West in the Thirteenth and early Fourteenth Centuries," *Past and Present* 94 (1982), 4–26.

34. On children in Marie de France see Burgess, *Marie de France*, 169–70.

35. Lombard, *Sententiarum*, 4.30.3, (PL, 192:918, Q.2:441). To 1 Cor. 7: . . . causa vero propter quam contrahi debet est: procreatio prolis, et vitatio fornicationis. Sunt et alie cause honeste ut inimicorum reconciliatio, pacis reintegratio. *Glossa ordinaria*. To 1 Cor. 7:11: . . . causa propter quam contrahi debet est: prolis procreatio, fornicationis vitatio, inimicorum reconciliacio et huiusmodi bona eiusdem sunt fides, proles, sacramentum. Fides ne cum alio vel alia coheatur proles ut religiose educetur. Chanter, Paris Mazar. 176, fol. 180va. Sequitur de causa finali matrimonii illa scilicet propter quam contrahitur matrimonium que multiplex est. Una est prolis susceptio, alia fornicationis evitatio, tercia caritatis dilatatio, quarta inimicorum reconciliatio, v. pacis et federis confirmatio. . . . Courson, *Summa* XLII, 5, fol. 132va.

36. Andreas Capellanus, *De amore* III, p.300.

37. *De glorioso rege Ludovico* in *Vie de Louis le Gros par Suger*, ed. Auguste Molinier (Paris, 1887), 147, 149.

38. Chanter, *Summa*, 3(2a):101. Baldwin, *Masters, Princes, and Merchants*, 1:173.

39. Jean Renart, *Escoufle*, vv. 2150–96, 2792–93, 2166; *Roman*, 3036–95, 3504–41. In Marie de France's *Equitan* the king is reproached by his subjects for not marrying (vv.197–201) and the seneschal's wife eloquently articulates the social disparity between herself and the king (vv.120–48). On Louis VII's daughters see Alexander Cartellieri, *Philipp II. August, König von Frankreich* (Leipzig, 1899), 1:Beilagen 49.

40. *Piramus et Tisbé*, ed. C. de Boer, Classiques français du moyen âge (Paris, 1921), vv.234ff.

41. Chobham, *Summa confessorum*, 152.

42. See above for the Chanter pp.220 and 321n.35 and MS Bamberg, Cod. Misc. Patr. 136, in Müller, *Paradiesesehe*, 296.

43. (See above n.35 for the beginning) . . . vi efficacior est omnibus scilicet discernendorum discretio et ordinate caritatis exhibitio, quia nisi esset matrimonium nemo sciret discernere heredem a non herede vel liberos ab advenis. Nam si passim omnibus et licite concessus esset quibuslibet vagus coitus, non esset maior discretio inter homines quam inter bruta. Unde quilibet attendens matrem suam fuisse expositam libidini multorum non posset dividicare quis esset pater eius, et ita non posset adimplere mandatum illud: honora patrem et matrem etc. De hiis habitur C.32, q.2, c.10 [Augustine, *De bono coniugali* c.6]. Courson, *Summa* XLII, 5, fol. 132va.

Simile de facto accidit de principe huius regni qui consensit matrimonialiter in filiam imperatoris pro qua ancilla enim fuit ei supposita et illam ancillam duxit in uxorem ex qua spurios suscepit filios qui postmodum subverterunt regnum. . . . Ibid. XLII, 12, fol. 137va.

Andreas Capellanus, *De amore* I, 6; III, pp.172, 300.

44. Burgess, *Marie de France,* 186.

Conclusions

1. Augustine, *De civitate dei* I, 9.

2. C.21 in Mansi, 22:1007–10.

3. From a multifaceted study Henry Ansgar Kelly concludes that, contrary to these findings in twelfth-century France, love and marriage were fundamentally compatible in fourteenth-century England. His texts include not only the contemporary poets Chaucer and Gower and their immediate sources but also Ovid, André, romances, and canon lawyers in common with the twelfth century. Beyond the possibility of differences between the texts of the fourteenth and twelfth centuries, his thesis is supported by means of three general propositions. (1) He introduces a distinction between literature that takes love "seriously" and texts that take it lightly or satirically. By discounting the latter (for example: Ovid's *Amores, Ars amatoria,* and *Remedia amoris,* the fabliaux and selected tales in Boccaccio's *Decameron*), he is able to reduce the apparent divergences. (2) Much of the seeming adultery in literature (for example: Tristan and Iseut, Cligès and Fenice) can be interpreted simply as the practice of clandestine marriage. And (3) the stern views of marital sexuality in the canonists were widely ignored, a conclusion that agrees with my own. *Love and Marriage in the Age of Chaucer* (Ithaca, 1975). See 333–34 for a summation of his conclusions.

4. On the feminine orientation of Marie's alimentary practices see Caroline Walker Bynum, *Holy Feast and Holy Fast: The Religious Significance of Food to Medieval Women* (Berkeley, Calif., 1987), chs. 3, 4, esp. pp.115–16, 119.

5. For a preliminary sketch of this sexual reciprocity see John W. Baldwin, "Consent and the Marital Debt: Five Discourse in Northern France around 1200," *Consent and Coercion to Sex and Marriage in Ancient and Medieval Societies,* ed. Angeliki Laiou (Washington, D.C., 1993), 257–70.

6. James A. Brundage, "Implied Consent to Intercourse," in *Consent and Coercion,* 245–56.

7. Froma I. Zeitlin, "The Poetics of Eros: Nature, Art, and Imitation in Longus' Daphnis and Chloe," *Before Sexuality: The Construction of Erotic Experience in the Ancient Greek World,* eds. David M. Halperin, John J. Winkler, and Froma I. Zeitlin (Princeton, 1990), 417–64. John J. Winkler, *The Constraints of Desire: The Anthropology of Sex and Gender in Ancient Greece* (New York, 1990), 101–26. Michel Foucault, *The History of Sexuality, 3: The Care of the Self* (New York, 1988), 228–32.

8. Robert W. Hanning, "Marie de France and the Wound of the Narrative: Risk and Vulnerability in the *Lais*" (unpublished paper).

9. The comprehensive study of Aristotle's influence on gender is Allen, *Concept of Woman.* For Aristotle's impact on the thirteenth century see 413–70.

10. For example, when Roger Dragonetti urges his reader to listen to that voice of the medieval romance which speaks "to the heart and ears," he assumes that the medieval listener-reader heard the same voice. *Le mirage des sources: L'art du faux dans le roman médiéval* (Paris, 1987), 7. When Jean Renart displaced Lïenor from the center of his romance, Roberta L. Krueger finds an identity between the romancier's poetics and the modern critics' theories. How Jean's contemporary female

audience actually "received" Jean's message is left to further inquiry. How Krueger will demonstrate that reception is left equally unresolved. "Double Jeopardy: The Appropriation of Woman in Four Old French Romances of the 'Cycle de la Gageure,'" *Seeking the Woman in Late Medieval and Renaissance Writings: Essays in Feminist Contextual Criticism,* ed. Sheiler Fisher and Janet E. Halley (Knoxville, Tenn., 1989), 44–45.

11. Hans Robert Jauss, *Toward an Aesthetic of Reception,* trans. Timothy Bahti, Theory and History of Literature 2, (Minneapolis, 1982), 3–45.

12. See explications of Aristotle and Galen in Michael Boylan, "The Galenic and Hippocratic Challenges to Aristotle's Conception Theory," *Journal of the History of Biology* 16 (1983), 83–112, and Elisabeth A. Clark, "Vitiated Seeds and Holy Vessels: Augustine's Manichean Past," *Ascetic Piety and Women's Faith: Essays on Late Ancient Christianity* (Lewistown, Queenston, 1986), 291–349.

13. Linda Cooper, "L'ironie iconographique de la coupe de Tristan dans *Escoufle,*" *Romania* 104 (1983), 157–76. What Cooper finds remarkable about the passage is not the interpretation of Tristan but the context of *Escoufle* in which the passage is inserted.

14. This is the argument in John W. Baldwin, "Jean Renart et le tournois de Saint-Trond: Une Conjonction de l'histoire et de littérature," *Annales: Economies, sociétés, civilisations* 45 (1990), 581; Ruth H. Cline, "The Influence of Romances on Tournaments in the Middle Ages," *Speculum* 20 (1945), 204–11; and Michel Stanesco, *Jeux d'errance du chevalier médiéval: Aspects ludiques de la fonction guerrière dans la littérature du moyen âge flamboyant,* Brill's Studies in Intellectual History 9 (Leiden, 1988), 11–102.

15. Paul Robinson's *The Modernization of Sex: Havelock Ellis, Alfred Kinsey, William Masters and Virginia Johnson* (New York, 1976) touches upon the subject.

INDEX

Abelard: 3, 119; castration, 69; clerical
    lover, 58; foreplay, 164; fornication, 64;
    reproduction, 217
Agnes de Méran, xiii
Alain, master, 130–33
Alain de Lille, 45, 308n.123
Albert the Great, 46, 234
Albertanus of Brescia, 19
Alexander Neckham, 10, 12, 22
Alexander III, pope, 7, 62, 77
Alfanus, archbishop of Salerno, 90
Aloul, 56, 76, 109–10, 179, 285n.42,
    288nn.80, 83, and 86
Amaury de Bène, 5
Anatomia magistri Nicolai, 12, 92, 94
Anatomia Richardi Salerniti, 12, 92
Anatomia vivorum, 90, 95, 234
André de Saint-Victor, xxv
André the Chaplain: xix–xx, xxii; adultery,
    65–66, 227; *ars amatoria,* 25; biography
    and works, 16–20; body, 99–100; bour-
    geoisie, 52; clergy, 58–60; clerical
    celibacy, 28; coitus, 189, 197; desire, 137–
    43, 150, 226; female desire, 233; food and
    drink, 184; foreplay, 164; fornication, 64;
    health, 186; hermeneutics, xxvi, 25; legit-
    imacy, 223; love sickness, 142; marriage
    politics, 220; *mésalliance,* 55; misogny,
    143; old age, 48–49; peasants, 51–52;
    promiscuity, 78; prostitutes, 79; pubes-
    cence, 47; rape, 204; three orders, 51;
    vagina, 111; vision, 49, 140–41
Angers, synod of (1217–19), 95, 286nn.53
    and 58, 287nn.67–68, 90nn.117 and 125,
    308n.123, 313n.26, 316n.66

Anselme de Laon, 3, 117
Anselm of Canterbury, 119
Arabic medical treatises, 11–12
Aristocracy: xviii–xix, 35, 39, 41, 50–57,
    54, 61, 112, 229; adultery, 69–73; food
    and drink, 181–82; love sickness, 133,
    142; marriage, 74, 77, 220–24
Aristotle: homologies, 90, 96, 230–31;
    homosexuality, 46; male supremacy,
    233–34; natural works, 5; sperm, 94, 206,
    231, 236
Arnoul d'Orléans, 21, 50, 98, 104, 286n.57
Art d'amours, 13, 23, 136, 143, 195–96
Auberee, 38, 56, 162, 222, 285n.41, 288n.85
Augustine: xix, xx; body, 88; coitus, 174;
    concupiscence, 116–21; contraception
    and abortion, 212–13, 217; female desire,
    136–37; male superiority, 230; orgasm,
    117–18; prostitutes, 80, 85; reproduction,
    210–11; sexuality, 225; sperm, 95,
    230–31; unnatural intercourse, 45;
    works, 3–4
Averroës, 234
Avicenna: 13–14, 131–32, 302n.38; contra-
    ception, 215; homologies, 90; male
    supremacy, 233; sperm, 95

Baudouin, (II) count of Guines, 42
Baudouin, (VI) count of Hainaut, (IX)
    count of Flanders, xix, 73, 34, 221,
    278n.86
Bédier, Joseph, 41
Beguines, 9
Bele m'est la voiz altane, 28, 156
Bella, (III) king of Hungary, 16

325